Science

FOR AQA

David Glover **Jean Martin** Helen Norris

CAMBRIDGE
UNIVERSITY PRESS

CAMBRIDGE UNIVERSITY PRESS
Cambridge, New York, Melbourne, Madrid, Cape Town, Singapore, São Paulo

Cambridge University Press
The Edinburgh Building, Cambridge CB2 2RU, UK

www.cambridge.org
Information on this title: www.cambridge.org/9780521686730
© Cambridge University Press 1997, 2001, 2006

First published 1997
Second edition 2001
Third edition 2006

Printed in the United Kingdom at the University Press, Cambridge
Cover and text design by Blue Pig Design Ltd
Page layout by Kamae Design, Oxford

A catalogue record for this publication is available from the British Library

ISBN-13   978-0-521-68673-0 paperback
ISBN-10   0-521-68673-3 paperback

Chemistry

Physics

■ An introduction for students and their teachers

This book is divided into Biology, Chemistry and Physics.
Within each subject, you will find three different types of material

- boxes containing ideas from your studies of Science at Key Stage 3
- scientific ideas that all Key Stage 4 students need to know
- information to help you understand How Science Works.

■ Ideas from your studies at Key Stage 3

You need to understand these ideas before you start on the new science for Key Stage 4.
But you will <u>not</u> be assessed <u>directly</u> on these Key Stage 3 ideas in GCSE examinations.

Some ideas will take a whole page like this.

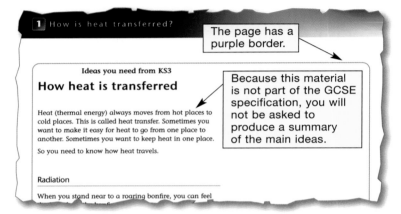

> 1 How is heat transferred?
>
> The page has a purple border.
>
> **Ideas you need from KS3**
>
> ### How heat is transferred
>
> Heat (thermal energy) always moves from hot places to cold places. This is called heat transfer. Sometimes you want to make it easy for heat to go from one place to another. Sometimes you want to keep heat in one place.
>
> So you need to know how heat travels.
>
> Because this material is not part of the GCSE specification, you will not be asked to produce a summary of the main ideas.
>
> **Radiation**
>
> When you stand near to a roaring bonfire, you can feel

Some ideas will not take up a whole page. They are shown in a purple box like this. In such cases, the Key Stage 3 material is included in a box, usually at the start of the Key Stage 4 topic.

> **REMEMBER FROM KS3**
>
> A **species** is a group of similar organisms that can interbreed.

■ Scientific ideas that all Key Stage 4 students need to know

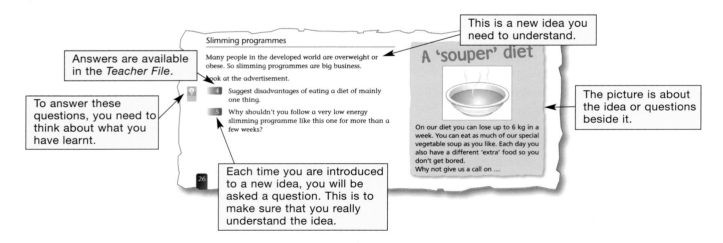

> **Slimming programmes**
>
> Many people in the developed world are overweight or obese. So slimming programmes are big business.
>
> Look at the advertisement.
>
> 4 Suggest disadvantages of eating a diet of mainly one thing.
>
> 5 Why shouldn't you follow a very low energy slimming programme like this one for more than a few weeks?
>
> 26

This is a new idea you need to understand.

Answers are available in the *Teacher File*.

To answer these questions, you need to think about what you have learnt.

The picture is about the idea or questions beside it.

Each time you are introduced to a new idea, you will be asked a question. This is to make sure that you really understand the idea.

> **A 'souper' diet**
>
> On our diet you can lose up to 6 kg in a week. You can eat as much of our special vegetable soup as you like. Each day you also have a different 'extra' food so you don't get bored.
> Why not give us a call on …

You should keep answers to <u>What you need to remember</u> sections in a separate place.
They contain all the ideas you are expected to remember and understand in examinations.
So they are very useful for revision.

It is very important that these summaries are correct.
You should always check your summaries against those provided on pages 329–344 of this book.

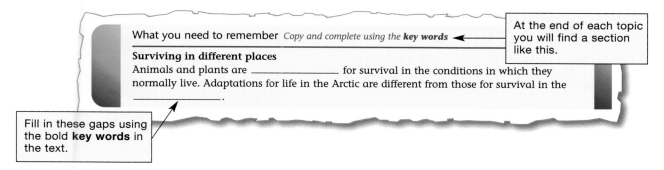

At the end of each topic you will find a section like this.

What you need to remember *Copy and complete using the **key words***

Surviving in different places
Animals and plants are _____ for survival in the conditions in which they normally live. Adaptations for life in the Arctic are different from those for survival in the _____ .

Fill in these gaps using the bold **key words** in the text.

■ Helping you to understand How Science Works

Some pages have information about how science works as well as the ideas that you need to learn.
They end with <u>What you need to remember</u> boxes like the one above.

Others are about how science and scientists work or let you practise scientific skills by answering different types of questions. They end with a different <u>What you need to remember</u> section.

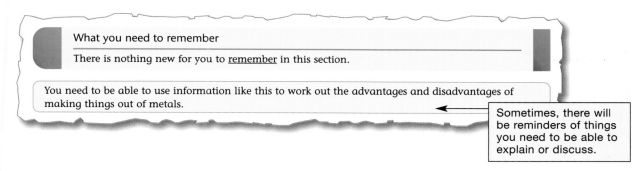

What you need to remember

There is nothing new for you to <u>remember</u> in this section.

You need to be able to use information like this to work out the advantages and disadvantages of making things out of metals.

Sometimes, there will be reminders of things you need to be able to explain or discuss.

Pages 312–322 also help you with How Science Works.

■ The back of this book

In the back of this book, you will find

- a section about How Science Works and handling data
- a section on revising for exams and answering exam questions
- a page about balancing equations
- a periodic table
- a page of important physics formulas
- completed 'What you need to remember' boxes
- a glossary of important scientific words.

■ CDs in the Science Foundations series

This book is accompanied by a *Science Teacher File* CD containing adaptable planning and activity sheet resources. There are also accompanying *Science* CDs of interactive e-learning resources including animations and activities for whole class teaching or independent learning, depending on your needs. The Additional Science specification is supported in a similar way.

1 Survival

Senses and common sense

Visitors to Death Valley are at risk of overheating and of losing too much water and salt. Park wardens suggest that visitors need to:

A cover up and wear sunscreen, a hat and sunglasses

B drink 4–8 litres of water a day

C watch out for signs of dehydration such as headaches and nausea (feeling sick)

D stay alert to prevent accidents on the rough ground

E watch and listen for snakes and other animals.

So, visitors' survival depends on their senses, their nervous systems and the ability of their bodies to control temperature, water and salt balance.

1 From the list above

    a what does suggestion **A** protect you against?
    b what protects you against dehydration?

Death Valley, California, is very hot and dry. Summer temperatures can reach 49 °C.

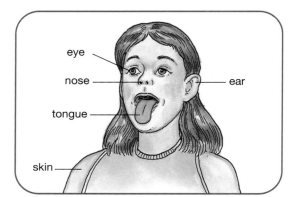

Receptors in sense organs detect what is going on around you.

Your senses

Humans and other animals have sense organs.

They contain special cells called **receptors** that receive **stimuli** from the **environment**.

For example, receptors in your eyes detect light.

2 Copy and complete the table.

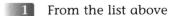

Sense organ	How it helps you to survive in Death Valley
eye	

How we see things

The diagram shows what happens when you see a tree.

3 Where are the light-sensitive cells in your eyes?

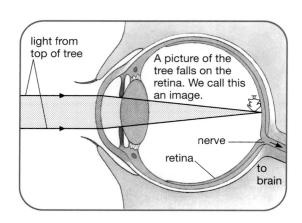

light from top of tree

A picture of the tree falls on the retina. We call this an image.

nerve

retina

to brain

Detecting chemicals (taste and smell)

There are thousands of taste receptors on your tongue. They detect chemicals dissolved in water and are in groups called taste buds.

4 Look at the diagram.
List the <u>four</u> different tastes that your tongue can detect.

Receptors inside your nose detect chemicals in the air (smell). You need to taste and smell to get the full flavour of food.

5 Food seems tasteless when you have a cold. Why do you think this is?

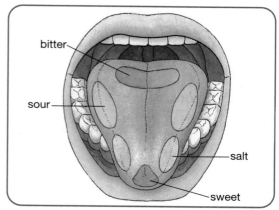

There are four different kinds of taste bud on your tongue.

Skin deep

Your skin, including the skin on your tongue, is sensitive to touch.

6 Write down <u>three</u> other stimuli your skin detects.

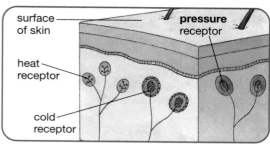

Pain and touch receptors are nearer to the skin's surface than pressure and temperature receptors.

Ears aren't just for hearing

Position and movement receptors in your ears and your muscles help you to detect changes in position and to keep your balance.

7 **a** Write down the <u>two</u> places in your ears where there are receptors.
b In each case, say what the receptors are for.

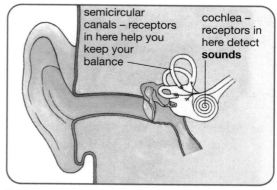

Ears contain position and movement receptors as well as sound receptors.

What you need to remember *Copy and complete using the* **key words**

Survival

You need sense organs to detect _____ – to make you aware of changes in your _____. Sense organs contain special cells called _____. Different receptors detect different stimuli. Some are sensitive to touch, to _____ or to temperature. Others detect light, _____, changes in position and chemicals.

You don't need to know the structure and function of sense organs such as the ear and eye.

2 Making decisions – coordination

From sense organ to brain

The receptors in your sense organs are connected to your **nervous** system.

> **1** Look at the diagram.
> Write down the parts of the nervous system.

Nerve fibres carry information from receptors to your brain and spinal cord. Your brain and spinal cord are the two parts of your central nervous system.

They make sense of the information and cause responses. We say that your brain **coordinates** your actions.

Suppose you are walking in Death Valley and see a snake. You stop walking and stand very still.
You can do this because of your nervous system.

> **2** Look at the diagram.
> What type of stimulus travels from the snake to your eye?

The receptors in your eyes send information as nerve impulses along nerve fibres to your brain.

A nerve impulse is a bit like a tiny electrical impulse.

What does your brain do next?

Your brain lets you react or respond. You decide what to do. Then your brain sends impulses to the muscles in your body to carry out your decision.

> **3** What is your response to seeing the snake?

> **4** Which parts of your body produce this response?

Your brain coordinates the actions of all the muscles you use to stop you moving. Then you have to use your brain to think what to do next!

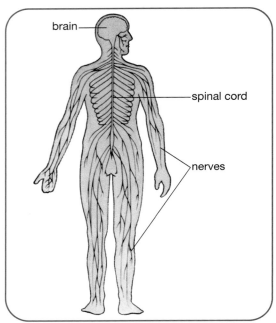

Your nervous system.

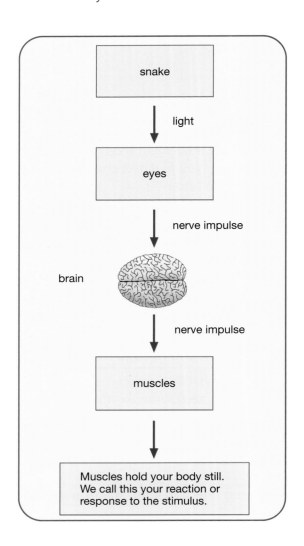

Getting information to and from your brain

Nerve fibres carry information to and from your brain. To do this, they need to be very long. Each nerve fibre is part of a cell called a nerve cell or **neurone**.

Sensory neurones carry impulses from your receptors to your brain. **Motor** neurones carry impulses from your brain to the muscles and glands that respond. We call them **effectors**.

5   Describe the difference between the job of a sensory and the job of a motor neurone.

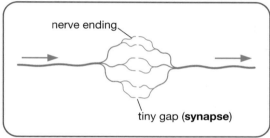

Nerves are made of bundles of nerve fibres.

Pathways in your nervous system

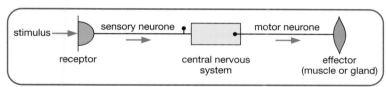

Your brain and spinal cord make up your central nervous system.

6   What is a synapse?

There is a tiny gap between one neurone and the next. A chemical released at the end of one neurone causes an impulse in the next one.

What you need to remember *Copy and complete using the key words*

Making decisions – coordination

Your _____ system allows you to react to your surroundings and _____ your behaviour.

Information from receptors passes along _____ neurones in _____ to your spinal cord and brain. Your brain coordinates the response. It sends nerve impulses along _____ neurones to the _____ that respond.

There is a tiny gap called a _____ between one _____ and the next.

3 Automatic responses

Ouch! That's hot

Some reactions are voluntary. You decide to do them. But if you touch a hot plate, you don't want to waste time thinking about it before you move your hand. The diagram shows what happens.

We call a rapid, **automatic** response like this a **reflex** action.

In this reflex action, the part of the central nervous system involved is the spinal cord.

1 Put the following sentences in the right order to explain what happens. Use the diagrams on this page and the next page to help you.

■ Receptors in the skin detect that the plate is hot.

■ Contraction of muscles makes the arm bend away from the hot plate.

■ Impulses from receptors travel along a sensory neurone to the central nervous system.

■ At **synapses**, relay neurones set up impulses along motor neurones to the arm muscle.

■ Impulses pass to a relay neurone.

Reflex actions such as blinking involve your brain. But you still don't have to think about them.

2 Copy and complete the table to show some reflex actions.

> **REMEMBER**
>
> Your brain and spinal cord make up your central nervous system.

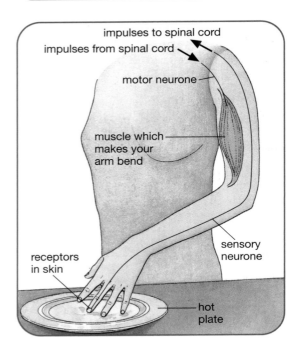

Stimulus	Automatic response
dust in eyes	
bright light shone at eyes	
food goes into windpipe	

Another reflex action

Look at the photograph. When someone taps just below your knee, your lower leg automatically jerks outwards. This doesn't seem to have survival value. It may have done in the past. Doctors sometimes use this reaction to test the health of your nervous system.

3 Describe, step by step, the knee-jerk reflex.

Tracing the pathway through the spinal cord

Look at the diagram.

4 Write down, in the order they act, the names of the <u>three</u> types of neurone in a reflex action.

5 Name the effector in this example.

Muscles respond to nerve impulses from **motor** neurones by **contracting**. Glands respond by **secreting** a useful substance.

6 When Liam saw his dinner, his mouth started to 'water' (his brain caused his salivary glands to secrete saliva).

    a Why is this reflex useful?
    b For this reflex, what is the
        i stimulus?
        ii receptor?
        iii coordinator?
        iv effector?
        v response?

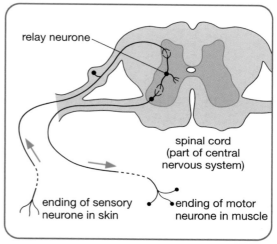

relay neurone

spinal cord (part of central nervous system)

ending of sensory neurone in skin

ending of motor neurone in muscle

What you need to remember *Copy and complete using the **key words***

Automatic responses

Fast, _____ responses to stimuli are called _____ actions.

Impulses pass from receptors to effectors via sensory, relay and _____ neurones.

At junctions between neurones, there are tiny gaps called _____.

Nerve impulses reach effectors very rapidly and cause the response.

If the effector is a muscle, it responds by _____. If it is a gland, it responds by releasing or _____ a chemical.

4 Keeping things the same in your body

To work properly, everything inside your body has to be kept at a **constant** level. Your body must be at just the right **temperature**. Your blood must contain just the right amounts of water, sugar and ions such as sodium ions.

Normally, your body automatically controls them. But you may have problems in hot, dry, windy conditions or when you are playing sports.

> **1** Write down <u>three</u> substances that your body needs to keep at a constant level.

> **2** Copy and complete the sentences.
>
> You take in water in _____ and
>
> _____ .
>
> You lose water in _____ ,
>
> _____ and _____ .
>
> Your _____ control your water balance.

Chemicals called **hormones** control the composition of your blood. Special glands secrete hormones into your blood. Your **bloodstream** carries them to the organs that use them. We call these **target** organs.

> **3** Look at the diagram. Then copy and complete the table.

Part of body	How it helps your body stay the same
skin	controls your body temperature
kidneys	
pancreas	
lungs	

Automatic control may fail in difficult conditions such as those in deserts like Death Valley, California. You have to make sure that it doesn't by

- taking in enough water
- taking in enough salt to provide ions
- getting enough shelter.

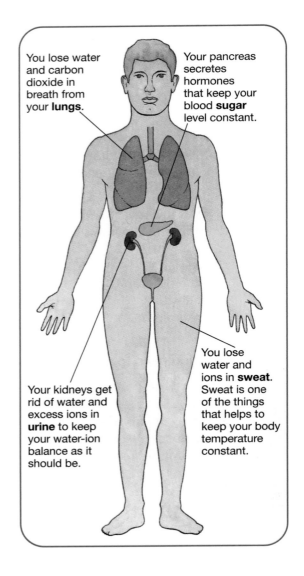

You lose water and carbon dioxide in breath from your **lungs**.

Your pancreas secretes hormones that keep your blood **sugar** level constant.

Your kidneys get rid of water and excess ions in **urine** to keep your water-ion balance as it should be.

You lose water and ions in **sweat**. Sweat is one of the things that helps to keep your body temperature constant.

Replacing water, ions and glucose

It's not just harsh places like Death Valley that cause problems for your body. Playing sports can have similar effects.

Your muscles work harder so they

- use more glucose
- release more energy.

As a result, you get hot. This makes you sweat, so your body loses more water and ions than usual.

4 Write down <u>three</u> substances that sports drinks are designed to replace.

5 Write down <u>two</u> reasons why some sports scientists don't recommend sports drinks.

Are you better off drinking water?

Manufacturers claim that their sports drinks give you an advantage. They replace the water and salts that you lose and the glucose in them gives you an 'energy boost'.

Some sports scientists suggest that it's better just to drink water or to make your own drink using water, salt and glucose. (There are recipes on the Internet.) They point out that sports drinks are expensive and people don't always buy the right one for the job. The wrong one can be harmful. Another problem is that they contain citric acid as a preservative – and citric acid rots your teeth.

Why must your body be at 37 °C?

Chemical reactions happen all the time in your body. **Enzymes** are substances that make these chemical reactions happen faster. Your enzymes work best at 37 °C. High temperatures damage enzyme molecules.

6 Copy the graph.
Mark where you think enzymes are damaged.

7 Why don't enzymes work as well below 37 °C?

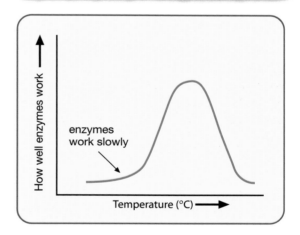

What you need to remember *Copy and complete using the* **key words**

Keeping things the same in your body

For it to work properly, everything inside your body must be kept at a _____ level. Special glands in your body produce chemicals called _____ to control the amounts of water, ions and _____ in your blood. Your _____ carries hormones to their _____ organs.

You lose water from your _____ in your breath. You lose water and ions from your skin in _____ and from your kidneys in _____.

For _____ to work at their best, your body _____ must be kept constant.

You need to be able to evaluate the claims of manufacturers about sports drinks.

5 The menstrual cycle

Monthly preparation for pregnancy

Hormones from the **pituitary gland** and **ovaries** control a woman's **menstrual cycle**.

About every 28 days

- an egg ripens in one of a woman's ovaries and is then released
- a thick lining develops inside her womb.

1 Look at the diagram, then copy and complete the sentences.

An egg travels from the ovary to the womb through the _____ _____.
This is where it can join up with a sperm and become _____.

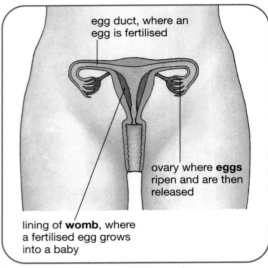

A woman can become pregnant if one or more of her eggs is fertilised by a sperm.

The lining of the womb thickens at the same time as an egg is ripening. If an egg is fertilised, the lining is ready to receive it.

If an egg isn't fertilised, the lining breaks down. This is a 'period'. The egg dies.

2 Copy and complete the table.

	What happens to the lining of the womb	What happens to the egg
egg is fertilised		
egg isn't fertilised		

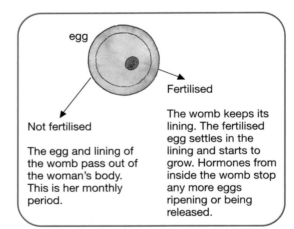

Not fertilised

The egg and lining of the womb pass out of the woman's body. This is her monthly period.

Fertilised

The womb keeps its lining. The fertilised egg settles in the lining and starts to grow. Hormones from inside the womb stop any more eggs ripening or being released.

Different hormones do different jobs

Some hormones

- stimulate – they make things happen
- inhibit – they stop things happening.

3 Look at the picture.
Then copy and complete the diagram below.

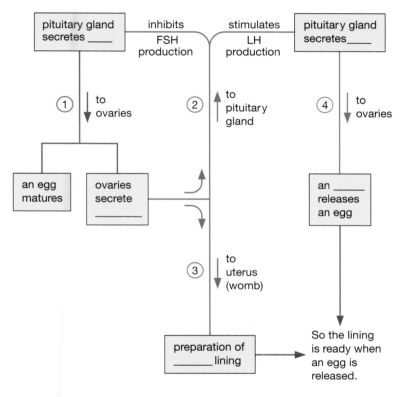

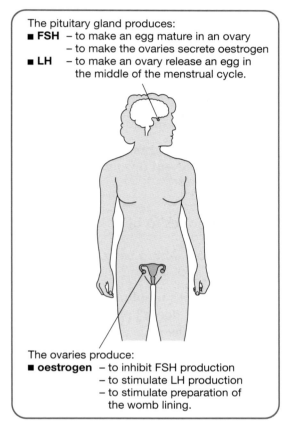

The pituitary gland produces:
- **FSH** – to make an egg mature in an ovary
  – to make the ovaries secrete oestrogen
- **LH** – to make an ovary release an egg in the middle of the menstrual cycle.

The ovaries produce:
- **oestrogen** – to inhibit FSH production
  – to stimulate LH production
  – to stimulate preparation of the womb lining.

Hormones travel around the body in the bloodstream.

4 Where in the woman's body is her pituitary gland?

5 How do hormones get from where they are made to where they make things happen?

What you need to remember *Copy and complete using the **key words***

The menstrual cycle

The pituitary gland secretes the hormones _____ and _____.
FSH affects the ovaries. It stimulates them to make _____ mature and to
produce hormones including _____. Oestrogen from the ovaries makes the
lining of the _____ thicken. It also inhibits FSH production and causes the
release of the hormone LH by the _____ _____. LH stimulates
the _____ to release an egg at about the middle of the _____
_____.

6 Using hormones to control pregnancy

Some women want to have a baby but can't become **pregnant**. Other women don't want to become pregnant. Both these problems can sometimes be solved using **hormones**. In other words, we can use hormones to control **fertility**.

1 Look at the diagram.
Which hormones could be used

   a to help a woman become pregnant?
   b to prevent a woman becoming pregnant?

Using hormones to help a woman become pregnant

Janet and Carl want a baby. They've been trying for a year.

Doctors at Janet's hospital have found out that her pituitary gland doesn't produce enough FSH, so her ovaries don't release eggs. There isn't much chance of her becoming pregnant. She is infertile.

Her doctor has decided to treat Janet by injecting the hormone **FSH** into her blood. The hormone should make her ovaries release eggs. We call this fertility treatment. It has helped many women to have the babies they want.

2 Why is Janet not becoming pregnant?

3 What will fertility treatment do to help?

4 Write down <u>two</u> problems there can be with fertility drugs.

Janet's friend Sushila had even more problems becoming pregnant. Her egg tubes were damaged so the eggs she produced couldn't reach her womb. The only way for Sushila to become pregnant was to have her eggs fertilised in a dish and then put into her womb to grow. We call this IVF treatment.

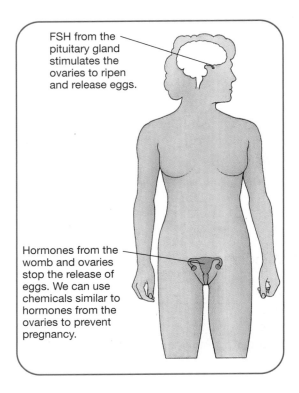

FSH from the pituitary gland stimulates the ovaries to ripen and release eggs.

Hormones from the womb and ovaries stop the release of eggs. We can use chemicals similar to hormones from the ovaries to prevent pregnancy.

A fertility **drug** doesn't always work. But sometimes it works too well. Several eggs may be released at once so a woman has several babies at the same time. We call these multiple births.

How doctors helped Sushila

Sushila had to take hormones to make more eggs mature than usual. Then the doctor collected them from her ovaries for IVF. She was lucky. She had a healthy baby at the first attempt.

5 Suggest which hormone Sushila had to take.

6 Suggest why
   a the doctor collected lots of eggs
   b Sushila had two embryos put into her womb.

In IVF, sperm fertilise eggs in a dish. The fertilised eggs grow for a few days to make sure that they are alive and growing. Then the doctor puts one or two embryos into the woman's womb.

Using hormones to prevent pregnancy

Some couples want to have sexual intercourse but don't want the woman to become pregnant. The woman can take **contraceptive** pills – or oral contraceptives. These contain hormones that inhibit FSH production. So they stop **eggs** maturing.

However, the pills can have side effects such as sickness and headaches. In a very few women, they cause serious heart problems or even death. Also, a woman must remember to take the pills regularly. If she doesn't, she may become pregnant.

7 Write down <u>two</u> reasons why a couple might not want the woman to become pregnant.

8 Some women who don't want to become pregnant don't want to use pills.
Suggest <u>two</u> reasons why.

Couples may want to plan when they have their children.

Some couples already have children and don't want any more.

What you need to remember *Copy and complete using the **key words***

Using hormones to control pregnancy
Some women use _____ to control their _____.
FSH is a fertility _____ for women who don't produce enough _____ of their own.
It helps a woman to become _____ by stimulating her ovaries to make eggs mature. Oral _____ pills contain hormones that inhibit FSH production. They stop _____ maturing.

You should be able to describe and explain some of the problems and benefits of using hormones to control fertility, including IVF.

1 A healthy diet

Ideas you need from KS3

We often see or hear in the media, 'You are what you eat'. There is some truth in this. But we are also a product of our <u>genes</u>, our <u>environment</u> and our <u>lifestyles</u>.

A healthy diet contains everything your body needs. It shouldn't contain things that harm you.

All the food you eat is your diet. So everyone is on a diet, not just people trying to lose weight.

Some nutrient groups in your food	What your body needs it for
carbohydrates	energy
proteins	growth and replacing cells (you use excess for energy)
fats	energy and making cell membranes
vitamins	healthy cells

1 Write down <u>four</u> nutrient groups that a healthy diet should contain.

2 Plan a simple snack lunch that contains all these things. It should also contain other vitamins, fibre, water and minerals such as iron and calcium.

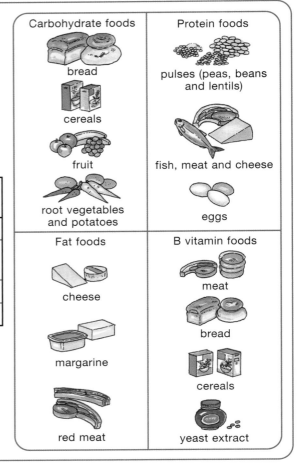

Different diets for different people

There are lots of ways of getting a healthy diet. Different people choose different types of food. Many people eat less red meat now than they did. Vegetarians don't eat any meat at all.

3 Why do you think people become vegetarians?

4 A diet without meat may be healthier. Explain why.

5 What can vegetarians eat to get enough

    a protein?
    b B vitamins?

The only way vegetarian food is ever likely to give you a heart attack.

Eating too much animal fat may cause heart disease.

What is the right balance?

The diagram shows what the Food Standards Agency recommends.

6 Draw and complete a table with these headings.

Food group	Suggested proportion

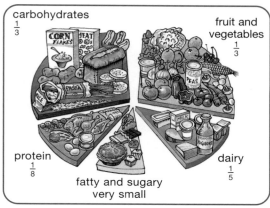

The proportions of different **food groups** in a healthy diet.

What if you don't get enough of a nutrient?

Shortage of energy foods can make you too thin.
Shortage of proteins affects your growth.
The amounts of vitamins you need are small. But if you don't get enough your body won't work as it should.

We call a problem caused by lack of a particular nutrient a **deficiency disease**. The table shows a few of these diseases.

7 Write down the deficiency disease caused by lack of vitamin C.

8 What is anaemia?

Nutrient	Deficiency causes ...
vitamin A	poor night vision (night blindness), dry skin
vitamin B_3	wasting, skin and mental problems (pellagra)
vitamin C	weakness, bleeding (scurvy)
vitamin D	soft bones (rickets)
iron	tiredness owing to lack of haemoglobin (anaemia)

What if you get too much?

Eating more **energy** foods than you need makes you put on weight. You store the excess as fat. Too much of nutrients such as vitamin A or vitamin D can actually poison you.

9 Why is there a warning on many vitamin pills packs not to exceed the stated dose?

It's the balance of your diet over days that matters, not what you eat in just one meal. Continually having too much or too little of a nutrient makes your diet unbalanced. You become **malnourished**.

What you need to remember *Copy and complete using the key words*

A healthy diet
A healthy diet contains the right balance of the different _____ _____ and the right amount of _____.
We say that a person whose diet is not balanced is _____.
A malnourished person may be too fat, too thin or have a _____ _____.

LIB

2 Energy balance

A balanced diet!

Even if your diet is varied and contains all the vitamins and minerals you need, your diet could still be unbalanced in terms of energy.

1 Write down

   a the <u>two</u> main groups of energy foods
   b <u>two</u> things that affect the amounts you need.

2 What happens to your body mass if you

   a use more energy than the amount of energy in your food?
   b use less energy than the amount of energy in your food?

Energy needs vary

The amount of energy you need varies with:

- the temperature – you need less **energy** food in warm weather
- the amount of exercise you do – the more exercise you do, the more energy food you need.

If you are one of those people who can eat lots without increasing your body mass, it may be that the rate of chemical reactions in your cells is high. We say that you have a high **metabolic rate**.

3 Write down <u>three</u> things that affect the amount of energy food you need.

4 Copy and complete the sentences.

   People with a high _____ rate tend not to gain body _____ easily.
   This is because the rate of _____ _____ in their cells is high.
   Their cells quickly break down _____ and sugars.

5 Write down <u>three</u> things that affect your metabolic rate.

> **REMEMBER**
>
> You use energy released in respiration from carbohydrates, fats and excess proteins in your diet for:
>
> - moving
> - growing
> - keeping warm.

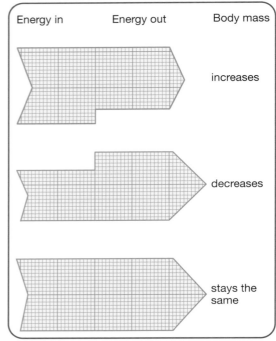

If you take in more energy in food than you use, you store the extra as fat. To keep your body mass the same, your energy intake and use should balance.

> Some things that affect your metabolic rate are:
>
> - **inherited** factors (your genes)
> - the amount of exercise you do (regular exercise can increase your metabolic rate)
> - the proportion of **muscle** to fat in your body
> - your hormones.

More benefits of exercise

You have seen that **exercise** increases your metabolic rate. Even when you've finished exercising, your metabolic rate stays high for a while. The longer you exercise for, the longer it stays high.

Exercise also increases the size of your muscles.
The more muscle cells you have and the more active they are, the more glucose they respire.

People who exercise regularly are usually **fitter** than people who don't. They can exercise for longer without getting tired and out of breath.

6 What are the benefits of having a body with

  a more muscle?
  b less fat?

7 Look at the photographs of the cells.

  a Which <u>two</u> cell types respire fastest?
  b Which cell type has a low metabolic rate?

Some people are overweight because the rate of chemical reactions such as respiration in their cells is low.
They respire energy foods slowly and store the excess in fat cells.

8 Suggest <u>two</u> things that these people can do to lose body mass.
Give reasons for your suggestions.

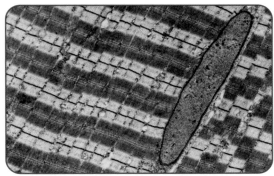

Muscle cells use the energy released in respiration to contract. They have a <u>high</u> metabolic rate.

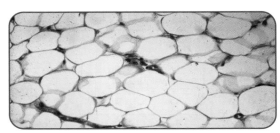

White fat cells are energy stores. They form useful insulation and padding – a bit like cushions around delicate organs. They have a <u>low</u> metabolic rate.

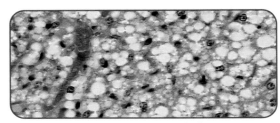

Brown fat cells have a <u>high</u> metabolic rate. They store fat in many small globules and can break it down quickly to release lots of heat (thermal) energy.

What you need to remember *Copy and complete using the **key words***

Energy balance
The rate at which chemical reactions happen in your cells is called your

_____ _____.

It depends on

- how active you are
- the proportion of _____ to fat in your body
- your genes (_____ factors).

_____ increases your metabolic rate and it stays high for some time after you finish exercising.
If you take regular exercise, you are likely to be _____ than people who don't.
The less exercise you take and the warmer it is, the less _____ food you need.

3 More about body mass

What is normal body mass?

As with other features of the human body, there is a range of normal body mass. It depends on your sex, height, age and skeleton.

1 Use the chart to find out the range of normal body mass for a female who is 1.60 m tall.

2 At what body mass do we say that a male 1.70 m tall is underweight?

> Doctors and fitness experts use several ways of assessing body mass.
> They use
>
> - height–weight charts
> - body mass index (BMI)
> - skin fold measurements.

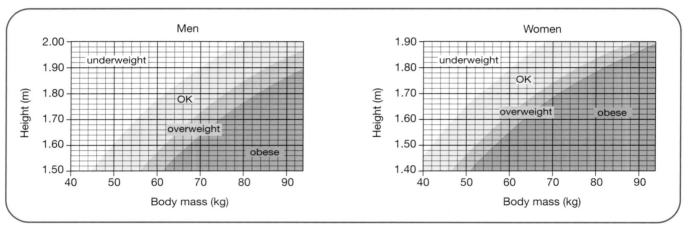

These charts are for adults. During puberty, body mass increases before the growth spurt.
So, at that time, a higher body mass than shown on the chart may be normal.

What if your body mass is too low?

In the developed world, people who are underweight are either ill or have deliberately dieted to lose weight.

In the developing world, some people have no choice. They rarely get enough to eat. This may be because

- their crops have failed
- they are too poor or have no land
- there just isn't any food to buy.

Their **health** suffers. Children and old people are often the worst affected.

3 Copy and complete the sentences.

People who don't get enough _____ are often ill because their _____ to infection is _____. Women's periods become _____.

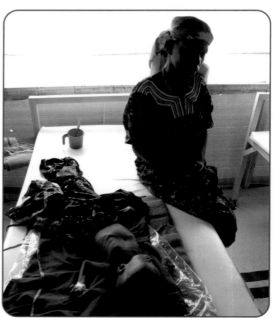

Lack of food means that this family have poor resistance to **infection**. The mother's **periods** are irregular.

What if your body mass is too high?

In places such as the UK in the developed world, many people eat too much and take too little **exercise**. So many people are **obese**.

If you are fat (**overweight**) or very fat (obese), you are more likely to have health problems.

4 Look at the photographs. Then copy and complete the table.

Result of being overweight	Effect on health
too much weight on limbs	
fat deposits in arteries	
narrowing of arteries	
cells take up sugars slowly	

Narrow arteries cause **high blood pressure** (blood pressure of more than 140/90 mm Hg).

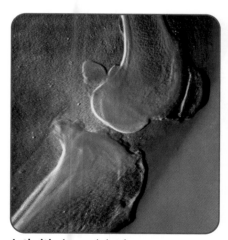

Arthritis (worn joints).

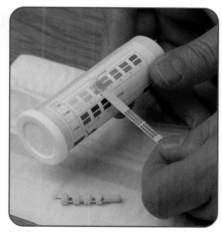

Diabetes (too much sugar in the blood).

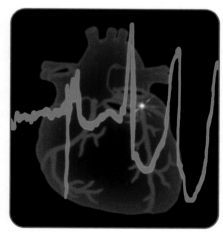

Heart disease.

What you need to remember *Copy and complete using the **key words***

More about body mass

In the developed world many people eat too much and take too little _____.
They easily become _____ and develop health problems.
People who are _____ are at greater risk of getting diseases linked with excess weight such as _____, _____, _____ _____ and _____ _____ _____.
In the developing world, some people have _____ problems linked to lack of food. They may have poor resistance to _____. Women may have irregular _____.

4 How can you lose body mass?

In the developed world, more people are worried about being overweight than being underweight. So at any one time thousands of people are on slimming diets.

The United Nations suggests that adults need a diet containing 8800 kilojoules of energy a day. In the USA and Europe, there are people who live on less than half of that and still don't lose body mass. This is because constant dieting and lack of exercise have lowered their metabolic rates. 5000 kJ a day is a starvation diet in the developing world. It's not enough for people who are active and have a normal metabolic rate.

1 Suggest why, when they eat the same amount, some people gain and others lose weight.

In theory, you can lose body mass if you

- eat only 5000 kilojoules a day (you are taking in less energy than you use)
- take more exercise (your cells release more energy in respiration).

2 Write down two reasons why exercising can help you to lose weight.

3 How can people who have failed to slim on 5000 kilojoules a day lose body mass?

These two people have very similar diets. The one on the right does very little exercise and has a low metabolic rate.

Exercise increases your metabolic rate and helps you to build muscle.

Slimming programmes

Many people in the developed world are overweight or obese. So slimming programmes are big business.

Look at the advertisement.

4 Suggest disadvantages of eating a diet of mainly one thing.

5 Why shouldn't you follow a very low energy slimming programme like this one for more than a few weeks?

A 'souper' diet

On our diet you can lose up to 6 kg in a week. You can eat as much of our special vegetable soup as you like. Each day you also have a different 'extra' food so you don't get bored.
Why not give us a call on …

Sensible slimming

There are lots of different slimming programmes. Many involve 'calorie counting' in order to eat a very low-energy diet.

> **REMEMBER**
>
> Carbohydrates, fats, proteins, vitamins, minerals, fibre and water are all important for your health.

6 Which nutrients may be in short supply in a low-energy (calorie counting) slimming diet?

7 What can a slimmer do to get enough of these nutrients?

The Atkins way – no need to feel hungry

On the Atkins diet, you can eat as much meat and fatty foods as you like. Cut out the carbohydrates and you'll lose weight!

Slimming club diets

Joining the club benefits you in lots of ways. You learn how to change your eating habits and put together a low calorie diet that you'll enjoy. The exercise classes are safe and you have other people to turn to help when you them.

8 Look at the newspaper cuttings.

  a Write down <u>two</u> benefits of joining a slimming club and suggest <u>two</u> problems.

  b A high-fat diet may be bad for your heart. Which diet is high in fat?

9 What can you do to make sure that you don't put the weight back on when you stop dieting?

Food replacement diets

Some people slim by replacing two meals a day with drinks containing proteins, vitamins and minerals. This ensures that they get all the essential nutrients. But when they go back to their old eating habits, they put the weight back on.

When slimming goes too far

With a good slimming programme, you usually eat less but have the normal number of meals. You don't usually become too slim. A few people do. Their body mass drops low enough for it to put their health and their lives at risk.

They use up all the stores of carbohydrates and fats in their bodies. Then they start to break down the proteins in their muscles, including their hearts. They have anorexia.

10 If you use up all your carbohydrate and fat stores

  a what is your energy source?

  b how does this harm your health?

What you need to remember

How can you lose body mass?
There is nothing new for you to <u>remember</u> in this section.

> You need to be able to evaluate claims made by slimming programmes.

5 Diet and heart disease

Risk factors

Diet is just one of the risk factors for **heart disease**.
It's not the only one that you can control.

> **1** Write down <u>three</u> things that affect the health of
> your heart that
>
> **a** you can't change
> **b** you can change.

Processed foods, including fast foods such as burgers, often
contain a lot of **salt** and **fat**. Having too much fat can raise
your **blood pressure** and increase your risk of heart disease.
Salt does the same in about 30% of people.

However

- salt and fat both make food more tasty
- we need fats in our diet. We can't make cells
  without them.

> **2** Why do people choose fatty and salty foods rather
> than healthier foods?

> **3** Look at the food label. Write down <u>two</u> good things
> and <u>two</u> bad things about the nutrients in this food.

> **4** Which groups of fats <u>may</u> be healthier for your
> heart, and why?

FACT FILE
What affects the health of your heart?

- Inherited factors – the amount of
  cholesterol your **liver** makes depends
  on your genes as well as on your diet.
- Your age – the older you are, the
  greater the risk.
- Your sex – until the menopause,
  women are at lower risk.
- Your lifestyle – including diet,
  exercise, smoking, alcohol and stress.

Cauliflower Cheese

NUTRITION			
Typical Values	per pack	per 100 g	
Energy Value	1560 kJ	390 kJ	
(Calories	375 kcal	95 kcal)	
Protein	22 g	6 g	HIGH
Carbohydrate	14 g	3 g	LOW
(of which Sugars	3 g	0.8 g)	
Fat	26 g	6 g	HIGH
(of which Saturates	16 g	4 g)	HIGH
Fibre	4 g	1 g	MEDIUM
Sodium	1.0 g	0.2 g	HIGH
Salt	2.4 g	0.6 g	HIGH

This label is from a single serving of cauliflower
cheese.

A healthy diet includes plenty of unprocessed foods and lots of fresh fruit and vegetables. It should be
low in red meat, fat, salt and sugars. Fish, including oily fish, are beneficial.

Animal fats are rich in **saturated** fat
and <u>may</u> increase the amount of blood
cholesterol.

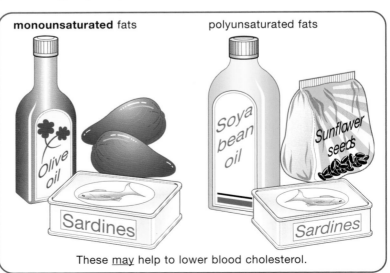

monounsaturated fats   polyunsaturated fats

These <u>may</u> help to lower blood cholesterol.

Cholesterol isn't all 'bad'

The **cholesterol** in your blood doesn't all come from your food. You also make it in your liver. It's a normal body fat and it travels in the blood as **lipoproteins**, a combination of protein and fat. There are two kinds. 'Bad' or <u>LDL</u> cholesterol can form deposits in arteries and cause heart disease.

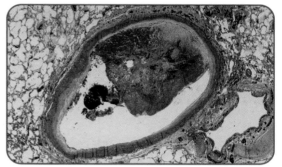

The narrowing of the space inside this artery causes blood pressure to rise.

Look at the picture.

5 When cholesterol deposits form, what happens to the space inside an artery?

6 What effect does this have on blood pressure?

7 What happens to heart muscle when it doesn't get a good supply of oxygen?

We sometimes call <u>HDL</u> cholesterol 'good' because it protects your arteries against becoming blocked. People at risk of heart disease may be sent for a cholesterol test. This measures the LDL, HDL and total cholesterol in their blood.

The LDL/HDL balance is important. Ideally, LDL cholesterol should be below 3 mmol per dm^3 and total cholesterol at or below 5 mmol per dm^3.

8 Why would a doctor think that a blood LDL cholesterol reading higher than 3 mmol per dm^3 was a problem?

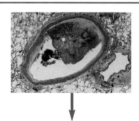

It would take only a small blood clot to block this artery.

If an artery to part of the heart muscle (a coronary artery) is blocked, the blood supply to that part stops.

That part of the muscle doesn't get the oxygen it needs so it stops working. Then it dies. This is a heart attack.

> Doctors suggest that people with too much cholesterol in their blood should
>
> - eat a diet low in saturated fat to lower the amount of LDL cholesterol
> - take plenty of exercise to raise the amount of HDL cholesterol

What you need to remember *Copy and complete using the **key words***

Diet and heart disease

Processed foods often contain a high proportion of _____ and _____.
For about 30% of the population, too much salt can cause an increase in

_____ _____.

The fat in your diet and inherited factors affect the amount of _____ your
_____ makes. Two types of _____, LDL and HDL, carry cholesterol around
your body. High levels of LDL (bad) cholesterol increase your risk of blood vessel damage
and _____ _____. HDL (good) cholesterol protects your arteries.
Eating polyunsaturated and _____ fats may lower blood cholesterol and help to
improve the LDL / HDL balance that is important for heart health. Eating _____
fats can increase blood cholesterol.

1 People and drugs

A **drug** is a substance that can change the way your body or mind works. Most drugs have some harmful and some beneficial effects. Some, such as painkillers and antibiotics, are mainly beneficial but can cause **harm**. Others such as tobacco and cannabis, which some people use to help them relax, increase the risk of ill health.

1 Write down

    a <u>two</u> types of drug that are mainly useful

    b <u>two</u> types of drug that are mainly harmful.

People have been using drugs for thousands of years. We know that people made beer in Babylon 8000 years ago. Look at the Egyptian picture writing about alcohol from nearly 4000 years ago.

2 What dangers of drinking alcohol are mentioned in this writing?

People in many parts of the world made alcohol from sugar. They used whatever source of sugars they found where they lived.

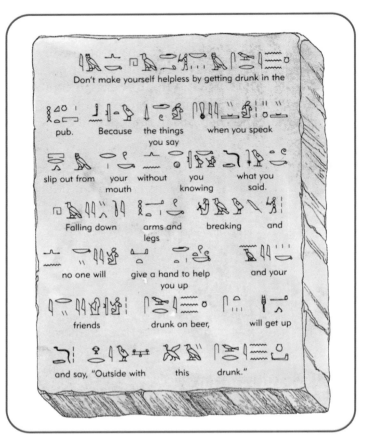

Don't make yourself helpless by getting drunk in the pub. Because the things you say slip out from your mouth without you knowing what you said. Falling down arms and legs breaking and no one will give a hand to help you up and your friends drunk on beer, will get up and say, "Outside with this drunk."

Egyptian picture writing (hieroglyphics).

More drugs from plants

Indigenous people found ways of using other **natural** substances found in their local plants. 500 years ago, the Incas in the Andes of South America chewed coca leaves. It helped them to work hard in difficult places and it stopped them feeling hungry.

3 What do we use the coca plant for now?

4 Suggest why the Chinese used a plant called artemesia to treat malaria, but South American Indians used bark from the cinchona tree.

We now use plants from around the world to make our medicines. Scientists gather the knowledge of indigenous people about their plants. Then they develop new drugs from them.

5 Suggest why drug companies are particularly interested in saving habitats such as rain forests.

We now get anaesthetics and cocaine from the coca plant.

Legal and illegal drugs

Some people use drugs for relaxation and **recreation**.
Some drugs are legal. Others are **illegal**.
Look at the table.

Although people start off using them for enjoyment, drugs soon cause problems for many users. Drugs such as heroin, cocaine and nicotine are addictive. In the longer term some drugs, such as tobacco and alcohol, increase the risk of health problems such as heart disease, stomach ulcers and some cancers. There may be a link between cannabis and mental health problems.

Group	Effects	Examples
stimulants	speed up the body	amphetamines (speed), cocaine, crack, ecstasy, <u>caffeine</u>, <u>nicotine</u>
depressants	slow down the body	<u>alcohol</u>, opiates, cannabis
hallucinogens	make you see, hear or feel unusual things	LSD (acid), cannabis, magic mushrooms
opiates	painkillers; also act as both depressants and hallucinogens	heroin, morphine

Legal drugs are underlined in the table. Some others are legal on prescription. Far more people use **legal** than illegal drugs.
So legal drugs have more impact on our health and the National Health Service (NHS).

6 Write down

a <u>two</u> drugs that are legal
b <u>two</u> drugs that are illegal.

7 Copy and complete the table below.

Drug	Possible health problems
alcohol	stomach ulcers, liver disease
cannabis	
cocaine	
heroin	
tobacco	

What you need to remember *Copy and complete using the **key words***

People and drugs
A substance that can change the way your body works is called a _____.
Many drugs come from _____ substances. _____ (native) peoples usually know about their local sources of drugs and have used them for thousands of years.
Some drugs are beneficial but can also _____ our bodies.
Some people use drugs for _____. Some are more harmful than others. Some are legal, some _____. The overall impact of _____ drugs on health is much greater than the impact of illegal drugs, because more people use them.

You need to be able to evaluate the different types of drugs and why some people use illegal drugs for recreation.

2 What's your poison – alcohol?

Beers, wines and spirits like whisky contain alcohol. Alcohol is a drug.

1 Look at Morton's description of how alcohol affects behaviour. Make a table with these headings and then complete it.

Number of drinks	How Morton says people behave	What do you think he means?

One drink and you act like a monkey; two drinks, and you strut like a peacock; three drinks, and you roar like a lion; and four drinks – you behave like a pig.
Henry Vollam Morton (1936)

It's just the same now. The Government is very concerned about heavy drinking. Look at the picture.

2 Write down <u>three</u> aspects of antisocial behaviour shown by binge drinkers.

Some more effects of alcohol

Alcohol affects your **nervous system**. Even small amounts make you sleepy and slow your **reactions**.

Larger amounts can make you lose self-control or consciousness, or even go into a **coma**. In one raid, robbers forced a postmaster and his wife to drink a bottle of whisky between them to 'knock them out'. His wife died from alcohol poisoning.

3 What does alcohol do to your body that makes it dangerous to drink and drive?

4 What can happen if you drink too much alcohol?

Your liver breaks down alcohol into harmless substances. But if you drink too much, alcohol can damage organs before your liver gets rid of it.

5 Which organs does alcohol damage?

Binge drinking leads to antisocial behaviour.

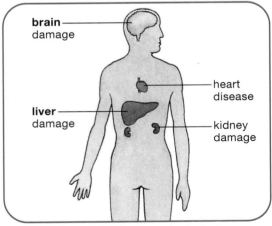

brain damage

liver damage

heart disease

kidney damage

Longer-term effects of too much alcohol.

How much alcohol is there in different drinks?

Different alcoholic drinks contain different amounts of alcohol. When health workers suggest limits for the maximum amounts that adults should drink, they talk about units.

6 Tony drinks two pints of ordinary beer.
Alex drinks one pint of strong beer and one single whisky.
Nassia drinks two glasses of wine.
How many units of alcohol does each person drink?

| $\frac{1}{2}$ pint ordinary beer or cider | $\frac{1}{3}$ pint strong brew | 1 glass of table wine | 1 glass of sherry | 1 single whisky |

Each drink contains one unit of alcohol.

What is reasonable drinking?

Alcohol is a poison. It slows your reactions and it affects your behaviour. You can become dependent on alcohol. When you can't do without it, we say you are <u>addicted</u> to it.

But small amounts of alcohol can help some people to relax. The diagram shows how many units of alcohol many health workers think it is safe for adults to drink each week.

7 **a** What is the maximum number of units a man should drink each week?
b How much strong beer is this each day?

8 Paula drinks three glasses of wine and a single whisky each day.

a How many units of alcohol is this in a week?
b What advice would you give Paula?

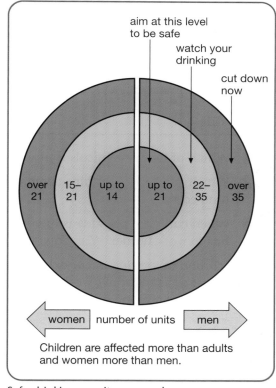

aim at this level to be safe
watch your drinking
cut down now

over 21 | 15–21 | up to 14 | up to 21 | 22–35 | over 35

women | number of units | men

Children are affected more than adults and women more than men.

Safe drinking – units per week.

What you need to remember *Copy and complete using the* **key words**

What's your poison – alcohol?
Alcohol can damage organs such as your _____ and _____. It also affects your _____ _____.
Your _____ become slower and you may lose self-control. You may even lose consciousness and go into a _____.

3 Legal but harmful – tobacco

What is in cigarette smoke?

Cigarette smoke contains many harmful chemicals.
Look at the table.

Chemical	Addictive drug	Poison	Effect on body
tar (4000 different chemicals)		✓	**carcinogens** (cause cancers)
nicotine	✓	✓	increases blood pressure, raises pulse rate
carbon monoxide		✓	blood can carry less oxygen

1 Which of these chemicals is an addictive drug?

2 Which substance contains chemicals that cause lung cancer?

3 When carbon monoxide is in your blood, your heart has to work harder. Why do you think this is?

It is the carbon monoxide in car exhaust fumes that can kill people. If gas fires aren't working properly they can also release carbon monoxide.

Some insecticides contain nicotine.

Nicotine is a natural poison found in many plants.
The plants produce it to stop insects eating them.

4 What effect does nicotine have on your body?

5 Why do gardeners find nicotine useful?

6 Draw a table with these headings. Complete it using the information in the diagram.

Organ affected	Name of disease	What the disease does

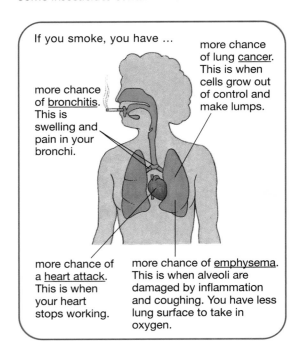

If you smoke, you have …

more chance of lung cancer. This is when cells grow out of control and make lumps.

more chance of bronchitis. This is swelling and pain in your bronchi.

more chance of a heart attack. This is when your heart stops working.

more chance of emphysema. This is when alveoli are damaged by inflammation and coughing. You have less lung surface to take in oxygen.

Does it matter whether you smoke?

The table shows how smoking affects your chance of getting lung cancer.

Number of cigarettes smoked per day	Increased risk of cancer compared with non-smokers
5	4 ×
10	8 ×
15	12 ×
20	16 ×

7 Explain, as fully as you can, what the table tells you.

8 Look at the photograph.
What message is the photograph trying to get across to people?

9 The fetus (developing child) inside a pregnant woman who smokes is likely to get less **oxygen** than it should. Why is this?
(Hint: Look at the table on page 34.)

10 Write down <u>one</u> effect of lack of oxygen on the baby.

FACTS AND FIGURES

■ Out of every 1000 teenagers who smoke, about 250 will eventually die of smoking-related diseases.
■ On average, smokers die 10–15 years earlier than non-smokers.
■ Over 90% of people who die from lung cancer are smokers.
■ The babies of pregnant women who smoke weigh, on average, 200 g less than the babies whose mothers do not smoke. We say that the babies have a low **birth mass**.
■ Pregnant women who smoke are more likely to have a miscarriage or stillbirth.

Would you like a cigarette?

No!

What you need to remember *Copy and complete using the **key words***

Legal but harmful – tobacco
Tobacco smoke contains

■ _____ – an addictive substance
■ _____ – substances that cause cancer
■ _____ _____ – which reduces the amount of oxygen your blood can carry.

When a pregnant woman smokes, the fetus can be deprived of _____ so the baby may have a low _____ _____.

4 Smoking and lung cancer

Sir Walter Raleigh brought tobacco to Britain in the 16th century. People smoked it in pipes. Cigarettes became popular during and after the 1914–1918 War. Few women smoked before 1920.

Deaths from lung cancer increase

In the years after the 1914–1918 War, the number of men dying from lung cancer increased. At first many people thought that it was because doctors were getting better at diagnosing lung cancer. This could have explained some of the increase. But people began to look for other reasons.

1 Look at the graph.
What was the death rate from lung cancer in

   a 1920?
   b 1940?

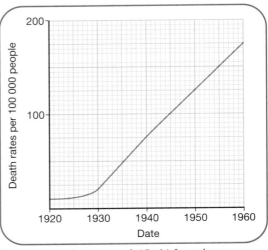

Death rates of men aged 45–64 from lung cancer in England and Wales.

Why were deaths from lung cancer increasing?

About 50 years ago in Britain, Professor Richard Doll and Dr Bradford Hill thought that there might be a link between cigarette smoking and lung cancer.

Other scientists were thinking about and working on similar ideas in the USA.

2 Suggest why did Doll and Hill started to suspect that smoking and lung cancer were linked.

What Doll and Hill did

They decided to test their idea by doing a survey.

- They selected a group of men with lung cancer.
- As a control group, they selected a group of men of similar ages and backgrounds who didn't have lung cancer.
- They asked both groups the same questions.

---

3 What was the idea that Doll and Hill were testing?

4 Why did they need a control group?

5 Look at the table.
Do the results support the idea that there is a link between smoking and lung cancer?

	Lung cancer patients	Control group
smokers	99.7%	95.8%
non-smokers	0.3%	4.2%

Looking for more evidence

In 1951, Doll and Hill decided to do some longer-term studies. They studied the smoking habits, health and death rates of a group of doctors over 5 years.

	Deaths of doctors from lung cancer (per 100 000)
non-smokers	7
light smokers	47
moderate smokers	86
heavy smokers	166

6 Look at the table.

   a Which group of doctors was at most risk from lung cancer?
   b How many times greater was the risk of lung cancer for heavy smokers than for non-smokers?

At the same time as Doll and Hill were researching the health of doctors, scientists at New York University found that many of the chemicals in tobacco smoke caused cancers in animals.

In 1962, the Royal College of Physicians produced a report. It concluded that there was a link between lung cancer and smoking. Not everyone agreed.

7 What was the report called?

Following the report, there was only a 4% fall in the number of cigarettes smoked. But doctors took notice. Large numbers gave up smoking. The death rate of doctors from lung cancer fell.

8 What did many doctors do that provided further evidence of a link between smoking and lung cancer? Explain your answer.

9 Some groups of people didn't want to accept that there was a link between smoking and lung cancer. Suggest <u>two</u> reasons for this.

By the end of the 20th century, even the tobacco companies had to agree that smoking increases the risk of developing lung cancer.

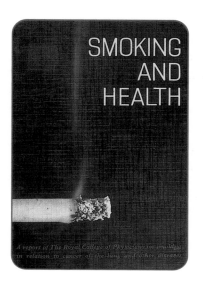

Some people don't want to give up smoking.

What you need to remember

Smoking and lung cancer
There is nothing new for you to <u>remember</u> in this section.

You need to be able to explain how the link between lung cancer and smoking gradually became accepted.

5 Addiction

Illegal drugs

Cannabis, opium and cocaine are ancient drugs from plants.

Plant	One named drug
cannabis	cannabis
opium poppy	**heroin**
coca leaves	**cocaine**

Heroin and cocaine are very addictive drugs.
They change some **chemical** processes in the body.
The bodies of addicts no longer make some of the chemicals they need to keep them feeling well. So addicts feel very ill when they can't get their drug. That's why it's so hard for people **addicted** to hard drugs such as cocaine and heroin to quit.

1 Name <u>two</u> addictive drugs.

2 Look at the photograph.
What are withdrawal symptoms?

Cannabis may cause other problems. Scientists can't agree on whether or not there is a link between cannabis and later health problems and addiction to <u>hard drugs</u>.

3 Write down <u>two</u> problems that may be linked to using cannabis.

4 Look at the newspaper article.

    a Write down <u>three</u> mental health problems that may be linked to use of cannabis.

    b Suggest another explanation for the results of these studies.

5 **a** Why do some people want to use cannabis as a medicine?

    b Suggest some problems that this may cause.

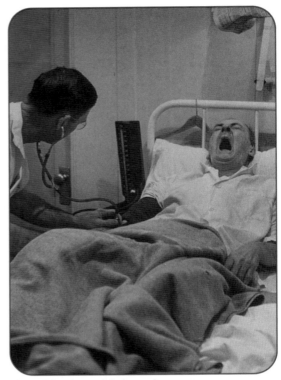

This addict has **withdrawal symptoms**.
He is desperate, sick and in pain.

Does cannabis cause mental health problems?

The results of three recent studies suggest that using cannabis as a teenager may increase the risk of mental health problems in later years.
The figures show that people who smoked cannabis are more likely to develop depression, anxiety or schizophrenia than people who didn't.

Some people use cannabis to ease the pain of cancer or to relieve the symptoms of multiple sclerosis.

Legal drugs

It's not just illegal drugs that are addictive. Some people become dependent on alcohol or the nicotine in tobacco. We call someone addicted to alcohol an alcoholic. More people smoke and drink alcohol than use hard drugs.

6 Suggest why

    a many people want to give up smoking

    b more people are trying to give up smoking than other drugs.

Giving up smoking

More people are trying to give up smoking than any other drug. The NHS is so keen to help people to stop smoking that it offers several forms of help:

- nicotine replacements, including gum or patches
- lozenges that make cigarettes taste foul
- counselling (one-to-one or in a group)
- a website, helplines and leaflets for advice.

7 Suggest why the NHS offers so many different kinds of help.

8 Write down some advantages and disadvantages of using nicotine patches.

9 Choose <u>one</u> other way of stopping smoking. Write down the advantages and disadvantages of this method.

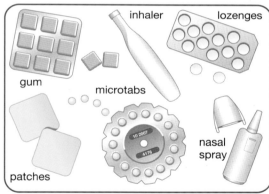

What you need to remember *Copy and complete using the **key words***

Addiction

Drugs change the _____ processes in people's bodies so they may become dependent or _____ to them.

They may suffer _____ _____ without them.

_____ and _____ are very addictive.

You need to be able to evaluate studies about links between cannabis use, health and addiction to hard drugs. You need to be able to evaluate the different ways of trying to stop smoking.

6 Making sure medicines are safe

We all want to know that any medicinal drugs we use are safe, work and have no serious **side-effects**. That's why it takes years to develop a new drug.

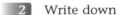 **1** Copy and complete the sentence.

Scientists test drugs to find out if they work against the _____, have no serious _____, are not poisonous and are _____ to use.

Finding and testing suitable molecules

Scientists start by studying a disease and looking at earlier treatments. Often this gives them some idea of the shape of a molecule that might work. Then they look for molecules with similar shapes. Often they find them in plants or even in existing drugs.

The next stage is to **test** these molecules. Scientists use computer modelling, then tests on human cells. Many drugs fail because they are poisonous (**toxic**). Others fail because they don't work well.

2 Write down

   a <u>two</u> sources of new drugs
   b <u>two</u> aims of the laboratory tests.

Next, scientists use animals to test the compounds that passed the laboratory tests. Many people disagree with this, but it has to be done by law.

Antibiotics are drugs to treat diseases. Scientists test a new antibiotic
- in different concentrations
- on different types of infected human cells.

We call these <u>in vitro</u> tests.

Clinical trials

If any compounds pass all the tests, they go for a series of trials on humans called clinical **trials**.

3 Write a list of reasons for clinical trials.

4 In 3rd stage trials, doctors give some patients the old drug and some the new one. Why?

Trial	To find out if …	Tried on …	Number of people
1st	• the drug is safe • there are side-effects	volunteers (some may have the disease)	Up to 50
2nd	• the drug works well • there are side-effects	people with the disease	40–100
3rd	• the new drug is better than the current best treatment	new patients with the disease	several thousand

Clinical trials take years.

The thalidomide story

Scientists developed **thalidomide** as a sleeping pill. It also prevented '**morning sickness**' in pregnant women. It completed the standard tests for the time. In 1957, doctors started to prescribe it. Soon, babies were being born with abnormal **limbs**. About 12 000 babies were born with birth defects before doctors found out that thalidomide affected developing fetuses. The drug was then banned.

> **5** Describe the effects of thalidomide on fetuses.

The original tests on rats hadn't shown up any birth defects. Later tests on rabbits and monkeys did.

> **6** Suggest why the original tests on thalidomide didn't show up the problem of birth defects.

In 1965, an Israeli doctor used thalidomide as a sedative to help a **leprosy** patient with a painful and inflamed infection. By morning, the swelling and pain were reduced. Now, more doctors prescribe it.

Cancers depend on the growth of new blood vessels. So doctors are now researching thalidomide as a treatment for cancer. They also want to find a chemical with a similar structure but without the side-effects.

> **7** Which leprosy patients can't take thalidomide?

> **8** Why might thalidomide be useful against cancer?

'Thalidomide babies' had tiny limbs (arms or legs) like flippers or missing fingers or toes.

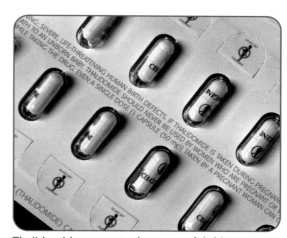

Thalidomide seems to do two useful things.
- It blocks the proteins that cause inflammation (redness and swelling).
- It slows the growth of blood vessels.

What you need to remember *Copy and complete using the key words*

Making sure medicines are safe

Scientists _____ new medicinal drugs in the laboratory to make sure they are not _____. Then they do _____ on human volunteers to find any _____.

Sometimes drug tests fail to show up problems. _____ is a drug that was developed as a sleeping pill. Doctors discovered that it also helped to relieve _____ _____ in pregnant women. Sadly, when pregnant women took it, their babies were born with abnormal _____. The drug was banned. Recently, doctors have started to prescribe it to treat _____.

7 Drugs to prevent problems

The problem of blood cholesterol

If fatty deposits narrow your arteries, you've got <u>cardiovascular disease</u>. You are at greater risk of coronary heart disease and stroke.

> 'Cardio' means to do with the heart.
> 'Vascular' means to do with the blood vessels.

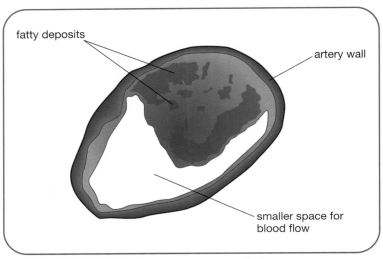

Narrowed arteries in the heart (coronary arteries) can cause coronary heart disease including pain (angina) and heart attacks.

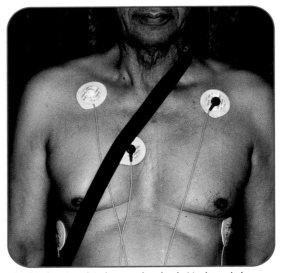

Abid is having his heart checked. He hasn't been able to work since he had a heart attack when he was 30.

1 What is the effect of fatty deposits in arteries on blood pressure?

According to the World Health Organisation, cardiovascular disease causes about one-third of all deaths worldwide. That's 18 million deaths a year.
It also causes a lot of ill health and disability.

2 Write down <u>three</u> effects of cardiovascular disease on

a people's lives
b the economy.

3 Look at the photo on the right. Caring for Sue costs the NHS and the local authority a lot of money. Suggest at least <u>five</u> ways they have to help her.

Narrowed arteries increased the blood pressure in the blood vessels in Sue's brain. One of them burst and damaged part of her brain. Now she can't walk or speak.

Finding out who's at risk

There is a test for the amount of cholesterol in your blood. It's recommended for middle-aged and older people, particularly those with raised blood pressure. If a person's blood cholesterol is too high, the first thing to do is to look at their lifestyle.

4   What changes in lifestyle might a doctor suggest to a person with raised blood cholesterol?

If lifestyle changes don't work, the doctor can prescribe statins. Statins have some side-effects and aren't suitable for everyone. People with liver disease or who drink a lot of alcohol or are pregnant can't take them.

5   Why do doctors prefer patients to make lifestyle changes rather than to take drugs?

How well do statins work?

The table shows the combined results of four studies. Statins were compared with a placebo. A placebo doesn't contain an active drug, but just taking a pill sometimes has an effect.

6   Why did some people have a placebo?

7   What can you conclude from these results?

8   From these studies, why can't you say that statins benefit all groups of people?

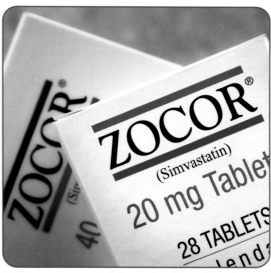

Statins are a group of drugs that lower blood cholesterol. They work by blocking an enzyme that is necessary for the production of LDL cholesterol.

Study	Age	Number of people	Time (years)	Percentage with heart problems	
				Statin	Placebo
1	65+	8998	4.9–6.1	12.0	16.4
2	65–70	4891	5	20.9	27.2
3	over 70	5806	5	23.6	28.7
4	70–82	5804	3.2	14.1	16.2

What you need to remember

Drugs to prevent problems
There is nothing new for you to <u>remember</u> in this section.

You need to be able to evaluate the effects of statins on cardiovascular disease.

1 The problem of infection

In 19th century Europe, the causes of disease were a mystery. Look at the picture. There was no <u>evidence</u> to support any of the ideas.

> **1** Suggest what might make people think that bad (or smelly) air might cause disease.

Doctors spread disease

Ignaz Semmelweiss was a Hungarian doctor who worked in a hospital in Vienna in the 1840s. It was common then for women to die in the hospital soon after having babies. The disease was called 'childbed fever'.

Semmelweiss knew that doctors didn't wash their hands between examining one patient and the next. So he thought that doctors were spreading the disease. He insisted that doctors washed their hands in a solution of 'chloride of lime' and the death rate fell.

> **2** What can you conclude from the fall in death rates? Choose between **a** and **b**.
>
> **a** Doctors spread childbed fever on unwashed hands.
>
> **b** Doctors spread microorganisms that caused childbed fever.

When Semmelweiss left the hospital, doctors stopped bothering to wash their hands. Death rates increased.

> **3** Look at the picture. Women are less likely to catch an infection during childbirth now than they were 100 years ago.
> Write down <u>two</u> reasons for this.

Malaria

Malaria is a disease associated with swamps – which are smelly. The word malaria means 'bad air'.
We know now that malaria is an infection spread by mosquitoes that breed in swamps.

God uses disease as a punishment.

Bad air causes disease.

Microorganisms cause disease.

The link between microorganisms and infection

Showing that doctors passed on childbed fever wasn't evidence that microorganisms caused the disease. Semmelweiss didn't show <u>what</u> the doctors were passing on.

It was Louis Pasteur who made the link. He infected healthy silkworms with material from diseased ones. When he examined the silkworms under a microscope, he found microorganisms in diseased silkworms but not in healthy ones.

4 Scientists before Pasteur had suggested that microorganisms caused disease but few people had listened.
Explain why they took notice of Pasteur.

Pasteur worked on diseases of humans and other animals, too. He published a scientific paper about the link between microorganisms and infections.

Other scientists read about his ideas. One of them was Joseph Lister. He was the surgeon who first used an antiseptic in his operating theatre. Antiseptics slow the growth of the microorganisms that cause infections. Before the use of antiseptics, up to half of patients died from infections following operations.

5 Explain how Joseph Lister's work supports Pasteur's microorganism theory of disease.

Operating theatres have changed in lots of ways.

Hospitals now

People still catch infections in hospital. Treating these infections takes up valuable staff time and hospital beds – and it's not always successful. So prevention is better than cure.

6 Write down <u>two</u> things that people who work in hospitals can do to reduce a patient's risk of catching an infection in hospital.

Ward hygiene and thorough hand-washing with alcohol gel can reduce the spread of infections in hospital.

What you need to remember

The problem of infection
There is nothing new for you to <u>remember</u> in this section.

You need to be able to relate the contribution of Semmelweiss in controlling infection to solving modern problems with the spread of infection in hospitals.

2 Invading microorganisms

Small but dangerous

Following the work of Louis Pasteur, we know that some microorganisms cause **disease**. We call them **pathogens**. Bacteria and viruses are examples. When they get into your body, they may make you ill.

Know your enemies

The cells of **bacteria** are much smaller than the cells of your body.

1 a Measure the length of the bacterium. Then work out how long it really is.
b Measure the size of the virus. Then work out how big it really is.
c How many times bigger than a virus is a bacterium in real life?

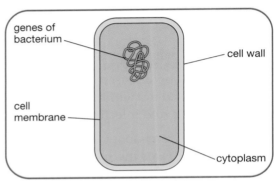

A bacterium. This is about 8000 times longer than real life.

Viruses are even smaller than bacteria. They are made of a few genes in a coat made of protein.

2 Look at the picture of a bacterial cell infected by a virus.
Which part of the virus goes into the cell?

Viruses can't **reproduce** by themselves. They need to invade living cells and use them to make more viruses. They **damage** the cells as they escape.

3 Why are viruses usually harmful?

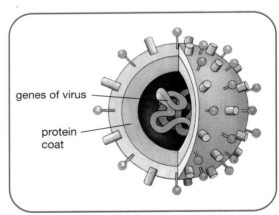

A virus. This is about 300 000 times bigger than real life.

Bacteria are everywhere

Like you, bacteria need food and water to survive.

Many of them need oxygen too. Most grow best when it's warm. We find bacteria in places where there are all the things they need.

4 Write down <u>three</u> places where you would expect to find bacteria.

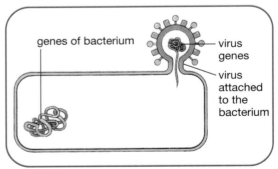

Viruses are so small that they can even infect a bacterium.

You cannot escape

Your body is full of places where bacteria can live and reproduce.

5 Why is your body a good home for bacteria?

Millions of bacteria live between the cells of even the cleanest skin. Some are useful, most do no harm and others make your sweat smelly. Bacteria in other parts of your body can cause diseases such as sore throats and food poisoning.

6 Why can't you wash all the bacteria off your skin?

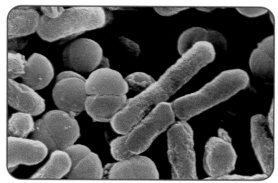

Bacteria that live in the human body.

Do pathogens always make you ill?

When the number of microorganisms is small, you often don't notice any effect. Many are easily destroyed by your **white blood cells**. Some are harder to destroy.

But microorganisms can breed very quickly. Many release poisons or **toxins**. As their numbers get larger, the toxins and the increase in your temperature begin to make you feel ill. This may take a few hours, days or even weeks.

7 What kind of cell destroys microorganisms?

start	1
after 20 minutes	2
after 40 minutes	4
after 60 minutes	8

How quickly can bacteria breed?

Bacteria reproduce by dividing into two.

8 Imagine you have eaten a pie with 50 bacteria in it. At human body temperature, they divide every 20 minutes.
Copy and complete the table.

Time (min)	Number of bacteria
0	50
20	
40	
60	

What you need to remember *Copy and complete using the **key words***

Invading microorganisms

Microorganisms such as _____ and _____ can get into your body.
They may multiply rapidly, releasing _____ (poisons) into your tissues. These
make you feel ill. Viruses can _____ only inside living cells. The newly produced
viruses burst out of the cells, causing _____.
The microorganisms that cause _____ are called _____.
_____ _____ _____ help to defend our bodies against them.

3 How do we treat diseases?

When we get an infection, we often take liquids or tablets called medicines. These contain useful drugs.

Some of these drugs help to ease **symptoms** such as aches and pains. Others kill the microorganisms that cause the disease.

> **1** Look at the photographs, then copy and complete the table.

	What it does	Examples
painkiller		
antibiotic		

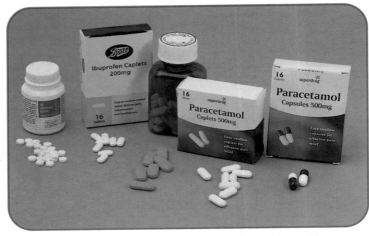

These are **painkillers**. They relieve pain but don't kill **pathogens**.

More about antibiotics

Antibiotics such as **penicillin** kill bacteria but they don't kill **viruses**. Viral pathogens live and reproduce inside cells. So it's hard to find drugs that kill them without damaging body cells and **tissues**.

Most antibiotics kill some kinds of bacteria but not others. Doctors usually know which one to use to treat a particular infection. If an antibiotic upsets your stomach or you are allergic to it, the doctor can give you a different one.

> **2** Explain why we need a range of antibiotics.

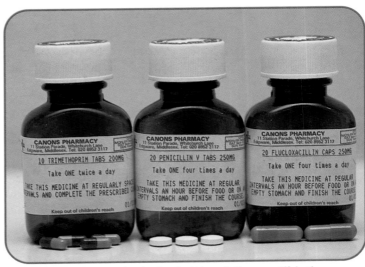

These kill bacteria inside the body. We call them **antibiotics**.

Sometimes antibiotics no longer kill the bacteria they used to. The bacteria that cause tuberculosis (TB) are hard to kill. An antibiotic called streptomycin worked well for many years. But the course of treatment lasts six months so many people stop taking it too soon and some of the bacteria survive. These are the ones that are most resistant to streptomycin – and they spread to other people.

> **3** Why is it important to complete a course of antibiotics?

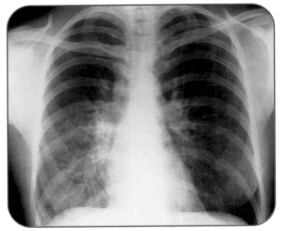

Tuberculosis is a serious lung infection.

Choosing a treatment

Kelly and Tom both have influenza. The symptoms are a raised temperature and aches and pains all over. Influenza is a virus infection.

Tom also has a severe sore throat caused by a bacterial infection. He probably caught it because the influenza virus weakened him. We call it a secondary infection.

The doctor told them both to rest, to keep warm and to drink plenty of fluids. She suggested taking painkillers such as paracetamol to ease the aches and pains. She warned them not to take too many.

4 The doctor also prescribed an antibiotic for Tom, but not for Kelly. Explain why.

Look at the photograph.

5 **a** What is the maximum dose of paracetamol in one day?
 b Why is it dangerous to take more than this?

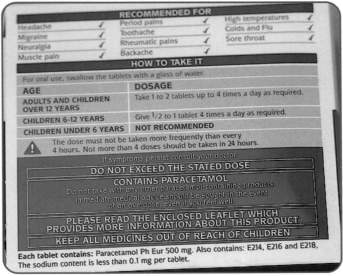

RECOMMENDED FOR		
Headache ✓	Period pains ✓	High temperatures ✓
Migraine ✓	Toothache ✓	Colds and Flu ✓
Neuralgia ✓	Rheumatic pains ✓	Sore throat ✓
Muscle pain ✓	Backache ✓	

HOW TO TAKE IT

For oral use, swallow the tablets with a glass of water.

AGE	DOSAGE
ADULTS AND CHILDREN OVER 12 YEARS	Take 1 to 2 tablets up to 4 times a day as required.
CHILDREN 6-12 YEARS	Give 1/2 to 1 tablet 4 times a day as required.
CHILDREN UNDER 6 YEARS	NOT RECOMMENDED

⚠ The dose must not be taken more frequently than every 4 hours. Not more than 4 doses should be taken in 24 hours.

If symptoms persist consult your doctor.

DO NOT EXCEED THE STATED DOSE

CONTAINS PARACETAMOL
Do not take with any other paracetamol-containing products. Immediate medical advice should be sought in the event of an overdose, even if you feel well.

PLEASE READ THE ENCLOSED LEAFLET WHICH PROVIDES MORE INFORMATION ABOUT THIS PRODUCT

KEEP ALL MEDICINES OUT OF REACH OF CHILDREN

Each tablet contains: Paracetamol Ph Eur 500 mg. Also contains: E214, E216 and E218. The sodium content is less than 0.1 mg per tablet.

An overdose of paracetamol is poisonous. It kills by damaging the liver and kidneys.

What you need to remember *Copy and complete using the* **key words**

How do we treat diseases?
Doctors prescribe some medicines to help relieve _____ of a disease.
For example, _____ relieve aches and pains but they don't kill the
_____.
_____, including _____, kill bacteria inside the body. They can't kill
_____ because they live and reproduce inside cells. It's hard to find drugs that
will kill them without damaging body _____.

4 Bacteria and viruses change

Bird influenza

This is a virus infection that mainly affects birds such as chickens. Doctors first identified a strain of the same virus in humans in Hong Kong in 1997. In the years that followed, small numbers of people caught the disease from birds. Half of these people died, because they had no immunity to this virus.

The World Health Organisation warned governments that the virus might mutate or change into a strain that could spread from person to person.

> **1** What is a mutation?

> **2** What is a pandemic?

> **3** Why does bird flu kill so many of the people infected?

> **4** Suggest why diseases spread so rapidly around the world now.

We develop immunity to viruses such as the influenza virus.

↓

But viruses mutate. The ones that our white blood cells don't recognise survive and we pass them on.

Epidemics (outbreaks of flu) ——→ Pandemics (worldwide outbreaks of flu)

Mutant bacteria

Bacteria also mutate to produce new strains. Many of these strains are resistant to antibiotics. Some strains of the bacteria that cause TB are examples.

Antibiotics kill off the non-resistant strains. The resistant ones survive, reproduce and pass on resistance. This is an example of 'survival of the fittest'. We call it evolution, or change by **natural selection**.

There are now strains of many different kinds of bacteria that are resistant to one or more antibiotics. This is what happens when we use antibiotics incorrectly or use them when we don't really need to. We say that we **over-use** them.

> **5** Write down <u>two</u> ways we over-use antibiotics.

> **6** Why do we need to develop new antibiotics?

Some farmers feed antibiotics to animals that aren't ill. This prevents infection and makes the animals grow faster.
This over-use could lead to more antibiotic resistance in bacteria. Some resistant bacteria in animals could also infect humans.

Resistance affects all of us

If you catch a strain of a bacterium that is **resistant** to the antibiotic that normally kills it, taking that antibiotic won't cure you. It will be a few days before you find out that you need a different antibiotic.

7 Read the cutting from a Medical Research Council Update.

    a What does 'multiple drug resistance' mean?
    b Why does the writer call it 'alarming'?

8 Because of resistance to streptomycin, doctors now have to treat patients with TB with a mixture of four antibiotics.
Suggest why this is.

9 In New York, some people are paid to go to a clinic regularly to take their antibiotics.
Suggest why the medical authorities decided to do this.

> Until recently, most strains of drug-resistant TB have been resistant to only one of the drugs available and so patients could be treated effectively using different drugs. But the emergence early this decade in New York City of multiple drug resistance is altogether more alarming. Patients were found to be infected with TB that was resistant to virtually all known drugs.

Superbugs

When *Staphylococcus aureus* gets inside our bodies, it may cause blood poisoning. Many strains are resistant to penicillin. A strain called **MRSA** is also resistant to the alternative antibiotic methicillin. There is another antibiotic that usually kills it. But over 20% of people who get MRSA infections die.

10 Suggest why hospitals have to report cases of MRSA. Explain as fully as you can.

11 Some hospitals won't operate on carriers of MRSA until they are free of it. Suggest why.

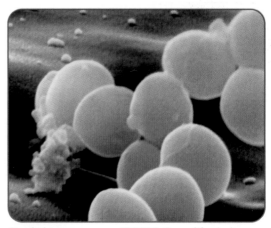

Staphylococcus aureus (25 000 times life size). About 10% of us have the bacterium *Staphylococcus aureus* in our noses and on our skin, where it does no harm. In some cases, it is MRSA (methicillin-resistant *Staphylococcus aureus*).

What you need to remember *Copy and complete using the **key words***

Bacteria and viruses change
Many strains of bacteria, including _____, have become _____ to antibiotics as a result of _____ _____. To prevent even more bacteria developing resistance, it is important not to _____ antibiotics.

You need to be able to relate epidemics and pandemics of diseases such as bird flu (a virus infection) to mutation of bacteria and viruses.

5 Immunity and vaccination

Who discovered vaccination?

Edward Jenner (1749–1823) was a Gloucestershire doctor. He is usually credited with the discovery of vaccination against smallpox.

In fact, the Chinese used something similar against smallpox 800 years before Jenner. Some Turkish, Greek, English and Indian people used it 100 years before Jenner. In England, Lady Mary Wortley Montague described what happened in Turkey and recommended it to her friends in 1717.

The Jenner story goes something like this. There was an old wives' tale that dairymaids who caught cowpox from cows never got smallpox.

In 1796, Jenner took some pus from a cowpox spot and scratched it into the arm of a boy called James Phipps. Two months later, he tried to infect the boy with smallpox. He didn't succeed because the boy was **immune**.

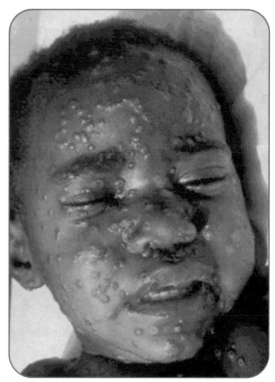

People feared smallpox. It killed 12–30% of the people who caught it. The survivors were left badly scarred.

1 What clue does the story give you that the viruses that cause cowpox and smallpox are similar?

2 Jenner's experiment wouldn't be allowed now. Why not?

3 Suggest some reasons why Jenner usually gets the credit for discovering vaccination.

4 Look at the picture. What does this tell you about what some people thought of vaccination?

Now we have vaccines to protect us against many bacterial and virus infections. However, there are still some people who refuse to be vaccinated.

Why we have vaccinations

Doctors try to prevent viral and bacterial diseases by **vaccination**. Prevention of viral infections is particularly important because there are few treatments for them. Viruses cause measles, mumps and German measles (rubella).

> **5** Look at the pictures.
> Write down <u>one</u> example of a vaccine made from
>
> **a** dead bacteria
> **b** weakened viruses.

> **6** Write down <u>two</u> ways of vaccinating people.

Vaccination doesn't just protect the people who are vaccinated. If enough people are **immunised** against it, a pathogen has fewer people to spread to. An outbreak or epidemic of the disease is less likely.

Vaccination campaigns got rid of smallpox from one country after another. By the mid-1970s, it only existed in Ethiopia, Somalia and parts of the Indian subcontinent. The World Health Organisation (WHO) decided to wipe it out.

> **7** Explain how other countries benefit from getting rid of smallpox altogether.

Teams of WHO health workers tracked down cases of smallpox and vaccinated everyone within a 2 mile radius. This was to stop the disease spreading. By 1977, the smallpox virus existed only in laboratories.

> **8** People with smallpox were difficult to find because their families hid them.
> Suggest why.

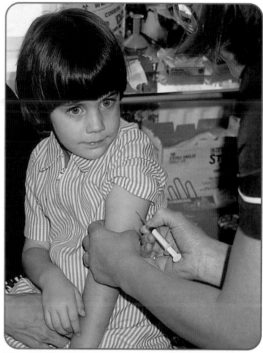

The **vaccine** being injected is made from **dead** whooping cough bacteria.

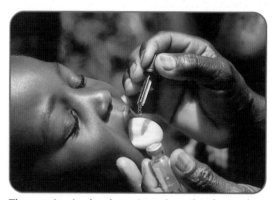

The vaccine in the drops is an **inactive** form of the polio virus.

What you need to remember *Copy and complete using the **key words***

Immunity and vaccination

Having a disease makes you _____ to another infection by that disease. You can also become immune by being _____. Doctors and nurses put small amounts of _____ or _____ forms of a pathogen into your body as a _____. We call this _____. After vaccination, your body responds to future infection by the pathogen as though you have already had the disease.

6 Humans against microorganisms

Which diseases do we vaccinate against?

Virus infections like measles and rubella can spread very quickly. In the UK and many other countries, there are vaccination programmes against them.

1 Write down <u>two</u> reasons why health workers want parents to have their children vaccinated.

2 Why do some parents find it difficult to decide whether or not to have their children vaccinated?

> Vaccination doesn't just protect your child. If all children are vaccinated a disease has no-one to spread to.
>
> But don't some children have side effects from the vaccine?
>
> But some children are badly affected by diseases too. Some even die from them.

The MMR vaccine

Look at the extract from a Health Education leaflet about **MMR**. This is a combined vaccine.

3 Why is the vaccine called MMR?

The MMR vaccine has both benefits and problems. It is cheaper than three separate vaccines and children need fewer injections. This could mean that more children will be vaccinated.

Some people think that the combined vaccine produces more side-effects than the separate vaccines. Others don't want their children vaccinated against measles.

The measles vaccine causes fits in a few children. However, infection with measles is ten times more likely to cause fits than the vaccine.

4 Suggest why

   a the Department of Health in the UK decided to use only the combined MMR vaccine

   b some parents ask for separate vaccines.

5 Rubella is usually a mild disease. Some girls and boys aren't vaccinated as children.
Why are they offered the vaccine before they leave school?

MMR vaccine

This is given when your child is between 12 and 15 months and again when your child is 3 to 5 years old.
The MMR vaccine protects your child against Measles, Mumps and Rubella (German measles).

What is measles?
The measles virus is very infectious. It causes a high fever risk and a rash. About one in 15 children who get measles are at risk of complications which may include chest infection, lung and brain damage. In severe cases measles can kill.

What is mumps?
The mumps virus causes swollen glands in the face. Before immunisation was introduced, mumps was the commonest cause of viral meningitis in children under 15. It can also cause deafness and swelling of the testicles in boys and ovaries in girls.

What is rubella?
Rubella, or German measles, is usually very mild and isn't likely to cause your children any problems. However, if a pregnant woman catches it in her early pregnancy, it can harm the unborn baby.

More about immunity

You become immune to a disease either by having it or by being vaccinated against it. What happens in your blood is the same. Look at the pictures.

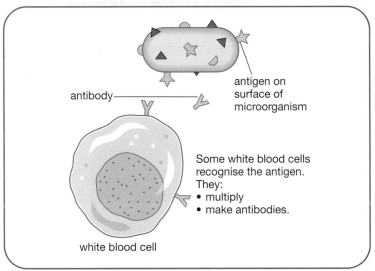

antibody —

antigen on surface of microorganism

Some white blood cells recognise the antigen. They:
• multiply
• make antibodies.

white blood cell

White blood cells respond to proteins on the surface of both active and inactive **pathogens**.

> **6** Write down <u>three</u> ways that white blood cells protect you against pathogens and their toxins.

When a new kind of pathogen gets into your body, white blood cells have to start making new kinds of antibodies and antitoxins. This takes time. That's why it takes time to become **immune**. Next time the <u>same</u> pathogen gets in, your white blood cells can respond rapidly. They start making the correct antibodies and antitoxins straight away.

> **7** Normally, a vaccine makes you immune to only one kind of pathogen. Suggest why.

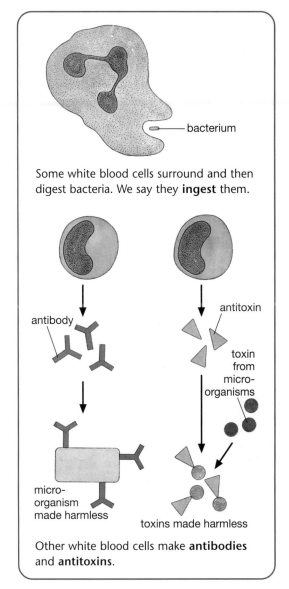

bacterium

Some white blood cells surround and then digest bacteria. We say they **ingest** them.

antibody

antitoxin

toxin from micro-organisms

micro-organism made harmless

toxins made harmless

Other white blood cells make **antibodies** and **antitoxins**.

What you need to remember *Copy and complete using the **key words***

Humans against microorganisms

When pathogens get into your body, your white blood cells help to defend you against them. Some white blood cells take pathogens into their cells. We say they _____ them. Some produce _____ to destroy particular viruses or bacteria. Others make _____ to counteract the poisons (toxins) the pathogens release.

Having a disease, or being vaccinated against it, makes you _____ to that particular disease. When you meet it again, your body responds fast enough to stop you being ill. An example of a vaccine is _____, which is used to protect children against measles, mumps and rubella.

You need to be able to evaluate the advantages and disadvantages of being vaccinated against a particular disease.

7 How has the treatment of disease changed?

Egyptians 4000 years ago knew about the problems of infections. They didn't know the causes, but they had some ways of treating them. They used myrrh, honey or an ore of copper called malachite to treat infected wounds. We now know that these substances slow down the growth of bacteria.

People in other countries and at other times also knew about infection and had some of their own remedies. Doctors used whatever treatments were fashionable at the time. Some worked, others didn't.

> **1** Look at the pictures.
> Write down <u>two</u> ways of treating infections that doctors no longer use.

Now, we know that microorganisms cause infectious diseases. With vaccination and the use of antibiotics, we expect to be better protected against them. Still, millions of people die every year from infectious diseases. A worldwide vaccination programme got rid of smallpox. But other diseases continue to spread.

Doctors in the past used leeches. They still use them now – but not for treating infections.

People thought breathing through scented nosegays protected them against 'bad' air that caused disease.

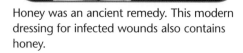

Honey was an ancient remedy. This modern dressing for infected wounds also contains honey.

The fall and rise of tuberculosis (TB)

People in the UK used to call the lung disease tuberculosis 'consumption' because it seemed to consume the body. People with this disease lost weight, became weaker and seemed to waste away. As towns grew and overcrowding increased, it became more and more common. At its worst, it caused as many as a quarter of all deaths in Europe.

> **2** Suggest why fresh air and a good diet helped some patients.
>
> **3** What was the benefit of keeping tuberculosis patients away from other people?

When penicillin was found to cure many other infections, doctors hoped that it would also cure TB. But it didn't work.

The treatment for TB in the early 20th century was fresh air and a good diet. Special hospitals called sanatoriums kept TB patients away from other people. Infection rates started to fall.

A new cure

Eventually scientists discovered an antibiotic called streptomycin that did work. If patients took it for 6 months, they had a good chance of being cured. As a result, the number of deaths from tuberculosis went down further. Now, it's going up again.

4   Look at the pictures. Write down <u>four</u> reasons why deaths from tuberculosis are increasing.

5   AIDS is a major cause of the spread of tuberculosis. Explain this as fully as you can.

6   In 1993, the World Health Organisation declared that tuberculosis was a global emergency. What do you think they meant?

Prevention is better than cure

We can prevent many infectious diseases, including tuberculosis, by vaccination. TB vaccination doesn't always work. Sometimes the immunity doesn't last for long. Many people have never been vaccinated against TB. So there are lots of people for it to spread to.

7   Write down <u>two</u> reasons why vaccination against TB hasn't stopped its spread.

It is only in the past 50 years that scientists have found out how vaccines work. They are using this knowledge to try to develop new and better vaccines.

Reasons for the increase in TB include …

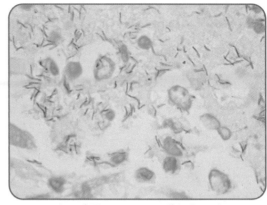

Some strains of TB are now antibiotic resistant.

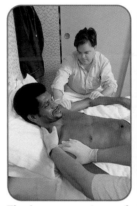

The immune systems of AIDS patients don't work properly.

TB spreads where there is overcrowding, poverty and homelessness.

Recycling air in aircraft can spread infections like TB.

What you need to remember

How has the treatment of disease changed?
There is nothing new for you to <u>remember</u> in this section.

When you are given information, you need to be able to explain how treatment of disease has changed as a result of increased understanding of antibiotics and immunity.

1 Surviving in different places

Plants and animals can only live, grow and reproduce in places where conditions are suitable for them. They have to be **adapted** to the conditions in which they live. That's why different kinds of animals and plants live in different places.

Cold places, hot places

The Arctic fox is adapted to live in the cold, but the Fennec fox is adapted to live in the heat of the Sahara desert.

1 Look at the pictures.
Write down <u>two</u> differences between the Arctic and Fennec foxes.

2 Copy and complete the table.

To help them to stay cool, Fennec foxes have …	… because they have …
a large surface area for heat loss …	a b
little insulation to prevent heat loss …	a b

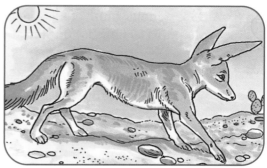

Fennec foxes have long bodies and ears. This means that they have a large surface area. They have hardly any fat and very short fur.

The small surface area of the Arctic fox reduces heat loss. Its fat and fur are good for stopping heat escaping. We say that fat and fur are good insulators.

3 Make a table, like the one in question 2, to show how Arctic foxes stay warm in a cold climate.

The colours of some animals match their surroundings. We say that they have good camouflage.

4 Arctic foxes have white coats in winter and dark coats in summer.
Explain how this helps them to survive.

Arctic foxes have a short body and small ears, lots of fat and thick fur.

Some other adaptations to desert life

In the **desert** there is very little water. Gerbils and snakes survive by living in burrows. The burrows stay cool during the day. Droplets of water (condensation) collect on the walls. Each day a gerbil produces only one or two drops of very concentrated urine.

5 Gerbils and some snakes can survive the shortage of water in the desert.
Write down:

a <u>two</u> adaptations that help the gerbil to survive
b <u>two</u> adaptations that help the snake to survive.

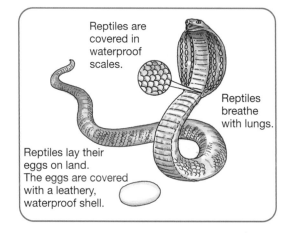

Reptiles are covered in waterproof scales.

Reptiles breathe with lungs.

Reptiles lay their eggs on land. The eggs are covered with a leathery, waterproof shell.

A camel's hump is a fat store. It can break down fat to release water.

A camel can drink large amounts of water.

Its mouth is tough so it can eat thorny plants like cacti.

Coarse wool on top of its body protects the camel from the Sun

Short hair underneath the camel lets heat escape.

Its big flat feet stop it sinking into the sand.

6 Camels are well adapted to life in the desert. Copy and complete the table to show how.

Adaptation	How it helps
can drink large amount drink of water	doesn't have to drink very often

What you need to remember *Copy and complete using the **key words***

Surviving in different places
Animals and plants are _____ for survival in the conditions in which they normally live. Adaptations for life in the Arctic are different from those for survival in the _____ .

You need to be able to use these and similar ideas to suggest how other animals are adapted to the conditions in which they live.

2 Adapt and survive

The place where a plant or animal lives is called its habitat. To survive, a plant or an animal must be **adapted** to survive in its habitat. That means it can get the **materials** and the energy that it needs from

- its surroundings
- other organisms that live there.

An animal gets its materials and energy from food – the plants and other animals in its habitat.

1 Write down <u>two</u> materials that plants take in from their surroundings.

2 What is a plant's energy source?

Many plants and animals have special features that help them to survive.

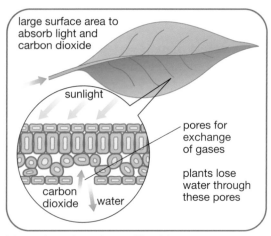

large surface area to absorb light and carbon dioxide

sunlight

pores for exchange of gases

plants lose water through these pores

carbon dioxide   water

Many plants have leaves like this.

Why does a cactus have spines?

One thing that you may not realise is that the spines of a cactus are actually its leaves. Unlike most leaves, the spines have a very small surface area. This means that they lose less water.

The green part of a cactus is its stem. The stem is swollen with water storage tissues.

3 Copy and complete the table.

Adaptation of a cactus	How this helps it to survive
its _____ are spines or thorns	**a** spines protect it against grazing animals. **b**
its _____ is green and fleshy	**a** it can make food in photosynthesis **b**
its roots are very long	

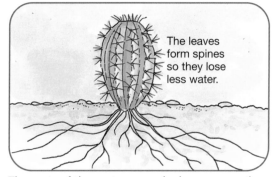

The leaves form spines so they lose less water.

The roots of the cactus spread a long way so they can take in nutrients from a bigger volume of soil. A cactus also stores water in its tissues.

Eat and be eaten

Animals get their food from plants and other animals. So plants and animals have adaptations

- to help them get their food
- to avoid being eaten.

You have already seen that some plants have spines or **thorns** to try to stop animals eating them.

But some animals like camels are adapted to cope with the thorns.

4 Suggest <u>two</u> ways a hedgehog avoids being eaten by a predator.

Wasps have a different way of protecting themselves. They have stings that inject a poison that causes pain and inflammation. When an animal such as a frog catches a wasp, it gets stung. Next time it sees one, it will recognise its **warning colours** – and leave the wasp alone.

5 What are 'warning colours'?

6 Hoverflies don't sting. Explain how 'warning colours' help hoverflies to survive.

7 Why do some plants contain poisonous chemicals in their tissues?

When attacked by **predators**, hedgehogs roll into a ball.

Hoverflies look a bit like wasps. We say they mimic them.

The nicotine in tobacco plants is a poison to put insects off eating it.

What you need to remember *Copy and complete using the* **key words**

Adapt and survive

To survive, organisms need to obtain _____ from their surroundings and from the other plants and animals that live there.

Animals and plants may be _____ in special ways to cope with particular features of their habitats. Examples of adaptations are _____, poisons and _____ _____ to deter _____.

You need to be able to use these and similar ideas to suggest how organisms are adapted to the conditions in which they live.

3 Different places, different plants

You may be asked to suggest reasons why animals and plants live where they do. You need to think about the environmental conditions, then about particular features of the animal or plant that enable them to survive in those conditions.

steep hill
(thin, dry soil)

flat, marshy
ground
(very wet soil)

river

pasture (grassy field)
(deep, moist soil)

A walk in the country

Imagine you are walking up the hill from the river in the drawing above.

1 Copy the table. Then complete it to describe the three types of land you walk through.

	What the soil is like	What grows there
flat, marshy ground		
pasture		
steep hill		

2 Explain, as fully as you can, why

a oak trees grow on the hill but not by the river
b alder trees grow by the river but not on the hill.

3 Suggest where you may find

a rabbits
b squirrels.

Write down the reasons for your suggestions.

Alder trees can survive in wet soil. They don't survive so well on drier soil, where other trees grow better.

To survive, oak trees need well-drained soils.

Why don't trees spread to the pasture?

Sheep are eating the grass in the field. They are grazing. Seeds from the trees fall on the pasture and some of them start to grow. Sheep eat the tops of the tiny trees.

Look at the drawings of these plants.

4 Sheep usually kill young trees.
Explain why.

5 Grass can survive grazing by sheep.
Explain why.

6 What would happen to the pasture if there were no sheep on it for several years?
Explain your answer.

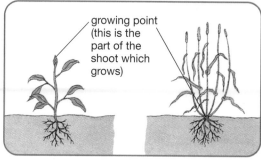

Tree seedling.   Grass plant.

Into the woods

It gets darker as you go into the wood. The plants are different from those in the field. They are adapted to different conditions.

7 Write down <u>two</u> differences between conditions in the wood and in the field.

To the mountains

As you go over the top of the hill you can see mountains in front of you. The trees above you are all conifers. As you walk up the mountain it gets colder and more windy.

Water evaporates more quickly in windy places. Trees living in windy places can easily lose too much water. To survive they have to lose as little water as possible.

8 Write down <u>two</u> ways conifers are adapted to stop them losing water from their leaves.

9 Higher up the mountain there are no trees at all. Why do you think this is?

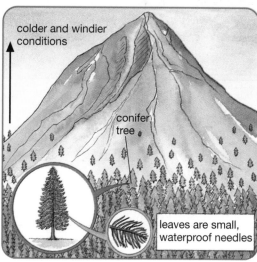

What you need to remember

Different places, different plants
There is nothing new for you to <u>remember</u> in this section.

You need to be able to explain why plants and animals live where they do.

4 Why weed the garden?

What are weeds?

Weeds are plants that are growing where they are not wanted. People plant poppies in their flower gardens, but poppies are weeds in a farmer's crop.

1 Write down the names of <u>three</u> weeds in the picture on the right.

Gardeners don't like weeds because they take the things that flowers, fruit and vegetables need to grow.
They **compete** with the gardeners' plants. Gardeners try to get rid of weeds so that their plants can grow better.

2 Write down <u>four</u> things the crops and weeds compete for.

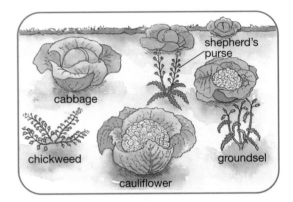

cabbage · shepherd's purse · chickweed · cauliflower · groundsel

Pull them up.

Cut them down.

Use weedkiller.

3 Write down <u>three</u> ways of getting rid of weeds.

Weeding is a constant battle

A garden is overgrown.
The weeds are all crowded together (1).

A family clears the weeds and plants vegetables (2).

Picture 3 shows the same garden a few months later.

4 Describe <u>two</u> differences between the weeds in pictures 1 and 3.

5 Why are there weeds in the garden a few months later?

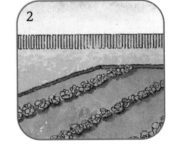

This weed grew from a seed blown into the garden.

This weed grew from a bit of root that was left in the soil.

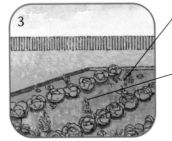

How weeds can start to grow again.

Competition between weeds

The groundsel plants on the right were taken from the garden shown on the opposite page. Both of these plants took three months to grow.

6 Describe <u>one</u> way in which they are similar.

7 Describe <u>one</u> difference between them.

The first plant has grown tall because the garden was overcrowded. The plant was competing with many other plants.

8 What are the plants competing for when they grow tall?

9 Which parts of the plant would you expect to grow bigger in the competition for water and nutrients?

Plants compete for **light** as well as for water and nutrients from the soil. Plants can get what they need more easily if they have plenty of space.

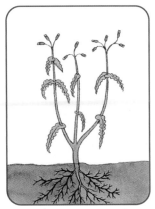
Groundsel from a very weedy garden.

Groundsel from a less weedy garden.

What happens if we never weed a garden?

This picture shows the same garden again, but it has not been weeded for many years.

10 What plants have taken the place of many of the smaller weeds?

11 Why do you think the smaller weeds died out?

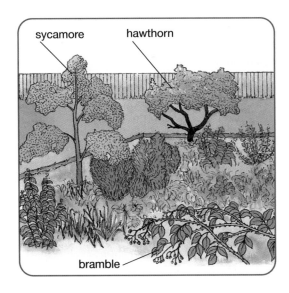
sycamore   hawthorn

bramble

What you need to remember *Copy and complete using the **key words***

Why weed the garden?
Plants need the right conditions to grow well. They need materials such as
_____ and _____ from the soil and plenty of _____.
They _____ with each other for these things.

You need to be able to suggest what plants are competing for when you are given information about a particular habitat.

5 Competition between animals

Animals often have to **compete** with each other for the things that they need. Animals that can't compete very well don't survive.

A male robin competes with other male robins for a territory. Having a territory means that it has a place to nest and find food. Then it can attract a **mate**.

Some animals defend territories

In some species of animals, a pair, a family or a pack may occupy a particular area called their **territory**. They stop other members of their species getting in. So they keep out the animals that compete with them for exactly the same **food**. But they have to spend time keeping watch for rivals. Sometimes they have to fight and may get injured.

1 Write down <u>three</u> advantages of having a territory.

2 What are the disadvantages of being territorial?

Seabirds defend only their nesting sites

Seabirds such as gannets and penguins compete for nesting sites on land. They don't have feeding territories at sea.

3 Suggest why seabirds don't need feeding territories.

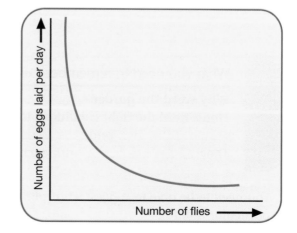

The gannets in this colony defend only the small space they need for their eggs and young.

Competition between flies

Animals that don't compete very well often don't breed.

Some scientists keep fruit flies for breeding experiments. The graph shows what happens if they keep too many flies in a cage.

4 **a** What happens to the number of eggs that the fruit flies lay as the number of flies goes up?

b Suggest why this happens.

Competition between squirrels

So far we have looked at animals of the same kind, or **species**, competing with each other. But as well as competing with members of their own species, animals compete with those of other species.

If two different species compete for exactly the same things they can't live together. One of the two species will win the competition and so survive.

The graph shows what happens when grey squirrels arrive in an area where red squirrels live.

5 Describe what happens to the numbers of the two types of squirrel.

This may happen because the two types of squirrel are in competition. But some scientists think that disease is an important factor. Grey squirrels are more resistant than red squirrels to a serious infection.

6 What do you think that these two species of squirrel could be competing for?

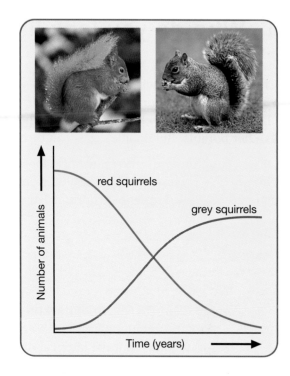

Competition between birds

Blackbirds and song thrushes eat similar food.
But they can still live together in the same places.

7 What <u>two</u> differences in their diet mean that blackbirds and song thrushes can live in the same place?

Song thrush eats		Blackbird eats
snails		✗
insects		insects
slugs		slugs
worms		worms
and a few berries		and a lot of berries

What you need to remember *Copy and complete using the **key words***

Competition between animals
Animals of one species often _____ with each other. They also compete with members of other _____ . They compete for _____ , water, a _____ and _____ .

When you are given information about a particular habitat, you need to be able to suggest what the animals in it are competing for.

1 Who do you look like?

Children look like their **parents** in many ways. We say they have many of the same features or **characteristics**. The child in the picture has brown eyes just like her parents. But people's eyes can be other colours.

Other young animals and plants also look like their parents. The characteristics passed on from parents to children are called inherited characteristics.

1 Write down

    a <u>two</u> characteristics that the kitten shares with its parents and all other cats

    b <u>two</u> features that the kitten shares with its parents but does not share with all other cats.

How are inherited characteristics passed on?

To produce a young animal, a sex cell from the father must join up with a sex cell from the mother. These **sex cells** are called **gametes**.

Plants can also produce young from sex cells.

- The male sex cell of a plant is in a pollen grain.
- The female sex cell is in an ovule.

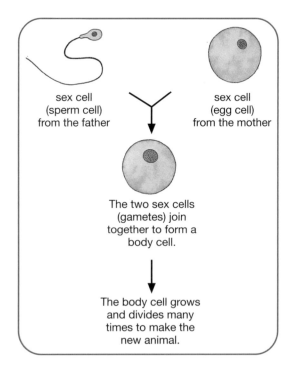

sex cell (sperm cell) from the father

sex cell (egg cell) from the mother

The two sex cells (gametes) join together to form a body cell.

The body cell grows and divides many times to make the new animal.

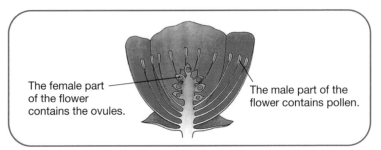

The female part of the flower contains the ovules.

The male part of the flower contains pollen.

2 Copy the table and complete it.

	Sex cells (g_____)	
	Male	Female
Animals		
Plants	in the	in the

The information in sex cells

This information controls how the body cells of the young animal or plant develop.

3 Look carefully at the picture of a mother, father and son. Then copy and complete the table.

	Nose shape	Hair colour	Eye colour	Skin colour
Mother			brown	
Father	long and straight			
Gary				

mother   father

their son Gary

4 Which of Gary's characteristics were controlled

a mainly by information from the egg?
b mainly by information from the sperm?
c by information from both egg and sperm?

Genes carry the information

Information in cells is carried in units called **genes**. Different genes control different characteristics.

5 Copy and complete these sentences.

Some characteristics can be controlled by just _____ gene.
Most characteristics are controlled by _____ genes.
An example of this is _____ colour.

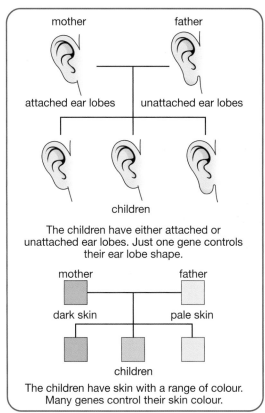

mother   father

attached ear lobes   unattached ear lobes

children

The children have either attached or unattached ear lobes. Just one gene controls their ear lobe shape.

mother   father

dark skin   pale skin

children

The children have skin with a range of colour. Many genes control their skin colour.

> **REMEMBER FROM KS3**
> The environment also affects some characteristics.

What you need to remember *Copy and complete using the **key words***

Who do you look like?
Young plants and animals have similar characteristics to their _____.
This is because parents pass on information to their young in the form of genes in their
_____ _____ (_____).
Different _____ control the development of different _____.

2 Passing on genes

Where are our genes?

The **genes** in our cells contain information that tells **cells** how to develop. So they control our **characteristics**.

1. Copy the diagram of the cell.

2. Copy and complete the sentences.

   Genes are parts of _____.
   These are inside the _____ of each cell.

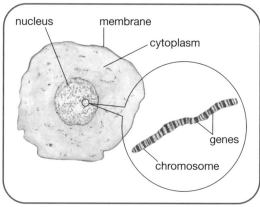

Genes are on **chromosomes** in the **nucleus** of a cell.

Looking at genes

The diagram shows some genes on the chromosome of a fruit fly.

3. Copy and complete the table.

Gene	Characteristic the gene controls

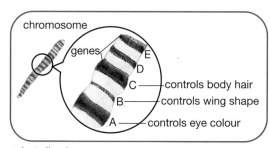

A fruit fly chromosome.

4. Look at the different fruit flies.
   What features could genes D and E control?

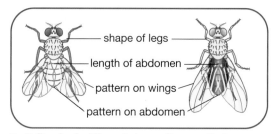

Fruit flies look different depending on their genes.

How many chromosomes?

The nuclei of different animals and plants contain different numbers of chromosomes. In body cells, chromosomes are always in pairs. So genes come in pairs too.

5. Copy and complete the sentences.

   Chromosomes are in _____ in body cell nuclei.
   Fruit fly cells have _____ pairs of chromosomes.

Look at the picture of human chromosomes on the next page.

6. How many pairs of chromosomes are there in a human body cell nucleus?

The Human Genome Project

An organism's complete set of genes is called its genome. In June 2000, scientists finished the first draft of a map of the human chromosomes to show where all the genes are.

Before this work, they thought that humans had about 50 000 genes. Now they think that there are only 20 000 to 25 000.

7   What is a genome?

8   About how many genes are there in the human genome?

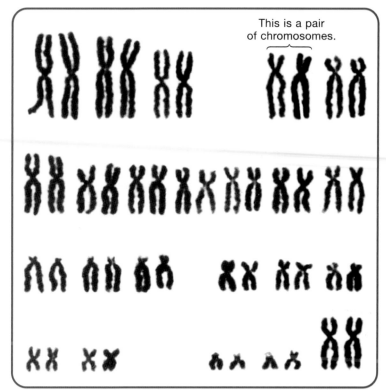

This is a pair of chromosomes.

The pairs of chromosomes of a human female.

The next step

Scientists now want

- to find out what each of the genes does
- to identify faulty genes.

They have already found out some of this information and made some discoveries that help doctors to prevent and treat some diseases.

9   Suggest why doctors and scientists are putting a lot of effort into finding out more about our genes.

What you need to remember *Copy and complete using the* **key words**

Passing on genes
Living things are made of _____.
The _____ of a cell contains many pairs of _____.
Chromosomes carry the _____ that control the _____ of animals and plants.

3 Two kinds of reproduction

Sexual reproduction

A woman and a man produce a baby when the man's
sperm joins with the woman's egg.
We call this sexual reproduction.

Sex cells

Look at the diagram, then answer these questions.

1 **a** Where are sperm cells made?
   b Where are egg cells made?

2 In humans, how many chromosomes are there in
   each sperm cell and in each egg cell?

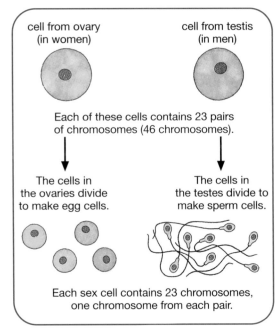

Making sex cells.

Passing on life

This diagram shows what happens when a sperm cell and
an egg cell join together.

3 Copy and complete the sentences.

Another name for sperm and egg cells is
_____. These sex cells join or fuse
to make one cell.
This cell grows into a baby by _____
many times. Each body cell in the baby contains
_____ pairs of chromosomes (46 in
total).
One of the chromosomes in each pair comes from
the _____. The other chromosome in
each pair comes from the _____.
So the baby has a mixture of genes from the
_____ parents.

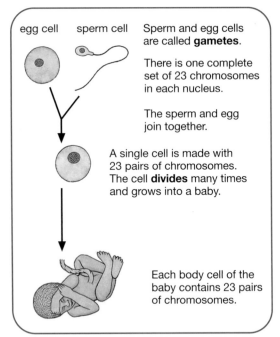

Why a baby has a mixture of **genetic information**
from two parents.

Reproducing without sex

Some plants and animals reproduce without making sex cells. We call it **asexual reproduction**. (Asexual means non-sexual.) There is no joining of gametes and a single **parent** produces the young.

An amoeba is a tiny animal that has just one body cell. It can split into two to make two amoebas.

4 **a** Describe how an amoeba reproduces.
b Explain why the new amoebas are identical.

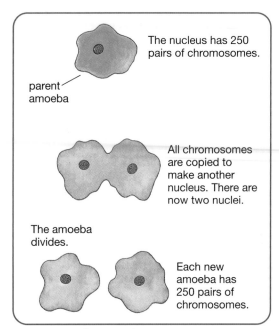

The nucleus has 250 pairs of chromosomes.

parent amoeba

All chromosomes are copied to make another nucleus. There are now two nuclei.

The amoeba divides.

Each new amoeba has 250 pairs of chromosomes.

How an amoeba reproduces.

Some plants and animals with many cells can also reproduce without using sex cells. Tiny new plants or animals may grow from the body of the parent. These then split off to make new plants or animals.

New strawberry plants can grow from runners. The parent and the runners are **genetically** identical.
We say the runners are **clones** of the parent plant.

5 How many parents does a strawberry runner have?

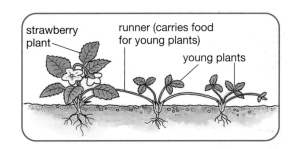

strawberry plant

runner (carries food for young plants)

young plants

We can also grow strawberry plants from seeds. They then have two parents.

6 Strawberry plants grown from seeds will all be slightly different from each other. Explain why.

7 A gardener has a strawberry plant that produces large, tasty strawberries.
How can she grow more plants exactly like it?
Explain your answer.

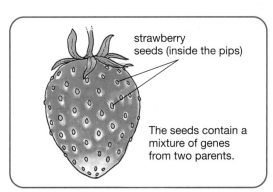

strawberry seeds (inside the pips)

The seeds contain a mixture of genes from two parents.

What you need to remember *Copy and complete using the **key words***

Two kinds of reproduction
In sexual reproduction, male and female sex cells or _____ join (fuse). The cell produced _____ to produce a new individual. The offspring from sexual reproduction have a mixture of _____ _____ from two parents, so they vary.

_____ _____ involves one _____. So there is no fusion of gametes, no mixing of genetic information and no variation in the offspring. We call these _____ identical offspring _____.

4 Using asexual reproduction

New plants don't always grow from sex cells.
They sometimes grow from the ordinary cells of plants.
Some do this by themselves. We can produce new plants
from parts of older plants, too.
We call these parts **cuttings**.

When we grow plants from seeds, we don't know what the
plants will be like. But cuttings have the same
characteristics as the plant we take them from.

1 Why do plants from cuttings look exactly like the
plant they came from?

2 Making new plants from cuttings is called asexual
reproduction. Explain why.

Taking cuttings from plant shoots

Myalee wants to take cuttings from a geranium plant.
The diagram shows what she needs to do.

Cuttings from the same plant have exactly the same **genes**.
We say they are **genetically** identical.
We call them **clones**.

3 Write down the following stages in the right order.
Use the diagram to help you.

- Plant the cutting in compost.

- Dip the cut end of the shoot into rooting hormone.

- Cut a young shoot from the parent plant.

- Cover the cutting with a polythene bag.
Cuttings need to be in a damp atmosphere until
the roots grow.

- Take off some of the lower leaves.

4 What does rooting hormone do?

5 Plants wilt and may die if they don't have enough
water. What <u>two</u> things should Myalee do to stop
the plant losing water?

> **REMEMBER**
> - Genes control what plants look like.
> - Cells from the same plant contain
>   the same genes.
> - We call reproduction without sex
>   cells asexual reproduction.

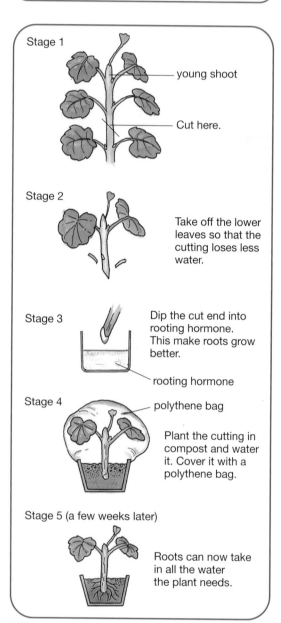

Stage 1 — young shoot — Cut here.

Stage 2 — Take off the lower leaves so that the cutting loses less water.

Stage 3 — Dip the cut end into rooting hormone. This make roots grow better. — rooting hormone

Stage 4 — polythene bag — Plant the cutting in compost and water it. Cover it with a polythene bag.

Stage 5 (a few weeks later) — Roots can now take in all the water the plant needs.

Taking a geranium shoot cutting.

Using other parts of a plant for cuttings

We take cuttings because it helps us to produce many plants **quickly** and **cheaply**.

We can take cuttings from leaves and roots as well as shoots.

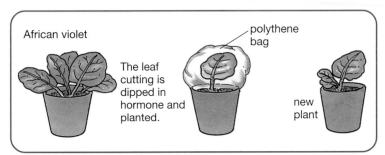

Gardeners often grow African violets from leaf cuttings.

6 Write down <u>three</u> reasons why plant nurseries usually grow African violets from cuttings rather than by sowing seeds.

7 The diagram shows how you can make new rhubarb plants.

   a Which part of the rhubarb plant is used to make cuttings?

   b When is the best time to take these cuttings?

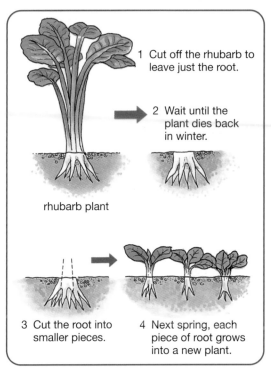
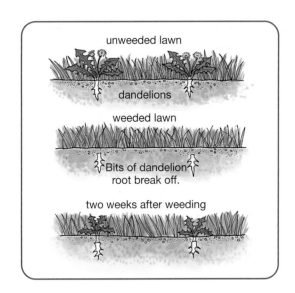

1 Cut off the rhubarb to leave just the root.

2 Wait until the plant dies back in winter.

rhubarb plant

3 Cut the root into smaller pieces.

4 Next spring, each piece of root grows into a new plant.

Making new rhubarb plants.

Reappearing dandelions

Cuttings can sometimes grow where you don't want them. When you dig up dandelions from a flower bed or lawn, they often grow again.

8 Look at the diagram.
Why did the dandelions reappear after two weeks?

unweeded lawn

dandelions

weeded lawn

Bits of dandelion root break off.

two weeks after weeding

What you need to remember *Copy and complete using the* ***key words***

Using asexual reproduction
We can grow more plants from parts of older plants. We call them _____.
Cuttings from the same plant all have exactly the same _____.
Plants with exactly the same genes are _____ identical.
We call them _____.
Taking cuttings helps us to produce new plants _____ and _____.

5 More about cloning

New varieties of potatoes

The parts of potato plants that we eat are underground stems called tubers. The plants produce them by asexual reproduction, so they are **clones**. Farmers plant these tubers to grow more potatoes. So, if a farmer plants a type of potato called Desiree, the whole crop will be Desiree potatoes.

> **1** Look at the picture.
> Write down <u>two</u> advantages of growing a potato crop by cloning.

Potato plants also have flowers which produce seeds. So, scientists produce new types called varieties of potatoes by sexual reproduction. They breed from plants with the characteristics they want. They grow new plants from the seeds and choose the best plants to breed from. This is called selective breeding. When they find a useful variety, they clone it to produce potato tubers for the farmers to plant.

> **2** Why do plant breeders grow potatoes from seeds rather than clones?

> **3** Suggest <u>two</u> characteristics of potatoes that they may want to select.

Another way of cloning plants

A way of growing a large number of identical plants even more quickly than from cuttings is by using **tissue** culture.

Scientists can sterilise the surface of cells without damaging them. Then they grow the cells on sterile jelly called agar so that there aren't any bacteria or fungi.

The cells divide to produce a mass of identical cells. The scientists separate them to produce lots of new plants.

> **4** Write down <u>two</u> reasons why bacteria and fungi don't grow in the culture tube.

> **5** Scientists add different chemicals to the agar at each stage. What do they add and why?

Cloning produces a large number of genetically identical tubers fairly quickly.

Scientists grow the new plants on agar containing nutrients and hormones that make shoots grow.

Then they transfer the plants to agar with nutrients and hormones that make roots grow.

We can clone animals too

Angora goats produce valuable wool. So, they are expensive. If a breeder buys only a few goats, it will be a long time before he has a big herd.

The diagram shows how scientists clone Angora goat embryos, then **transplant** the clones into the wombs of ordinary goats. These goats give birth to the more expensive Angora kids.

6 Copy and complete the sentences.

The cells of an early embryo are _____.
So each cell can grow into a complete

_____.

The new embryos are _____ into the wombs of host mothers. So farmers produce several _____ from one Angora embryo.
These kids are part of one _____.

7 Cloning and embryo transplants allow a farmer to build up a herd of Angora goats more quickly and cheaply than by ordinary breeding. Explain why.

Dolly the sheep was a different kind of clone. Scientists produced Dolly by fusing the nucleus from a body cell of an **adult** sheep with an unfertilised egg cell that had had its own nucleus removed. You can find out more about Dolly on page 80.

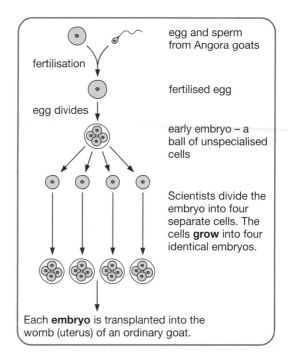

egg and sperm from Angora goats

fertilisation

fertilised egg

egg divides

early embryo – a ball of unspecialised cells

Scientists divide the embryo into four separate cells. The cells **grow** into four identical embryos.

Each **embryo** is transplanted into the womb (uterus) of an ordinary goat.

Angora kid.

Ordinary nanny goat.

What you need to remember *Copy and complete using the **key words***

More about cloning
Modern cloning techniques include:

■ _____ culture. This is growing new plants from small groups of cells.
■ _____ transplants. Scientists separate the cells from a developing animal embryo before they become specialised. Then they _____ the identical embryos or _____ into the wombs of host mothers.
■ producing embryos by fusion of nuclei from _____ cells with egg cells.

You may be asked to interpret information about cloning techniques and to consider economic issues concerning cloning.

6 Genetic engineering

Finding genes

Each of your 23 pairs of chromosomes is made of a large number of genes. Scientists have made a first draft of a map of the chromosomes to show where the genes are. This is the Human Genome Project. It should help scientists to detect and treat some inherited diseases.

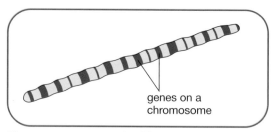

genes on a chromosome

Chromosomes are made of long molecules of DNA. A gene is a section of this DNA. It is a code that determines the order of amino acids in a protein.

1   **a**   Where exactly are your genes?
      b   What are they made of?
      c   What does a gene do?

2   Why do scientists want to map chromosomes?

Using genes

When scientists find out where a gene is, they can **'cut' it out** and make copies. They use **enzymes** to make the 'cuts'. They use different enzymes to make the copies. Then they can **transfer** the copies into the cells of other living things. These cells may then make proteins that they wouldn't normally make.

We call this **genetic engineering**.

The hormone insulin is a protein. Scientists have transferred the human insulin gene to bacteria, which then make the protein insulin. Now, many people with diabetes use this 'human' insulin. In the past, they used insulin from animals.

3   Look at the diagram, then copy and complete the sentences.

Scientists 'cut out' the human insulin _____.
They transfer it to _____.
We call this _____ _____.
The gene continues to make _____ in the bacterial cells. Scientists grow large numbers of bacteria to produce lots of insulin.

4   Some people think that it is wrong to use insulin from animals.
Write down some possible reasons for this.

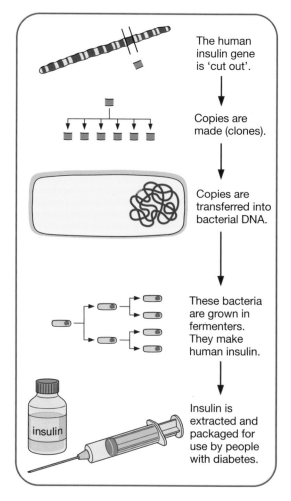

The human insulin gene is 'cut out'.

Copies are made (clones).

Copies are transferred into bacterial DNA.

These bacteria are grown in fermenters. They make human insulin.

insulin

Insulin is extracted and packaged for use by people with diabetes.

More gene transfers

Some scientists have transferred genes for different proteins into fertilised sheep eggs. These cells make copies of the gene when their nuclei divide. So, all the new nuclei of the embryo contain the new gene. Examples of human genes transferred to sheep include those for producing the proteins needed for

- treating cystic fibrosis (a genetic disorder)
- blood clotting (factors VIII and IX).

Doctors hope to find a way to transfer genes into human cells. For example, if they could transfer normal genes into enough cells of cystic fibrosis patients, these people could live healthy lives. We call this gene therapy.

Scientists can transfer useful genes into plants too. For example, they put a gene for herbicide resistance from a bacterium into sugar beet cells at an early stage of their **development** in tissue culture. The crops grown from these cells are genetically modified (changed). We call them **GM** crops.

5 Describe <u>one</u> example of gene transfer in an animal and <u>one</u> in a plant.

6 Many farmers save money by planting seeds from a previous year's crop. Some charities think that herbicide-resistant crops are bad for farmers in poor countries.
Why is this?

Scientists hope that this sheep will secrete human factor IX in its milk.

This sugar beet will not be killed when the farmer sprays the field with herbicide (weedkiller).
But the farmer has to buy new seeds and the matching weedkiller each year. Saved seeds do not grow.

What you need to remember *Copy and complete using the **key words***

Genetic engineering
Scientists can find a useful gene in an animal or plant and _____
_____ _____ using _____.
They can make copies of the gene and _____ them to the cells of organisms such as bacteria.
They can also transfer genes into the cells of animals and plants at an early stage of their _____ so that they develop with the characteristics that they want. For example, they do this to produce _____ crops with particular features.
All these are examples of _____ _____.

You may be asked to interpret information about genetic engineering techniques and to consider economic, social and ethical issues concerning genetic engineering, including GM crops.

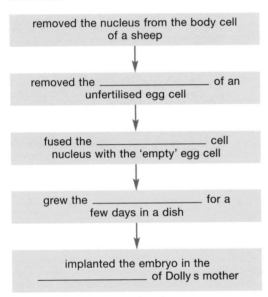

7 Advances can cause problems

New discoveries, techniques and inventions may bring problems as well as benefits.

Problems with clones

There was great excitement when Professor Ian Wilmut and his team cloned Dolly the sheep.

1 Copy and complete the flow chart.

Scientists:

> removed the nucleus from the body cell of a sheep
>
> ↓
>
> removed the _____ of an unfertilised egg cell
>
> ↓
>
> fused the _____ cell nucleus with the 'empty' egg cell
>
> ↓
>
> grew the _____ for a few days in a dish
>
> ↓
>
> implanted the embryo in the _____ of Dolly s mother

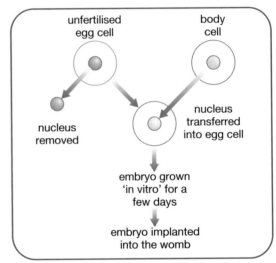

The embryo grew into Dolly – a clone of the adult sheep.

When Dolly was born, she seemed to be normal. But she aged quickly, and had arthritis by the time she was $5\frac{1}{2}$ years old. Other cloned animals have had similar problems. Perhaps nuclei from body cells are too old to start with.

In theory, making human clones from body cell nuclei is now possible.

Read the newspaper cutting.

2 The United Nations wants to ban cloning of adult humans. Suggest some reasons based on

   a practical issues
   b ethical issues.

3 Suggest reasons why some countries are for and others against cloning to produce cells to treat patients.

United Nations vote suggests human cloning ban

The UN has been debating human cloning for 2 years. Many countries want a legally binding worldwide ban on reproductive cloning of humans from adult cell nuclei. However, they want to allow cloning to produce cells to treat disease and repair damage.

Other countries want to ban all cloning. They see cloning to produce cells as the deliberate creation and destruction of human beings. They say that it is not ethical.

In March 2005, UN members voted for a voluntary ban on human cloning.

Problems with cloning

We produce animals and plants with the characteristics that we want by

- selective breeding
- cloning
- genetic engineering.

All these things reduce variety in a species. In other words, they reduce the number of different genes in a population.

If conditions change, plants and animals that we have selected for farming may not grow as well as they did. They may need different forms of genes to survive in the new conditions. But, if these genes have been bred out of the population, they are lost forever. This is why

- organisations save seeds from old or wild varieties of plants
- some farmers keep rare breeds of animals.

The Millennium Seed Bank is at Wakehurst Place in Sussex.

4 Explain why some governments and other organisations have set up 'seed banks'.

5 Wild potatoes are smaller and less appetising than modern varieties.
   Explain, as fully as you can, why plant breeders are interested in them.

Wild potatoes come in a wide range of sizes, colours and shapes.

What you need to remember

Advances can cause problems
There is nothing new for you to <u>remember</u> in this section.

You need to be able to interpret information about cloning techniques and to consider economic, social and ethical issues concerning cloning.

1 Change in nature

How populations change

Plants and animals usually produce more offspring than there is space or food for. So, only a few of the offspring survive long enough to breed.

1 **a** Describe the <u>two</u> forms of moth in the picture.
  b Which one is the more likely to die before it can breed?
  Explain your answer.

Only the moths that breed pass on their characteristics. It looks as if nature – or the environment – has 'selected' moths with the useful characteristics. So we call it natural selection.

2 In a place with trees like the ones in the picture, what would you expect most moths to be like?

3 Suppose pollution killed the lichens and blackened the tree trunks. What could happen to the moth population?
  Explain your answer.

Peppered moths rest on tree trunks during the day. Only the best camouflaged moths escape being eaten by birds.

These moths are resting on light coloured trees that are covered in lichen.

A more worrying change

We use antibiotics to kill the bacteria that cause disease. Sometimes mutations in bacteria stop an antibiotic killing them. We say the bacteria have become antibiotic resistant.

In 1972, there was an epidemic of typhoid in Mexico. Normally, an antibiotic called chloramphenicol would have cured it. This time it didn't work. Over 14 000 people died. Eventually, they found an antibiotic that worked.

4 Explain, as fully as you can, why chloramphenicol didn't control this epidemic.

The changed moths and bacteria are not new species. But sometimes changes in a population are big enough to produce new species.

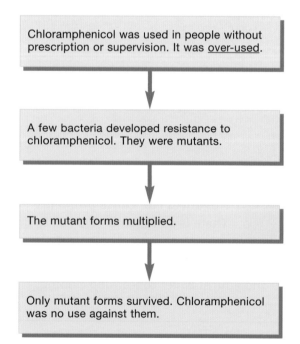

Chloramphenicol was used in people without prescription or supervision. It was <u>over-used</u>.

A few bacteria developed resistance to chloramphenicol. They were mutants.

The mutant forms multiplied.

Only mutant forms survived. Chloramphenicol was no use against them.

Evidence for new species

You can find fossils like the ones in the picture at Whitby on the Yorkshire coast. The people of Whitby used to say that an ammonite was a snake turned into stone by St Hilda. They called another fossil a devil's toenail.

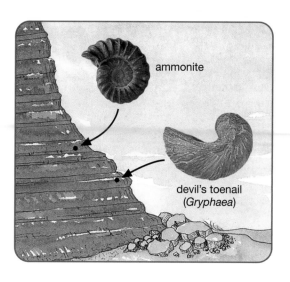

ammonite

devil's toenail
(*Gryphaea*)

What do scientists think fossils are?

Scientists think that **fossils** are the remains of dead plants and animals from millions of years ago.

They have evidence that *Gryphaea* and the ammonite both lived in the sea over 180 million years ago.

5 What are fossils?

Evidence from fossils shows that *Gryphaea* evolved from an ancient oyster. Scientists think that both are related to modern oysters. They lived in similar conditions. Scientists call them different species because they don't look exactly the same and lived so far apart in time.

Animals exactly like *Gryphaea* don't exist today. We say that they are **extinct**.

6 Scientists can't be certain that ancient and modern oysters and *Gryphaea* are all different species. Why is this?

> **REMEMBER FROM KS3**
>
> A **species** is a group of similar organisms that can interbreed.

What you need to remember *Copy and complete using the key words*

Change in nature

We can observe change in _____. We call the remains of ancient species _____. Most scientists agree that fossils provide _____ of how much (or how little) species have changed. They also show that many ancient life forms have died out or become _____.

You need to understand that there are questions that scientists can't answer, for example, whether or not living things separated in time belong to the same species.

2 Three billion years of life

Scientists aren't sure when life on Earth began, but it was a lot further back in time than 180 million years.
They think that

- the Earth formed about 4600 million years ago
- life on Earth began over 3000 million (3 **billion**) years ago.

1 For about what fraction of its history has there been life on Earth? Choose from half, more than half and less than half.

Look at the fossil stromatolites.
Similar microorganisms are alive today.

2 What is the evidence that life on Earth began over 3 billion years ago?

3 Why can't scientists be sure when life on Earth began?

New forms of life

Fossils can also tell us how life on Earth has changed.
Most scientists think that all species of living things on Earth today came from earlier, simpler species. We say that living things have **evolved**.

4 Where do scientists think that life began?

5 Copy and complete the sentences.

Simple forms of life _____ into plants and animals. These then evolved into bigger and more _____ plants and animals.

Studying similarities and differences between species helps us to understand how closely **related** they are. Then we can suggest which earlier species a new one may have evolved from.

Few soft-bodied creatures leave any trace. These fossil stromatolites are the remains of mats of microorganisms that lived 3500 million years ago. Most remains in very old rocks have been destroyed by heat and pressure.

These present-day stromatolites in Australia are built by plant-like microorganisms.

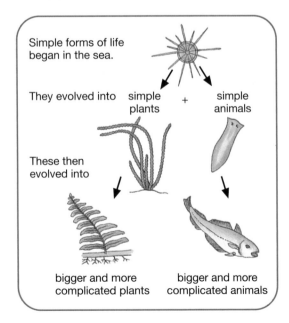

Simple forms of life began in the sea.

They evolved into simple plants + simple animals

These then evolved into

bigger and more complicated plants | bigger and more complicated animals

Which plants and animals lived when?

Scientists can use fossils to tell them which plants and animals lived when. The diagram shows some of the things scientists have found out.

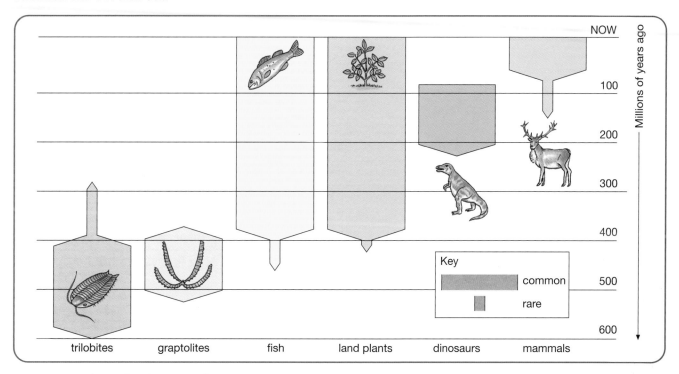

You can see from the diagram that graptolites were very common between 500 million and 400 million years ago. Then they died out. We say they became **extinct**.

6 When did trilobites first appear?

7 When did trilobites become extinct?

8 Which group of animals first appeared about 220 million years ago?

9 Name a group of animals which became common between 400 and 300 million years ago.

10 How long ago did the first mammals appear?

What you need to remember *Copy and complete using the **key words***

Three billion years of life

Scientists think that simple life forms developed on Earth over 3 _____ years ago.

Then they changed or _____ to produce all the species that are alive today plus lots of species that are now _____.

Scientists study similarities and differences between species. This helps them to see how closely _____ they are. This helps them to understand evolutionary relationships between species.

3 Some puzzles

To explain <u>how</u> life developed, scientists and others are interested in

- how life on Earth began
- how the millions of species developed
- how new variations within a species arise.

The beginnings of life

For life as we know it, there must be ...	Scientists think they could have come from ...
water	■ the sea or water in pores in rocks
chemicals such as amino acids	■ chemical reactions in the atmosphere and the sea ■ space – chemicals arrive on Earth in meteorites
a source of energy	■ chemical reactions in the sea around hot springs ■ the Sun

1 Write down <u>two</u> places where life on Earth may have begun.

Some scientists think that it wasn't just the chemicals of life that arrived on Earth from space. They think that life itself began somewhere else in the solar system. It arrived on Earth deep inside meteorites. Then it continued to develop underground in the water in the pores of rocks.

2 If life developed underground or around deep sea vents, what could its energy source be? Explain your answer.

In some experiments in the 1950s, scientists passed sparks through a mixture of gases they thought was like the Earth's early atmosphere. There was great excitement when they produced amino acids. But ideas about the gases in the early atmosphere have changed. No-one has produced amino acids using the new mixture.

3 Suggest a source of 'sparks' in the atmosphere.

Meteorites (rocks from space) usually burn up in the atmosphere. Some land on the Earth. Some scientists think that is how life arrived on Earth.

Deep sea vent. Hot water springs bring minerals up from deep inside the rocks. This is where some scientists think life started – in iron sulfide 'bubbles' that formed a framework for cell membrane formation.

A structure for life

Another suggestion is that the chemicals need to come together on a framework. This would make it easier to build structures such as cell membranes. Two possible frameworks that scientists are thinking about are those formed by clay minerals and by iron sulfide bubbles.

> **4** Scientists have suggested clay minerals or iron sulfide bubbles as a framework for life.
> Why do they think a framework is needed?

So, there are many theories about how life on Earth began. All the scientists can give reasons for their theories. But there isn't enough evidence to conclude that any of the theories is correct. So all we can say is that scientists can't be certain about where or how life began.

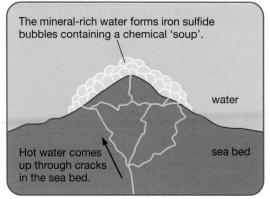

The mineral-rich water forms iron sulfide bubbles containing a chemical 'soup'.

water

Hot water comes up through cracks in the sea bed.

sea bed

Mike Russell of Glasgow University has found evidence of iron sulfide bubbles in ancient sea floor rocks.

Variation and change

There is plenty of evidence of both variation and change, now and in the past. The puzzles were how and why new variation appeared and what made living things change or evolve.

> **5** Copy and complete the sentences.
>
> We know now that living things vary as a result of differences in their _____ and their _____. Changes in the environment mean that living things _____.

The next two pages show you how scientists found out about change and about the problems they had.

What you need to remember

Some puzzles
There is nothing new for you to remember in this section.

You need to understand that there are questions that scientists can't answer and to be able to suggest reasons why scientists can't be sure about the origin of life on Earth.

4 Explaining change

Ideas about evolution

In the 18th and 19th centuries, scientists found out more and more about fossils.

Many accepted that fossils were the remains of ancient plants and animals. So they wanted to know why new ones appeared and others became extinct.

The Church taught that species didn't change.

1 a What was Cuvier's explanation of new species and extinctions?
  b Why were few people willing to suggest other explanations at the time?

Lamarck thought that organs changed when they needed to. For example, giraffes developed long necks because they needed to reach up into the trees for food. But he couldn't explain how. He also thought that the characteristics that an animal developed during its life were passed on to its offspring.

Charles Darwin and Alfred Russel Wallace were the first to explain <u>how</u> changes could happen. They came up with the same explanation at the same time. They called it **evolution** by **natural selection**. Another name for it is 'the survival of the fittest'. Darwin gets most of the credit because he collected a lot of evidence about changes in plants and animals, too.

Many people mocked the idea because it went against the teaching of the Bible. Now, many people do accept it, but not everyone.

2 Why do you think that so many people were thinking about changing species in the 18th and 19th centuries?

3 Lamarck and Darwin both suggested theories of evolution, but they explained it in different ways. Describe the differences.

4 Why did it take so long for the idea of evolution to become widely accepted?

An 18th century French naturalist called Georges Louis de Buffon thought that the Earth was much older than the Bible suggested and that species had changed. The Church forced him to say that he was wrong.

A French scientist called Georges Cuvier suggested that a series of Noah's floods and creations explained the fossil record.

Another French scientist called Jean Baptiste Lamarck observed artificial selection. He thought that something similar might happen in nature.

Charles Darwin thought that the animals or plants best suited to their **environments** would survive, breed and pass on their characteristics.

The natural selection of giraffes

Thousands of years ago, the animals that evolved into giraffes were not as tall as giraffes are now. Over a long period of time, giraffes developed longer and longer legs and necks. They could reach leaves high in the trees, as well as reaching down for water.

5 Copy and complete the diagram below.

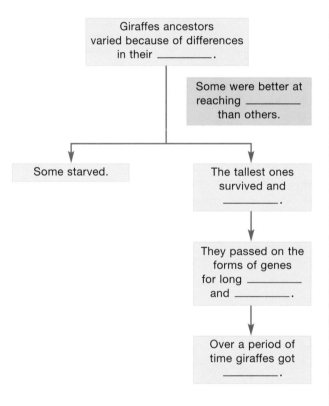

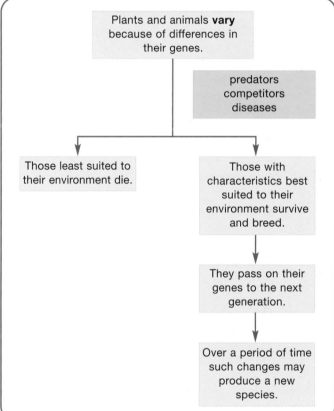

| Giraffes ancestors varied because of differences in their _____. |
| Some were better at reaching _____ than others. |

| Some starved. | The tallest ones survived and _____. |

They passed on the forms of genes for long _____ and _____.

Over a period of time giraffes got _____.

Plants and animals **vary** because of differences in their genes.

predators
competitors
diseases

Those least suited to their environment die.

Those with characteristics best suited to their environment survive and breed.

They pass on their genes to the next generation.

Over a period of time such changes may produce a new species.

How natural selection can produce new species. (This was Darwin's idea of natural selection, except that he didn't know about **genes**.)

What you need to remember *Copy and complete using the **key words***

Explaining change

Individuals in a species _____ because of differences in their _____.
Those with characteristics best suited to their _____ are the most likely to survive, breed successfully and pass on their genes to the next generation. The least suited die. Over a period of time a species changes. This is _____ by _____ _____.

You need to be able to identify differences between different theories of evolution and to suggest reasons for different theories.

5 New tricks and old

Some species have changed very little

We know from **fossils** that some plants and animals are very like their ancestors. They have **changed** very little. Others are very different. Scientists think that species alive today evolved from ancient species.

1 Show which fossils were the ancestors of the modern plants and animals in the diagram.
For example:
A = ginkgo

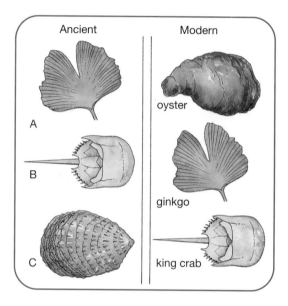

Others have changed a lot

Scientists think that modern horses evolved from small mammals that ate soft leaves from bushes. Fossils from older rocks are of animals with four toes and few tooth ridges. Those from younger rocks have longer teeth with strong ridges for grinding tough grass.

2 Copy and complete the table.

Older fossils	Modern horses
small animals	_____ animals
_____ teeth	longer teeth
teeth with _____ ridges	teeth with _____ ridges
_____ toes	_____ toe

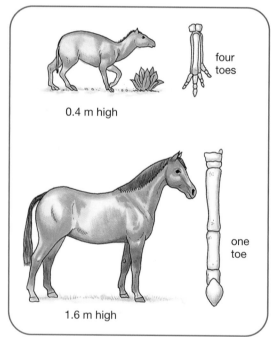

Small animals can dodge and hide amongst bushes to escape predators. Horses with longer legs can run faster.

Scientists think that these changes happened because the environment changed. Modern horses are suited to grassy plains, while their early ancestors lived amongst trees and bushes.

3 Copy and complete the sentences.

The horses that were best at feeding on _____ and running fast _____. They bred and passed on their _____. Their young also had these useful _____.

Others didn't change enough

Plants and animals that couldn't adapt to changes in their **environment** died out. Whole groups became extinct. Dinosaurs and mammoths are examples. This was more likely to happen when the environment changed suddenly or over a fairly short period of time.

This happened in the past and is happening now. Many plant and animal species are in danger of extinction.

4 Why do some species die out?

Why did dinosaurs become extinct?

Dinosaurs became extinct about 65 million years ago. Scientists argue about the reason.

Look at some of their ideas.

5 Choose one of the ideas that you think is not very sensible. Explain why you think it is probably wrong. (Use the 'Information' box to help you.)

6 Explain, as fully as you can, how a meteorite could have made dinosaurs extinct.

Ideas that could explain the extinction of dinosaurs
- New **predators** killed them.
- A very big meteorite hit the Earth and dust blocked out the Sun.
- New **diseases** killed them.
- New **competitors** took over their food.

Information to help you
- Plants can't grow without the Sun.
- The biggest dinosaurs were bigger than other animals at that time.
- Most dinosaurs ate plants.
- Dinosaurs probably couldn't survive very cold weather.

What you need to remember *Copy and complete using the **key words***

New tricks and old
We can learn from _____ how much (or how little) plants and animals have _____ since life began on Earth.
Species may become extinct if the _____ they need to survive changes.
Extinction can also happen because of new _____, new _____ or new _____.

You need to be able to interpret evidence about evolutionary theory just as you have done in this section and those before it.

6 How new features arise

Genes control features or **characteristics** such as tooth ridges and height. So to produce new features, genes must change.

We sometimes make a mistake when we copy a sentence. A small mistake can make a big difference.

Look at the drawings.

1. Sentence **B** is a copy a student made of sentence **A**. How many letters did she copy wrongly?

2. What difference did it make to the reindeer?

A Your nose is not red.   **B** Your nose is now red.

Mis-spelled genes?

Before it divides, a nucleus makes a new copy of its chromosomes. Sometimes there are mistakes in these copies. We call these mistakes **mutations**.

A mutation, or change, in a gene can cause a change in the protein it controls. So, it is possible for a mistake in a gene to cause a size or colour change in a plant or animal.

Amongst the billions of sex cells produced, there will be many mutant genes. Many of them are harmful.
As a result, the sex cell itself or the resulting embryo doesn't survive.

Not all mutations are harmful

Mutations happen all the time in nature.
Scientists sometimes use radiation to cause extra mutations in seeds such as wheat. They see the effects when they grow the seeds.

3. Look at the picture. The scientists are very pleased with wheat plant C.
Why is this?

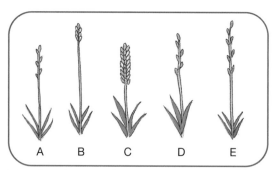

Mutations increase the amount of variation. They increase the number of different characteristics to select from.

Mutation and change

So, mutations can be

- harmful
- useful
- of no importance at the time they happen.

4 Write down <u>two</u> mutations that are harmful.

Mutations that are immediately useful may cause more rapid change in a **species**.

Other mutations that survive just increase the amount of **variation** in a population. If the **environment** changes, this may help a whole species to survive. When there is a lot of variation, there are likely to be a few animals or plants that are suited to the changed conditions. They will

- survive
- **breed** successfully
- and **pass on** their genes.

Many individuals will die, but the <u>species</u> will survive.

5 When there is little variation, a species may not survive a change in the environment.
Explain why.

6 Mutations that seem to have little effect when they happen, sometimes become useful.
Suggest reasons why.

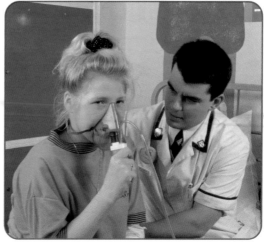

Carol has a disorder called cystic fibrosis caused by a mutant gene. To survive, she now needs a lung transplant.

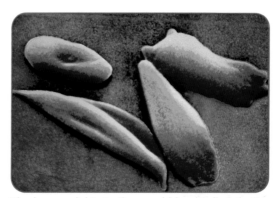

The haemoglobin in these red blood cells is faulty so the cells can't do their job properly.
A mutation in a gene is the cause.

What you need to remember *Copy and complete using the **key words***

How new features arise

Sometimes genes change to produce new forms. We call these changes _____.
They may cause more rapid change in a _____.
Mutations increase the amount of _____ in a population. A species with a varied population is more likely to survive a change in the _____. It is more likely to include individuals with _____ suited to the environment. These individuals are likely to survive, _____ successfully and _____ _____ their genes.

1 Humans take over

After the last Ice Age, 60% of the British Isles was woodland. The maps show how this had changed by the year AD 1086.

1 Copy and complete the sentences.

In 7000 BC, _____ of Britain was covered with trees. By AD 1086, this had fallen to 20%. This means that there were _____ times as many trees in 7000 BC as in AD 1086.

2 Was more woodland lost from the north or the south of Britain?

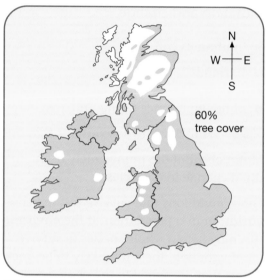

7000 BC – the British Isles after the last Ice Age.

What happened to the trees?

From 7000 BC, people cleared the land of trees for animals to graze and then later to grow crops.

In 500 BC, people started to make charcoal to get iron from iron ore. As the number of people increased, they cleared more land for **farming** and used even more wood for building.

3 Write down <u>three</u> reasons for cutting down trees.

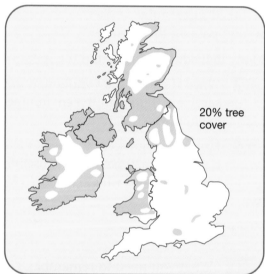

AD 1086 – the time of the Domesday survey.

Twentieth-century forests

During World War I, timber was needed for pit props in coal mines, for paper and for building. Millions of acres of trees were cut down. The war ended in 1918. By then, trees covered only 4% of the British Isles.

4 What was done, after 1918, to increase the numbers of trees in Britain?

About 10% of Britain is now covered by trees.

The Forestry Commission was set up after World War I. Large areas of new forest were planted.

Effects of losing the trees

Many woodland plants and animals can survive only in shady and damp conditions. When woods are cut down, there are fewer places for them to live.

5 Some woodland plants survive in hedges.
Why do you think this is?

6 During the last 50 years farmers have pulled up many hedgerows to make bigger fields.
Why do you think many people are worried about this?

Hedgerows.

Open fields.

What else do people use land for?

As well as using land for farming, we use it for **building** and for roads. We also use it for **quarries** to get stone and for **landfill** sites, where we dump rubbish.

When we do this, we destroy the **habitats** of many plants and animals. So the number of different species falls. We say that **biodiversity** is reduced.

The map shows land use in a small area.

7 What is most of the land in this area used for?

8 What is shown in square B4?

9 In which squares can you find evidence that we use land for quarrying and for dumping waste?

10 What do we mean when we say that biodiversity is reduced?

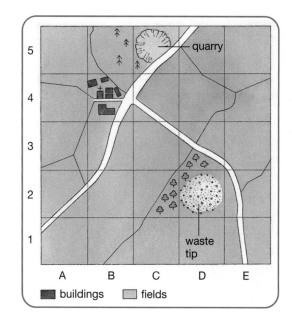

What you need to remember *Copy and complete using the key words*

Humans take over
Humans reduce the amount of land available for other animals and for plants by cutting down trees and using the land for _____ and _____, taking stone from _____ and dumping waste in _____ sites. All these things can destroy the _____ of animals and plants and reduce _____.

You need to be able to analyse the effects of humans on the environment just as you have done here.

2 More people, more problems

More people, fewer trees

Nowadays, people have a much bigger effect on the **environment** than they used to. One reason for this is that there are a lot more people. In 1850, there were over 1000 million people in the world. Some scientists estimate that there will be about nine times as many people by 2050.

As the human **population** increases, more land is used for growing food and more timber is needed. The last great forests in the world are in danger.

1 **a** What are these forests called?

b How long will they last if we keep chopping them down at the present rate?

Rain forests provide habitats for lots of different species. The variety of habitats and the **biodiversity** may be higher than any other on land.

When the forests disappear, so do the plants and animals that live in them. Scientists are still exploring these forests for new species. They are particularly interested in forest plants as sources of new drugs.

2 Write down <u>two</u> reasons why loss of biodiversity matters.

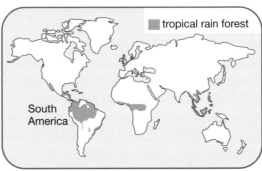

The biggest area of tropical rain forest is in South America. About 1% is cut down each year.

More farming means more pollution

Using more land for farming means that we pollute **water** more.

Look at the pictures.

3 Write down <u>three</u> types of chemical that farmers use that drain into water and pollute it.

4 There is much less pollution of water when land is covered with trees. Explain this as fully as you can.

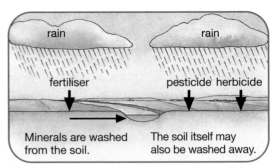

Minerals are washed from the soil.

The soil itself may also be washed away.

Farming land

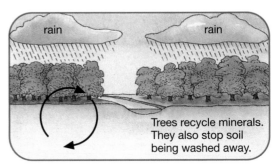

Trees recycle minerals. They also stop soil being washed away.

Forest

We all use more things

There are a lot more people in the world than there used to be. Many of us have a lot more things like fridges, cars and TV sets. We say we have a higher **standard** of living. This affects the world around us.

5   **a**   Where do we get the raw materials to make all these things?
      b   What will eventually happen to the supply of these raw materials?

The things we use eventually wear out.

6   What further problem does this cause?

More energy means more air pollution

We use so much energy to make and use things that we are using up the Earth's **non-renewable** energy resources (fuels) such as coal and oil. Also, the more fuel we burn, the more waste gases we produce and the more we pollute the air.

7   Copy the headings. Then complete the table.

Waste gases	Environmental problem

Humans have always affected the local area where they live. But there are now many more people, and they are having a bigger effect.

8   **a**   How does burning fuels in Britain affect nearby countries?
      b   How does it affect the whole Earth?

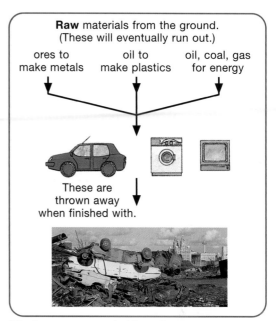

Raw materials from the ground. (These will eventually run out.)
ores to make metals   oil to make plastics   oil, coal, gas for energy

These are thrown away when finished with.

We throw **waste** and old products away. They pollute the **land**.

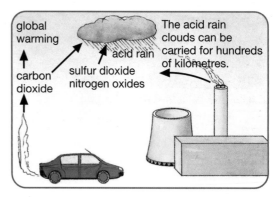

global warming   acid rain   The acid rain clouds can be carried for hundreds of kilometres.
carbon dioxide   sulfur dioxide nitrogen oxides

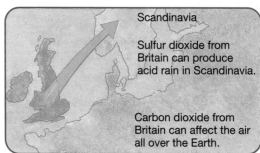

Scandinavia

Sulfur dioxide from Britain can produce acid rain in Scandinavia.

Carbon dioxide from Britain can affect the air all over the Earth.

What you need to remember *Copy and complete using the **key words***

More people, more problems
As the human _____ and the _____ of living increase, so does our effect on the _____. Loss of forest and other habitats leads to reduction in _____. Some of the plants and animals lost may have been of use in the future.
We use up _____ materials, including _____ energy sources faster.
We also produce more _____. Unless we handle the waste carefully, we will cause more pollution of the air, _____ and _____.

3 Sustainable development

Nowadays, we seem to be more aware of our effects on the environment. But we still want to travel about and to have more possessions. As the population increases and as we all try to improve our standard of living, the problem gets worse.

In 1983, an international commission on environment and development was set up. Gro Harlem Brundtland was in charge.

In 1987, the Commission produced a report called 'Our Common Future'. The report talked about the needs of human beings, the environment and the Earth's resources. It pointed out that there was a difference between what humans want and what they actually need to live comfortably.

> ### People's basic needs
> - A safe, secure water supply.
> - Enough nutritious food.
> - An energy source for cooking and keeping warm.
> - Shelter.
>
> Many people don't have these things.

Gro Harlem Brundtland, former Prime Minister of Norway.

1 Look at the pictures. Which one should be labelled 'I need' and which 'I want'?
Explain your answer.

In 1992, the Earth Summit in Rio de Janeiro agreed on a document called Agenda 21. This document sets out what we need to do to make sure that humans can survive in the 21st century.

To meet the needs of the poor, there must be economic development. But this must be done in a way that won't damage the **environment** and so that development can keep going. The **people** of the future will then have what they need.
We call this **sustainable** development.

2 What is sustainable development?

3 Brundtland said 'It is both futile and indeed an insult to the poor to tell them that they must live in poverty to protect the environment.'

a What do you think she meant?
b Do you agree with her?

I need some Nike trainers.

I haven't eaten today. I need some food.

Think globally, act locally

This title is another of Gro Harlem Bruntland's messages. What she means is that we can all do our bit for global sustainable development.

4   Think about the energy and materials we all use, the waste we produce and the pollution we cause. Write down <u>three</u> things that <u>you</u> could do to help to conserve the Earth's resources.

National and local authorities in the UK have policies concerning the environment and resources. Planners have to work within these policies because new roads, buildings, water supplies, and so on

- take up land
- affect wildlife by destroying habitats or making them too small to provide enough food or space
- cause pollution.

5   Why do we need policies on the environment?

It's difficult for the United Nations to get countries to agree and to co-operate. Countries are keen to look after their own interests. For example, the Kyoto agreement on climate change came into force at the end of 2004, 7 years after it was agreed. Only 151 countries signed up to the agreement to cut greenhouse gas emissions. Those countries produce 55% of the emissions. The USA didn't sign.

6   Suggest reasons why some countries refused to sign the Kyoto agreement.

The United Nations Environment Programme attempts to set standards and bring about co-operation between countries on environmental issues such as biodiversity, conservation of resources and climate change.

The UK government has policies on environmental issues such as biodiversity.

In the UK, **local** authorities have to have policies on issues such as land use and recycling.

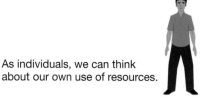

As individuals, we can think about our own use of resources.

What you need to remember *Copy and complete using the* **key words**

Sustainable development

We need _____ development to improve the quality life of _____ now and in the future and to avoid damaging the _____.
To manage sustainable development, we need to plan at _____, regional and global levels.

You need to be able to weigh evidence and form balanced judgements about environmental issues including sustainable development. Think about <u>sustainable development</u> as you study the environmental issues in the following sections.

4 Make Poverty History

This is a 21st century campaign supported by over 200 groups including well-known charities and religious groups, and many individuals, including celebrities.

Campaigners argue that trade, debt and aid policies cause a lot of the problems in developing countries. They hope to force developed countries to take responsibility for ending poverty around the world.

1 Suggest why so many people support this campaign.

To end poverty, we need to share resources more fairly. So we need to live in a more sustainable way.

The Make Poverty History rally in Trafalgar Square, London, on 3 February 2005.

Can we meet our needs in a sustainable way?

We all need a source of energy.

2 We can burn wood, fossil fuels or biogas made from organic waste. Which one of these is <u>not</u> sustainable? Explain your answer.

3 Why is it more sustainable to make electricity from wind or solar energy than by burning fuel?

4 We can burn fossil fuel, wood and organic waste. Write down <u>one</u> better use for each one.

> **REMEMBER**
> - We make compost from organic waste.
> - We make many things from wood.
> - We use chemicals from fossil fuels to make plastics, paints, dyes and many other things. (You learn about this in chemistry.)

Collecting and growing food has energy costs too.
To survive, people must gain more energy from their food than they use getting it. Hunter–gatherers gain 5–10 times more energy from food than they use to get it. So they can collect enough food for a family.

A European farmer grows enough food for many families. But the farmer will have used up lots of energy from fossil fuels. Processing food and transporting it large distances also uses fuel.

5 Look at the picture. Write down <u>three</u> ways that farming uses the energy from fossil fuels.

6 Suggest how we could feed ourselves in a more sustainable way. Explain your answer.

It takes a lot of energy to make and use equipment and chemicals. Some chemicals harm the environment too.

What you need to remember

Make poverty history
There is nothing new for you to <u>remember</u> in this section.

You need to be able to form balanced judgements about sustainable development.

5 The energy problem

Acid rain

As we use more energy, we burn more fuel.
The more fuel we burn, the more **waste gases** we produce and the more we pollute the **air**.

> **1** Write down <u>three</u> places where we make waste gases.

> **2** How are these waste gases produced?

Fuels often contain sulfur. When we burn fuels

- sulfur reacts with oxygen to produce **sulfur dioxide**
- nitrogen and oxygen from the air react to form **nitrogen oxides**.

> **3** Look at the diagram. Then copy and complete the sentences.
>
> Burning fuels produces smoke and waste gases called _____
> _____ and _____
> _____. These gases
> _____ in rain and make it
> _____. Acid rain can kill
> _____. It also makes lakes
> and rivers too _____ for
> plants and animals to survive.

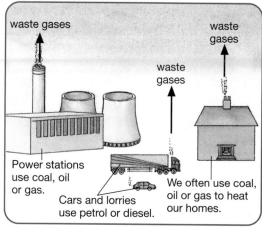

Burning fuels produce smoke and waste gases. These go into the air.

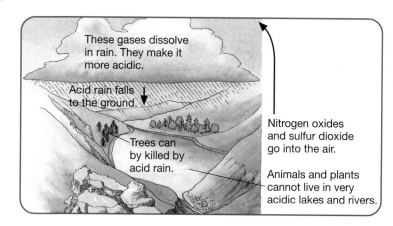

These gases dissolve in rain. They make it more acidic.

Acid rain falls to the ground.

Trees can by killed by acid rain.

Nitrogen oxides and sulfur dioxide go into the air.

Animals and plants cannot live in very acidic lakes and rivers.

What can we do about acid rain?

To make rain less acidic, we must put less sulfur dioxide and nitrogen oxides into the air.
The diagram shows some ways of doing this.

> **4** Write down <u>two</u> ways of reducing the amount of sulfur dioxide we put into the air.

> **5** **a** How can we remove nitrogen oxides from car exhaust fumes?
>
> **b** What harmless gases are produced from this?

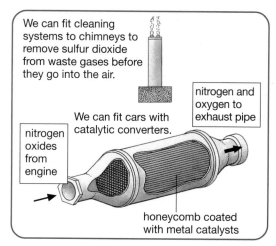

We can fit cleaning systems to chimneys to remove sulfur dioxide from waste gases before they go into the air.

We can fit cars with catalytic converters.

nitrogen and oxygen to exhaust pipe

nitrogen oxides from engine

honeycomb coated with metal catalysts

Using low sulfur fuels and removing waste gases can both help to reduce **acid rain**.

What you need to remember *Copy and complete using the **key words***

The energy problem
Burning fuels produces smoke and _____ _____ which pollute the
_____. These gases include the _____ _____ and
_____ _____ that contribute to _____ _____.

6 Are we changing the climate?

Is the Earth getting warmer?

There is plenty of climate data for the past hundred years or so that seems to suggest that global warming is happening. But we need evidence going much further back than that.

The data in the charts comes from

- tree growth rings
- air trapped in Antarctic ice
- ocean sediments and corals
- historical records.

1 Suggest which <u>two</u> sets of records provide evidence for the past 1000 years only.

The average temperature of the Earth seems to be rising. But it could be just normal variation.

2 Write down <u>one</u> piece of evidence from the charts which supports the idea that

   a global warming is happening
   b the rise in temperature is part of a natural cycle of temperature changes.

How good is the evidence?

Scientists discussing global warming need to think about whether this data is

- reliable – they are more likely to trust it when data from different sources match
- valid evidence for global warming – a rise in the average temperature of the whole Earth.

3 Write down <u>one</u> piece of evidence that increases in temperature were widespread, or global.

4 Suggest why many scientists think that the climate change data on this page is reliable.

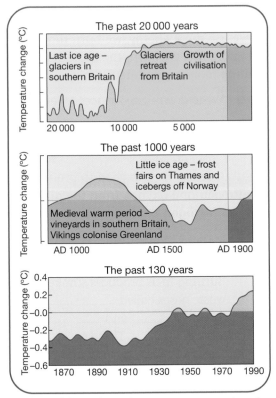

- The red lines show the average temperature in the second half of the 20th century.
- The scales on the three graphs are different.
- During the 'little ice age', it was so cold in the winter that the River Thames froze and people could take part in activities on the ice.

How does the Earth warm up?

Energy reaches the Earth's surface from the Sun. Most of the **energy** is re-radiated by the surface as infra-red waves. These are absorbed by methane and **carbon dioxide** in the atmosphere.

Like the glass in a greenhouse, the gases stop energy escaping. So we call them greenhouse gases. They cause the **greenhouse effect**, which is what keeps the Earth warm.

Without its **atmosphere**, the average temperature of the Earth would be about 38 °C cooler than it is.

5 Look at the diagrams.

   a What kind of rays does the Earth radiate?

   b Write down <u>two</u> things that can happen to this radiation.

   c How does this affect the average temperature of the Earth?

Measurements show that the amounts of the greenhouse gases in the atmosphere are increasing.

Some scientists think that this will make the Earth warmer than it otherwise would be. This is **global warming** – or an increase in the **average** temperature of the Earth.

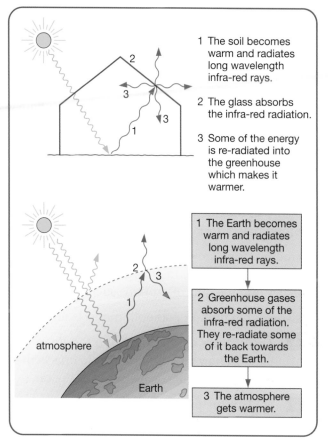

1 The soil becomes warm and radiates long wavelength infra-red rays.

2 The glass absorbs the infra-red radiation.

3 Some of the energy is re-radiated into the greenhouse which makes it warmer.

1 The Earth becomes warm and radiates long wavelength infra-red rays.

2 Greenhouse gases absorb some of the infra-red radiation. They re-radiate some of it back towards the Earth.

3 The atmosphere gets warmer.

atmosphere

Earth

What you need to remember *Copy and complete using the **key words***

Are we changing the climate?

Methane and _____ _____ in the Earth's atmosphere absorb most of the _____ that the Earth radiates. Some of this energy is re-radiated to the Earth's surface.

It keeps the Earth warmer than it would otherwise be. This is called the _____ _____ .

The amounts of methane and carbon dioxide in the _____ are increasing.
This may be increasing the _____ temperature of the Earth.
We call it _____ _____ .

You need to be able to evaluate methods of collecting environmental data and to analyse and interpret the data about environmental issues such as global warming. You need to ask yourself whether the data is valid and reliable.

7 More about global warming

Why are the amounts of greenhouse gases increasing?

The amount of carbon dioxide in the atmosphere depends on

- the amount of **fuel** (including wood) burned
- the amount of decay of waste by **microorganisms**
- the amount of photosynthesis.

The carbon dioxide taken up by tree leaves for photosynthesis 'locks up' carbon in wood for many years.

Microorganisms growing without oxygen put methane into the atmosphere. These microorganisms live in rice fields, marshes and the guts of animals such as cattle.

The size of the human population affects all of these things.

1 The pictures tell the story of a family in Java. Explain how each thing they do affects the amount of carbon dioxide or methane in the air.

2 Look at the pie charts.
Write down the two main sources of

   a carbon dioxide
   b methane.

3 Many people blame deforestation in tropical countries for the increase in the amount of carbon dioxide in the atmosphere. Are they right to do so? Use evidence from this page to support your ideas.

4 Write down two gases that cause the greenhouse effect.

An increase in the amounts of these gases in the atmosphere may cause **global warming**.

We cut down some trees and sold them for timber. | We burnt the rest of the trees to get rid of them.

We grow rice on some of the land. | We also keep some cattle.

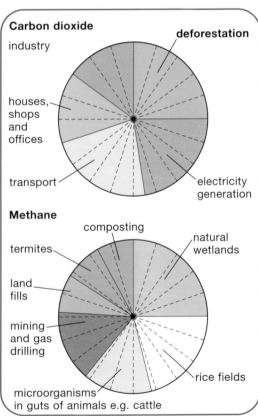

The pie charts show the percentage of the increase in greenhouse gases in the atmosphere caused by various activities.

Some effects of global warming

The temperature will only have to increase by a few degrees Celsius to cause big changes on Earth. It may

- melt a lot of ice so that the **sea level** rises
- affect the **climate** (the patterns of temperature, winds and rainfall)
- affect the winds and the lengths of the seasons
- affect the types of plants that grow in different parts of the Earth.

5 a Write down <u>three</u> effects of global warming.

b Write a few sentences about how these changes may affect humans.

6 Look at the maps. Describe how the vegetation in Britain may change.

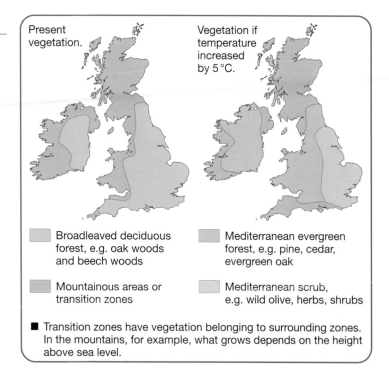

Present vegetation.

Vegetation if temperature increased by 5 °C.

- Broadleaved deciduous forest, e.g. oak woods and beech woods
- Mediterranean evergreen forest, e.g. pine, cedar, evergreen oak
- Mountainous areas or transition zones
- Mediterranean scrub, e.g. wild olive, herbs, shrubs

■ Transition zones have vegetation belonging to surrounding zones. In the mountains, for example, what grows depends on the height above sea level.

What can we do about global warming?

We need to take action to reduce the amounts of greenhouse gases such as carbon dioxide and methane in the atmosphere.

7 Look back over pages 97 to 105, then copy and complete the table on the right.

Increases amount of greenhouse gases	What we, as individuals, can do
loss of trees	grow and/or protect plants

What you need to remember *Copy and complete using the* **key words**

More about global warming

Burning _____, _____ and decay of waste by _____ all <u>add</u> carbon dioxide to the air.

Trees <u>remove</u> _____ _____ from the air and 'lock it up' in their wood. So fewer trees reduces means less carbon dioxide is removed from the atmosphere.

Keeping cattle and growing rice increase the amount of _____ in the air.

Greater amounts of carbon dioxide and methane in the Earth's atmosphere may cause _____ _____. As well as causing quite big changes in the Earth's _____ it may lead to a rise in _____ _____.

You need to be able to weigh evidence and form balanced judgements about environmental issues such as global warming.

8 Waste can pollute water

Why we need to treat sewage

In the UK, we treat most of our sewage so that it doesn't pollute rivers and seas. The diagram shows what can happen when untreated **sewage** gets into a river.

1 What happens to fish in a river polluted with large amounts of sewage?

2 Why isn't there enough oxygen in the water?

We also pollute water with the chemicals we use on farms and in factories.

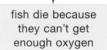

untreated sewage goes into a river

↓

microorganisms which break down the sewage need a lot of oxygen

↓

the amount of oxygen dissolved in the water goes down

↓

fish die because they can't get enough oxygen

Chemicals we use on farms

Farmers spray chemicals on to their crops. **Pesticides** and **herbicides** are two examples of these chemicals.

Farmers use pesticides to kill the insects and other animals that feed on their crops.

They use herbicides to kill weeds.

Pesticides and herbicides are **toxic**.
This means that they are poisonous.

3 Why do farmers want to get rid of weeds?

4 Organic farmers try not to use chemicals on their crops. Why is this?

These poppies are competing with the wheat crop. They take some of the water, minerals and light.

Pesticides and herbicides pollute land and water

Farmers spray pesticides and herbicides on their crops. This pollutes the land.

Look at the picture.

> **5** How do pesticides and herbicides get into streams and rivers?
>
> **6** What other chemicals can also get into streams and rivers?
>
> **7** Where do the chemicals eventually end up?

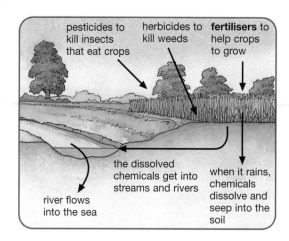

pesticides to kill insects that eat crops

herbicides to kill weeds

fertilisers to help crops to grow

the dissolved chemicals get into streams and rivers

when it rains, chemicals dissolve and seep into the soil

river flows into the sea

Industrial waste

Waste from factories also causes pollution. In the 1960s, a chemical factory in Minamata Bay, Japan, let out poisonous waste containing mercury into the sea. By 1969, many people were ill and 68 people had died.

> **8** How did the mercury get into people's bodies?

waste from the factory

local people catch fish in the bay

Acid rain

Many lakes in Europe now have no fish.

> **9** Why have the fish in these lakes died?

The rain is more acidic than it should be because people have polluted the air with sulfur dioxide. Acid rain makes lakes more **acidic**.

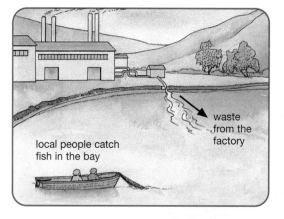

There are now no fish in this lake. The water has become too acidic.

What you need to remember *Copy and complete using the **key words***

Waste can pollute water
Humans are producing more and more waste.
Unless we handle it properly we will cause more pollution.
We pollute water with untreated _____.
Farmers use _____ to make their crops grow better. The _____ and
_____ they use to protect their crops are _____. All these chemicals
drain from the land into the water.
Dissolved waste gases such as sulfur dioxide make the water _____.

9 Indicators of pollution

Monitoring pollution

Many scientists monitor pollution of water, air and land. Some are researchers in universities. Others work directly for

- international environmental organisations
- governments
- local authorities
- organisations such as power companies.

I monitor air pollution for the local council. When air pollution rises too high, we suggest that people with asthma stay indoors.

1 Write down <u>three</u> reasons why we monitor pollution.

2 Suggest why power companies employ scientists to check that air pollution stays fairly low.
Answer as fully as you can.

I work for a power company. My job is to collect and analyse data on the spread of gases leaving the power station. We have to ensure that people in the surrounding area arent harmed.

Ways of monitoring pollution

Some of the scientists monitoring pollution use data recorders to measure changes in concentration of particular chemicals. They can see how pollution changes from hour to hour and from day to day.

Others survey groups of animals and plants to find out how polluted air and water are. We call these plants and animals **indicator** organisms. These scientists are looking at the longer-term effects of pollution.

Invertebrate animals are good indicators of the amount of **water pollution**. Some can live in very polluted water, others only in clean water.

Look at the picture.

3 If rat-tailed maggots live in a stream, what does that tell you?

4 Which invertebrates live only in clean water?

I work for the Environment Agency. I sample river water to make sure that nobody is polluting it. The river is important for drinking water as well as for wildlife.

I work in the local planning department. We have to plan for sustainable development. So, when we consider applications for new factories, roads, airports and so on, we need data on pollution and wildlife.

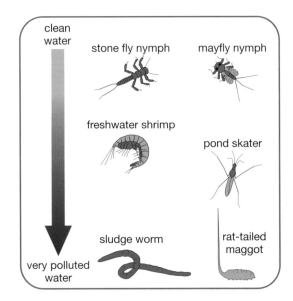

clean water

stone fly nymph   mayfly nymph

freshwater shrimp

pond skater

sludge worm   rat-tailed maggot

very polluted water

Indicators of air pollution

Lichens are very sensitive to the amount of sulfur dioxide in the air. Some species are more sensitive than others. So the species present and the number of different species give scientists clues about the amount of air pollution. We say that **lichens** are indicators of the amount of air pollution.

Lichens grow very slowly. They indicate the long-term purity of the air. Scientists also monitor the amounts of pollutants in the air directly with chemical tests. This gives them day-by-day information about the amounts of gases such as sulfur dioxide in the air.

5 If you can't find any lichens on trees and walls, what can you say about the air?

6 A local authority inspector suspected that emissions of sulfur dioxide from a factory were increasing. Should she use a lichen survey or chemical tests to find out. Explain your answer.

7 Which lichen in the chart indicates the cleanest air?

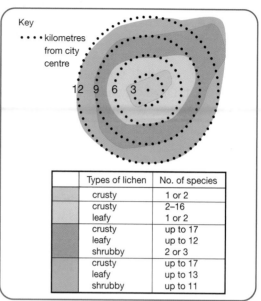

	Types of lichen	No. of species
	crusty	1 or 2
	crusty	2–16
	leafy	1 or 2
	crusty	up to 17
	leafy	up to 12
	shrubby	2 or 3
	crusty	up to 17
	leafy	up to 13
	shrubby	up to 11

As you go outwards from a city centre, the amount of air pollution usually decreases. So the number of species of lichens increases.

low ——————————————— pollution ——————————————→ high

Shrubby lichen.

Leafy lichen.

Crusty lichen.

What you need to remember *Copy and complete using the **key words***

Indicators of pollution

We can use _____ organisms to show how much pollution there is, including

- _____ as indicators of air pollution
- invertebrate animals as indicators of _____ _____.

You need to be able to evaluate methods of collecting environmental data and consider their validity and reliability.

10 Looking to the future

We get raw materials such as fuels and minerals from the Earth's crust. Once we've used these natural resources, they can't be replaced. We say that they are <u>non-renewable</u>. For sustainable development, we must use them more carefully. In other words, we must <u>conserve</u> them.

> **1** When we say that we should conserve fuel, what does that mean?

> **2** Write down <u>two</u> reasons why we need to conserve natural resources.

What can <u>we</u> do to conserve non-renewables?

A lot of things end up as waste in landfill sites when we are finished with them. But <u>we</u> could reuse or recycle many of them.

> **3** Explain the difference between reusing and recycling.

> **4** Write down <u>three</u> things that we can
>
> **a** recycle
> **b** reuse.

> **5** Write down <u>two</u> benefits of recycling materials
>
> **a** to people
> **b** to the environment.

> **6** A family has these rules.
>
> ■ If it's less than a mile away, we walk.
> ■ If we can go where we want when we want by public transport, we don't use the car.
>
> Explain how these rules help the environment and the health of this family.

> **7** Suggest how
>
> **a** a family can also save energy at home
> **b** saving energy like this benefits the family.

REMEMBER

To be sustainable, development must

■ allow development to continue
■ not damage the environment.

We can pass many items on to other people or to charity shops for reuse.

If we recycle waste, such as bottles and aluminium cans, these materials will not run out as quickly. Using recycled materials uses less energy than using new raw materials.

If some of the people going to town in these cars went on the bus, the amount of fuel used would be smaller.

Development versus the environment

We also need to think about how we use the land.
New roads and buildings

- take up land
- affect wildlife by destroying habitats or making them too small to provide enough food or space
- cause pollution.

8 Explain why a species might not survive if we

    a halve the size of its habitat

    b pollute the habitat.

So we can't just build wherever we want to. Whenever anyone applies for planning permission to build or extend something like a road, a factory or an airport, they have to report on the risk to the environment.

Filling in ponds destroys habitats for newts. Even making ponds smaller can mean that they don't provide enough food or space for newts.

"My reports include a scientific study of the main features of the area, data on the wild plants and animals, and any air or water pollution. When the company needs data on pollution or particular animals and plants, it pays specialists to do field studies.

Then I use this data to predict the effects of any proposed plans. A development could put an endangered species at risk. It could cause an increase in pollution. If so, neither the company nor the planners would want it to go ahead."

Andrea is a scientist working for a chemical company. She writes the company's environmental reports.

Andrea

9 Write down <u>two</u> reasons why

    a we need planning permission for building

    b authorities sometimes refuse planning permission.

10 Suggest why Andrea's company wants to do all it can to protect the environment.

For <u>sustainable</u> development we need to assess the benefits against the harm to the environment of building a new motorway here.

What you need to remember

Looking to the future

There is nothing new for you to <u>remember</u> in this section.

You need to be able to form balanced judgements about sustainable development.

1 Limestone for building

Limestone is a very useful **rock**. People all over the world have used it for thousands of years. We use it for **building** and as a raw material for making other things.

> 1 Copy and complete the table.

Part of the world	Name of the limestone building

St Paul's Cathedral, London.

A Pyramid, Egypt.

All of these buildings are built from limestone.

Empire State Building, New York.

Everyday places, too

It's not just famous buildings which are made from limestone. We use it for building everyday things too.

This village is in the Cotswold Hills. If you dig down through the soil, you find limestone.

> 2 Write down <u>four</u> things in the picture that are made from limestone.

> 3 Why do you think limestone is the most common building material in this village and not granite?

Using limestone

Limestone is not a very hard rock so we can cut it into blocks and slabs quite easily.

This makes limestone very useful for building.

But there is a problem with using limestone for building, as the pictures show.

4   Why is limestone a useful building material?

5   What is the problem of using limestone for building?

6   Why is this problem worse today than it was hundreds of years ago?

New materials from limestone

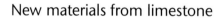

We add limestone to other substances to help us make many other building materials.

Weather changes limestone. Acid rain makes it change even more quickly.

7   Look at the pictures.
Write down the names of <u>three</u> building materials which are made using limestone.

We make **cement** by heating limestone with clay.

The Millennium Bridge in Gateshead sits on 19 000 tonnes of **concrete**, made using limestone.

The Gherkin contains a large amount of **glass**. One of the raw materials for making glass is limestone.

What you need to remember *Copy and complete using the **key words***

Limestone for building

Limestone is a type of _____.

It is very useful for _____ because it is easy to cut into blocks.

Many other useful building materials can be made from limestone, for example _____, _____ and _____.

2 Where do we get limestone from?

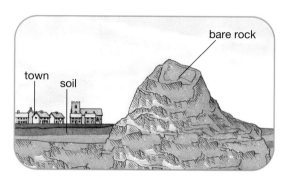

We don't usually see the rock that's under our feet. This is because it's often covered with soil. We also cover the ground with roads, pavements and buildings. If you dig down far enough you always reach solid rock, like limestone.

The photo shows how we get limestone from the ground.

1 Copy and complete the following sentences.

We remove limestone from the ground in places called _____.

Large chunks of rock are blasted off using _____.

Limestone is a very important building material. Quarries provide jobs, but they are not always popular with local people.

We get limestone from **quarries**. Rock is blasted off the quarry face using explosives.

Camberdale News

Lawson to expand Field View quarry

Five hundred local people marched through the centre of Camberdale this morning. They wanted to draw attention to plans for a local quarry expansion.

Quarry operators, Lawson, plan to expand the Field View quarry. Quarry manager James Shore said today, 'local builders and industries can't get enough of our limestone. We'd be mad not to take this opportunity to expand. New chemicals from limestone can help to improve our environment, too.'

Camberdale residents are worried about the increase in noise and dust which the quarry will cause. Some residents say that the quarry also pollutes local rivers and streams.

I lead walks in the area. People come here on holiday because the countryside is so beautiful.

I study the wildlife in this area. The oldest parts of the quarry have been well restored and there are lots of rare orchids growing there.

If the quarry expands I'll open a new shop in the area. The other one is already very busy.

I worry about my boy when he goes off with his friends – that quarry is so dangerous.

I farm right up to the edge of the quarry.

I live on the main road. A bigger quarry will mean more traffic. Those heavy lorries are so noisy.

I leave school next year and I'd like to work nearby.

The new quarry workers and their families will need houses. That's more work for my building firm.

2   Make a large copy of the table. Use the information from the newspaper article and the people's opinions to help you complete it.

Advantages of the Field View quarry	Disadvantages of the Field View quarry

3   Imagine that you are the quarry manager. Write a letter to the Camberdale News explaining how you think expanding the quarry will be good for the area.

What you need to remember *Copy and complete using the **key words***

Where do we get limestone from?
We get limestone from places called _____.

You need to be able to use information like this to say how using limestone affects local people, the environment and the amount of money in an area.

3 What's it all made from?

All chemical substances, including limestone, are made from tiny **atoms**. There are about 100 different kinds of atoms in nature.

If a substance is made from just one kind of atom, we call it an **element**.

> **1** How many elements do you think there are? Give a reason for your answer.

We burn the element carbon on the barbecue.

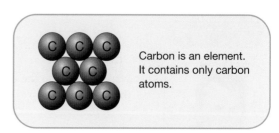

Carbon is an element. It contains only carbon atoms.

Using letters to stand for elements

We can save time and space by using our initials instead of writing our full name.

In science we often use the initials of an element instead of the whole word. We call these letters the **symbols** of the elements.

The table shows some of these symbols.

> **2** What is the symbol for
>
> **a** carbon?
> **b** sulfur?
>
> **3 a** What are the symbols for calcium and for silicon?
> **b** Why do you think these elements need to have a second, smaller letter in their symbols?

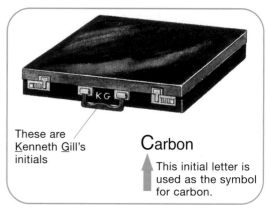

These are Kenneth Gill's initials

Carbon

This initial letter is used as the symbol for carbon.

Kenneth Gill's briefcase.

Some of the symbols we use come from the old names of the elements.

> **4** Copy and complete the table.

Element	Old name	Symbol
	cuprum	
sodium		

Element	Symbol we use	
carbon	C	
calcium	Ca	
copper	Cu	from cuprum, the old name
nitrogen	N	
oxygen	O	
sulfur	S	
silicon	Si	
sodium	Na	from natrium, the old name

Elements in the periodic table

Group 1	Group 2												Group 3	4	5	6	7	Group 0
					H hydrogen													He helium
Li lithium	Be beryllium												B boron	C carbon	N nitrogen	O oxygen	F fluorine	Ne neon
Na sodium	Mg magnesium												Al aluminium	Si silicon	P phosphorus	S sulfur	Cl chlorine	Ar argon
K potassium	Ca calcium	Sc scandium	Ti titanium	V vanadium	Cr chromium	Mn manganese	Fe iron	Co cobalt	Ni nickel	Cu copper	Zn zinc		Ga gallium	Ge germanium	As arsenic	Se selenium	Br bromine	Kr krypton
Rb rubidium	Sr strontium	Y yttrium	Zr zirconium	Nb niobium	Mo molybdenum	Tc technetium	Ru ruthenium	Rh rhodium	Pd palladium	Ag silver	Cd cadmium		In indium	Sn tin	Sb antimony	Te tellurium	I iodine	Xe xenon
Cs caesium	Ba barium	elements 57–71	Hf hafnium	Ta tantalum	W tungsten	Re rhenium	Os osmium	Ir iridium	Pt platinum	Au gold	Hg mercury		Tl thallium	Pb lead	Bi bismuth	Po polonium	At astatine	Rn radon
Fr francium	Ra radium	elements 89+																

5 How many groups can you see in the periodic table?

The periodic table shows all of the elements that we know about. Over the years, scientists have studied the elements and arranged them in order.

In the periodic table, many of the elements have been placed into vertical **groups**.

Using the periodic table

The periodic table is very useful. We can use it to make good guesses about elements we have never seen.
This is because there are patterns we can understand in the table. For example, elements in the same group are very much alike. We say they have similar **properties**.

6 Lithium and sodium are both in Group 1 and are very similar. Which other elements will be much like lithium and sodium?

What you need to remember *Copy and complete using the key words*

What's it all made from?
All substances are made from tiny _____.
If the substance has atoms that are all of one type we call it an _____.
There are about 100 different elements.
We use letters to stand for elements. We call these _____. For example, Na stands for one atom of _____ and O stands for one atom of _____.
The periodic table shows all of the elements. Each column contains elements with similar _____. We call each column a _____.

4 What's in limestone?

What are compounds?

When atoms of different elements join together we get a substance called a **compound**.
Most substances are compounds.

The diagrams show some compounds. Each compound has its own formula.

The formula of a compound tells us

- which elements are in the compound
- how many atoms of each element there are in the compound.

1 Copy the table. Then complete it to include all of the compounds shown on this page.

Name of compound	Formula	Atoms in the compound
carbon dioxide	CO_2	1 carbon atom 2 oxygen atoms
water		
ammonia		
calcium oxide		
copper sulfate		
calcium hydroxide		

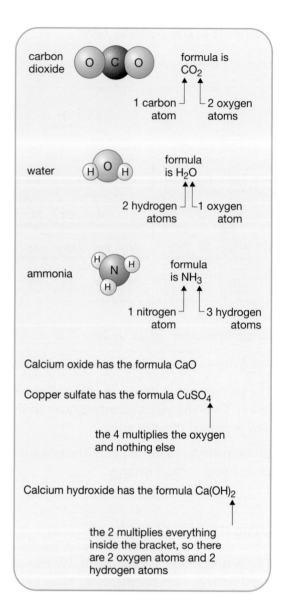

carbon dioxide — formula is CO_2 — 1 carbon atom — 2 oxygen atoms

water — formula is H_2O — 2 hydrogen atoms — 1 oxygen atom

ammonia — formula is NH_3 — 1 nitrogen atom — 3 hydrogen atoms

Calcium oxide has the formula CaO

Copper sulfate has the formula $CuSO_4$

the 4 multiplies the oxygen and nothing else

Calcium hydroxide has the formula $Ca(OH)_2$

the 2 multiplies everything inside the bracket, so there are 2 oxygen atoms and 2 hydrogen atoms

So what's limestone made from?

The picture shows some pieces of limestone from different places.

2 Which compound do we find in all these pieces of limestone?

Even though these rocks look different, they all contain the compound **calcium carbonate**.

Calcium carbonate

The **formula** for calcium carbonate is CaCO₃.

3 Copy and complete the table to show which atoms of each element make up the compound calcium carbonate.

Symbol			
Element			
Number of atoms			

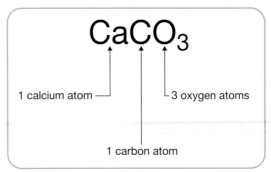

The compound calcium carbonate has the formula **CaCO₃**.

How to test for limestone

We cannot always tell if a piece of rock contains calcium carbonate just by looking at it.

4 Look at the picture.

How can we test a rock to see if it contains calcium carbonate?

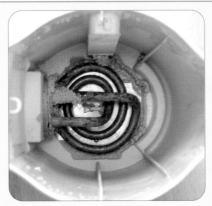

Drops of acid fizz when they are added to a lump of limestone.

DID YOU KNOW?

The scale in your kettle is calcium carbonate too. The chemical we add to remove the scale is an acid, which makes the calcium carbonate fizz.

What you need to remember *Copy and complete using the key words*

What's in limestone?

Limestone contains a chemical _____ called _____
_____.

The _____ of a compound shows the number of atoms it contains.
The formula for calcium carbonate is _____.

5 Heating limestone

People have been heating limestone to make chemicals for thousands of years. It's still an important chemical process today.

1 Write down <u>one</u> group of ancient people who heated limestone.

2 Why did they do this?

Ancient writings show that, even in 4000 BC, the Egyptians heated limestone. They used it to make plaster for the Pyramids.

The lime kiln

If we make limestone really hot we can change it into **quicklime**. We use a lime kiln to do this.

3 A lime kiln is heated in <u>two</u> ways. Write them down.

A word equation for the reaction is

limestone + $\langle$ heat energy $\rangle$ → quicklime + carbon dioxide

The chemical name for limestone is calcium carbonate.

The chemical name for quicklime is **calcium oxide**.

4 Write down the word equation using the chemical names for limestone and quicklime.

A reaction that uses heat (thermal) energy to break down a substance into new substances is called **thermal decomposition**.

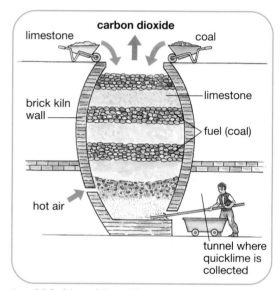

An old-fashioned lime kiln.

What you need to remember *Copy and complete using the **key words***

Heating limestone

When we heat limestone strongly in a kiln it breaks down into _____ and

_____ _____.

We call this kind of reaction _____ _____.

The chemical name for quicklime is _____ _____.

6 Describing reactions 1

In a chemical reaction, the **reactants** are the substances we use at the start. These turn into **products**, which are the substances left at the end.

If we heat copper carbonate

- there is one reactant – copper carbonate
- the products are copper oxide and carbon dioxide.

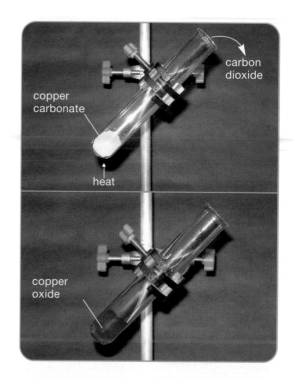

1 Copy the headings. Then complete the table to include the reaction with zinc carbonate shown in the photographs.

Reactant(s)	Product(s)
copper carbonate	copper oxide carbon dioxide

Writing word equations

When we heat copper carbonate it breaks down to produce copper oxide and carbon dioxide.

The **word equation** for this reaction is

copper carbonate → copper oxide + carbon dioxide

2 Write down a word equation for the reaction that happens when zinc carbonate is heated.

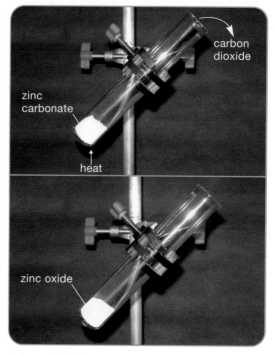

What you need to remember *Copy and complete using the key words*

Describing reactions 1
We can describe a chemical reaction using a _____ _____.
The substances that react are the _____.
The new substances that are produced are the _____.

7 Using quicklime

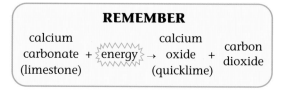

If we heat a piece of limestone strongly, it changes into a new material called **quicklime**.

1 **a** What is the chemical name for quicklime?
  b What other substance is produced when we heat limestone to make quicklime?

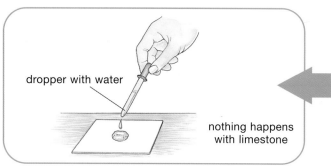

dropper with water

nothing happens with limestone

pieces of limestone (calcium carbonate)

Many other **carbonates** also split up (decompose) when we heat them.

2 What <u>two</u> substances are produced when we heat copper carbonate?

Quicklime looks almost the same as limestone, but when you add a few drops of water you can see the difference.

3 What happens when you add a few drops of water to limestone?

4 What happens when you add a few drops of water to quicklime?

The quicklime <u>reacts</u> with the water to form a new material.

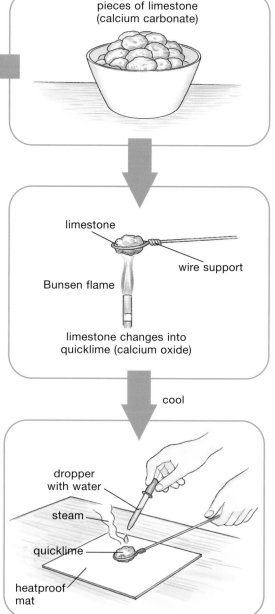

limestone

wire support

Bunsen flame

limestone changes into quicklime (calcium oxide)

cool

dropper with water

steam

quicklime

heatproof mat

What is the new material?

The new material formed from quicklime is called **slaked lime**.

5 Copy and complete the word equation.

quicklime + _____ → _____ + energy

The chemical name for slaked lime is calcium hydroxide.

6 Write down the word equation using the chemical names for quicklime and slaked lime.

What use is slaked lime?

We can use slaked lime to make a type of **mortar**. Mortar is the 'glue' which builders use to hold bricks or stone together.

We know that the Romans used mortars that were made from slaked lime.

7 Which other substance did the Romans add to slaked lime when they made mortar?

A Roman architect called Vitruvius wrote that mortar should be made like this:

> When the lime is slaked, let it be mingled with the sand in such a way that three of sand and one of lime is poured in ... For in this way there will be the right proportion of the mixture and blending.

Lime mortar or cement?

Instead of using lime mortar, builders can also use cement to hold bricks together.

Cement has different properties from lime mortar.

8 Which sets more quickly, lime mortar or cement?

9 Which substance would you use for repairing a brick built canal wall? Explain your answer.

10 Which substance would allow any damp to escape from an old building?

Substance	How fast does it set?	How strong is it?	Does it allow water to pass through?
cement	very quickly, even under water	very strong	no
lime mortar	slowly, over several weeks	not as strong as cement	yes

What you need to remember *Copy and complete using the **key words***

Using quicklime

When you heat limestone, it decomposes into _____ and carbon dioxide.

Many other _____ decompose in a similar way when you heat them.

Quicklime (calcium oxide) reacts with cold water to form _____ _____ (calcium hydroxide).

We can use slaked lime to make _____.

You need to be able to weigh up the advantages and disadvantages of using materials like cement for building.

8 Cement and concrete

Many of the things we build today are made from concrete.

When wet concrete sets, it becomes as hard as stone. When we mix concrete, it can be poured into moulds. This is how we make concrete into lots of different shapes.

> **1** Write down <u>two</u> things we can make using concrete.

> **2** Write down <u>two</u> reasons why concrete is useful for making these things.

To make concrete we need **cement**.

Cement is made from limestone.

Making cement

We need to use two materials from the ground to make cement. Look at the diagram.

These are the raw materials.

> **3** What <u>two</u> raw materials do we need to make cement?

> **4** What do we have to do to these raw materials to turn them into cement?

> **5** Write down <u>two</u> reasons why the kiln rotates all the time.

Making concrete

The diagram also shows how we can make **concrete**.

> **6** What <u>four</u> things must we mix together to make concrete?

These were made using concrete.

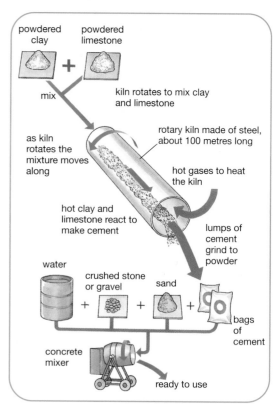

Using limestone to make cement and concrete.

Using concrete

Once we have mixed some concrete, we need to make it the right shape. The diagram shows how we can do this. The water **reacts** slowly with the cement to make the concrete set hard as stone. This can take a few days.

7 How can we keep the sides of the new concrete step straight?

8 Why should we wait a few days before removing the wooden frame?

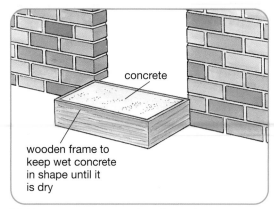

Making a concrete step for a house.

More about concrete

After water, concrete is the second most used substance on the Earth. Every year, one tonne of concrete is used for every person on the Earth. The reason we use it so much is that it is cheap and has many useful properties.

When designing a building, it is very important to think about its resistance to fire. Many large buildings are built using large steel columns.

Look at the table.

9 What is the fire resistance of a column that is only made from steel?

10 If a steel column is filled with concrete, what effect does this have on its fire resistance?

11 What else can be added to the column to make it even more fire resistant?

What the steel column is filled with	Fire resistance
no filling	12–20 minutes
concrete	1–2 hours
concrete and steel fibres	2–3 hours

This table shows the fire resistance of hollow steel columns used for building.

What you need to remember *Copy and complete using the* **key words**

Cement and concrete
We heat limestone and clay together in a hot kiln to make _____.
A mixture of cement, sand, rock and water gives _____.
The water _____ with the cement and makes the concrete set solid.

You need to be able to weigh up the advantages and disadvantages of using materials like concrete for building.

9 Glass in buildings

Making glass

Glass is another very useful material that we can make using limestone.

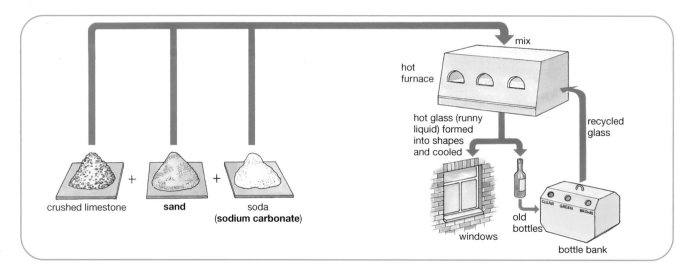

crushed limestone + **sand** + soda (**sodium carbonate**)

mix
hot furnace
hot glass (runny liquid) formed into shapes and cooled
recycled glass
windows
old bottles
bottle bank

1. What are the <u>two</u> other raw materials we need to make glass?

2. Why is it easy to make glass into lots of different shapes?

3. Why do companies that make glass collect old glass from bottle banks?

Building with glass

The Egyptians were able to make glass beads as early as 12 000 BC.

4. Write down <u>two</u> reasons why large amounts of glass are used in buildings.

5. What is a problem with using glass in buildings?

6. How can we reduce the amount of heat lost through a window?

Glass can also have a special metal coating to reflect heat back into the building.

7. How can coated glass help to prevent a building from losing heat?

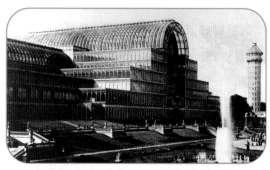

Most buildings use large amounts of glass to allow the light in. In 1851, the Crystal Palace was built from glass to make it look attractive.

Heat can escape from a building through the windows. Many windows are now double glazed. This means that the window has two layers of glass with an air gap in between.

Making glass safer

The London Eye was forced to close one evening after a piece of metal fell off. The metal hit a canopy and showered visitors with glass.

The attraction reopened the next day after engineers found out what had happened and made some repairs.

Four teenagers, who were boarding the Eye, were hit by some pieces of glass. Luckily they were not injured.

A spokesman for the London Eye said, 'I'm very pleased to say that the toughened glass worked well.'

8 Why is toughened glass safer than normal glass?

9 Why did the spokesman say that the toughened glass had 'worked well'?

When it's broken, toughened glass breaks into small pieces (called dice).
The pieces do not have sharp edges like normal broken glass.

What you need to remember *Copy and complete using the* ***key words***

Glass in buildings
We can use limestone to make _____.
To make the glass we heat a mixture of limestone, _____ _____ and _____.

10 Describing reactions 2

Understanding symbol equations

There are two ways to write down what happens in a chemical reaction.

For the reaction in which we heat calcium carbonate, the two kinds of equation look like this:

calcium carbonate $\rightarrow$ calcium oxide + carbon dioxide

$$CaCO_3 \quad \rightarrow \quad CaO \quad + \quad CO_2$$

In the second equation, we have replaced the names of the reactants and products with a **formula**.

We call the second equation a **symbol equation**.

> **1** Write down the formula for
>
> **a** calcium carbonate
> **b** calcium oxide
> **c** carbon dioxide.

In the box are the symbol equations for heating two other carbonates.

> **2** Copy each of the symbol equations from the box.
>
> Write the name of each chemical compound under its formula.

> **REMEMBER**
>
> The substances that react are the reactants.
> The substances that are produced are the products.
> The symbol for copper is Cu.
> The symbol for zinc is Zn.

> $CuCO_3 \rightarrow CuO + CO_2$
> $ZnCO_3 \rightarrow ZnO + CO_2$

Adding state symbols

There are three states of matter – solid, liquid and gas. Reactants and products can be solids, liquids or gases, or they can be dissolved in water.

We can show this in an equation by using state symbols.

In the calcium carbonate reaction

- calcium carbonate and calcium oxide are both solids
- carbon dioxide is a gas.

We can now write the equation like this:

$CaCO_3(s) \rightarrow CaO(s) + CO_2(g)$

> **3** Add the state symbols to the symbol equation for the reaction of copper carbonate. Copper carbonate and copper oxide are both solids.

(s)	means	**solid**
(l)	means	**liquid**
(g)	means	gas
(aq)	means	aqueous – this means solutions of substances dissolved in water, e.g. HCl(aq)

What state symbols mean.

A chemical reaction with quicklime

We can show what we make when we add water to calcium oxide if we use a word equation.

calcium oxide + water → calcium hydroxide

We can write this as the symbol equation below.

$CaO(s) + H_2O(l) \rightarrow Ca(OH)_2(s)$

4 What do the following symbols mean?

    a (l)
    b (s)

REMEMBER

Adding water to calcium oxide (quicklime) makes calcium hydroxide (slaked lime).

REMEMBER FROM KS3

In a chemical reaction, no mass is lost and no mass is gained. The **mass** of the products is the same as the mass of the **reactants**.

Why symbol equations need to be balanced

Atoms don't just appear or disappear during chemical reactions. So there must be exactly the same number of each type of atom in the products as there was in the reactants.

In other words, symbol equations must be **balanced**.

The equation shows what happens when we react hydrogen with oxygen. It is balanced.

5 Copy the table. Complete it to show the numbers of atoms in the reactants and products.

6 Copy the symbol equation below. Then show that it is balanced.

    $Mg + 2HCl \rightarrow MgCl_2 + H_2$

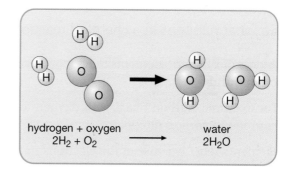

hydrogen + oxygen   water
$2H_2 + O_2$ ⟶ $2H_2O$

Reactants	Products
_____ hydrogen atoms	_____ hydrogen atoms
_____ oxygen atoms	_____ oxygen atoms

What you need to remember *Copy and complete using the **key words***

Describing reactions 2
For a chemical reaction, we can write a word equation and a _____ _____.
We replace the name of each chemical with a _____.
In a symbol equation, (s) stands for _____, (l) stands for _____, _____ stands for gas and _____ stands for aqueous solution.
Atoms do not appear or disappear during chemical reactions.
The _____ of the products is the same as the mass of the _____.
This means that when we write an equation it must be _____.

You need to be able to explain what is happening to the substances in this topic using ideas about atoms and symbols. You can learn more about balancing equations on page 326.

11 Chemical reactions up close

What's inside an atom?

The diagram shows what is inside an oxygen atom. In the centre of the atom is the **nucleus**.

Electrons move in the space around the nucleus.

1. How many electrons are there in an oxygen atom?

2. What is the electrical charge on an electron?

3. Write a sentence about the mass of an electron.

So what happens in a chemical reaction?

Atoms of different elements react together to form **compounds**.

For example, carbon reacts with oxygen to produce the compound carbon dioxide.

Elements react because of the electrons in their atoms.

Sharing electrons

The diagram shows how atoms of carbon and oxygen react together by **sharing** electrons.

4. How many atoms of oxygen react with one atom of carbon?

5. What is the name of the new compound that is made in the reaction?

REMEMBER

Everything is made from atoms. There are about 100 different kinds of atom. In an element, all of the atoms are of one kind.

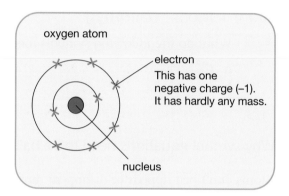

oxygen atom

electron
This has one negative charge (–1). It has hardly any mass.

nucleus

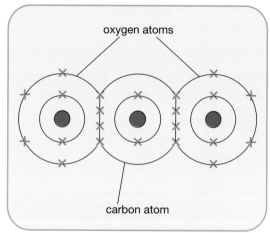

oxygen atoms

carbon atom

The carbon atom has reacted with two atoms of oxygen to make the compound carbon dioxide. The elements have made **chemical bonds**.

Give and take

Not all atoms react by sharing electrons. Sometimes atoms react by **giving** electrons to the atoms of another element.

The other element reacts by **taking** the electrons.

6   Copy and complete the following sentences.

In the reaction between sodium and chlorine, the sodium atom _____ an electron to a chlorine atom.
The chlorine atom takes an electron from the _____ atom.

7   What is the name for the new compound that is made in the reaction?

8   What is the everyday name for the compound that is made when sodium and chlorine react?

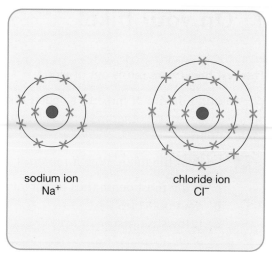

sodium ion
Na⁺

chloride ion
Cl⁻

Sodium has reacted with chlorine to make the compound sodium chloride. The sodium atom has given one electron to the chlorine atom. The elements have made a chemical bond.

We know the compound sodium chloride as common salt. We use it on our food!

What you need to remember *Copy and complete using the **key words***

Chemical reactions up close

In the centre of an atom there is the _____.
Around the nucleus there are particles called _____.
Atoms react with atoms of other elements to produce _____.
They do this by _____ electrons with another atom or by _____ or _____ electrons.
We say that the elements have made _____ _____.

1 On your bike!

The first bikes were made out of wood.

We wouldn't dream of making wooden bikes for adults now because we can use other materials. The table shows you some options.

One of the first bikes, made in 1817, was called the 'hobbyhorse'. It had wooden wheels and a wooden frame. You had to push it along with your feet – but it was faster than walking.

1 Look at the table. Which material

a is the most dense (has the greatest mass per m³)?
b does not corrode?
c is the strongest?

Material	Strength (MPa)	Mass of 1 m³ (kg)	Cost of 1 m³ (£)	Does it corrode?	Bendy or stiff?
wood	25	600	1000	no, it rots	quite bendy
steel	1100	7700	2000	yes	very stiff
aluminium	30	2700	4000	some corrosion	quite bendy
titanium	1000	4510	100 000	no	quite stiff

2 Write down <u>three</u> disadvantages of using wood to build a bike.

Bikes from metal

Later bikes, like the boneshaker in 1870, had frames made from cast iron.

Boneshaker bike from 1870.

By 1890, bikes were made from steel. They looked similar to those we use today.

3 Look at the table. Write down <u>two</u> reasons why we still use steel to build many bikes.

Bikes from around 1900.

Modern bikes

Some modern bikes have steel parts but many now contain large amounts of aluminium.

4   Look at the table on page 132.
    Write down <u>two</u> advantages an aluminium bike has over a steel bike.

Many people believe that titanium is the best modern metal for making bikes.

5   Look at the table.
    What properties does titanium have which make it an excellent choice for a bike?

6   Copy and complete the sentence.

    We don't make all bikes from titanium because it is very ——————.

Aluminium is the most popular material for building mountain bikes.

This bike is made from titanium. Many of the fastest cyclists ride bikes like this.

How bendy?

We can show information about 'how bendy a material is' in several ways. The words in the table do not give us as much information as the rank order shown.

7   What information can we get more easily from the rank order than from the results in the table?

8   What information does the rank order of materials still not tell us?

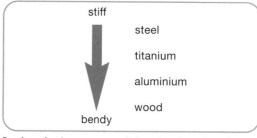

stiff

steel

titanium

aluminium

wood

bendy

Rank order is one way of showing how bendy a material is. It gives us more information than the words in a table

---

What you need to remember

On your bike!
There is nothing new for you to <u>remember</u> in this section.

You need to be able to use information like this to work out the advantages and disadvantages of making things out of metals.

2 Where do we get metals from?

Where do we find metals?

There are metals mixed with rocks in the Earth's **crust**.
We find gold in the Earth's crust as the metal itself.
The pieces of gold in rocks contain just gold and nothing else.
Gold is a very rare metal. Many other metals are much more common than gold.

Look at the pie chart.

1 Which are the <u>two</u> most common metals in the Earth's crust?

2 Why don't we show gold in the pie chart?

Most metals, including iron and aluminium, are in the Earth's crust as metal **ores**. In the ore the metal is joined with other **elements** as **compounds**.

Metals are often joined with oxygen in compounds we call metal oxides. For example, most iron ores contain iron oxide. Metals may also be joined with sulfur in compounds we call metal sulfides.

Looking at metal ores

In the first photograph there is a common iron ore.

3 **a** What is the name of this iron ore?
b There are <u>two</u> elements in the ore. What are they?

Now look at the photographs showing two other metal ores.

4 Copy and complete the table.

Name of the ore	Metal in the ore	Other elements in the ore

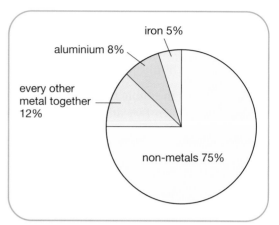

Elements in the Earth's crust. Gold makes up only three parts in every billion (thousand million) parts of the Earth's crust.

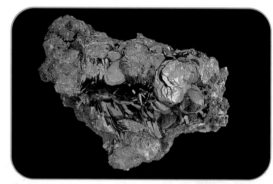

Haematite contains iron. This ore is a type of iron oxide (iron combined with oxygen).

Galena is lead sulfide (lead combined with sulfur).

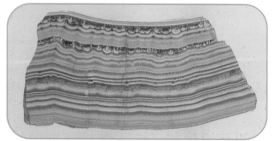

Malachite is copper carbonate (copper combined with carbon and oxygen).

How much metal is there in metal ores?

Metal ores contain rock as well as the valuable metal compounds. Different ores contain different amounts of rock.

5 How much metal compound is there in 100 g of each of the ores shown?

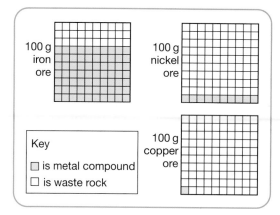

Metals and the environment

Without metals our lives would be very different.
But producing useful metals can also cause problems.

Iron ore mine in Australia.

Potash mine in Germany.

Gold mine in Brazil.

Mining metals and metal ores can make huge holes in the ground.

Quarrying and digging of the metal ore produces a lot of dust, which pollutes the air.

Huge heaps of waste rock may be left behind. Wastes still contain metal compounds. These can pollute streams and harm living things.

6 Write down <u>three</u> problems that mining metals and metal ores can cause.

What you need to remember *Copy and complete using the* **key words**

Where do we get metals from?

Metals are found in the Earth's _____ .

Most metals, except gold, are found joined with other _____ as

_____ .

Rocks containing metal compounds are called _____ .

You need to be able to think about the effects that mining metal ores can have on the environment.

3 Extracting metals from their ores

To get pure metals from ores, we must split up the metal compound in the ore. A **chemical reaction** must take place.

We can release, or **extract**, some metals by heating their oxides with the element **carbon**.

Iron metal from iron oxide

We extract iron from iron oxide in a **blast furnace** using carbon. The carbon reacts with the oxygen in the **iron oxide**. This leaves iron metal.

1   **a**   What other substance is produced?
   b   Write a word equation for this reaction.

When we remove oxygen from a metal oxide like this we call it **reduction**. We say that the carbon has reduced the iron oxide.

2   Copy and complete the sentence.

   When carbon removes oxygen from a metal oxide it is an example of _____ .

Extracting other metals

We can also use carbon to extract other metals from their oxides, for example lead:

lead oxide + carbon → lead + carbon dioxide

3   Which substance has been reduced in this reaction?

We pour carbon and iron oxide into the blast furnace. The iron oxide turns into iron metal. The reaction also makes carbon dioxide gas.

The reactivity series

Some metals are very reactive. This means that they burn easily and react with water and acid.

Look at the diagrams.

4   Which metal is the most reactive with acid?

5   Put the <u>four</u> metals in order, the most reactive first and the least reactive last.

The reactivity series for metals shows many metals in order of their **reactivity**.

6   Which is the most reactive metal in the series?

7   Which is the least reactive metal?

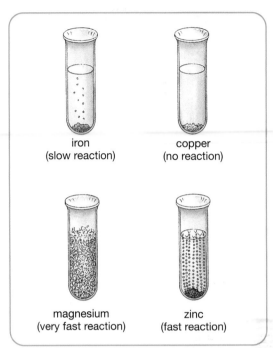

iron
(slow reaction)

copper
(no reaction)

magnesium
(very fast reaction)

zinc
(fast reaction)

Four different metals reacting with dilute acid.

Carbon in the reactivity series

Carbon isn't a metal, but we can put it in the reactivity series.

It can remove oxygen from some metal oxides, like iron oxide. It can only remove the oxygen from the metals which are **below** it in the reactivity series.

8   Can we use carbon to extract aluminium from aluminium oxide?
Explain your answer.

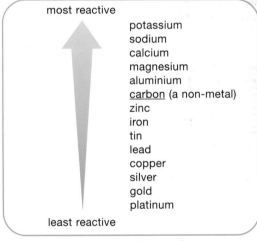

most reactive

potassium
sodium
calcium
magnesium
aluminium
<u>carbon</u> (a non-metal)
zinc
iron
tin
lead
copper
silver
gold
platinum

least reactive

This is the reactivity series for metals.
We can also put the non-metal carbon in the list.

What you need to remember *Copy and complete using the **key words***

Extracting metals from their ores
To split up a metal from its ore we need a _____ _____.
We say we _____ the metal.
To extract iron we heat _____ _____ with _____.
We do this in a _____ _____.
When we remove the oxygen from a metal oxide we call it _____.
We can put metals in order to show how reactive they are, or their _____.
We can only extract metals using carbon if they are _____ it in the reactivity series.

4 Is it worth it?

How pure is the ore?

We find metal ores in rocks. A rock must contain enough of a metal ore to make it worth mining. The purer the ore, the larger the percentage of metal in it.

How much does it cost?

Mines and extraction works need people to work in them. It mustn't cost too much to mine the ore, and it mustn't cost too much to extract the metal from the ore. We say it must be **economic**.

An ore that contains only a small amount of metal may still be worth mining if the metal is valuable enough.

What is the best source of copper?

The owner of a copper extraction works near Ambertone needs a new supply of copper ore.

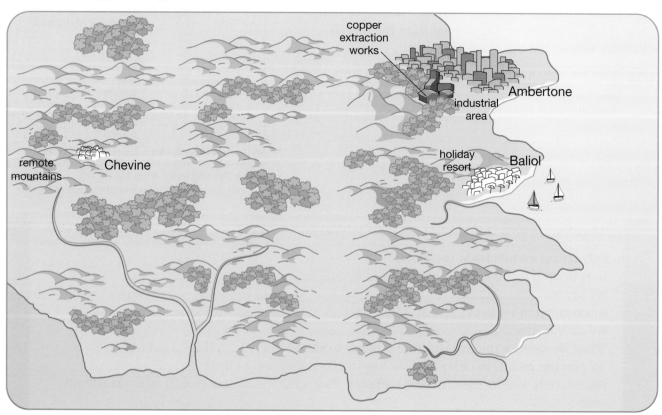

Here is part of the report he received about mines in the area.

Where the mine is	% copper in the ore	Cost of transport to the works	Population of the area	Estimated supply of the ore
Ambertone	1.1	£	very large	about 3 years
Baliol	2.3	££	large in holiday periods	about 6 years
Chevine	5.8	£££	very small	about 15 years

1   Which mine supplies the ore with the greatest amount of copper in?

2   Write down two problems there would be with mining ore in this region.

3   Which mine is closest to the copper extraction works?

4   Write down two problems there would be with mining ore in this region.

5   Are there any other factors, not in the report, which might affect your choice of mine?

6   Which factors could be different in 5 years' time?

7   Copy and complete the sentence.

I think the works owner should choose the mine in _____ to supply his ore.

Write down two reasons for your answer.

Too expensive

The works owner ends up paying much more for his copper ore than he was paying in the past.

8   What effect may this have on

   a   local businesses who buy copper from the works?
   b   workers at the extraction works?

Price of copper ore soars

Half of the workers at our local copper extraction works may lose their jobs.
'The price of my copper ore has doubled. I'll have to put up the price of my copper,' said works owner Dan Shaw today. 'If I lose customers, I'll have to lay off some workers'.

What you need to remember *Copy and complete using the **key words***

Is it worth it?
It is important to decide if it is worth extracting a metal from its ore.
We say it must be _____ to extract the metal. This changes over time.

You need to be able to use information like this to think about the effects of mining and making use of metal ores on local people and the amount of money in an area.

5 Iron or steel – what's the difference?

Steel is a strong, tough material. It is mostly **iron**.
We turn most of the iron that we make into steel.
We make iron in a blast furnace.

Material	% carbon	Properties
iron from the blast furnace	4.0	**brittle**
mild steel	0.4	tough

1 How much carbon is there in the iron from the blast furnace?

2 Why do you think that mild steel is a more useful material than iron from the blast furnace?

Removing the impurities

To change the iron from the blast furnace into steel, we must first remove the impurities. This makes pure iron.

3 How are the atoms arranged in pure iron?

4 Explain why pure iron is so easy to shape.

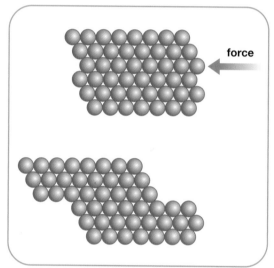

force

This is a model of the atoms in pure iron.
The atoms are in a pattern and the layers can **slide** over each other.
This makes it **soft** and easy to shape.

Turning the iron into steel

Pure iron is too soft to be useful. We must mix it with other elements to change it into steel.

The properties of a particular steel depend on what other elements we add and how much of these elements we add.

5 a Name three elements that we can add to iron to make steel.

   b Which of these three elements is not a metal?

6 Copy and complete the sentences.

Steels are not pure metals. They are _____.

About steels

- Steel is made by mixing iron with one or more other elements.
- The elements we mix with iron to make steel include **carbon** and **metals** such as nickel and chromium.
- There are many different types of steel.
- Steels are mixtures of elements, so we say they are **alloys**.

Steel has different properties from iron

Different elements have atoms that are different sizes.

7 **a** How do the other atoms in the steel affect the layers of iron atoms?

b What happens when we apply a force to the steel?

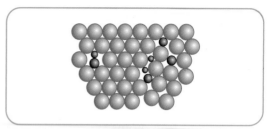

Other atoms in the steel **disrupt** the regular pattern of the iron atoms. They stop the iron layers from sliding so far when we apply a force.

Carbon steels

The cheapest and most common types of steel are made by mixing carbon with iron. The more carbon we add, the **harder** the steel becomes. We can use low carbon steel (0.2%) to make car bodywork. It's easy to press into **shape**. High carbon steel (1.5%) is very **hard** but brittle. We can use it to make knife blades.

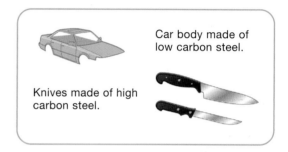

Car body made of low carbon steel.

Knives made of high carbon steel.

8 Copy and complete the table.

Type of steel	Properties	Uses

Stainless steel

9 Which elements can we add to iron to make stainless steel?

10 Which properties of stainless steel make it useful in the kitchen?

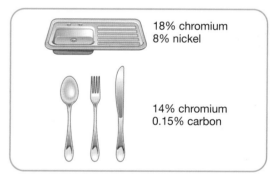

18% chromium
8% nickel

14% chromium
0.15% carbon

Stainless steel is useful because it doesn't **corrode** easily. It stays looking bright and shiny.

What you need to remember *Copy and complete using the **key words***

Iron or steel – whats the difference?

Iron from the blast furnace is about 96% iron. It contains impurities which make it
_____. We remove these impurities to make pure _____, which is quite
_____. The layers of atoms in pure iron can _____ over each other.
Steels are a mixture of iron with other _____ or with the non-metal element
_____. We say that steels are _____. The different sized atoms _____ the
layers in the iron. The layers don't slide over each other so easily.
We can add carbon to steel to make it _____.
Low carbon steels are easy to _____ while high carbon steels are _____.
Stainless steel is an alloy which does not _____ easily.

You need to be able to explain how the properties of other alloys are related to the way in which the atoms are arranged just like you did for steel.

6 More about alloys

Like everything else, metals are made up from atoms. Pure metals are elements because they contain just one type of atom. For example, iron is an element because it only contains iron atoms.

1 Write down the names of <u>two</u> other metal elements.

Many of the metals we use every day are not elements. They are **alloys**.

An alloy is a mixture of metals. By mixing metals together we can make metals harder and stronger.

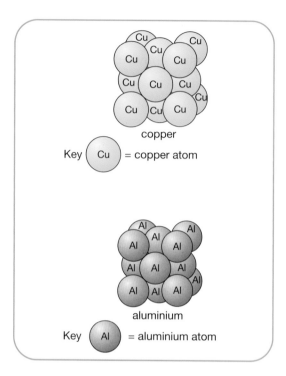

copper

Key (Cu) = copper atom

aluminium

Key (Al) = aluminium atom

Alloys of gold

There are many alloys of gold.

2 What other name do we give to pure gold?

3 Why do we commonly use 9 carat gold for jewellery?

4 Which <u>three</u> elements are added to gold to make it into 9 carat gold?

This ring is 24 carat gold. This tells us that it is 100% gold.

These rings are made from 9 carat gold. The gold also contains the metals silver, copper and zinc. Nine carat gold is less expensive and harder than pure gold.

Alloys of copper

Many of our everyday 'silver' coins are made from alloys of copper.

5 **a** Why don't we use pure silver to make coins?
   b Why don't we use pure copper to make coins?

6 Which metal do we add to copper to make the centre of a 1 euro coin and the 50p piece?

We often make 'silver' coins from a copper alloy called cupro-nickel. It contains 75% copper and 25% nickel. The alloy is much **harder** than pure copper.

Alloys of aluminium

We often make aluminium into an alloy called Duralumin. Duralumin contains copper and magnesium as well as aluminium.

Metal	Strength (MPa)
aluminium	30
Duralumin	150

7   Copy and complete the sentences.

Duralumin is a useful alloy of _____.
It has a greater _____ than aluminium.

8   Write down why we use Duralumin to make aircraft and not pure aluminium.

New alloys

We use many alloys in our everyday lives and scientists are always looking for new ones.

We can now buy glasses with frames made from a **shape memory alloy**.

9   Copy and complete the sentences.

An alloy which returns to its normal shape after bending is called a _____
_____ _____.

This type of alloy is useful for making _____.

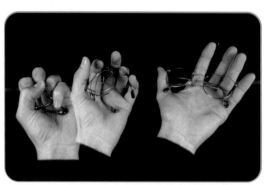

The frames of these glasses are made from a shape memory alloy. When we bend the alloy it still goes back to its original **shape**.

What you need to remember *Copy and complete using the **key words***

More about alloys

We can make metals more useful to us by mixing them with other metals.
Many of the metals we use are mixtures, or _____.
Pure copper, gold and aluminium are quite soft. We can add small amounts of other metals to these metals to make them _____.
Scientists often develop new alloys, for example _____ _____
_____.

We can bend this type of alloy and the metal will still return to its original _____.

You need to be able to weigh up the advantages of using smart materials like shape memory alloys.

7 The transition metals

Metals in the periodic table

This table shows us all of the elements in the natural world.

1. **a** How many elements are there altogether?
   b How many of these elements are metals?
   c Would you say that about a quarter, about a half or about three-quarters of the elements are metals?

2. What do you notice about where the non-metals and metals are in this table?

Which are the transition metals?

Most of the metals that we meet in everyday life are transition metals. We can find these in the **central block** of the periodic table.

These metals are useful for making many things because of their **properties**.

3. Write down the names of <u>five</u> transition metals.

Using transition metals

All transition metals are good conductors of **heat** and **electricity**. We can also bend or hammer them into **shape**. Two transition metals that we use a lot are iron and **copper**.

4. **a** Write down <u>one</u> reason why we use copper to make pipes.
   b Write down <u>three</u> reasons why we use copper to make electrical cables.

> **REMEMBER**
>
> The periodic table shows all of the elements. Each column contains elements with similar properties. We call each column a group.

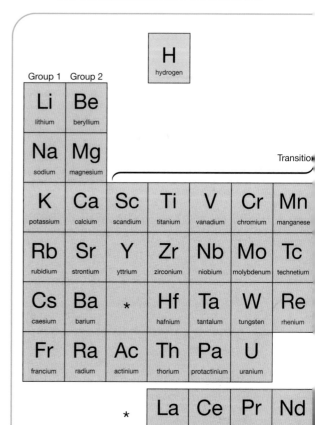

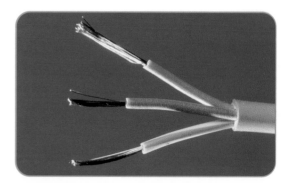

Copper is easy to shape into pipes and wires.
Copper pipes and wires are easy to bend.

Most of the transition metals are **strong**. Iron is one of the strongest, particularly when it is made into steel.

Iron is also easy to hammer or bend into shape.

5 Copy and complete the sentences.

We use steel to make bridges because it is _____.
Steel is easily shaped so we can use it to make _____.

We use more steel than any other metal.

| Key | metals |
| | non-metals |

				Group 3	Group 4	Group 5	Group 6	Group 7	Group 0
									He helium
				B boron	C carbon	N nitrogen	O oxygen	F fluorine	Ne neon
				Al aluminium	Si silicon	P phosphorus	S sulfur	Cl chlorine	Ar argon
o alt	Ni nickel	Cu copper	Zn zinc	Ga gallium	Ge germanium	As arsenic	Se selenium	Br bromine	Kr krypton
h lium	Pd palladium	Ag silver	Cd cadmium	In indium	Sn tin	Sb antimony	Te tellurium	I iodine	Xe xenon
r um	Pt platinum	Au gold	Hg mercury	Tl thallium	Pb lead	Bi bismuth	Po polonium	At astatine	Rn radon

m rium	Eu europium	Gd gadolinium	Tb terbium	Dy dysprosium	Ho holmium	Er erbium	Tm thulium	Yb ytterbium	Lu lutetium

What you need to remember *Copy and complete using the key words*

The transition metals
We find the transition metals in the _____ _____ of the periodic table.
Transition metals have all of the usual _____ of metals.
They are good conductors of _____ and _____. They are also easy to _____.
_____ has properties that make it useful for plumbing and wiring.
We use transition metals like iron as structural materials because they are _____.

8 Extracting copper

Just like iron, copper is below carbon in the reactivity series. This means that we can use carbon to extract copper from copper oxide.

The carbon reacts with the oxygen in the copper oxide. This leaves copper metal.

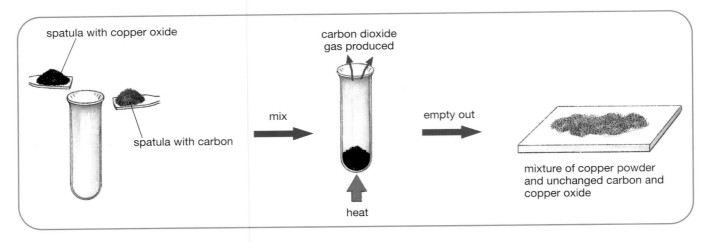

spatula with copper oxide

spatula with carbon

mix

heat

carbon dioxide gas produced

empty out

mixture of copper powder and unchanged carbon and copper oxide

> **1** **a** What other substance is produced?
>
> **b** Write a word equation for this reaction.

Using electricity to extract copper

The copper that we produce when we extract it with carbon is not very pure. We often need pure copper, especially when we use it to conduct electricity.

We extract most of the copper we need using **electricity**. We call this **electrolysis**.
The copper we make by electrolysis is 99.9% pure.

One disadvantage of using electrolysis is that it uses large amounts of electricity. This makes it an expensive process.

> **2** Copy and complete the sentences.
>
> We often need to produce copper which is
>
> _____.
>
> To do this we have to use _____.
> We call this process _____.
>
> **3** Why is it expensive to extract copper in this way?
>
> **4** How does the pure copper look different from the impure copper?

Pieces of copper before extraction by electrolysis.

New ways to extract copper

Some ores only contain a small amount of copper.
We call them low grade ores. Often we don't use **low grade**
ores because it would cost too much to get the copper out.

5   Which living things can help us to extract copper
from low grade ores?

We can use **bacteria** like these to extract metals
from low grade ores and waste from processing
plants.

No ugly mine?

Most people think of mines as huge holes in the ground
surrounded by piles of waste material. New ways of
extracting copper, like those which use bacteria, can cause
less damage to the **environment**.

Another new method involves extracting copper under the
ground, and the mining hardly disturbs the surface at all.

We can use this method to extract the copper from low
grade ores.

6   What can still happen on the land above the copper
'mine'?

You would never guess that under this cotton
field, copper metal is being extracted.

What you need to remember *Copy and complete using the key words*

Extracting copper
We usually use _____ to extract copper. We call this process _____.
Some ores contain only small amounts of the metal. We call these _____
_____ ores. We can use _____ to help us extract copper from
these ores.
New methods of extracting copper have less effect on the _____ than traditional
mines.

9 Aluminium and titanium

Aluminium – shiny and lightweight

Another metal that we use a lot of is aluminium. It's not a transition metal but it has many uses.

Aluminium is has a **low density** (it's lightweight). It doesn't **corrode** easily.

1 Copy and complete the sentences.

Aluminium is a light metal and so we can use it to build _____. Aluminium is also suitable for wrapping food in because it does not

_____.

Titanium – shiny, lightweight and expensive!

Titanium is a transition metal. It has

- high strength
- low density
- good resistance to corrosion.

2 Which properties of titanium make it better than steel or aluminium for

  a replacement hip joints?
  b engine parts in space rockets or high-tech aircraft?
  c covering important buildings?

We make aeroplanes from aluminium because it has a low density. The same volume of steel would weigh much more. The plane would never get off the ground!

Aluminium foil stays shiny because it doesn't corrode easily.

Comparing the properties of some metals

Metal	Density (kg/m^3)	Strength of strongest alloy (MPa)
titanium	4500	1400
iron/steel	about 7800	1340
aluminium	2700	300

Titanium and titanium alloys are even more resistant to corrosion than aluminium (and aluminium alloys).

The Guggenheim Museum in Bilbao is covered with titanium.

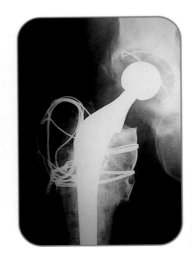

Titanium is often used for replacement hip joints.

So how do we extract reactive metals?

We can't extract **reactive** metals like aluminium and titanium using carbon. This is because both of them are above carbon in the reactivity series.

3 Write down the names of two metals which we

 a can extract using carbon
 b can't extract using carbon.

Extracting aluminium is not simple. There are many **stages** involved. We use a lot of thermal energy to melt the ore. Then we pass large amounts of electricity though the ore to extract the aluminium.

To extract titanium from its ore, we use a reactive metal like sodium or magnesium. The process has many stages. Extracting metals like sodium and magnesium uses a lot of energy.

It is very **expensive** to extract the metals aluminium and titanium from their ores.

4 Copy and complete the table.

Metal	Do we need large amounts of **energy** to extract it?	Is the extraction simple or are there many stages?
aluminium		
titanium		

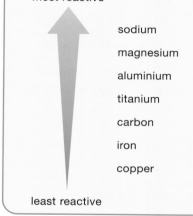

REMEMBER

Carbon can remove oxygen from some metal oxides, like iron oxide. It can only remove oxygen from the metals which are below it in the reactivity series.

most reactive

sodium

magnesium

aluminium

titanium

carbon

iron

copper

least reactive

Aluminium ingots.

What you need to remember *Copy and complete using the key words*

Aluminium and titanium

Titanium and aluminium are very useful metals. This is because both metals have a
_____ _____ and they will not _____ easily.
However, aluminium and titanium are both _____ metals.
Extracting them from their ores is very _____.
This is because

- there are many _____ to the extraction
- the process uses a lot of _____.

10 New metal from old

What is recycling?

We all throw away rubbish and things which we don't want any more. Many of these things are made from materials which we can use again, or **recycle**.

  1   Write down <u>three</u> metal objects which we get rid of.

  2   How can we reuse waste metal?

There are many important reasons why we should recycle metals.

We can recycle most things made from metal. First we separate the metals, then we chop the metal up and melt it down.

Recycling protects our environment

Every year we throw away millions of tonnes of waste metal. One way that we can deal with the waste is to bury it in the ground.

  3   Write down <u>three</u> ways in which landfill sites affect the environment.

Each household throws away about 2 kg of metal each week. By recycling metal, we reduce the amount of waste that we need to bury.

That landfill site really looks a mess.

My dad remembers when there were wildflowers and butterflies in that field.

Harmful chemicals from the rubbish soak into the ground, too.

If we recycle metals, we have to extract less ore

There are <u>two</u> ways we can get the metals we need.

■ We can extract them from ores.
■ We can recycle metal things which we no longer need.

Mining metal ores and extracting the metal affect our **environment**.

Once we've used all of the metal ores up, we can't **replace** them.

  4   Write down <u>two</u> reasons why it is better to recycle metals than to extract them from their ores.

Recycling metals saves energy

Extracting aluminium from its ore is very **expensive**.
It uses large amounts of **energy**.

5 Copy and complete the sentences.

We have to _____ the aluminium ore.
We have to _____ the ore to melt it down.
We use _____ to extract the aluminium from the ore.
We can save energy by _____ the metal.

Recycling one can won't make any difference. Where do you recycle metals, anyway?

Did you know that recycling just one aluminium drinks can saves enough energy to run a TV for 2 hours?

6 What difficulties are there with recycling metals?

7 What percentage of the steel that we use is recycled?

8 What percentage of the aluminium that we use is recycled?

9 Recycling metals saves energy.
Which saves more energy, recycling steel or aluminium?

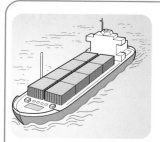

We have to transport aluminium ore from the mine to the extraction plant. This is often across the sea.

We have to melt the ore by heating it to a high temperature.

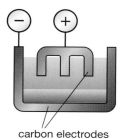

carbon electrodes

We extract aluminium from the molten ore using electricity.

alu

Of course, recycling aluminium also uses energy, but only about a twentieth.

Name of metal	How much of the metal that we use is recycled (%)	Energy saving (%)
steel	42	62–74
aluminium	39	95

What you need to remember *Copy and complete using the **key words***

New metal from old
We should reuse or _____ metals instead of extracting them from their ores.
Extracting metals affects our _____ and uses up substances which we cannot
_____. It is also _____ because it uses large amounts of
_____.

You need to be able to use information like this to consider the effects of recycling metals on the environment, local people and the economy.

1 Crude oil – a right old mixture

Crude oil is a mixture of lots of compounds.
The compounds are all very useful but we can't use them until we've separated them.

> **1** Write down the <u>two</u> main uses for the compounds in crude oil.

Most of the compounds in crude oil are liquids at room temperature.

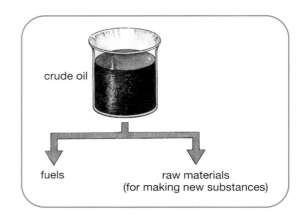

What's in a mixture?

When two or more substances are mixed together but not joined together with a chemical bond we say they make a **mixture**.

When we mix things together there isn't a chemical reaction between them. The properties of each substance are **unchanged**. This means that we can **separate** them again.

> **2** Which substances are mixed together in
>
> **a** steel?
> **b** sea water?

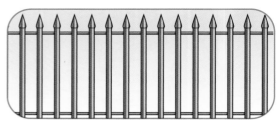

This steel is a mixture of the **elements** carbon and iron.

Sea water is mainly a mixture of the **compounds** water and sodium chloride.

How to separate a mixture of liquids

To separate a mixture of liquids we need to heat it up. When we heat up a liquid it changes to a vapour. We say it evaporates. When a liquid is boiling it evaporates very quickly.

When we cool a vapour, it changes back into a liquid. We say that it condenses.

> **3** Copy the diagram on the right. Then complete it.

We can use distillation to help us separate a mixture of liquids.

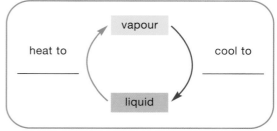

Evaporating a liquid and then condensing it again is called **distillation**.

Separating the liquids in wine

Wine is a mixture of liquids.

4 Which <u>two</u> liquids are mixed together in wine?

The diagram below shows how we can separate alcohol from wine. The alcohol we collect is called brandy.

Wine is a mixture of water, alcohol and small amounts of other chemicals.

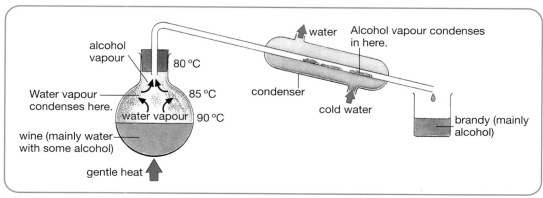

We can separate alcohol and water like this because they have different **boiling points**. Water boils at 100 °C and alcohol boils at 78 °C.

5 Copy and complete the sentences.

The wine contains two liquids called _____ and _____.
The liquid alcohol boils at _____. It turns into alcohol _____.
Droplets of alcohol form in the _____.
Water boils at _____.
Any water vapour _____ in the neck of the flask.

When we separate a mixture of liquids into parts or fractions we call it **fractional distillation**.

What you need to remember *Copy and complete using the **key words***

Crude oil – a right old mixture
Crude oil is a _____ of a very large number of compounds. A mixture is made from two or more _____ or _____.
The substances in a mixture are not joined together with a chemical bond. The chemical properties of each substance in the mixture are _____ so we can _____ them.
Evaporating a liquid and then condensing it again is called _____.
Separating a mixture of liquids into different parts is called _____ _____.
The liquids in the mixture must have different _____ _____.

2 Separating crude oil

We use **fractional distillation** to separate crude oil into different parts or fractions. The different fractions boil at different **temperatures**.

1 a Which fraction of crude oil has the highest boiling point?
  b Which fraction has the lowest boiling point?

2 Explain why we can separate crude oil by fractional distillation.

3 Why is separating crude oil into fractions more difficult than making brandy?

Fraction of crude oil	Boiling points (°C)
dissolved gases	below 0
petrol	around 65
naphtha	around 130
kerosene	around 200
diesel oil	around 300
bitumen	over 400

An oil fractionating tower

In Britain, 250 000 tonnes of oil are produced every day! To separate all of this oil into its fractions, we use enormous fractionating towers.

The diagram shows one of these.

4 Copy and complete the sentences.

Crude oil is heated to about _____ °C.
The fractions in the crude oil condense at different _____.

Bitumen has a _____ boiling point so it falls straight to the bottom of the tower.
Methane has a _____ boiling point so it goes straight to the top of the tower.
Fractions with in-between boiling points _____ partway up the tower.
The lower the boiling point of a fraction, the _____ it goes up the tower before it condenses.

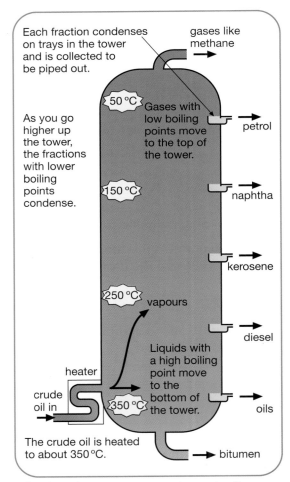

Each fraction condenses on trays in the tower and is collected to be piped out.

gases like methane

50 °C Gases with low boiling points move to the top of the tower.

petrol

As you go higher up the tower, the fractions with lower boiling points condense.

150 °C

naphtha

kerosene

250 °C vapours

diesel

Liquids with a high boiling point move to the bottom of the tower.

oils

heater

crude oil in

350 °C

bitumen

The crude oil is heated to about 350 °C.

A fractionating tower to separate crude oil. Each fraction in the oil condenses at a different temperature.

What's it really like?

It's difficult to imagine the size of a fractionating tower.

5 The bus in the picture is 4 m high.
About how tall is the fractionating tower?

6 Write down <u>two</u> places in Britain where you would find fractionating towers.

Looking at the fractions

Each fraction in crude oil contains molecules which are a similar **size**. For example, all of the molecules in diesel are quite small.
Some **properties** of the fractions depend on the size of their molecules.

In Britain, we can see fractionating towers like this in Essex, Milford Haven, Teesside, Grangemouth, Fawley and Killingholme.
The bus is to give you an idea of the size of the tower.

Oil fraction	petrol	diesel	lubricating oil	bitumen
Boiling point	low	quite low	quite high	high
Size of molecules	small	quite small	big	very big
Appearance				
How easy is it to ignite a few drops?	Catches fire very easily. We say it is very flammable.	Catches fire quite easily.	Hard to light.	Hard to light.

7 Which fraction has the lowest boiling point?

8 Which fraction has the highest boiling point?

9 Which fraction has the smallest molecules?

10 Which fraction has the largest molecules?

11 As the size of the molecules increases, what happens to

a the boiling point of the fraction?
b how easy the fraction is to ignite?

What you need to remember *Copy and complete using the **key words***

Separating crude oil
We separate crude oil into fractions by _____ _____.
The oil evaporates in the fractionating tower. Different fractions condense at different
_____. The fractions we collect contain molecules of a similar _____.
The fractions in crude oil have different _____ which depend on the size of the molecules.

3 What are the chemicals in crude oil?

Most of the chemicals in crude oil are **compounds** made from just two kinds of atom.

The smallest part of each compound is called a **molecule**. Look at the picture of the two molecules.

> **1** Which <u>two</u> kinds of atom do these molecules contain?
>
> **2** What is the difference between the two molecules?
>
> **3** Write down the formula of
>
> **a** the smaller molecule
> **b** the larger molecule.

Molecules made only of **hydrogen** atoms and **carbon** atoms are called **hydrocarbons**. Most of the molecules in crude oil are hydrocarbons.

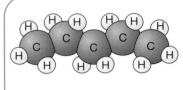

This molecule has 5 carbon atoms and 12 hydrogen atoms. We write this C_5H_{12}. This is the formula of the compound.

Key — carbon atom (C), hydrogen atom (H)

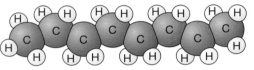

This molecule has 8 carbon atoms and 18 hydrogen atoms.

More about the hydrocarbons in crude oil

The hydrocarbon molecules in crude oil are all different sizes. This means that they all have a different **boiling point**. Most of the hydrocarbons in crude oil belong to a group called the **alkanes**.

> **4** What do you notice about the names of the alkanes?
>
> **5** Copy and complete the table.

Hydrocarbon	Formula	Boiling point in °C
butane		
hexane		
decane		

> **6** Copy and complete the sentence.
>
> The alkanes with the biggest molecules boil at the _____ temperatures.

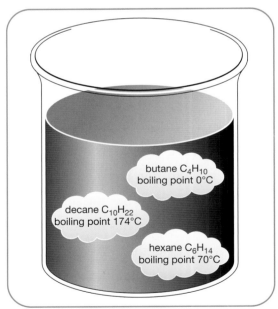

butane C_4H_{10} boiling point 0°C

decane $C_{10}H_{22}$ boiling point 174°C

hexane C_6H_{14} boiling point 70°C

These are some of the molecules we find in crude oil. We call them the alkanes.

More about alkanes

The alkane called ethane contains two carbon atoms and six hydrogen atoms.

7 Write down the molecular formula for ethane.

8 Draw the structural formula for ethane.

9 What does the structural formula tell us about a molecule?

10 Copy and complete the table.

Name of alkane	Molecular formula	Structural formula
propane		H H H | | | H – C – C – C – H | | | H H H
butane	C_4H_{10}	

We say that the alkanes have the general formula C_nH_{2n+2} where n is the number of carbon atoms.
An alkane with five carbon atoms has the formula C_5H_{12}.

11 What is the molecular formula for the alkane with eight carbon atoms?

12 What does the word saturated tell us about hydrocarbons?

Formulae for the alkanes

We can show alkane molecules in two ways.

- The molecular formula, e.g. C_2H_6 for ethane.
  This tells us the numbers of each type of atom in a molecule
- The structural formula, e.g.

$$H-\underset{\underset{H}{|}}{\overset{\overset{H}{|}}{C}}-\underset{\underset{H}{|}}{\overset{\overset{H}{|}}{C}}-H$$

This shows us how the atoms are arranged in a molecule.

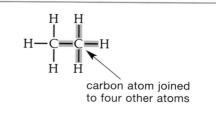
carbon atom joined to four other atoms

Alkanes are **saturated** hydrocarbons. This means that each carbon atom has used up all of its four bonds to link to other atoms.

What you need to remember *Copy and complete using the **key words***

What are the chemicals in crude oil?

Crude oil contains many different _____. The smallest part of a compound is called a _____.

Most of the compounds in crude oil are _____. This means that the molecules are made from atoms of _____ and _____ only.

Many of these hydrocarbons are compounds called _____.

We can show the structure of alkanes like ethane in two ways:

- by writing the molecular formula _____
- by drawing the structural formula _____

The alkanes have the general formula _____. We say that they are _____ hydrocarbons.

The more carbon atoms there are in an alkane molecule, the higher its _____.

4 Burning fuels – where do they go?

Too big to be useful

Crude oil contains many compounds which have large molecules. These are not very useful as fuels.

1 What size are the molecules in bitumen?

2 Copy and complete the sentences.

Compounds with large hydrocarbon molecules are not very _____ as fuels.
We do not use bitumen as a fuel because it is hard to _____.

Useful fuels from crude oil

We get gases, petrol and diesel from crude oil. These have small molecules and are all useful fuels. When we burn them, energy is released and new substances are produced.

Look at the diagram.

3 What reacts with petrol to make it burn?

4 What happens to the new substances that are produced?

5 Copy and complete the word equation.

petrol + _____ → waste gases + energy

All the fuels we get from crude oil produce the same new substances when they burn.

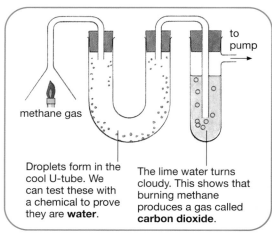

Waste **gases** from exhaust go into the air.

oxygen from the air

petrol

engine

petrol tank

What new substances are made when fuels burn?

To find out what new substances are made when fuels burn, we need to trap them. The diagram shows how we can do this.

6 What two substances are made when methane burns?

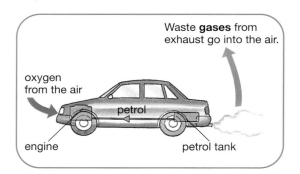

to pump

methane gas

Droplets form in the cool U-tube. We can test these with a chemical to prove they are **water**.

The lime water turns cloudy. This shows that burning methane produces a gas called **carbon dioxide**.

Trapping the new substances we make when we burn methane.

7 Copy and complete the word equation.

methane + oxygen → _____ _____ + _____ + energy

What happens to molecules when fuels burn?

The diagram shows what happens to a methane molecule when it burns.

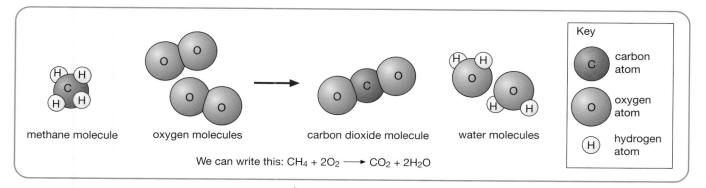

methane molecule   oxygen molecules   carbon dioxide molecule   water molecules

We can write this: $CH_4 + 2O_2 \longrightarrow CO_2 + 2H_2O$

Key

C carbon atom

O oxygen atom

H hydrogen atom

8 Copy and complete the sentence.

When fuels like methane burn

■ the carbon in the fuel makes the gas

_____ _____

■ the hydrogen in the fuel turns into

_____.

The water that is produced in the reaction is water vapour.
It turns into water, or condenses, when it cools down.

Burning other fuels

Fuels from crude oil are all hydrocarbons.
The diagram shows two hydrocarbon molecules.

9 Burning hydrocarbons always makes water and carbon dioxide.
Why does this happen?

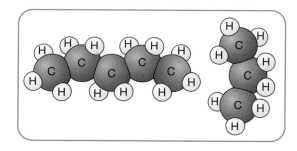

What you need to remember *Copy and complete using the key words*

Burning fuels – where do they go?

How we use hydrocarbons as fuels depends on their _____.

When we burn fuels we make new substances that are mainly _____.

Most fuels contain carbon and hydrogen. When they burn, they produce _____ _____ and _____ vapour.

5 It's raining acid

Acids are dangerous chemicals. We know that they can 'eat away' at some things.

1   **a**   What has happened to the statue in the photograph?

    b   What has caused this to happen to the statue?

Acid rain is a serious problem in many countries, including Britain. As well as damaging buildings, acid rain can harm animals and plants.

2   Write down <u>two</u> ways acid rain can harm living things.

We need to prevent acid rain from forming.
To do this we have to understand what causes it.

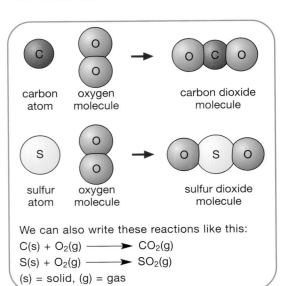

Acid rain can kill trees and the fish in lakes.

What turns our rain into acid?

When fuels burn they react with oxygen.
Atoms in the fuel join with oxygen atoms in the air.
New substances called oxides are made.

Most fuels contain carbon atoms.

3   What new substance do the carbon atoms make when a fuel burns?

Many fuels also contain some sulfur atoms.

4   **a**   What new substance do the sulfur atoms make when the fuel burns?

    b   Write down a word equation for this reaction.

Sulfur dioxide is a gas that can turn rain into acid.

We can also write these reactions like this:
$$C(s) + O_2(g) \longrightarrow CO_2(g)$$
$$S(s) + O_2(g) \longrightarrow SO_2(g)$$
(s) = solid, (g) = gas

How sulfur dioxide makes acid rain

5 Copy and complete the sentences.

Some fuels contain sulfur.
When we burn these fuels we make a
_____ called sulfur dioxide.
This goes into the _____.
The sulfur dioxide reacts with oxygen and then
dissolves in droplets of _____.
This makes an acid called _____

_____.

Eventually the acidic droplets in the clouds fall as

_____ _____.

Acid rain doesn't usually fall where it's made.
Winds can blow the 'acid clouds' for hundreds of kilometres
before they fall as rain.

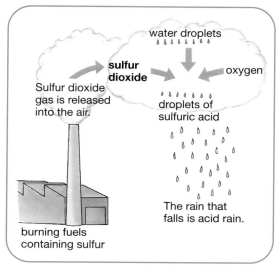

How rain turns into acid.

Pollution solutions

It is important to prevent sulfur dioxide from getting into
our air. We can do this in two ways.

We can remove **sulfur** from our fuels **before** we burn them. We can buy
petrol which has had much of the sulfur removed at the refinery.
The sulfur that's removed makes the gas which smells of rotten eggs!

We can remove the sulfur dioxide from gases
after we have burnt the fuel. Some power
stations have equipment to remove sulfur dioxide
before it escapes into the air.

What you need to remember *Copy and complete using the **key words***

It's raining acid
Many fuels contain atoms of sulfur. When we burn the fuel, we make the gas called
_____ _____. This gas can cause _____

_____.

To stop sulfur dioxide from getting into the air we can remove

- the _____ from the fuel _____ we burn it (e.g. in vehicles)
- the sulfur dioxide from the waste gases _____ burning the fuel.

6 Global warming, global dimming

When we burn fuels we put large amounts of **carbon dioxide** gas into the atmosphere.

The carbon dioxide acts like a blanket around the Earth. It stops heat from escaping and is making the Earth warmer. We call this **global warming**.

1 Write down <u>two</u> ways in which we burn large amounts of fuel.

2 Which element in fuels burns to make carbon dioxide?

A warmer Earth

The temperature on the Earth is beginning to rise. Scientists are making predictions about how the Earth will change, even in our lifetime. Here is what some people think could happen in Britain by 2080.

> **REMEMBER**
>
> When we burn fuels
>
> - the carbon in them turns to carbon dioxide
> - the hydrogen in them turns to water.

Our vehicles use a lot of fuel. We also burn fuel to make electricity in our power stations.

This is the second time we've been to the coast this March! It's 25 °C today.

I can grow Mediterranean fruits all year round.

This coast has changed a lot now the sea level has risen.

The temperature was over 40 °C in Kent again yesterday.

All that part of the town is under the water now.

Autumn doesn't start until late October these days. It's December and the grass is still growing.

It never snows here any more. Snow wasn't as bad as floods.

Rescuing people from floods is my full-time job. There's flooding in many towns in the winter because it rains so much.

Mosquitoes are everywhere. Malaria is a common disease in Britain now.

We only need to put the heating on for a few weeks each year.

3 Use the predictions for 2080 to copy and complete the table.

Advantages of global warming in Britain	Disadvantages of global warming in Britain

What about the rest of the world?

There are a few good points about global warming in Britain but the effects could be much more serious in many other parts of the world.

Scientists believe that Africa will be very badly affected.

4 What will happen to the African people if their farmland turns into desert?

It is already difficult to grow crops in parts of Africa. Global warming could turn much of Africa into a desert where nothing will grow.

Global dimming

When fuels burn they often release tiny **particles** into the air. Many of these are the tiny specks of carbon which we call soot.

We have some evidence to show that less and less sunlight is reaching the ground. This is known as **global dimming**.

Some scientists believe that global dimming is due to particles in the atmosphere.

5 Write down <u>three</u> effects that global dimming could have.

Plants need light to photosynthesise.

We need sunlight to provide solar power.

Even a small amount of dimming will affect how our crops ripen.

What you need to remember *Copy and complete using the **key words***

Global warming, global dimming
When we burn fuels we produce large amounts of the gas _____ _____.
This is making the Earth warmer. We call it _____ _____.
Burning fuels also releases tiny _____ into the air. These may be reducing the amount of sunlight that reaches the ground. We call this _____ _____.

You need to be able to weigh up the effects of burning hydrocarbon fuels on the environment. This is also covered on pages 160 and 166.

7 Better fuels

We need to find alternatives to the fuels that we make from crude oil. Burning hydrocarbons from crude oil pollutes our environment.

Fuels from crude oil are non-renewable – once they have been used we can't replace them.

1 Write down <u>two</u> reasons why we need to find alternative fuels.

2 Copy and complete the sentence.

Three substances which we make when we burn hydrocarbons from crude oil are _____

_____, _____

_____ and _____.

Many of our cars use petrol as a fuel, but cars can run on many different fuels.

Diesel vs petrol

Diesel is widely available and produces less carbon dioxide than burning petrol. We get it from crude oil.

3 Write down <u>one</u> advantage to the environment of using diesel as a fuel.

4 Copy and complete the sentence.

Diesel engines release a large number of _____ into the air.

Biodiesel

Biodiesel is a hydrocarbon fuel but it doesn't come from crude oil. It's made from the oils of plants like oilseed rape.

We can use it in the diesel cars we already have if we mix it with diesel.

5 Why is a biodiesel mixture better for the environment than ordinary diesel?

6 Why do you think very few diesel cars run on biodiesel in the UK?

> **REMEMBER**
>
> Burning hydrocarbon fuels produces
>
> - large amounts of carbon dioxide gas, which is causing global warming
> - particles of soot, which are causing global dimming
> - sulfur dioxide, which causes acid rain.

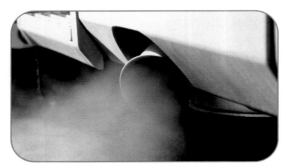

This car uses diesel as a fuel. The waste gases contain a lot more particles than those from a petrol engine.

This rapeseed is being grown to produce oil for biodiesel. Growing the crops uses carbon dioxide from the air.

Many people would like to run their cars on biodiesel. Unfortunately, in 2005, it was only available at about 150 filling stations in the UK.

Ethanol

In Brazil, 20 million cars already use an alternative fuel. The fuel that most cars use is petrol mixed with ethanol. Many new cars in Brazil can run on ethanol alone.

Ethanol is a type of alcohol. It burns more cleanly than pure petrol and gives out less carbon dioxide.

7 Which crop do Brazilians grow as a raw material to make ethanol?

8 Write down <u>one</u> advantage to the environment of using ethanol as a fuel.

> **DID YOU KNOW?**
> Poison is added to ethanol fuel.
> This is to stop drivers from drinking it!

The Brazilians make ethanol for their vehicles from sugar cane.

Hydrogen fuel cells

A hydrogen fuel cell makes electricity which we can use to power the motor of a car.

Fuel cell cars are already available in the UK. The only waste they produce is water.

9 Write down <u>one</u> big disadvantage with using fuel cell cars.

10 How can we overcome this disadvantage?

This car needs hydrogen to make it run. Making hydrogen uses a lot of energy and can cause pollution if we make it using fossil fuels. To prevent this pollution, we must use renewable energy, like solar power, to make the hydrogen.

What you need to remember

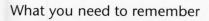

Better fuels
There is nothing new for you to <u>remember</u> in this section.

> You need to be able to weigh up the good and bad points about new fuels.

8 Using fuels – good or bad?

The Mont Blanc tunnel is an important road tunnel in the Alps. It connects France to Italy.

In March 1999, there was a terrible fire in the Mont Blanc tunnel. It killed 39 people. The tunnel remained closed for 3 years.

1 About how many vehicles used the tunnel every year before the fire?

No more traffic!

The tunnel was a vital link between north and south Europe. All of the traffic had to find another route.

Much less petrol and diesel was used in the area.

2 Write down <u>two</u> reasons people like to visit the Mont Blanc region.

3 What happened to the amount of money coming into the area after the fire?

Less asthma

We all know that burning fuels in vehicles causes pollution. Some doctors think that if a person has asthma, traffic pollution can make the disease worse for them.

4 What is asthma?

While the Mont Blanc tunnel was closed, many local doctors reported that childhood asthma decreased.

5 Copy and complete the sentences.

Closing the Mont Blanc tunnel had an effect on childhood _____. This could have been due to the decrease in traffic _____ from vehicles.

Smoke billowing out of the entrance to the Mont Blanc tunnel during the fire in 1999. Before the fire, 2 million vehicles passed through the tunnel each year.

Every year many tourists visit the area around the tunnel to ski and enjoy the mountains. Local businesses lost money when the tunnel was closed. Restaurants and hotels took less money. Property prices fell.

Stacey has asthma. Asthma makes it hard for her to breathe.

More light

While the tunnel was closed, a photographer who worked in the area noticed a big change.

6 What did the photographer observe?

7 What do fuels produce which can affect the amount of light reaching the ground?

8 Why did closing the tunnel have this effect on the air quality?

A local photographer reported that the light quality in the area was much better when the tunnel was closed. Much more light was reaching the ground.

Reopening the tunnel

Some local people did not want the tunnel to reopen. They could see the effects of the traffic.

When the tunnel was open, the snow around the entrance was always stained black. In the winters, while it was closed, the snow stayed very white.

Some people claimed that wildlife was returning to the area now there was less traffic.

There were also many people who needed the tunnel to reopen. It reopened in 2002.

9 Copy and complete the sentences.

Closing the tunnel really affected the _____ people.
They had to transport their goods using other _____ .

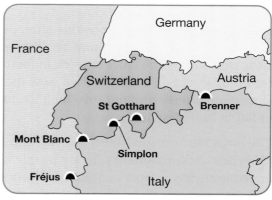

Closing the tunnel caused congestion in other tunnels and on mountain passes.
It particularly affected the Italians, who needed the tunnel for transporting goods to northern Europe.

What you need to remember

Using fuels – good or bad?
There is nothing new for you to <u>remember</u> in this section.

You need to be able to weigh up the effects of using fuels on the environment, local people and the amount of money in an area.

1 Crude oil – changing lives

Since 2001, China has increased the amount of trade it does with other countries. Companies in China have been able to sell many more of their goods overseas. The Chinese also use more imported goods.

Because of all of their new business, the Chinese are making more and more goods. To do this they need oil.

1 Write down the names of three foreign companies that are doing business in China.

2 How much oil did China use every day in

    a 1992?
    b 2002?

3 Write down the two main reasons why China needs more oil.

Oil – good for the people?

Because of all the new business, there are lots more jobs.

People who live in the countryside often find it hard to get work. So huge numbers of people have moved into the cities to work in factories, restaurants and on building sites. Now they can earn more money and improve their standard of living and lifestyle.

The large number of workers moving into the cities has caused problems. Many people have ended up living in poor conditions. Many businesses pay the new workers badly and expect them to work long hours.

4 Copy and complete the table.

Advantages of moving to the city	Disadvantages of moving to the city

Many foreign companies are now doing business in China, like Ikea, B&Q, Unilever and BP.

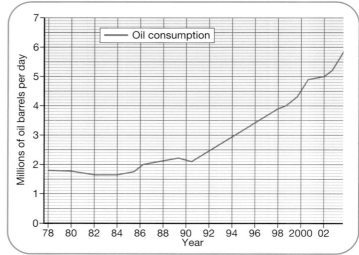

This graph shows us how much oil China has used in the past 24 years. The oil is needed for fuels and as a raw material to make materials like plastics.

Money, money, money

China can't produce enough oil for all of its industries so it has to buy it from other countries. One place it gets oil from is Kazakhstan.

5   How does China get the oil from Kazakhstan?

People in Kazakhstan have become much richer because they are selling their oil to China.

In the main towns of Kazakhstan, restaurants and bars are opening. There are also many new building sites.

6   What are <u>two</u> signs that more money is coming into an area?

China has built a 1240 km pipeline to bring oil from Kazakhstan. That's further than the distance from Land's End to John O'Groats!

Winners and losers

In China, millions of very poor people make a living by farming.

Less and less land is being used for farming. The people are getting even poorer and not enough crops are being produced.

7   Copy and complete the sentences.

Farmland in China is disappearing.
It is being replaced by _____,
_____ and _____.

8   Why do you think the Chinese government is trying to stop farmland from being used for building?

In recent years, more than 20 million Chinese farmers have been forced off their land to make room for roads, factories and houses.

What you need to remember

Crude oil – changing lives
There is nothing new for you to <u>remember</u> in this section.

You need to be able to weigh up the effects of using products from crude oil on people's lives and the amount of money in an area.

2 Making large molecules more useful

We use more crude oil for fuel than for anything else. However, there are lots of long hydrocarbon molecules in crude oil and these are not very **useful** as fuels.

1 Write down two reasons why large hydrocarbon molecules do not make good fuels.

We can make large hydrocarbon molecules into more useful substances if we break them down into smaller molecules. We call this **cracking**.

This is how we make most of the petrol that we use.

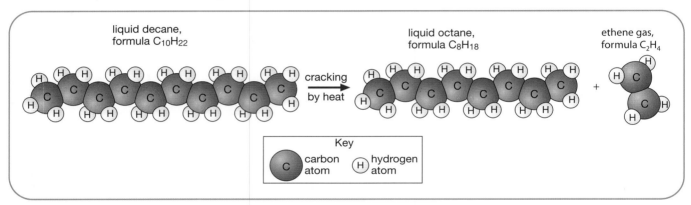

liquid decane, formula $C_{10}H_{22}$

liquid octane, formula C_8H_{18}

ethene gas, formula C_2H_4

cracking by heat

Key

C carbon atom   H hydrogen atom

2 Copy and complete this word equation.

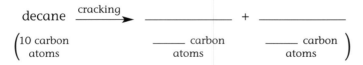

decane $\xrightarrow{\text{cracking}}$ _____ + _____

$\left(\begin{array}{c}\text{10 carbon} \\ \text{atoms}\end{array}\right.$ _____ carbon atoms _____ carbon atoms $\left.\right)$

It is simpler to write this equation using the formula of each compound.

3 Copy and complete the formula equation.

$C_{10}H_{22} \xrightarrow{\text{cracking}}$ _____ + _____

We have to heat large molecules to make them break down or decompose. So we call it **thermal decomposition**.

4 Explain why cracking is a thermal decomposition reaction.

Cracking hydrocarbons at a refinery

The diagram shows what happens in the part of a refinery where we crack hydrocarbons.

5 Put the sentences in the right order to explain how we crack hydrocarbons.
The first sentence is in the correct place.

- ■ We heat the liquid containing the long hydrocarbon molecules to a high temperature.

- ■ The long molecules **break down** into a mixture of smaller ones.

- ■ We pass the hydrocarbon vapour over a hot **catalyst**.

- ■ We separate the different small molecules produced.

- ■ The long hydrocarbons form a vapour. We say they **evaporate**.

6 Why do we use a catalyst in cracking?

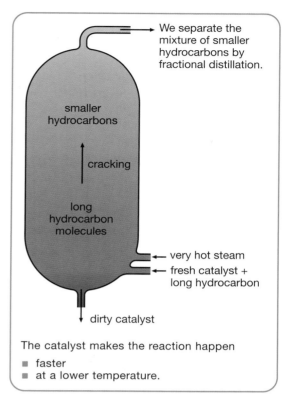

We separate the mixture of smaller hydrocarbons by fractional distillation.

smaller hydrocarbons

cracking

long hydrocarbon molecules

← very hot steam
← fresh catalyst + long hydrocarbon

↓ dirty catalyst

The catalyst makes the reaction happen
- ■ faster
- ■ at a lower temperature.

What you need to remember *Copy and complete using the **key words***

Making large molecules more useful
Large hydrocarbon molecules are not very _____ as fuels.
We can break them into smaller, more useful molecules.
We call this _____.
We heat the large molecules to make them _____.
We pass the vapours over a hot _____.
We separate and collect these smaller more useful molecules.
The large molecules _____ _____ to make smaller ones.
We call this _____ _____.

3 Small molecules

We can crack large hydrocarbon molecules to make smaller molecules. These are useful as **fuels**.

Some of the small molecules that we make by cracking belong to a family of hydrocarbons called the alkanes.

1. Write down the names of <u>two</u> alkanes.

2. Why are alkanes useful?

A different group of hydrocarbons

Another group of molecules that we make by cracking is called the **alkenes**.

The alkenes are not the same as the alkanes.
They contain a double bond between two carbon atoms.

We say the alkenes are **unsaturated** hydrocarbons.

3. Write down the name of the smallest alkene molecule.

4. Copy and complete the sentences.

In an alkane molecule, each carbon atom is joined to _____ other atoms.

We say the alkanes are _____ hydrocarbons.

In an alkene molecule there is a _____ bond between two of the carbon atoms.

We say the alkenes are _____ hydrocarbons.

5. a Copy the diagram of the ethene molecule. Draw the double bond in a different colour and label it.

   b Write the formula for ethene underneath your diagram.

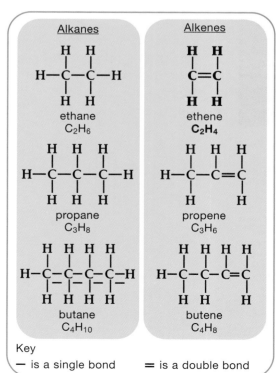

We use alkanes like butane as fuels.

Alkanes	Alkenes
ethane C_2H_6	ethene C_2H_4
propane C_3H_8	propene C_3H_6
butane C_4H_{10}	butene C_4H_8

Key
— is a single bond   = is a double bond

More about the alkenes

Because they have the same structure, the alkenes all have the same general formula (look at the box).

6 Without drawing the molecules, write down the formula for

a butene (four carbon atoms)
b hexene (six carbon atoms).

A general formula for alkenes

To find the number of hydrogen atoms in an alkene:

- count the number of carbon atoms (n)
- double this number ($2n$).

The general formula for an alkene is C_nH_{2n}.

The many uses of ethene

We use ethene to help us make many other useful chemicals like alcohol (ethanol) and plastics.

We can also use ethene to make fruit ripen.

7 Why do farmers pick fruit before it is ripe?

8 Copy and complete the sentences.

Unripe fruit is stored in an atmosphere which contains _____.
The ethene makes the fruit _____.

But I'm not ripe yet!

Farmers often pick fruit before it is ripe. Unripe fruit is firmer and not so easy to damage.
The fruit is transported when it's unripe. Then it is stored in an atmosphere which is rich in ethene.

What you need to remember *Copy and complete using the* **key words**

Small molecules
Some of the small hydrocarbon molecules we make by cracking are useful as

_____.

The small molecules belong to two groups, the _____ and the _____.
Alkenes contain a double bond between two carbon atoms. We say they are

_____.

We can show the structure of an alkene like ethene in two ways:

- by writing the molecular formula _____
- by drawing the structural formula _____

The general formula for the alkenes is _____.

4 Making ethanol

Ethanol is the chemical name for the kind of alcohol in drinks like beer and wine.

Ethanol has other uses too.

> **1** Write down <u>two</u> other uses for ethanol apart from alcoholic drinks.

In Brazil, ethanol is used as fuel for cars. It's called gasohol.

The chemicals that give a perfume its smell are dissolved in ethanol.

Making ethanol from ethene

We can make ethanol using ethene. This method is quick and easy.

ethene		
water	heat in furnace →	**ethene + steam** → **catalyst** at 300 °C → ethanol vapour + water vapour → condensed → ethanol + water

> **2** Copy and complete the sentences.
>
> To make ethanol we heat _____ and water in a _____ .
> This turns the water into _____ .
> We pass the vapours over a hot _____ .
> This makes a vapour which we condense.
> The liquid produced is a mixture of _____ and water.

Another way to make ethanol

We don't make the ethanol in wine or beer by heating ethene with steam. We make it using sugar.

We get sugar from crops like sugar beet.

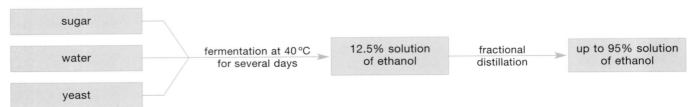

sugar / water / yeast → fermentation at 40 °C for several days → 12.5% solution of ethanol → fractional distillation → up to 95% solution of ethanol

> **3** Write down the name of the raw material which we use to make the ethanol in wine and beer.

Comparing the ways we make ethanol

4 Copy and complete the table.

How we make ethanol	From ethene and steam	By fermentation using sugar
Does it use a lot of energy? (Does it need a high temperature?)		
Could the raw materials run out? (Are they non-renewable?)		
Is it quick or does it take a few days?		

5 The managers of an ethanol factory in South America want to use raw materials which are renewable.
They decide to make the ethanol using sugar.
What is a renewable raw material?

6 Write down <u>two</u> more good reasons for using sugar to make ethanol.

7 Write down <u>two</u> problems of using sugar to make ethanol.

We can't easily get hold of ethene.

Our farmers are only just growing enough crops for the local people.

Using sugar to make ethanol is so slow!

Ethene comes from crude oil, which is non-renewable.

Using ethene needs lots of energy.

What you need to remember *Copy and complete using the **key words***

Making ethanol
Ethanol is a very useful chemical. We can make ethanol by reacting _____ and _____. We pass the vapours over a _____.

You need to be able to weigh up the advantages and disadvantages of making ethanol from renewable and non-renewable sources.

5 Joining molecules together again

We crack long hydrocarbon molecules to give us small, more useful molecules. We can use these small hydrocarbon molecules to make new, large molecules. We call the large molecules **polymers**.

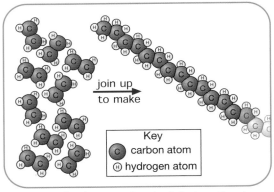

We make long molecules called polymers by joining together lots of smaller molecules. It's a bit like joining lots of daisies or paper clips to form chains.

One of the small molecules we get by cracking hydrocarbon molecules is called ethene. If we join many ethene molecules together, we get a very long molecule that is a useful plastic.

1 a What is the name of the plastic made from ethene?
   b Why does the plastic have this name?
   c Write down <u>three</u> items we make from poly(ethene).

The small molecules which join together to make a polymer are called **monomers**.

2 What is the monomer which goes to make up poly(ethene)?

3 What other name can we give the plastic poly(ethene)?

Lots of small ethene molecules join together to give a long molecule of **poly(ethene)**. 'Poly' means 'many'.

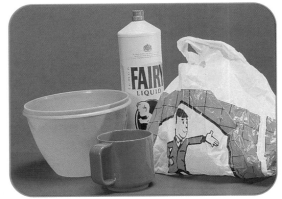

These are all made from poly(ethene). People often call this plastic polythene.

More useful polymers

Propene is another alkene. We can join together monomers of propene to make a polymer.

Different polymers have different **properties**, so we can use them for different things.

 **4** Write the name of the polymer made from propene.

5 Copy and complete the sentence.

Polymers like poly(ethene) and poly(propene) have different _____.

6 Why is it better to use poly(propene) than poly(ethene) for making ropes?

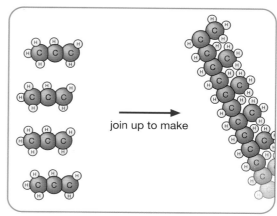

join up to make

Lots of small propene molecules join up to form **poly(propene)**. Poly(propene) does not stretch as much as poly(ethene) when it is pulled.

Making slime

We can make a polymer called 'slime' using PVA glue and borax. The properties of the slime depend on the amounts of these chemicals we add together.

7 Look at the table.
Copy and complete the sentences.

When we added 1 cm^3 borax to make the slime, it spread _____ cm^2 in 5 minutes.
It was not very viscous (hard to pour).
The more borax we added to the slime, the more _____ it became.

REMEMBER

If a liquid is viscous it is hard to pour. This slime is not very viscous!

Polymers can also have different properties depending on the **conditions** that we use to make them, for example the temperature and pressure.

Volume of borax we added in cm^3	Area of slime after 5 minutes (cm^2)
1.0	8
2.0	5
3.0	4
4.0	3
5.0	2

What you need to remember *Copy and complete using the key words*

Joining molecules together again
We can use alkenes to make long molecules or _____. Examples of polymers are
_____ and _____.
We call the small alkene molecules which join together the _____.
Different monomers make polymers with different _____.
The properties of a polymer also depend on the _____ that we use to make it, such as the temperature and pressure.

6 Useful polymers

You probably use lots of things made from polymers.
You may be sitting on a polymer, wearing polymers, having
some polymers in your lunch – the list is endless.

Scientists are always looking for new polymers with
different uses.

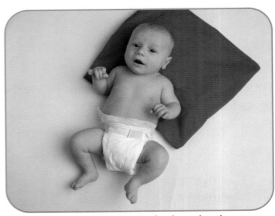

Disposable nappies contain hydrogel polymers.

Nappy technology

Disposable nappies contain a polymer which can soak up
water. We say the polymer is absorbent.

A **hydrogel** polymer is built into the nappy as a powder.
When the powder absorbs water, it turns into a gel (a bit
like jelly!).

> **1** Why are hydrogel polymers useful in nappies?

> **2** Write down <u>two</u> other uses for hydrogel polymers.

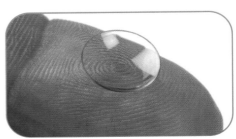

Soft contact lenses are often made from a hydrogel.

We can cover burns and blisters with a hydrogel
dressing. It provides the best conditions for the
wound to heal.

Smart polymers

Smart polymers can be sensitive to temperature, pH and
movement. They pick up signals and respond to them.
The Intelligent Knee Sleeve for athletes is an example.
This is designed to reduce injuries caused by jumping and
landing with your knee in the wrong position.

When the athlete bends his knee

- it stretches the polymer
- the sleeve beeps when it has bent far enough.

> **3** Copy and complete the sentences.
>
> The fibres of the 'Knee Sleeve' are made from a
> smart _____.
> The fibres in the sleeve respond when the athlete
> _____.

This footballer (Australian Rules) wears an
Intelligent Knee Sleeve during training.
You can see a strip on the front of the sleeve
that is coated with a smart polymer.

Shape memory polymers

Some smart polymers have one shape at a low temperature and change to a different shape at a higher temperature. We call these **shape memory** polymers.

Shape memory polymers are very useful for making support mattresses and surgical stitches.

4 What happens to the stitches as the body warms them up?

5 Why don't the stitches stay in the body forever?

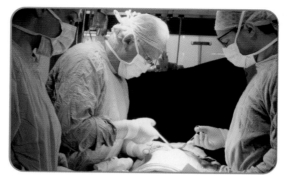

Surgeons can use shape memory polymers in surgery. The surgeon makes loose stitches using the polymer. As the body warms them, the stitches tighten up automatically. The body breaks the polymer down when the tissue has healed.

Dentists use polymers too

Dentists use polymers for building crowns and bridges on people's teeth.

6 Why are polymers better than some traditional dental materials?

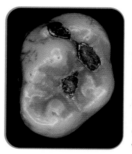

New **dental** polymers are being developed which are stronger and look more attractive than the metals in traditional fillings. Some of the metals dentists used were poisonous too!

Dry as a bone

We can make fabrics **waterproof** by coating them with a polymer. However, waterproof jackets can get damp inside because of the sweat we produce. Gore-Tex® won't let rain through but it lets warm water vapour out. This is because it contains tiny holes, or pores. It's important to keep Gore-Tex clean or the pores get clogged up.

7 How does Gore-Tex prevent damp from collecting inside the jacket?

8 What is a disadvantage with using Gore-Tex in a dirty environment?

These jackets are made from Gore-Tex.

What you need to remember *Copy and complete using the **key words***

Useful polymers

Polymers have many uses. New uses for polymers are being developed. For example

- _____ polymers which absorb water
- _____ polymers which respond to changes
- _____ polymers for repairing teeth
- _____ _____ polymers which change shape when they are heated
- _____ polymer coatings for fabrics.

7 Polymers and packaging

Modern packaging

Much of the **packaging** we use these days is made from polymers. There are many reasons for this.

1 Copy and complete the table.

Item	Why we use polymers for packaging it
cheese	
bleach	
mail order catalogue	

2 Write down <u>two</u> disadvantages of using polymers made from oil for packaging.

Smart packaging

Question: How do you tell if a fruit is ripe?

Answer: Squeeze it, of course!

This is a big problem for fruit sellers. When customers squeeze the fruit, they damage it.

Smart packaging can tell you how ripe the fruit is. The label detects the chemicals that ripe fruit release and changes colour.

3 What does a red label tell you about the fruit?

4 What colour does the label turn after 5 days?

5 Explain, as fully as you can, the advantages of this smart label.

Some properties of polymers
- Easy to shape and colour
- Cheap
- Flexible
- Lightweight
- Strong
- Hygienic
- Non-rusting
- Good resistance to corrosive chemicals
- The polymers we make from oil do not break down naturally

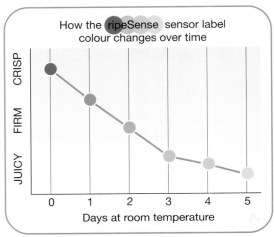

How the ripeSense sensor label colour changes over time

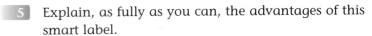

The sensor label on smart packaging changes colour as the fruit ripens.

Packaging from crops

Most of the polymers we use come from crude oil. However, scientists have developed new polymers from renewable sources like starch and sugar.

6 Where do we get starch from?

7 Why is it better to use starch than crude oil as a raw material for making polymers?

Bacteria feed on the starch and produce the polymer in a fermenter.

Scientists can control the process to produce polymers with different properties. Some polymers are suitable for making bottles and others for plastic films.

Getting the starch from crops could be cheaper and easier than using crude oil. This means there is a big demand for polymers made from renewable substances like starch.

8 Why might a packaging company be interested in the new polymer?

We can get starch from crops like corn and potatoes. We can use the starch as a raw material for making polymers.

Plastic mountains!

The polymers in most of our plastics don't break down naturally. We say that they are not biodegradable. This is an enormous problem for our environment because they take up a lot of room in our landfill sites. They also make up most of our litter.

Scientists have developed some plastics which will eventually break down.

9 **a** What is the plastic in this fork made from?
b What eventually happens to biodegradable plastics?
c How does this help the environment?

Just in the UK, we produce enough plastic waste to fill the Royal Albert Hall three times every single day.

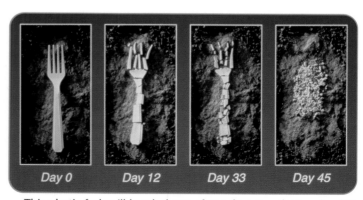

Day 0   Day 12   Day 33   Day 45

This plastic fork will break down after a few months in a landfill site. The plastic is biodegradable and made from sugar.

What you need to remember *Copy and complete using the **key words***

Polymers and packaging
Polymers are very useful as _____ materials.

8 What happens to waste polymers?

We bury a lot of our waste in landfill sites.

Microorganisms break down natural fibres like cotton and wool. So when we throw them away they rot. We say that they are **biodegradable**.

Most polymers don't rot. They are not biodegradable. Waste polymers can cause a problem to the environment.

If we bury cotton and polythene at the same time, the cotton will rot away but the polythene will not.

1 What happens when we bury

    a natural fibres like wool and cotton?
    b polymers like polythene?

Using carrier bags

Most supermarket carrier bags are made from the plastic called polythene.

People like to use carrier bags because they are hygienic, strong and convenient to use.

The bags are inexpensive to produce but it is important to remember that

- we use non-renewable fossil fuels to make plastics like polythene
- making plastics can produce harmful waste gases.

2 About how many bags does a household use each year?

3 Why do people use so many carrier bags?

> **REMEMBER**
>
> A fossil fuel is a fuel formed in the Earth's crust from the remains of living things, e.g. crude oil.

> **DID YOU KNOW?**
>
> Every year, each household uses an estimated 323 carrier bags!

Disposing of carrier bags

Most plastic carrier bags end up in landfill sites like this one. No one knows how long it will take for them to break down – probably more than 100 years.
Lots of plastic also ends up as litter.

4 Write down <u>three</u> problems of using landfill sites.

5 How can litter be harmful to children and animals?

Recycling carrier bags

In the UK we only recycle 5% of our plastic.
If we just melted down all of our plastic waste the new material would not be very useful.

6 Copy and complete the sentences.

It is more difficult to recycle _____ than materials like glass and metals.
This is because there are _____ different groups of plastics and they are hard to _____.

7 Where can you recycle carrier bags?

8 What could you do to reduce the number of carrier bags you use?

Landfill sites look ugly and take up land which we could use for other things like farming or building. It also costs a lot of money for local councils to deal with all the waste.

Recycling plastics is more difficult than recycling glass, newspaper and cans.
There are six different types of plastic and it's very difficult to sort them.
However, some supermarkets do have special bins for recycling carrier bags or plastic bottles.

There are many types of bag which are designed to be used over and over again.

What you need to remember *Copy and complete using the key words*

What happens to waste polymers?
Many polymers are not broken down by _____.
We say they are not _____.

You need to be able to weigh up how using, throwing away and recycling polymers can affect people, the environment and our economy.

1 Plants – not just a pretty face

We don't just grow plants because they look attractive. Everyone knows how important they are to us as a source of food.

Many plants contain enough oil to be worth harvesting. We can collect garlic from the wild to give us garlic oil. We can also grow crops like olives to give us olive oil.

Nuts like groundnuts (peanuts) give us oil which we can use for cooking.

What can we use plant oils for?

We can use plant oils such as groundnut oil for **food**. We use others to make paint, cosmetics, perfumes and lubricants.

1 Copy and complete the table.

Plant oil	Does the oil come from seeds, nuts or fruits?	What we can use the oil for

The African oil palm has **fruits** which give us palm fruit oil. We can use it to make cosmetics.

In the future, plants could be important to us for many more reasons. Some people already use them as **fuels**.

We are using up fossil fuels like crude oil so quickly that they are running out. Plants often contain **plant oils** which are similar to the chemicals in crude oil.

2 Which word do we use to describe fossil fuels which means that they cannot be replaced?

3 What do plants contain which are similar to the chemicals in crude oil?

> **REMEMBER**
> - Fossil fuels took millions of years to form
> - Once we have used them up they cannot be replaced.
> - We say that they are non-renewable resources.

The **seeds** from oilseed rape give us a useful oil. We can add it to diesel to give us a cleaner fuel.

How do we extract plant oils?

There are different ways to extract the oils from fruits, nuts and seeds.

First we must **crush** them.

Then, one way to extract the oil is by pressing.

4 Write down <u>two</u> ways we can press the oil out of soya beans.

To remove the oil from these soya beans, we can **press** them between heavy granite millstones. We can also use a modern stainless steel press.

We extract oil from lavender seeds by **distillation** using steam. We add water to the seeds and heat it to above 100 °C. The heat from the steam makes the globules of oil in the plant burst and the oil then evaporates.

> **REMEMBER**
>
> Evaporating a liquid and then condensing it again is called distillation.

5 Copy and complete the sentences.

When we distil lavender seeds, we collect a mixture of _____ and _____.
We can separate the liquids because the oil _____ on the water.
We pipe off the _____ into storage _____.

The lavender oil we produce by steam distillation is mixed with water. If we leave the mixture to settle, the oil floats on top of the water because it is less dense. The oil is piped off into storage containers.

Both pressing and distillation give us the plant oil mixed with **water** and **impurities**.
We have to remove these to produce the pure oil.

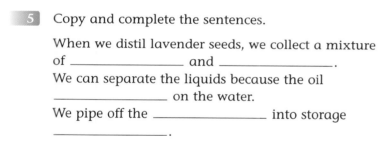

What you need to remember *Copy and complete using the **key words***

Plants – not just a pretty face
Many plants contain _____ _____ which can be very useful to us.
We can use plant oils for _____, _____ and many other things too.
Plant oils can come from the _____, _____ and _____ of the plant.
To extract the oil we often have to _____ the plant material.
Then we have to either _____ it to squeeze out the oil or remove it by _____ using steam.
Finally we remove any _____ or _____ from the plant oil.

2 Plant oils for food

Oils are fats which are liquid at room temperature.

1   Write down the names of <u>three</u> fats.

2   Write down the names of <u>four</u> oils.

The fats and oils in our diet can come from animals or plants. They are very important **foods** because they give us lots of **energy**. They also give us other important **nutrients**, for example sunflower oil is rich in vitamin E.

A name we can give to the oils from plants is **vegetable oils**. We eat many types of vegetable oil.

3   Copy and complete the sentences.

We all need _____ and _____ in our diet. This is because they provide large amounts of _____.
They also contain many important _____.

All of these substances are fats.

Not too much!

Although everyone needs some fat in their diet, it's important that we don't eat too much of it.
Large amounts of fat can give us health problems.

We all know that eating too much fat can make us overweight.

Fat is so full of energy that it is easy to eat too much of it. Many of the foods that we really enjoy contain large amounts of fat.

4   What mass of fat

   a should a teenage female eat each day?
   b should an adult male eat each day?
   c is contained in a meal of two pieces of fried chicken and one regular fries?

5   Copy and complete the sentences.

Like all fats, vegetable oils give us large amounts of _____.

If we eat more food than our body needs, we can become _____.

Food	Fat per serving (g)
Burger King 'Whopper'	34
McDonald's Big Mac	23
KFC chicken breast	19
regular fries	15

This information was taken from the various company websites in December 2005.

Age	Guideline daily amount of fat (grams)	
	Female	Male
15–18	80	105
Adult	70	95

Cooking using vegetable oils

We can cook a food like potatoes in different ways.

- We can boil them in water, which takes 20 minutes.
- We can fry them in a vegetable oil, which only takes a few minutes.

6 Why does it take less time to cook the potatoes in oil than in water?

Frying foods gives them a different flavour. It also changes the amount of **energy** in the food.

The water in the pan boils at 100 °C.

Food	Portion size (g)	Energy content per portion (kJ)
boiled rice	400	1092
fried rice	400	3242

7 What happens to the amount of energy we get from rice if we fry it rather than boiling it?

8 Why is it important to avoid eating too much fried food?

The oil in the fryer boils at a higher temperature than water does.

A healthy way to fry?

Stir frying is a popular way to cook meat and vegetables. It can be a healthy way to cook, but only if we use a small amount of vegetable oil.

9 Copy and complete the sentences.

Stir frying can cook food very _____.
This means that the cooked food still contains plenty of _____.
It is healthy to stir fry as long as we only use a small amount of _____ _____.

Stir frying cooks food very quickly. The more quickly we cook food, the less of the vitamins we destroy.

What you need to remember *Copy and complete using the **key words***

Plant oils for food
Plants give us oils which we call _____ _____. They are very important to us as _____.
Like other fats and oils, they give us lots of _____. They also contain important
_____.

We can cook using vegetable oils. This increases the amount of _____ in the food.

You need to be able to weigh up the effects of using vegetable oils in our food. You need to think about their effects on our diet and health. You will continue this on page 188.

3 Changing oils

We can't spread vegetable oils on bread or toast because they are too runny. We have to **harden** them.

Look at the Box.

> **1** Copy and complete the sentences.
>
> We can make vegetable oils harder if we react them with _____.
> The reaction needs a _____ catalyst and a temperature of _____.
> When oils have reacted with hydrogen we say they are _____.

Reacting an oil with hydrogen makes it a solid at room temperature. This is because hydrogenated oil has a **higher melting point** than the oil it was made from.

We can also use hardened oils for making **cakes** and biscuits.

> **2** Write down <u>two</u> uses for hardened vegetable oil.
>
> **3** What happens to the melting point of oil when it has reacted with hydrogen?

Vegetable oils – unsaturated fats

Vegetable oils will react with hydrogen because they contain **carbon–carbon double bonds**.

> **4** What do we call compounds which contain double bonds?
>
> **5** What happens to a double bond when a molecule reacts with hydrogen?

Although it's important to try to eat less fat, fats are essential in our diet.

Unsaturated fats like those in vegetable oils are much healthier for us than other types of fat.

The fats in dairy products and meat, and in cakes and biscuits are saturated fats.

> ### Hardening vegetable oils
>
> - To make vegetable oils harder, we react them with **hydrogen** at 60 °C.
> - We use a **nickel catalyst** to speed up the reaction.
> - After the reaction, the new oils contain more hydrogen. We say they are **hydrogenated**.

Sunflower oil is very useful for making **spreads** like margarine.

> ### REMEMBER
>
> Some molecules contain a double bond between two carbon atoms. We say they are **unsaturated**.

Double bonds can open up. This happens when unsaturated molecules react with hydrogen.

What's wrong with saturated fats?

If you eat too much saturated fat, like butter and cream, your body may make too much of a harmful type of cholesterol.

  6 What can happen to your arteries if your body produces too much cholesterol?

  7 How can this cause a heart attack?

It is important to keep the level of cholesterol in our bodies low. We can do this if we replace some of the saturated fats in our diet with unsaturated fats.

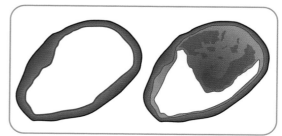

The artery on the right is partly blocked by cholesterol. This makes it difficult for the blood to flow through.
If an artery to your heart muscle becomes blocked, it can cause a heart attack.

Testing for double bonds

We can find out if a vegetable oil contains unsaturated fats using a chemical called **bromine**. We can also use **iodine** for this test.

Bromine can open up the double bond in unsaturated molecules and join with the molecule.

Bromine water is yellow–brown. It becomes colourless when the bromine in it reacts with the vegetable oil.

  8 Copy and complete the sentences.

To test for carbon–carbon double bonds, we use

_____ _____. When we mix

it with vegetable oil, it becomes _____.

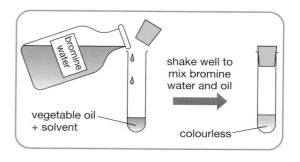

bromine water

shake well to mix bromine water and oil

vegetable oil + solvent

colourless

What you need to remember *Copy and complete using the key words*

Changing oils

We can _____ vegetable oils if we react them with _____. In this reaction, we use a _____ _____ at 60 °C.
We say that the hardened oils are _____. They now have a

_____ _____ _____ and are solid at room temperature.
We use the hardened oils to make _____ like margarine and for making

_____.

Vegetable oils can contain _____ _____ _____. We say that they are _____.
We can detect these double bonds using chemicals like _____ or _____.

You need to be able to weigh up the effects of using vegetable oils in foods and the impact that they can have on our diet and health.

4 Emulsions

When we add oil to water, it won't **dissolve**. However, we can mix oil and water together to make an **emulsion**.

> **1** What happens if you leave an emulsion of oil and water to settle?

Emulsions are **thicker** than either oil or water and have different **properties**.

The oil and water do not mix.

If we shake them together well, the oil forms tiny globules which are held up by the water. This is an emulsion.

Everyday emulsions

One reason that we use emulsions in foods is because they look good. We say they have a better **appearance** than oil or water. Emulsions can also feel good when we eat them – they have a pleasant **texture**.

> **2** Copy and complete the sentences.
>
> We make mayonnaise from _____ and _____. If we just mixed these two ingredients they would _____ again.
> We add _____ to the mixture to stop it from separating.
> Mayonnaise has an attractive, shiny _____.

If we leave the emulsion for a few minutes, the oil globules join up again and float back to the top of the water.

We can also use an emulsion of oil and vinegar to make **salad dressing**. The emulsion is thicker than either of the two liquids alone, so it's better for **coating** the salad.

> **3** Write down <u>three</u> examples of foods which are made from emulsions.
>
> **4** Why is salad dressing good for coating salads?

Ice cream is a frozen emulsion. That's why it has a smooth, creamy texture.

Mayonnaise is an emulsion we make from oil, vinegar and egg. The egg stops the oil and vinegar separating.

What you need to remember *Copy and complete using the **key words***

Emulsions

Oil won't _____ in water but we can mix oil and water together to make an _____.

Emulsions are _____ than oil or water. They are useful to us because they have special _____.

Emulsions have a good _____ and _____. They are also good for _____ foods. We use emulsions to make foods like _____ _____ and _____ _____.

5 Additives in our food

Many years ago, people mainly ate what they could collect, grow and store. They preserved some of their food to stop it from going bad.

1 How did people preserve food many years ago?

These days, a lot of the food we buy has been prepared and cooked in a factory. Some of it has been preserved in cans or packets, or by freezing. We call this processed food.

Most processed food contains **additives**. Manufacturers use additives in food

- to improve its **appearance** (how it looks, for example its colour)
- to improve its **taste** (sugars, acids)
- to improve its **shelf life** (make it keep longer)
- to stop the ingredients separating (emulsifiers).

2 What name do we give to an additive which makes a food keep for longer?

> ### DID YOU KNOW?
> On average, we eat 3.6 kg of additives every year.

3 Look at the pictures.
Then copy and complete the table.

Name of food	Why the additive was added

We can't eat all of this today!

Many years ago people preserved food by salting, drying or smoking it.

This jelly contains a colouring to make it look attractive.

This squash contains a sweetener to make it taste pleasant.

This bread contains a preservative to make it keep longer.

What you need to remember *Copy and complete using the **key words***

Additives in our food

Much of the food we eat is processed and contains _____.
Additives are put in food to improve its _____ (how it looks), its
_____ _____ (how long it lasts) and its _____.

6 Any additives in there?

Processed foods must have information on the label about any additives they contain. The additives should be listed with the **ingredients**.

> 1 Write down <u>three</u> of the additives in this processed cheese.

Food manufacturers can't put any old chemicals into our food. Many of the additives they are allowed to use have been given **E-numbers**. These mean that the additive has been tested for safety.

> 2 Copy and complete the table.

E-number	Other name	What it does	<u>Two</u> foods or drinks where we find it

Cheddar Cheese Slice (processed)
Vegetarian cheddar cheese, water, butter, milk proteins, natural cheese flavouring. Emulsifying salts: E331 trisodium citrate, E450 diphosphates, E452 polyphosphates. Lactose, salt. Preservative: E200 sorbic acid. Colour: E160(a) carotenes, E160(c) paprika.

This is the list of ingredients in a processed cheese. We have printed the additives in blue.

E406, or agar, is used to thicken food. We extract it from seaweed and use it in ice creams and tinned food. E951, or aspartame, is an artificial sweetener which is about 200 times sweeter than sugar. We find it in low-calorie drinks and desserts.

Chemical detectives

In February 2005, scientists discovered that a banned additive was being used in some foods. It was a dye called Sudan I. It had been added to a chilli powder from India.

Sudan I was banned because evidence showed it could increase our risk of cancer. When scientists discovered it in the chilli powder, shops were told to remove all the processed foods which contained it from their shelves. It turned out that it was in about 500 types of food!

To find out if foods contained Sudan I, samples were sent to laboratories. The laboratories carried out **chemical analysis** to test if the dye was present.

> 3 Why was Sudan I banned?

> 4 Write down <u>three</u> foods which contained the dye.

> 5 How did laboratories test for the dye?

ready-made spaghetti bolognaise

sausages

steak and kidney pudding

These are just some of the foods which had to be removed from shelves during the Sudan I scare.

Artificial colours

We add artificial colours or dyes to lots of our foods to make them look good.

Some people believe that additives like this can be harmful, particularly to children. But there are so many factors which affect children's behaviour that it is very difficult to do a fair test.

> **6** Write down <u>two</u> factors which could affect how a child behaves.

> **7** How could a parent try to find out if an artificial colouring was affecting their child?

Some evidence seems to show that additives do affect children's behaviour. Other scientists don't think that there is enough evidence to support this conclusion.

My little boy is so badly behaved, doctor. He won't go to bed until midnight and the only thing he wants to eat is sweets. Do you think the colours might be making him naughty?

Detecting artificial colours

We can use a technique called **chromatography** to help us

- find out if foods contain artificial colours
- identify which colours are in foods.

There are lots of ways to carry out chromatography. One method uses water to separate the colours in food colourings.

Look at the picture of a chromatography experiment.

> **8** Which of these food colourings contain only <u>one</u> colour?

> **9** What colours are in the green food colouring?

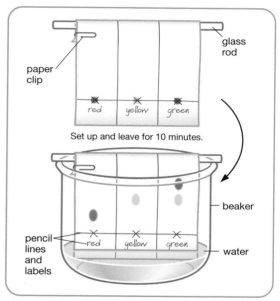

Colours in different food colourings.

What you need to remember *Copy and complete using the* **key words**

Any additives in there?
We can find out if a food contains additives by looking on the list of _____.
Many additives which are allowed in our food have been given _____.
We can find out which additives are in our food using _____ _____.
We can detect and identify artificial colourings using _____.

You need to be able to weigh up the good and bad points about using additives in foods.

7 Vegetable oils as fuels

Modern day living uses a lot of energy! We need to develop new fuels which we can use for our homes, industries and transport.

> **1** What name do we give to fuels like crude oil which were formed millions of years ago?

> **2** Write down <u>one</u> problem we will have if we continue to use these fuels.

There are many vegetable oils which we can use to produce **fuels**. Vegetable oils are **renewable** – they will not run out.

As long ago as 1895, an engine was invented which could use a fuel made from a vegetable oil. After the inventor died, scientists found that the engine could also run on a fuel from crude oil, so the idea was lost.

> **3** What type of vegetable oil was used to fuel the early engine?

Farms – the new oilfields?

Oilseed rape stores an oil in its seeds which we can change into a fuel. We can add the fuel to ordinary diesel. We call the new mixture biodiesel.

> **4** Copy and complete the list.
>
> There are several advantages to using biodiesel as a fuel.
>
> ■ We can use it in _____ engines without any changes.
> ■ Growing the crop uses the gas _____ _____ from the air.
> ■ When we burn biodiesel we produce less emissions like _____ _____, _____ _____ and _____.

This engine was designed to run on peanut oil.

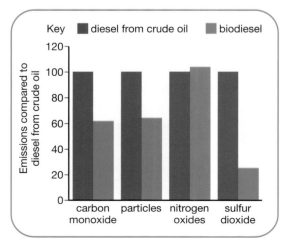

This graph compares the harmful substances produced when we burn biodiesel and diesel from crude oil.

Not all good

Some people believe that we could eventually **replace** our fossil fuels with fuels from vegetable oils. However, using vegetable oils to produce fuels has some problems.

Growing fuels in fields uses up a lot of land.
We have 5.7 million hectares of farmland in the UK.

5   Write down <u>two</u> problems we would have if we tried to use rapeseed oil to run all of our vehicles.

6   What could happen if oil companies offered our farmers more money to grow crops as fuels?

If we ran all our cars, buses and lorries using rapeseed oil, we would need 26 million hectares of farmland. We also need our farmland to grow crops for food.

What about palm oil?

Rapeseed oil isn't the only vegetable oil we can use to produce a fuel. We can also use palm oil. We already use it in many of our foods.

7   Which habitat is being destroyed by palm oil farming?

8   What happens if habitats are destroyed?

So, we can grow plants for oils to use as fuels. But there are other uses for the land. We have to balance the demand for food and fuels with the conservation of suitable habitats for plants and animals.

Much of the rain forest in Indonesia has been destroyed to grow oil palms. Animals like tigers and orang-utans used to live in the forest.

What you need to remember *Copy and complete using the **key words***

Vegetable oils as fuels
We can burn vegetable oils as _____. They could be used to _____ some of our fossil fuels.
Vegetable oils will not run out. We say that they are _____.

You need to be able to weigh up the good and bad points about using vegetable oils to produce fuels.

1 Ideas about the Earth

Scientists think that the Earth is made of different layers. They have carried out tests using the vibrations from earthquakes and explosions. The tests give them information about the layers.

1 Imagine you could drill a hole through the Earth to the centre. Copy and complete the sentences to say what you would find on the way through.

First, the drill would go through the solid rock in the Earth's _____.
Next, the drill would reach the layer called the _____.

About halfway through to the centre, the drill would reach the outer _____, which is _____.

The inner core is _____.

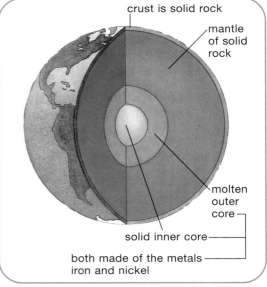

This is what the layers are probably like inside the Earth.

Changing ideas

Until about 200 years ago, most people believed that the mountains, valleys and seas on the Earth had always been just as they saw them then. Many people thought the Earth formed only a few thousand years ago.

Then geologists started to look at how rocks were being formed. They realised just how long it takes.
This made them think that the Earth must actually be many millions of years old.

2 Write down <u>two</u> reasons why geologists thought that the Earth must be very old.

3 What else did they then need to explain?

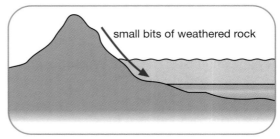

Sedimentary rocks form under water.
Geologists worked out that thick layers of rock must take millions of years to form.

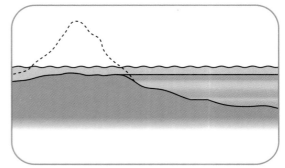

Geologists also realised that, over millions of years, mountains must be worn away. They needed to explain how new mountains form.

A cooling, shrinking Earth

The diagram shows one theory about how features such as **mountains** and oceans formed.

4 Write down the sentences in the correct order.

- The molten core carries on cooling, but more and more slowly. It shrinks as it cools.

- The Earth began as a ball of hot, molten rock.

- The shrinking core makes the crust wrinkle. The high places become mountains, the low places become seas.

- As the molten rock cooled, a solid crust formed.

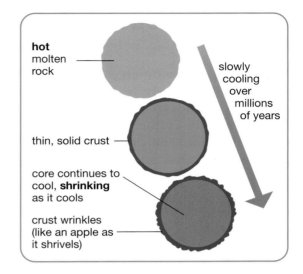

Problems for the shrinking Earth theory

According to this theory, the Earth can't be more than about 400 million years old or it would be cool and completely solid by now.

We can now date rocks, so we know that the Earth is a lot older than 400 million years. It's not solid because the Earth doesn't just lose heat, it produces it.

The Earth contains quite a lot of radioactive elements such as uranium. The atoms of these elements gradually break down. As they do so, they release heat.

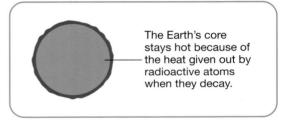

5 What effect does this heat have on the Earth?

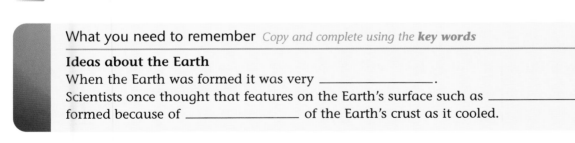

What you need to remember *Copy and complete using the **key words***

Ideas about the Earth
When the Earth was formed it was very _____.
Scientists once thought that features on the Earth's surface such as _____
formed because of _____ of the Earth's crust as it cooled.

2 Ideas about Earth movements

The idea of a moving crust

In 1912, a scientist called Alfred Wegener had a different theory about the Earth. He thought that, millions of years ago, the Earth had only one giant continent. Then it started to break apart. Over millions of years, the parts slowly moved to where they are today.

This idea was called the theory of continental drift.

> **1** Why was Wegener's theory about how the crust moves called continental drift?
>
> **2** What evidence did he have for continental drift?
>
> **3** Write down <u>two</u> reasons why most scientists didn't agree with Wegener's ideas.

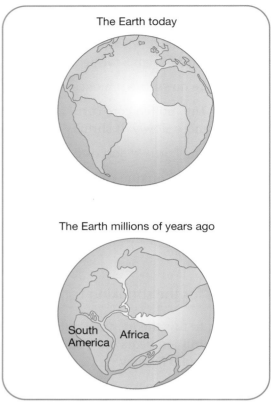

The Earth today

The Earth millions of years ago

South America   Africa

Wegener suggested that South America and Africa must once have been joined together. Most scientists said that there was no way the continents could have moved apart.
Also, Wegener was a meteorologist, not a geologist, so people didn't listen to him.

Evidence for Wegener's ideas

During the 1950s, scientists started to explore the rocks at the bottom of the oceans. The diagrams show what they found and how they explained it.

> **4** Copy and complete the sentences.
>
> Under the oceans are long _____ ridges. These are made of rock that is quite
>
> _____ .
>
> The sea floor under the ocean is moving
>
> _____ .
>
> Magma from below the Earth's _____ moves up to make new rock.

The new evidence convinced scientists that the Earth's crust is made of a small number of separate sections called **tectonic plates**. Under the oceans, these plates are moving apart. But in some places, the plates are moving towards each other. This pushes rock upwards to make new mountains.

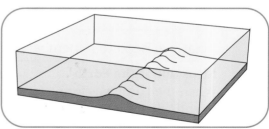

There are long mountain ridges underneath the ocean. They are made of young rocks.

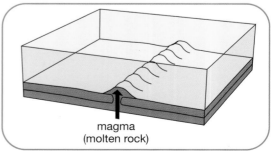

magma (molten rock)

Sections of crust on the sea floor are moving apart. New rock forms to fill the gap.

How can plates move?

Although the mantle is a solid, it is very hot and under great pressure. This means that it can flow very slowly, like a very thick liquid.

When the mantle flows, the tectonic plates **move** too.

5 Why can the mantle flow even though it's a solid?

6 Copy and complete the sentences.

Water _____ around when you heat it.
This is because hot water _____ and cold water moves _____ to take its place.

These movements are called **convection currents**.

Convection currents inside the Earth

Heat produced inside the Earth causes slow convection currents in the mantle.

Look at the diagram.

7 Copy and complete the sentences.

Convection currents in the mantle

- make plates A and B move _____
- make plates B and C move _____ .

The plates can move because they 'float' on top of the _____ .
There are very slow _____ currents in the mantle.

8 What heats up the mantle?

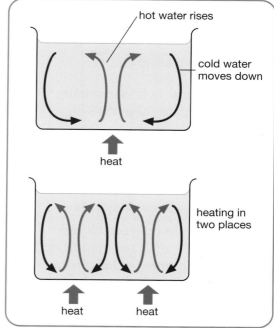

Scientists use models of heating liquids to help them explain how the mantle moves.
If a liquid gets hot, it moves around.
The diagrams show what happens.

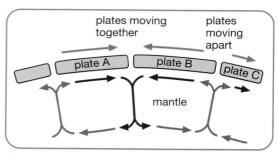

The tectonic plates move as the mantle flows.
The mantle is heated up by the breakdown of **radioactive** substances deep in the Earth.

What you need to remember *Copy and complete using the* **key words**

Ideas about Earth movements
The Earth's crust is made up from a number of large pieces. We call them _____
_____ .

The plates _____ as a result of _____ _____ in the mantle. Convection currents happen because the mantle is heated up by natural _____ processes.

You need to be able to explain why scientists didn't agree with the theory that the crust moves (continental drift) for many years.

3 Effects of moving plates

The Earth's unstable crust

Scientists eventually had to admit that Wegener's idea about moving continents was correct.

- They found evidence of movement.
- They were able to suggest how that movement could happen.

We now know that the Earth's crust and the upper part of the mantle are made up of a number of large pieces. We call these tectonic plates.

The map shows some of them. The plates move all the time. They don't move very fast, just a few **centimetres** (cm) each year. But these small movements add up to big movements over a long time.

1 Write down the name of the tectonic plate that Britain is on.

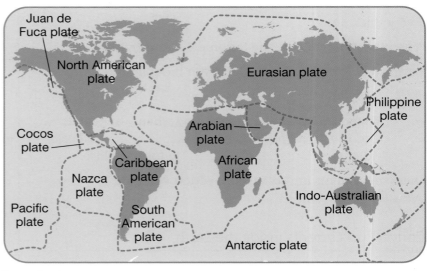

Tectonic plates.

Earthquakes and volcanoes

Sometimes the movements of the plates can be very **sudden**. These movements can cause **disasters**.

The places where tectonic plates **meet** are called plate boundaries. These are the places where plates are moving apart or pushing against each other. So they are the places where most **earthquakes** and **volcanic eruptions** happen.

2 Write down the names of <u>two</u> countries which regularly experience earthquakes and volcanic eruptions.

3 Why do some parts of the Earth, but not others, experience earthquakes and volcanic eruptions?

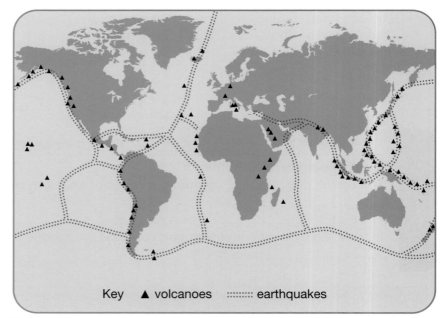

Key ▲ volcanoes ⋯⋯ earthquakes

Earthquakes and volcanoes in the world.

More about earthquakes

Earthquakes happen when plates move. The plates rub together and make the Earth shake.

One problem in an earthquake is that buildings collapse. People inside and out may be killed or injured.

There are often earthquakes in Japan. The shops, houses and offices are designed and built with special structures to help them withstand the movements.

> **4** Write down <u>two</u> ways that Japanese people try to prevent deaths from earthquakes.

In Japan, people are trained so that they know what to do in an earthquake.

Why can't we predict earthquakes?

Scientists have set up stations all round the world to record earthquakes automatically. The scientists use the records to find out exactly where each Earth movement happened. They also look for patterns in the records to try to predict when and where earthquakes will happen.

Even with all of these records, scientists still don't have enough information to predict earthquakes.

> **5** Why do you think a lot of time and money is spent trying to predict earthquakes?

> **6** What can happen if scientists make a wrong prediction?

They got it wrong.

They made 56 000 of us leave our homes.

Our shops and businesses had to close for two days.

We lost a lot of money.

In 1986, scientists wrongly predicted an earthquake in Italy.

What you need to remember *Copy and complete using the **key words***

Effects of moving plates

Tectonic plates move only a few _____ a year. But when they move, it can be _____. The movements can cause _____ like _____ and _____ _____. These happen at the places where the plates _____.

You need to be able to explain some of the reasons why scientists can't predict earthquakes.

4 Predicting disasters

Earthquakes are difficult to predict. So are volcanic eruptions. Scientists keep a close watch on volcanoes. They measure temperatures, pressures and the gases given off. This can be difficult and dangerous work.

Sometimes their measurements tell them there will be an eruption in the next few months. They cannot be more accurate than this because there are so many factors involved.

> **1** Write down <u>two</u> reasons why scientists cannot accurately predict volcanic eruptions.

> **2** Write down <u>one</u> way the people of Montserrat keep safe from the volcano on their island.

These houses and offices on the island of Montserrat were covered with ash from a volcanic eruption. Many people were forced to move to the north of the island where it is safer. Large numbers of people also went to live abroad.

Far-reaching effects

Being able to predict where and when volcanic eruptions and earthquakes will happen is important – and not just for people who live near them. Earthquakes and volcanic eruptions can have effects far from where they happen.

> **3** Write down <u>one</u> local and <u>one</u> worldwide effect of the Indonesian eruption in 1815.

Many of the volcanoes on the Earth are under the sea. When these erupt, they can cause a series of giant waves. We call this a tsunami.

Tsunami are most common in the Pacific Ocean, where there are more than half of the world's volcanoes.

> **4** Why do most tsunami happen in the Pacific Ocean?

An earthquake can also cause a tsunami.

On 26 December 2004, there was an enormous earthquake under the Indian Ocean. It was the biggest earthquake for 40 years. Nobody predicted the disastrous effect it would have.

In Indonesia in 1815, an enormous volcanic eruption like this one killed around 92 000 people. Ash from the volcano cooled the world for over a year. In some parts of the world, that year was called 'the year without a summer' because it was so cool.

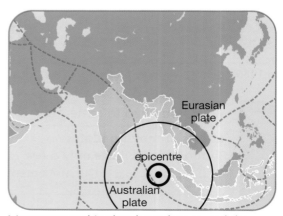

Movement at this plate boundary caused the tsunami in December 2004.

The wave spreads

In 7 hours, the wave caused by the earthquake spread thousands of kilometres. It moved at the speed of a jet plane. When it reached the coasts, it rose up into a giant wave taller than a double-decker bus.

5 Write down the names of <u>three</u> countries that this tsunami affected.

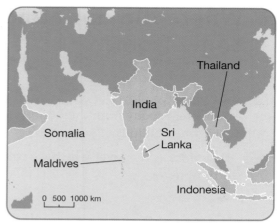

The Indian Ocean earthquake sent out waves which destroyed towns and villages on the coasts of these countries.

Every cubic metre of water has a mass of one tonne. That's as heavy as a small car. In these countries, the power of the wave flattened nearly everything that stood in its way. The tsunami killed more than a hundred thousand people. It also wrecked millions of lives.

6 Why did so many people lose their homes?

Still recovering

Nobody knows how long it will take for countries to recover after the tsunami.

People used to make a living from fishing and farming. All of the fishing boats were destroyed by the wave.

7 Copy and complete the table.

Way in which people made a living	How this was affected by the tsunami

Most of the buildings in the area were only built out of flimsy materials and were completely destroyed. Only a few well-built buildings remained.

The fields before (left) and after the tsunami. The salt water made the fields turn brown. Nobody knows when farmers will be able to grow crops on the land again.

What you need to remember

Predicting disasters
There is nothing new for you to <u>remember</u> in this section.

You need to be able to explain some of the reasons why scientists can't predict volcanic eruptions.

5 Where did our atmosphere come from?

The **atmosphere** is a layer of gas above the Earth's surface. It is very different today from the atmosphere when the Earth first formed billions of years ago.

> **1** How thick is the layer which we call our atmosphere?

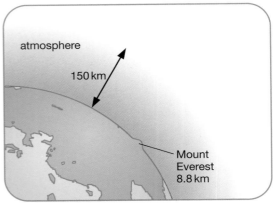

The Earth's atmosphere.

In the beginning

Scientists think that the Earth was formed about 4600 million years ago. This early Earth was so hot it was molten for millions of years. Then, as it cooled, a solid crust formed.
There were **volcanoes** everywhere.

> **2** Copy and complete the sentences.
>
> The early atmosphere came from _____ which were everywhere.
> They produced gases including _____
> _____.

As the Earth cooled, the water vapour in the atmosphere turned into liquid water. We say that it condensed. The water fell as rain and eventually collected on the surface of the Earth. It made the first lakes and **oceans**.

> **3** What happens to water vapour if we cool it down?
>
> **4** Explain how the oceans formed from the water vapour in the atmosphere.

For the first billion years after the Earth was formed volcanic activity was much greater than it is now. The volcanoes produced the **gases** which formed the early atmosphere, including **water vapour**.

> **DID YOU KNOW?**
>
> Some scientists think that most of the water actually came to Earth on comets and meteorites!

The early atmosphere

Some scientists believe that, 4000 million years ago, the atmosphere contained

- mainly **carbon dioxide** gas
- little or no **oxygen** gas.

In the atmosphere, there may also have been

- small amounts of **methane** and **ammonia**
- some **water vapour**.

Gas	Percentage in the atmosphere
oxygen	about 20
nitrogen	about 80
noble gases	small amount
carbon dioxide	tiny amount

The atmosphere today

5 Write down <u>two</u> differences between the Earth's early atmosphere and the atmosphere today.

The early atmosphere was a bit like the atmosphere on **Venus** today.

6 Copy and complete the sentence.

The atmosphere on Venus is mainly made from the gas _____ _____.

7 Explain why the Earth's early atmosphere was not suitable for humans and other animals.

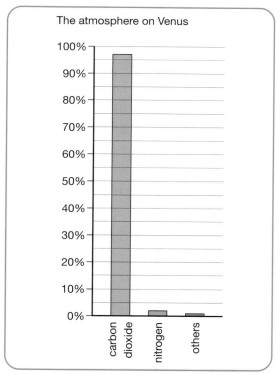

We need oxygen, but carbon dioxide poisons us. So we wouldn't be able to live on Venus.

What you need to remember *Copy and complete using the **key words***

Where did our atmosphere come from?
For the first billion years after the Earth formed, there were lots of _____.
These produced _____ which made up the early _____.
The _____ _____ that was made condensed to form the _____.

The early atmosphere was mainly made from _____ _____ gas.
There was very little _____, which living things need. This is like the atmosphere of _____ today.
There may also have been _____ _____ and small amounts of _____ and _____.

6 More oxygen, less carbon dioxide

3500 million years ago, there were plant-like microorganisms living in the sea. They used dissolved carbon dioxide to make their food. As a result, they started to 'pollute' the atmosphere with oxygen.

Later, tiny plants and then larger plants evolved in the oceans. Millions of years later, plants began to grow on the land too.

Plants use the gas **carbon dioxide** to produce their food (carbohydrate). We call this photosynthesis.

carbon dioxide + water → carbohydrate + **oxygen**

1   Write down the name of the gas that plants add to the atmosphere during photosynthesis.

2   What evidence do we have that oxygen levels were rising?

3   What was the percentage of oxygen in the atmosphere 400 million years ago?

4   What evidence is there that it was plants that took the carbon d.ioxide out of the atmosphere?

By 2200 million years ago, oxygen levels were high enough to oxidise iron. Banded red ironstone rocks are evidence of this.

The atmosphere 400 million years ago

- Oxygen level rising to 2% of the atmosphere.
- Carbon dioxide level falling.

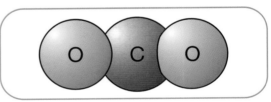

Carbon dioxide gas contains the elements carbon and oxygen.

Keeping carbon dioxide out of the atmosphere

By 200 million years ago, there was very little carbon dioxide left in the atmosphere. The **carbon** had become part of all of the living things on the Earth and their fossilised remains.

5   What are the two elements in the compound carbon dioxide?

When living things die, some rot and the carbon in them is recycled. Others may turn into **fossil fuels** like oil or coal. Then the carbon from the plants and animals is **locked up** in the fossil fuels until we burn them.

6   Where does the carbon that is 'locked' up in coal come from?

The tropical forests of the Carboniferous period formed much of the world's coal.

Where else is carbon dioxide locked up?

Between 600 million and 400 million years ago, fossil evidence shows us that many animals with shells evolved. The first animals were microscopic.
Fossils show us that, later, there were large animals such as corals and crinoids too.

Most of these animals had hard parts made of calcium carbonate. When these animals died and sank to the bottom of the sea as sediment, their shells formed carbonate rocks such as limestone and chalk.

These are **sedimentary** rocks. Carbon can stay 'locked up' in them for millions of years.

This limestone is made from the remains of crinoids or sea lilies. These animals are related to starfish.

7 **a** Write down the name of <u>one</u> carbonate rock.
   b What is the main carbon compound in this rock?

8 Look at the timeline showing the Earth's history. When did carbon start to become locked up in limestone?

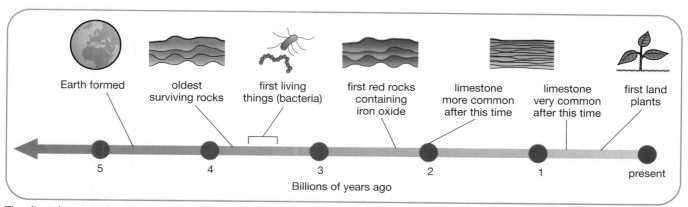

| Earth formed | oldest surviving rocks | first living things (bacteria) | first red rocks containing iron oxide | limestone more common after this time | limestone very common after this time | first land plants |

5   4   3   2   1   present
Billions of years ago

Timeline showing the Earth's history.

What you need to remember *Copy and complete using the* **key words**

More oxygen, less carbon dioxide
As plants began to grow on the Earth, they used up _____ _____ and produced _____.
Over billions of years the _____ in the carbon dioxide became _____ _____ as

■ _____ _____ like coal and oil
■ carbonates in _____ rocks.

So, the concentration of carbon dioxide in the atmosphere fell.

You need to be able to explain some ideas about how our atmosphere has changed and to weigh up some of the evidence to support these ideas.

7 Still changing – our atmosphere

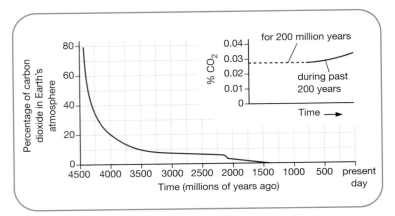

Today, tiny but very important changes are happening to our atmosphere.

Look at the graph. The concentration of carbon dioxide in the air fell for millions of years. Then, about 200 years ago, it started to rise.

> **1** Copy and complete the sentences.
>
> The percentage of carbon dioxide in the atmosphere 200 years ago was about _____.
> In the past 200 years, it has _____ to 0.033%.

> **REMEMBER**
>
> Carbon is 'locked up' in fossil fuels like oil and coal and in sedimentary rocks as carbonates.

Why is the carbon dioxide level rising?

Humans caused this rise by releasing the carbon locked up in the Earth's crust.

> **2** From which substances are we releasing carbon?

When we burn fossil fuels like oil, the carbon in them joins with oxygen to form carbon dioxide. We add this **carbon dioxide** to our atmosphere. We do the same thing when we break down limestone to make quicklime.

> **3** Copy and complete the sentences.
>
> Over the past 200 years, our use of fossil fuels like _____ has _____.
> So the amount of carbon dioxide in the _____ has increased.

Global warming

Most scientists believe that carbon dioxide acts like a blanket around the Earth. It reduces the amount of heat that escapes.

So, as the amount of carbon dioxide increases, the average temperature of the Earth's surface also increases.

We call this global warming.

We began to use more and more fossil fuels during the industrial revolution. This began in the 1800s. The new machinery used coal, oil and gas.

Evidence for global warming

One place we can look for evidence is deep in the ice in places like Antarctica and Greenland.

4 What is the length of some ice cores?

5 Copy and complete the sentence.

Ice cores can tell us information about the _____ and the _____ over thousands of years.

Evidence from ice cores suggests that the Earth is warmer now than it has been for thousands of years.

Scientists collect ice cores by driving a hollow tube up to 3 km into the ice. We can use the ice to find out about the climate and the atmosphere up to 750 000 years ago.

What's causing the Earth to warm up?

Some scientists think that the temperature increases are part of natural cycles. However, most scientists think that there is enough evidence to say that global warming is at least partly due to human activity.

6 Which <u>two</u> things are linked together by evidence from ice cores?

A link between two factors may not mean that one <u>causes</u> the other. For example, flu is more common in winter but winter is <u>not the cause</u> of flu (viruses are). Scientists need to explain how carbon dioxide, for example, could cause global warming. They also need to rule out other explanations. Human activity produces other gases which could also be adding to global warming, for example methane and nitrogen oxides. We call these greenhouse gases.

7 How could carbon dioxide cause global warming?

8 Suggest reasons why scientists still disagree about the cause or causes of global warming.

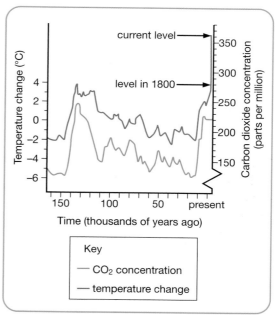

Evidence from ice cores tells us that there is a link between the temperature on the Earth and the concentration of carbon dioxide in the atmosphere.

What you need to remember *Copy and complete using the **key words***

Still changing – our atmosphere
Burning fossil fuels is increasing the concentration of _____ _____ in the atmosphere.

You need to be able to explain some ideas about how our atmosphere has changed and to weigh up some of the evidence to support these ideas, including the effects of human activities on the atmosphere.

8 The atmosphere today

Our atmosphere has been about the same for the past 200 million years.

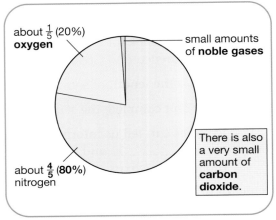

about $\frac{1}{5}$ (20%) **oxygen**

small amounts of **noble gases**

about $\frac{4}{5}$ (80%) nitrogen

There is also a very small amount of **carbon dioxide**.

What's in the air?

1 Copy and complete the sentences.

The two main gases in the air are _____ (about _____) and _____ (about _____). There is also a small amount of the _____ gases and an even smaller amount of _____ _____.

2 Why don't we show carbon dioxide on the pie chart?

Water vapour

Our atmosphere also contains **water vapour**. We can't show this on the pie chart because the amount varies. The most water vapour that air can hold is 4%.

3 Where in the world would you find air which contains 4% water vapour?

4 Why don't we show water vapour on the pie chart?

The noble gases

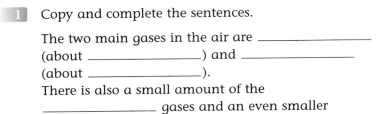

Periodic table showing the first 20 elements.

We find the noble gases in **Group 0** of the periodic table. These gases are very **unreactive** so we can't use them to make new substances.

5 Write down the names of <u>three</u> noble gases.

6 Why can't we use the noble gases to make new substances?

The air in the rainforest contains a lot of water vapour. We say it's very humid.

REMEMBER

A group is a vertical column in the periodic table.

Unreactive but useful

Because they are so unreactive, the noble gases have some important uses.

7   Copy and complete the table.

Name of noble gas	How we use the noble gas	Why we can use the gas like this
helium	used to fill balloons and airships	helium is lighter than air and does not burn

---

DID YOU KNOW?

Divers breathe a special mixture of helium and oxygen. This does cause a problem – the divers sound like a cartoon character!

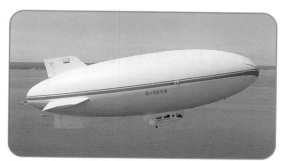

Helium is **less dense** than air. We can use it in airships and balloons. It is safe because it doesn't burn.

A tube filled with neon glows red when we pass electricity through it. We call tubes like these **electric discharge tubes**.

Filament lamps like this are filled with argon. The argon won't react with the filament, even when it's white hot.

What you need to remember *Copy and complete using the* **key words**

The atmosphere today

This table shows the gases in our atmosphere. There is also a small amount of

_____ _____ in the atmosphere.

The noble gases are in _____ _____ of the periodic table. They do not react with anything so we say they are _____ .

We can use the noble gases to make

_____ _____ _____ and _____

_____ . We can use _____ to fill balloons because

it is _____ _____ than air.

Gas	Amount
nitrogen	about _____
_____	about $\frac{1}{5}$ (20%)
_____	small amounts
_____	
_____	very small amount
_____	

Ideas you need from KS3

How heat is transferred

Heat (thermal energy) always moves from hot places to cold places. This is called heat transfer. Sometimes you want to make it easy for heat to go from one place to another. Sometimes you want to keep heat in one place.

So you need to know how heat travels.

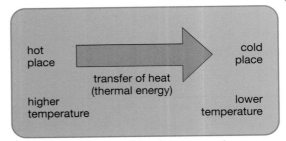

We often use the word 'heat' to mean the same thing as 'thermal energy'.

Radiation

When you stand near to a roaring bonfire, you can feel the heat from the bonfire falling on your face.

This happens because hot objects transfer heat by sending out rays. This method of energy transfer is called <u>radiation</u>.

1 What substance is required for heat transfer by radiation?

Thermal energy is transferred from the fire to your face by radiation. No substance (solid, liquid or gas) is needed, so the radiation can travel through empty space.

Conduction

If you put a solid between somewhere hot and somewhere cold, heat has to travel through the solid. This is called <u>conduction</u>. There has to be a substance there for conduction to happen.

Heat passes easily through some solids, for example metals. We call these conductors. Other solids conduct heat badly, and we call these insulators.

2 Look at the diagrams.

Copy and complete the table.

	Conductor or insulator?	Reason
bottom of pan		It will help transfer heat from the _____ to the _____.
table mat		It will cut down heat transfer from the _____ to the _____ surface.

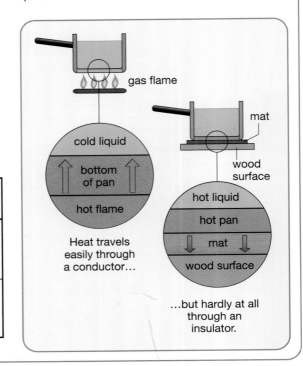

Heat travels easily through a conductor…

…but hardly at all through an insulator.

Convection in liquids

The water in a kettle is a liquid. Liquids can flow.

The heating element in an electric kettle is at the bottom, but it still heats up all the water in the kettle.

The diagrams show how it does this.

3 Draw <u>one</u> large diagram of the kettle.
Add arrows to show how hot water rises and cold water falls.
Label them or colour them in.
Use red for hot and blue for cold.

Each time the water moves around the kettle it gets a little bit hotter.

Hot liquids move and carry heat with them. This is called <u>convection</u>.

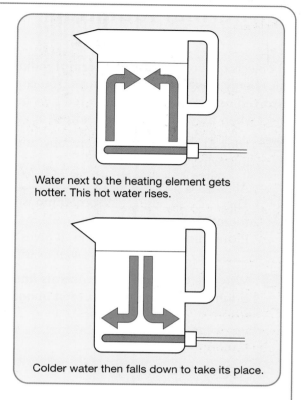

Water next to the heating element gets hotter. This hot water rises.

Colder water then falls down to take its place.

Convection in gases

The air in a room is a gas. Gases can also flow. Heaters are usually near the floor, but the whole of the room gets heated.

The diagrams show how heaters do this.

4 Draw <u>one</u> large diagram of the room and heater.
Draw arrows to show the hot air rising and the cold air falling.
Label or colour the arrows.

Hot gases, like hot liquids, move around and transfer heat by convection as they do so.

Convection only happens in liquids and gases.

It needs a substance that can flow.

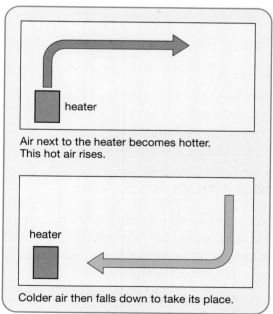

heater

Air next to the heater becomes hotter. This hot air rises.

heater

Colder air then falls down to take its place.

1 Thermal radiation

All objects give out energy as **thermal** radiation.
This energy travels as infra-red rays. You can't see
infra-red rays. You can feel infra-red rays from a hot
object when they raise the temperature of your skin.

1 Look at the diagrams. Then copy and complete the
following sentences.

All objects give out _____ radiation.
The _____ something is, the more
radiation it gives out.
If anything gets hot enough, it gives out
_____ rays as well as infra-red rays.

2 Why are the horse's eyes, nostrils and mouth the
brightest parts on the infra-red image?

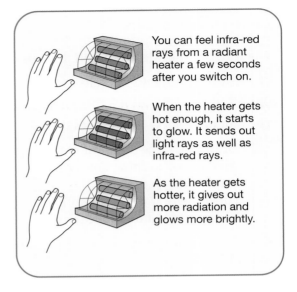

You can feel infra-red
rays from a radiant
heater a few seconds
after you switch on.

When the heater gets
hot enough, it starts
to glow. It sends out
light rays as well as
infra-red rays.

As the heater gets
hotter, it gives out
more radiation and
glows more brightly.

A wildlife photographer uses an infra-red camera
to film animals at night. An infra-red camera
shows that all objects give out infra-red rays.
Hotter objects give out more infra-red rays than
cooler ones. These appear brighter on the image.

Energy from the Sun

There is empty **space** between the Sun and us. Because
there is no substance to travel through, heat from the Sun
can't reach us by conduction or convection. Only radiation
can travel through empty space.

Some of the energy travels as light rays that we can see.
Some of the energy travels as infra-red rays that we can feel.

3 Energy can't be conducted or convected from the
Sun to Earth. Explain why not.

4 Write down another name for empty space.

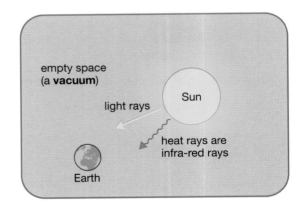

empty space
(a **vacuum**)

Sun

light rays

heat rays are
infra-red rays

Earth

How can you capture the energy in infra-red rays?

Dark, **matt** (dull) surfaces are good absorbers of infra-red rays. This means that they soak up infra-red radiation very well.

Light, **shiny** surfaces do not absorb infra-red rays very much. They are good at **reflecting** the rays away from themselves.

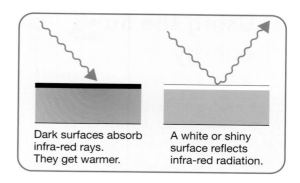

Dark surfaces absorb infra-red rays. They get warmer.

A white or shiny surface reflects infra-red radiation.

5   Look at the pictures below.
    Write a sentence to explain each one.

Dark clothes make you feel hot on a sunny day.

Astronauts wear shiny suits for space walks.

The tar on roads can melt in the summer sun.

Houses in hot countries are often white.

What makes a good radiator?

Dark, matt surfaces give out heat very well. We say that they are good emitters of infra-red rays. This means they give out infra-red rays very well.

Light, shiny surfaces don't give out as much radiation as dark surfaces at the same temperature. They are poor emitters of infra-red rays.

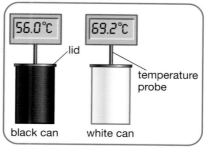

56.0°C   69.2°C   lid   temperature probe

black can   white can

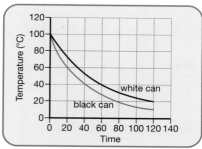

A student uses a temperature probe to record how fast hot water in two metal cans cools. One can is painted black, one white. Otherwise the cans are identical.

6   Look at the pictures. Which can cooled faster?

7   Explain the difference in the speeds at which the cans cooled.

What you need to remember *Copy and complete using the key words*

Thermal radiation

Infra-red rays can travel through empty _____.
Another name for empty space is a _____.
Heat radiation is also called _____ radiation.
A _____, _____ surface is good at absorbing and emitting infra-red radiation.
A _____, _____ surface is poor at absorbing and emitting infra-red radiation.
Light, shiny surfaces are good at _____ radiation.
The hotter something is, the more _____ energy it radiates.

2 Using the Sun's energy

Energy reaches the Earth from the Sun. We can make use of this energy if we trap it or concentrate it.

1 Describe <u>two</u> ways of concentrating the energy of sunlight.

2 How can we make use of this energy?

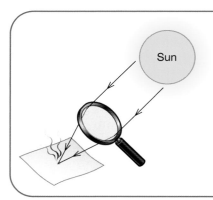

A lens <u>focuses</u> sunlight to a bright spot. The concentrated energy can set fire to paper.

Mirrors on this solar furnace <u>reflect</u> sunlight into a small space. It can reduce a temperature of 33 000 °C for scientific experiments.

How can we trap radiation from the Sun?

The diagram shows how a glass window can <u>trap</u> energy from the Sun inside a house.

3 Which kind of radiation can pass through glass – high temperature or low temperature?

4 Explain how a window traps the Sun's energy in a room.

5 Explain how this process can give us lower fuel bills.

infra-red radiation from very hot Sun

passes through glass

and is absorbed in room, making it warmer

low temperature radiation from room can't pass through glass

Solar cookers save lives

Refugees in some camps in Africa have no fuel wood. So they've been given solar cookers.
Their water is full of bacteria and must be heated above 65 °C for several minutes to make it safe.

The cooker is made from a curved card sheet.
The front surface of the card is painted silver or coated with metal foil. The card concentrates sunlight on a cooking pot at its centre. The pot is made from metal. Its outside surface is blackened.

6 Why is the concentrator painted silver or coated with shiny metal foil?

7 Why should the cooking pot be black, not white?

8 Would this be a good cooker in the UK? Give a reason for your answer.

9 What is the advantage of using a metal cooking pot rather than a clay one?

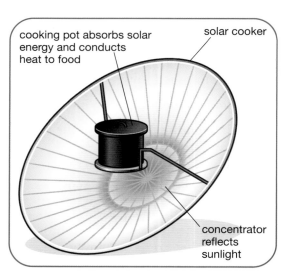

cooking pot absorbs solar energy and conducts heat to food

solar cooker

concentrator reflects sunlight

REMEMBER

Light, shiny surfaces are good reflectors and poor emitters.
Dark, matt surfaces are good absorbers and good emitters.

How does a solar panel work?

Some houses have solar panels on the roof.
These use energy radiated by the Sun to heat water.
The diagram shows how solar panels work.

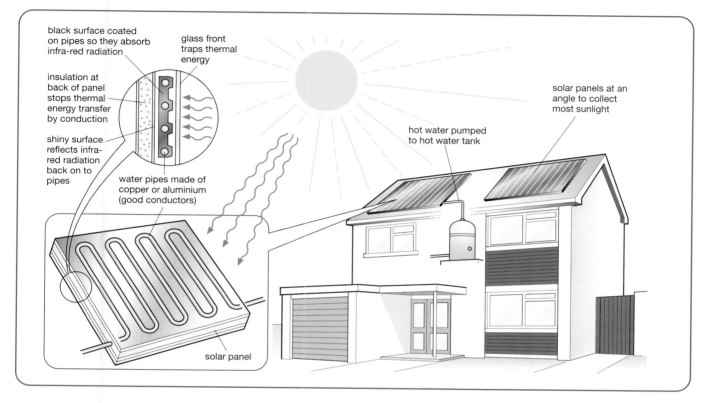

black surface coated on pipes so they absorb infra-red radiation

glass front traps thermal energy

insulation at back of panel stops thermal energy transfer by conduction

shiny surface reflects infra-red radiation back on to pipes

water pipes made of copper or aluminium (good conductors)

solar panels at an angle to collect most sunlight

hot water pumped to hot water tank

solar panel

10 Look at the diagram. Copy the series of boxes below.
Then fill in the missing words.

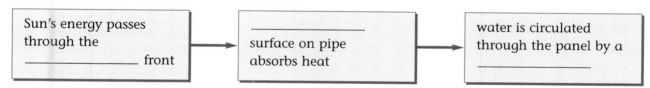

Sun's energy passes through the _____ front

→ _____ surface on pipe absorbs heat

→ water is circulated through the panel by a _____

11 Why is there a shiny surface behind the water pipes
in the solar panel?

12 Explain why there is a layer of insulation at the
back of the solar panel.

What you need to remember

Using the Sun's energy
There is nothing new for you to remember in this section.
You are using the ideas you have met earlier.
You will sometimes be asked questions like these in tests and examinations.

3 Explaining conduction, convection and radiation

Explaining conduction

If you put one end of a metal bar in a flame, heat moves from hot to cold – the far end of the bar soon gets hot too. Heat travels through the metal by **conduction**.

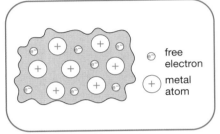

In metals, the electrons that carry electricity can carry heat too. This makes metals good heat conductors.

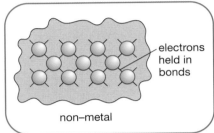

In non-metals such as plastic, wood and oil, all the electrons are held within atoms or molecules. They can't transfer energy, so these substances are poor conductors.

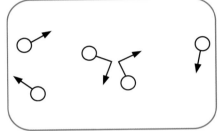

In gases, particles move about and collide with each other. But there are a lot fewer particles in each cm^3. So gases are poor thermal conductors.

Conduction is the movement of heat from **particle** to particle through a substance. Hot particles move faster than cold particles. They collide with their cooler neighbours and pass on energy.

> **1** How is heat transferred in conduction?
>
> **2** Why is metal a better conductor than plastic?
>
> **3** Explain why gases are poor thermal conductors.

Conduction happens in solids, liquids and gases.

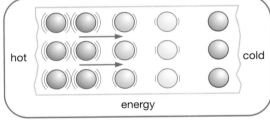

Particles with more energy pass on energy to neighbouring particles by colliding with them.

Explaining convection

Convection happens because **fluids** (liquids and gases) expand when they are warmer. The particles move about faster and take up more space. This means warm fluid is lighter than the same volume of cold fluid. A light fluid floats on top of a heavier one, so hot fluid will float upwards through cold fluid.

> **4** How is heat transferred by convection?
>
> **5** Why doesn't convection happen in solids?
>
> **6** Where is the best place to put the heating element in a kettle – at the top or at the bottom? Explain your answer.

Convection happens in fluids (liquids and gases). Hot water rises and cooler water sinks to take its place. This flow is called a convection current. The convection current carries heat from place to place.

Explaining radiation

Matter is made of particles. Some of the particles have a charge. Heat makes the particles jiggle about. When **charged** particles move like this, they give out electromagnetic **radiation**. The hotter something is, the faster its particles move and the more radiation it emits.

Electromagnetic radiation travels as **waves** through empty space. The radiation from a hot object is absorbed by the charged particles in any object it falls on. In this way, heat is transferred.

A hot mug emits thermal radiation that you can feel with your skin.

A very hot lamp filament emits light as well as thermal radiation.

7 Why is no medium (substance) required for heat transfer by radiation?

8 What kind of particles give out and absorb electromagnetic waves?

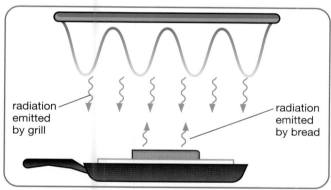

radiation emitted by grill

radiation emitted by bread

A red-hot grill and a slice of bread both emit and absorb radiation. But the grill emits more radiation than the bread. More heat transfers from the grill to the bread than from the bread to the grill, so the bread heats up.

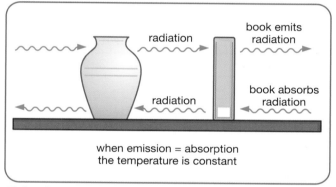

radiation

book emits radiation

radiation

book absorbs radiation

when emission = absorption the temperature is constant

All the objects in this room are at the same temperature. They all emit and absorb infra-red radiation at the same rate. This means there is no overall transfer of energy between them.

9 If all the objects in a room are giving out electromagnetic radiation, why do they stay at the same temperature?

What you need to remember *Copy and complete using the* **key words**

Explaining conduction, convection and radiation

_____ is the transfer of heat from particle to _____ through a material.

_____ is the transfer of heat in _____ by the movement of the particles in a convection current.

_____ is the transfer of heat by electromagnetic _____.

No substance is required between the objects that emit and absorb the radiation. Radiation is emitted and absorbed by _____ particles.

4 What factors affect heat transfer?

Choosing a table mat

A table mat protects a wooden table by reducing conduction from a hot pan to the table surface.

1 How do the **dimensions** of the mat affect the rate of heat transfer?

2 How does the **material** of the mat affect the rate of heat transfer?

Different materials transfer heat at different rates. We say that a good conductor like copper has a high **conductivity**. An insulator such as cork has a low conductivity.

Material	How many times better the material conducts heat than air
copper	20 000
glass	60
polythene	20
cork	6
air	1

The conductivity of different materials compared with air.

3 Which material is the better insulator – cork or polythene?

4 Suggest how you could you make a glass table mat as effective as a 3 mm cork table mat.

Why do elephants have big ears?

Elephants' large bodies produce a great deal of waste heat. They must have an effective way of getting rid of this heat.

5 Explain how the shape of the elephant's ears helps it get rid of waste heat.

6 In what shape container does a hot liquid cool more rapidly?

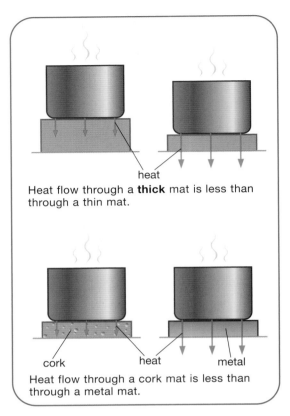

heat

Heat flow through a **thick** mat is less than through a thin mat.

cork   heat   metal

Heat flow through a cork mat is less than through a metal mat.

The elephant's ears are well supplied with blood vessels. Their flat shape provides a **large surface area** through which heat can escape.

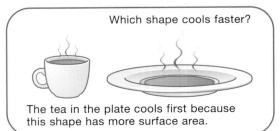

Which shape cools faster?

The tea in the plate cools first because this shape has more surface area.

Temperature difference

A hotplate gives out more heat each second when its temperature is high.

Heat transfers from hot to cold at a higher rate if the **temperature difference** is large.

7 Why must you increase the power supplied to a hotplate to increase its temperature?

8 What are the temperature differences between the room and the insides of the refrigerator and the freezer?

9 Explain why a freezer must be better insulated than a refrigerator.

A hotplate on a cooker heats up until the rate it gives out heat exactly balances the electrical power supplied.

When the plate is hotter, it loses heat to the surroundings more rapidly – so more power is needed.

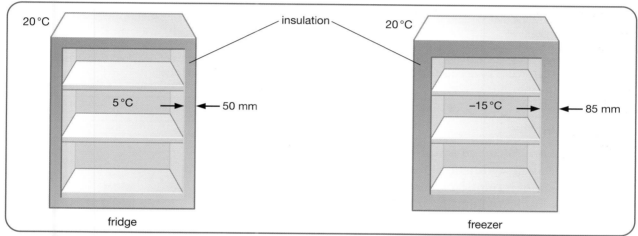

fridge

freezer

The temperature difference between the inside and the outside is bigger for a freezer than a fridge. The rate of heat flow into the freezer will be bigger. So it will use more power, unless it is provided with better insulation.

What you need to remember *Copy and complete using the **key words***

What factors affect heat transfer?

The rate of heat transfer through a material or to and from an object is affected by different factors. These include

- the _____ and shape of an object
- the kind of _____
- the _____ _____ between an object and its surroundings.

A good conductor has a higher _____ than a poor conductor.

A _____ _____ area transfers heat more quickly than a smaller one.

A thin sample transfers heat more quickly than a _____ one.

The higher the temperature difference, the greater the rate of heat transfer.

5 Keeping warm outdoors

Choosing a sleeping bag

You need a good sleeping bag and an insulating sleeping mat to keep warm when camping. The bag and the mat reduce heat transfer from your body to the surroundings.

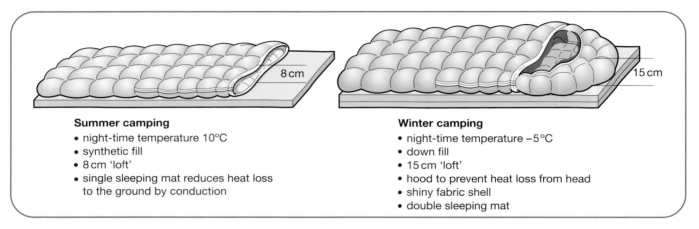

Summer camping
- night-time temperature 10°C
- synthetic fill
- 8 cm 'loft'
- single sleeping mat reduces heat loss to the ground by conduction

Winter camping
- night-time temperature −5°C
- down fill
- 15 cm 'loft'
- hood to prevent heat loss from head
- shiny fabric shell
- double sleeping mat

1 Explain why

a a down-filled bag is warmer than a similar bag filled with synthetic fibres

b 15 cm of insulation is more effective than 8 cm

c the inside and outside shells of the winter bag are made from shiny fabric

d a double sleeping mat is needed at −5 °C.

2 Which is the better filling to choose for a sleeping bag in wet conditions? Give a reason for your answer.

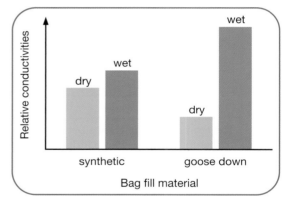

A hot drink

You can keep a drink hot all day in a vacuum flask. Its design prevents heat loss by conduction, convection and radiation.

3 Why is the flask made with a vacuum space between the glass walls?

4 Why are the inside and outside walls silvered?

5 How is heat loss from the liquid surface reduced?

6 Explain why heat cannot pass through a vacuum by conduction and convection.

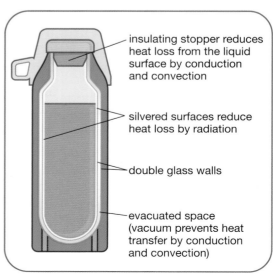

insulating stopper reduces heat loss from the liquid surface by conduction and convection

silvered surfaces reduce heat loss by radiation

double glass walls

evacuated space (vacuum prevents heat transfer by conduction and convection)

Keeping warm at the end of a race

In a marathon race, runners' bodies produce a lot of heat. They wear light clothes and sweat. This keeps them cool.

When they stop running, the combination of light clothes and wet skin means that they lose heat rapidly. There is a risk of hypothermia (dangerously low body temperature).

To prevent hypothermia, officials wrap the runners in space blankets as they finish.

7   Why is the space blanket silvered?

8   How does the space blanket reduce heat loss by convection?

9   How does it reduce heat loss by conduction?

10   Why is a space blanket more effective than a black bin liner?

11   Some athletes curl into a ball beneath their space blankets. How does this change their outer surface area? What effect does this have on their rate of heat loss?

When a liquid evaporates, it carries away heat. You can feel the cooling effect when perfume evaporates from your skin. The evaporation of sweat cools the body in the same way.

The silvered inner surface of the blanket reflects radiation back to the runner's body. The silvered outer surface reduces heat loss by radiation. Wrapping the blanket around the body creates a barrier to reduced heat loss by convection. It also traps an insulating layer of air to reduce heat loss by conduction.

What you need to remember

Keeping warm outdoors

There is nothing new for you to <u>remember</u> in this section.
You are using the ideas you met earlier.
You will sometimes be asked questions like these in tests and examinations.

6 Reducing heat loss from buildings

We're being robbed of our joules!

All buildings lose heat in various ways.

This costs money and wastes fuel.

1 Look at the diagram. Then, copy and complete the table. (A joule (J) is a unit of energy.)

Part of house	Heat lost each second (J)
ceiling	
window glass	
floor	
draughts	
walls	

2 Copy and complete the sentences.

Heat moves through walls by _____.
Draughts are caused by _____

_____.
Heat moves up to ceilings by convection and then moves through ceilings by _____.
Heat moves through window glass by _____ and through the floor by conduction. The biggest loss of heat is through the

_____.

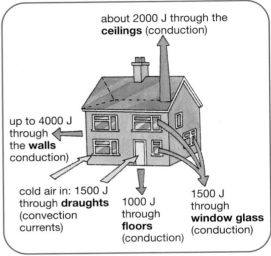

about 2000 J through the **ceilings** (conduction)

up to 4000 J through the **walls** (conduction)

cold air in: 1500 J through **draughts** (convection currents)

1000 J through **floors** (conduction)

1500 J through **window glass** (conduction)

Lots of thermal energy is lost each second from a badly insulated house on a cold day.

An energy-saving idea

The heat from the back of a radiator is transferred to the wall by radiation. The heat then moves through the wall by conduction. The diagram shows how to reduce this heat loss.

3 Copy and complete the sentences.

The shiny surface behind the radiator will _____ the infra-red rays back into the room. Plastic foam in wall cavities prevents heat loss by _____ without increasing heat loss by _____.

The most **effective** method is the one that reduces heat loss by the biggest percentage (%).

4 Which method of reducing the heat loss through the wall is the most effective?

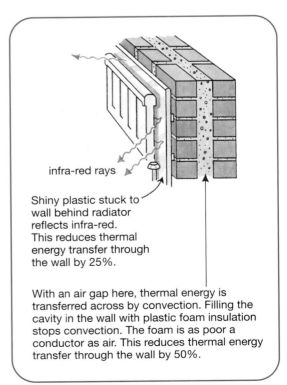

infra-red rays

Shiny plastic stuck to wall behind radiator reflects infra-red. This reduces thermal energy transfer through the wall by 25%.

With an air gap here, thermal energy is transferred across by convection. Filling the cavity in the wall with plastic foam insulation stops convection. The foam is as poor a conductor as air. This reduces thermal energy transfer through the wall by 50%.

There are several ways to reduce thermal energy loss through a wall.

More ways of reducing energy loss

5 Suppose that all the energy-saving ideas on these pages are used in the house shown at the top of page 224.

 a Draw a picture of the house and label the heat losses now that it is insulated.

 b What is the total thermal energy loss for the insulated house?

 c How does this compare with the uninsulated house?

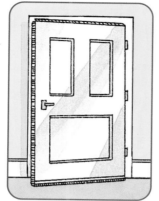

Draught excluders (strips) around doors and windows can save half of the heat lost through draughts.

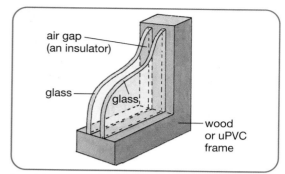

Double glazing can save about half of the thermal energy lost through windows.

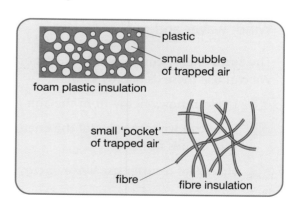

Insulating the loft with glass fibre 20 cm thick can save half of the thermal energy lost through the ceiling.

Why do foam and fibres make good insulators?

Air, like all gases, is a very poor **conductor**. But to use it as an insulator, we must stop it moving about.

Look at the diagrams of foam and fibre **insulation**.

6 Describe how the air is stopped from moving about in the foam and the fibre insulation.

7 Why is it important to stop the air moving about?

foam plastic insulation

small 'pocket' of trapped air

fibre   fibre insulation

What you need to remember *Copy and complete using the **key words***

Reducing heat loss from buildings

Heat can be lost from buildings by conduction through the _____, _____, _____ and _____ _____.

It is also lost by convection because of _____.

You can save heat by _____ the loft, fitting draught excluders, putting in cavity wall insulation and _____ _____.

Some methods reduce the amount of heat loss by a bigger percentage (%) than others. So we say that they are more _____.

Materials that are used for _____ often contain air. This air is trapped so it can't move about. A gas, such as air, is a very poor _____.

Ideas you need from KS3

All kinds of energy

We need energy to make things happen. When a lamp lights, a kettle boils, a plant grows or a band plays, there must be energy. Energy comes from different <u>sources</u>.

The Sun gives us energy

Most of the energy we use comes from the Sun.
Its heat and light reach us every day.

1 How do plants trap the energy of sunlight?

2 How can animals use this energy?

3 Copy and complete the sentences.

Coal, gas and oil are _____ fuels.
These fuels contain energy that was stored in the
bodies of _____ and _____
millions of years ago.

Wind, waves and rain

The Sun's energy causes winds, waves and rain.
We can use these as energy sources.

4 Explain how energy from the Sun produces wind.

5 How can we trap some of the energy that makes rain clouds form?

6 How does a surfer use wave energy?

No Sun needed

Some energy sources don't need the Sun.

7 Copy and complete the sentences.

We can use the radioactive substance
_____ as a nuclear fuel.
Energy taken from hot rocks is called
_____ energy.
The pull of the Moon's _____ is the
main cause of the tides.

Plants trap the energy of sunlight with their green leaves. Animals obtain this energy by eating plants.

Coal, oil and gas formed from the remains of dead plants and animals that were buried millions of years ago.

Energy from the Sun heats the ground. Hot air rises. Cool air takes its place. This is wind.

The sun evaporates water from the sea. Clouds form over high ground.

Water trapped behind a dam stores energy.

Wind causes waves. A surfer uses wave energy to produce motion.

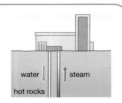

Radioactive substances keep the Earth hot. We can use uranium as a nuclear fuel.

A geothermal power plant uses hot rocks to make steam.

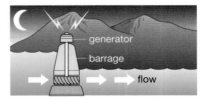

The tides are due mainly to the Moon's gravity. We can use them as an energy source.

Putting energy to work

When we use energy, we transfer it into different <u>forms</u>.
We use different machines and devices to do this.

8   Copy and complete the table.

Machine/device	Main form of energy produced
generator	
engine	
loudspeaker	
cooker	
LED	

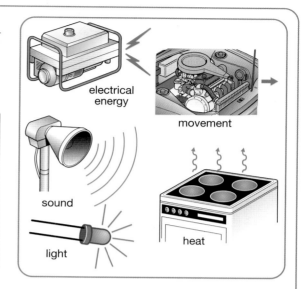

electrical energy

movement

sound

light

heat

Storing energy

Fuels store energy as <u>chemical energy</u>. We transfer this chemical energy into heat when we burn the fuel.

We can store energy in other forms too.

9   Copy and complete the sentences.

The water trapped behind a dam has _____ potential energy.

A squashed spring has _____ potential energy.

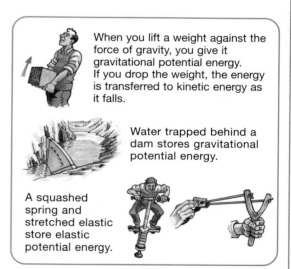

When you lift a weight against the force of gravity, you give it gravitational potential energy.
If you drop the weight, the energy is transferred to kinetic energy as it falls.

Water trapped behind a dam stores gravitational potential energy.

A squashed spring and stretched elastic store elastic potential energy.

Can we store electricity?

Electricity is a very useful form of energy, but we can't store it. When we need electricity, we must transfer another form of energy into electricity as we use it.

10   In what form does a battery store energy?

11   Name <u>two</u> forms of energy we can use to power a generator.

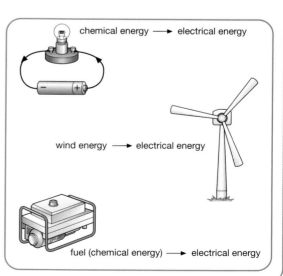

chemical energy ⟶ electrical energy

wind energy ⟶ electrical energy

fuel (chemical energy) ⟶ electrical energy

1 Does energy get used up?

When you 'use' energy, the energy does not get used up. It gets transferred into other forms. Some of it gets transferred into the form you want. For example a radio transfers electrical energy into sound.

1 Copy the crossword shape (use a piece of graph paper). Then read the clues and complete the crossword.

ACROSS
1 The form of energy you transfer to a bicycle when you pedal.
2 The form of energy you want from a battery.

DOWN
3 The main form of energy you want from a CD player.
4 The main form of energy you want from a torch.
5 The main form of energy you want from an electric fire.

2 Copy and complete this flow chart of the energy transfers in a model steam engine.

| chemical energy in fuel | → | | → | |

You don't always get just what you want

When you transfer energy, you don't get only the form of energy you want.

Usually, other energy transfers also happen.

3 Look at the TV in the picture.
Copy the table and complete it.

Energy put in	Useful forms of energy given out	Other forms of energy given out (waste energy)
_____	_____ and _____	_____

4 The TV is designed to let the waste energy get out easily. How is this done?

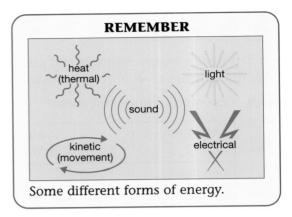

REMEMBER

Some different forms of energy.

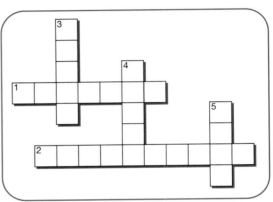

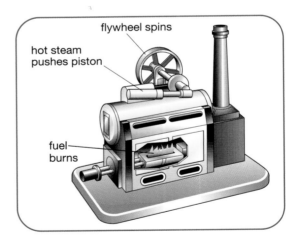

flywheel spins
hot steam pushes piston
fuel burns

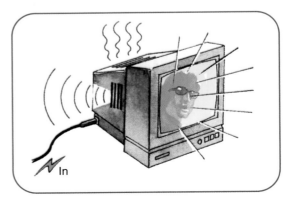

In

What happens to the energy we use?

Energy cannot be **destroyed**. It can only be transferred to other forms. When you watch television, the energy from it transfers to everything in the room, including your body. This energy makes everything a little bit warmer. All the energy ends up as thermal energy and spreads out.

5   Where does the kinetic energy of a car transfer to as it brakes?

6   What happens to all the light and sound energy at a show?

The car's kinetic energy is transferred to thermal energy in the brakes as it slows down.

Why can't we reuse energy?

When energy has spread out as thermal energy, it's almost impossible to **reuse** it. So, although energy can't be destroyed, it becomes less useful.

The sound and light energy of a show finally **spread out** as thermal energy. They make the theatre a little bit warmer.

Why do we always need an energy source?

Energy cannot be **created**. So we always need an energy **source** to supply the energy we need.

7   Why can't we reuse energy?

8   Why do we always need an energy source to supply energy?

9   How do we use gas as an energy source in our homes?

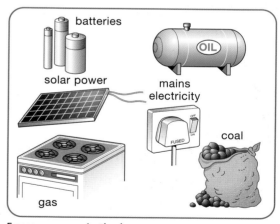

Energy sources in the home.

What you need to remember *Copy and complete using the* **key words**

Does energy get used up?

Energy can't be _____ or _____. It can only be transferred into other forms.

All the energy we use will finally _____ _____ as thermal energy.

We cannot _____ this energy and so we need an energy _____ to supply the energy we need.

2 How is energy wasted?

When we use energy, only part of it is transferred to useful forms. The rest is **wasted**.

Friction wastes energy

The moving parts of machines waste energy because of **friction**. The moving parts rub together and produce a lot of thermal energy and some sound.

1 Copy the diagrams of the bicycle and the skateboard. Mark with an X the places where friction between moving parts can waste energy.

2 How can we reduce the wasteful energy transfers on the bicycle and the skateboard?

lubrication reduces friction

Poor insulation wastes energy

A hot water tank wastes energy if it is not insulated. Thermal energy escapes through the tank walls, mainly by conduction. We need to supply more energy to keep the water hot if the tank is poorly insulated. We can improve the **insulation** with a tank jacket.

3 What is the daily saving made by fitting a jacket to the hot water tank?

4 What will the annual saving be?

5 Is the annual saving more or less than the cost of the jacket?

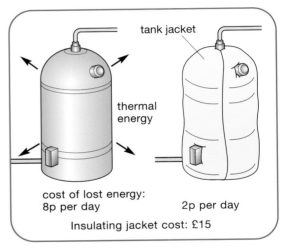

cost of lost energy:
8p per day   2p per day

Insulating jacket cost: £15

Poor design wastes energy

Modern kettles are designed to waste less energy than older models. The best design transfers the most thermal energy to the water. We say that this **design** is most **efficient**.

6 How does the material used for the older design waste energy?

7 Why is the shape of the new design more efficient?

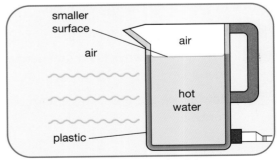

Plastic has a low thermal conductivity.
The smaller surface area reduces heat loss.

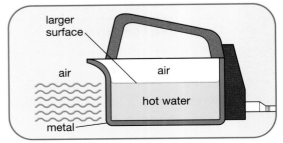

Metal has a high thermal conductivity.

Heating food efficiently

An efficient oven transfers as much energy as possible to food.

8 Look at the diagrams of the microwave oven and the ordinary electric oven.
Then copy and complete the sentences.

The microwave oven transfers electrical energy as radiation that heats the food. It also transfers some energy as _____, _____ and _____. But it does not waste much energy because only the _____ gets heated up.

The electric oven transfers electrical energy only as _____ energy. But lots of thermal energy gets lost by being _____, _____ and _____ through the sides and top.

So the microwave oven is more _____ than the ordinary electric oven.

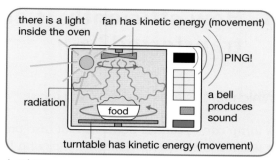
A microwave oven.

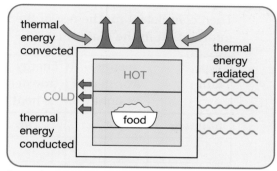
An ordinary electric oven.

Using lamps effectively

A light bulb isn't very efficient (see page 232) but we can still use a light bulb <u>effectively</u>. An effective lamp sends light to where we want it.

9 Look at the picture.
Which is the most effective way of using a light bulb

a for reading?
b for lighting the whole room?

Give reasons for your answers.

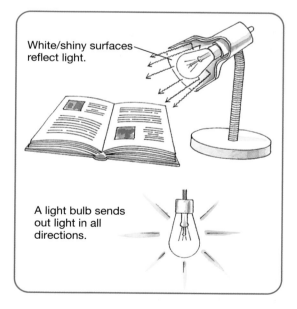

What you need to remember *Copy and complete using the **key words***

How is energy wasted?

Energy can be wasted by _____, poor insulation and poor _____.
We try to transfer energy in the most _____ way.
Any energy that is not transferred usefully is _____.

3 How efficiently is energy transferred?

REMEMBER

'Per cent' (%) means 'out of 100'.

Which lamps are most efficient?

A lamp can't produce light without also producing heat.
It **wastes** some energy. The efficiency of a lamp is the
fraction (or percentage) of energy that is transferred as light.

1 Copy the table.
Then complete it for the rest of the lamps, using the
information in the diagrams.

Type of lamp	Energy transferred as light (%)	Energy transferred as heat (%)	Efficiency (%)
filament	4	96	4

2 Write down the <u>three</u> types of lamp in order, starting
with the most efficient and ending with the least
efficient.

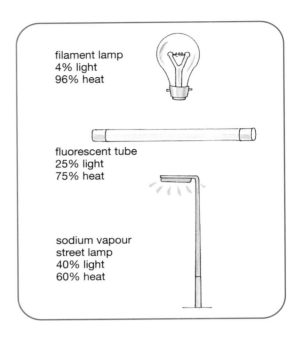

filament lamp
4% light
96% heat

fluorescent tube
25% light
75% heat

sodium vapour
street lamp
40% light
60% heat

What do you want from an engine?

You use an engine to do some sort of job for you. So you
want it to use most of its energy for that job. The less
energy the engine wastes, the more **efficient** it is.

Look at the engines in the diagrams.

3 Which engine is the most efficient?

4 What <u>two</u> sorts of 'waste' energy do all the engines
produce?

5 Railways changed from steam engines to diesel
engines and then to electric trains.
Why did this happen?

6 Imagine that you used 100 litres of petrol on a long
car journey.
How many litres would be doing useful work?

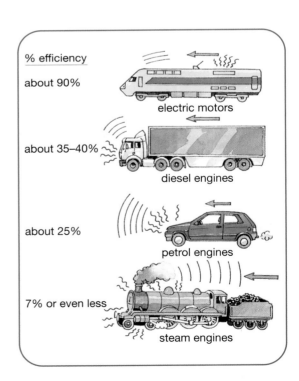

% efficiency

about 90%
electric motors

about 35–40%
diesel engines

about 25%
petrol engines

7% or even less
steam engines

How do we calculate efficiency?

The efficiency of a lamp or an engine is the fraction of the energy that is transferred as the form you want.

So:

$$\text{efficiency} = \frac{\text{useful energy out}}{\text{energy in}}$$

Suppose you get 1 joule of light out of the lamp for every 10 joules of electricity you put in. We can calculate the efficiency of the lamp like this:

$$\text{efficiency} = \frac{\text{useful energy out}}{\text{energy in}} = \frac{1}{10} = 0.1$$

The lamp transfers one-tenth of the energy into useful energy, so its efficiency is 0.1 or 10%.

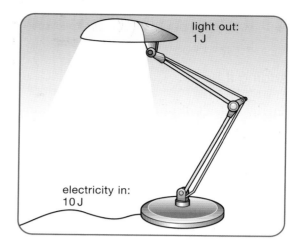

light out: 1 J

electricity in: 10 J

 7 Look at the diagrams of the different devices. Then copy and complete the table.

Device	Energy in	Useful energy out	Efficiency
electric motor			
petrol engine			
electric kettle			
fluorescent lamp			

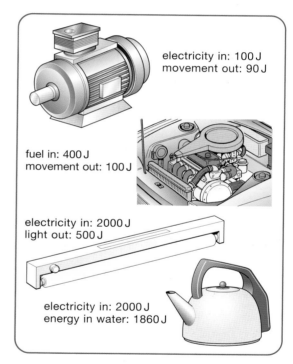

electricity in: 100 J
movement out: 90 J

fuel in: 400 J
movement out: 100 J

electricity in: 2000 J
light out: 500 J

electricity in: 2000 J
energy in water: 1860 J

What you need to remember *Copy and complete using the **key words***

How efficiently is energy transferred?

If a device is 100% _____ then it transfers all the energy it uses to useful energy.
A real device always _____ some energy.

You can work out the efficiency of a device with the formula $\text{efficiency} = \dfrac{\text{useful energy out}}{\text{energy in}}$

You need to be able to calculate the efficiency of a device, just like you have done on this page.

4 Keeping track of energy

Adding it up

Energy doesn't disappear, it just gets changed from one type of energy to another.

No energy gets lost – the total amount of energy you end up with is always **exactly** the same as the amount you started with.

1 Copy and complete the sentences.

The energy put into the television set is _____ % electricity.
The useful energy transferred is 40% as _____ and 10% as _____.
There is _____ % wasted as thermal energy.

The arrows on the diagram show how the television set transfers energy. The thickness of each arrow shows how much energy is transferred in that particular way.

The **wasted** and **useful** energy always add up to 100%.

2 Copy and complete the energy transfer diagrams below.

a filament lamp

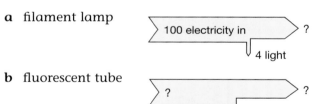

b fluorescent tube

Everything ends up as thermal energy

All the energy we use finally ends up as **thermal energy** that spreads out (see page 229). This makes everything in the surroundings a little bit **warmer**.

3 What has happened to the sound and light energy from a television set after you have seen and heard a programme?

4 Draw a diagram like the one opposite for a filament lamp. (Use a piece of squared paper.)

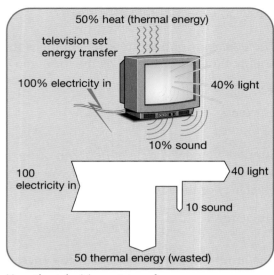

How the television set transfers energy.

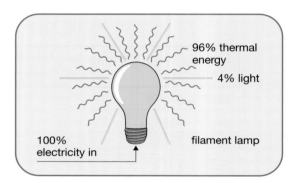

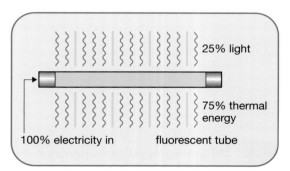

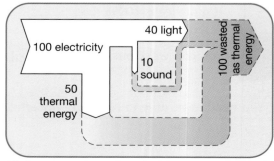

All the energy from the television set gets spread out and wasted as heat in the end.

5 Copy and complete the table of energy transfers. Don't forget that the wasted and useful energy add up to 100%.

Machine	Energy in (J)	Transferred energy (J)		
		Thermal energy	Movement	Sound
electric motor	100	5	90	
diesel engine	100			
petrol engine	100		25	10
steam engine	100	73	7	

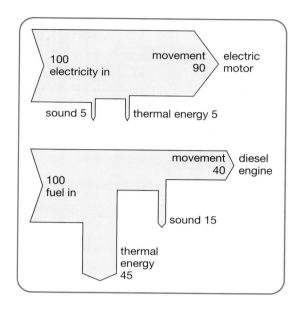

6 Draw a diagram like the ones opposite showing the energy transfers for the petrol engine. (Use a piece of squared paper.)

7 Which produces more waste thermal energy, a petrol engine or a diesel engine?

Can you use wasted energy for anything?

Sometimes you can make use of 'wasted' energy. Look at the diagram.

8 How can you use the wasted thermal energy from a car engine?

If a building is well insulated, the waste thermal energy from television sets, lamps, cookers and freezers can also help to keep it warm.

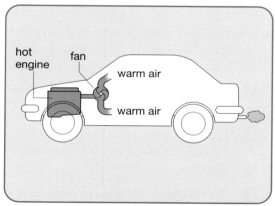

You can use waste thermal energy from a car engine to heat the inside of the car.

What you need to remember *Copy and complete using the key words*

Keeping track of energy

Some of the energy you put into a device will be transferred in a _____ way but some of it will be _____.

The useful energy plus the wasted energy always adds up _____ to the energy you put in.

All the energy eventually ends up as _____ _____, which makes everything a bit _____.

5 Making better use of energy

Why should we use less energy?

Most of our energy comes from the fossil fuels coal, oil and gas. These fuels are burnt to heat homes, power cars and produce electricity in power stations.

Many people think we should **conserve** (save) energy. Then we will burn less fuel.
Look at the pictures.

1 Give <u>two</u> reasons why using more fossil fuels may create problems for the future.

2 How does using less energy benefit householders today?

3 How much could an average household save by using 25% (one-quarter) less energy?

Six tonnes of carbon dioxide are produced to supply the energy for just one house for a year. That's like burning six large trees.

Fossil fuels will not last for ever. At present rates of use they will be gone in 50–200 years.

Fossil fuels release carbon dioxide into the atmosphere. This gas traps more of the Sun's heat. Increased fuel use may be linked to global warming. Sea levels will rise as the polar ice caps melt.

Efficient appliances

One way to save energy is to buy energy-**efficient** appliances. The energy label on a new appliance shows how efficient it is compared with similar appliances.

4 Which brand of fridge–freezer is more efficient (uses less energy)?

5 If 1 kW h (see page 245) of electrical energy costs 10p, how much does it cost to run each appliance for 1 year?

6 The Coldstar F1 is more expensive to start with but, if you run the appliances for 3 years, which brand is more expensive overall?

An average household spends £600 on energy each year.

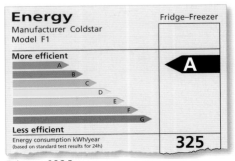

Energy   Fridge–Freezer
Manufacturer Coldstar
Model F1

More efficient

A

B

C

D

E

F

G

A

Less efficient
Energy consumption kWh/year
(based on standard test results for 24h)

325

Price = £235.

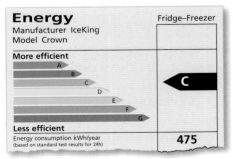

Energy   Fridge–Freezer
Manufacturer IceKing
Model Crown

More efficient

A

B

C

D

E

F

G

C

Less efficient
Energy consumption kWh/year
(based on standard test results for 24h)

475

Price = £199.

Switch it off

A set top box left on standby all the time wastes more than 80% of the energy it uses. A light left on in an empty room wastes energy. So do computers, televisions and DVD players left on standby.

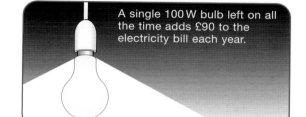

7 A room lit by a 100 W bulb is occupied for 12 hours each day.
What is the annual saving if the light is always switched off when the room is empty?

Electrical appliances should be turned off when not in use.

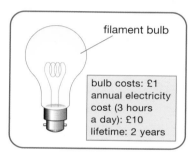

A single 100 W bulb left on all the time adds £90 to the electricity bill each year.

Change those bulbs

Energy-efficient light bulbs use about one-third of the energy of filament bulbs. But they are much more expensive to buy. This puts some people off changing.

8 Copy and complete this table.

Bulb type	Bulb cost (£)	Lifetime (years)	Number of bulbs used in 10 years	Annual electricity cost (£)	Total cost for 10 years (£)
filament	1	2	5	10	105
energy-efficient					

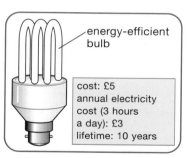

filament bulb

bulb costs: £1
annual electricity cost (3 hours a day): £10
lifetime: 2 years

energy-efficient bulb

cost: £5
annual electricity cost (3 hours a day): £3
lifetime: 10 years

An energy-efficient bulb is more expensive to start with but it costs less to run and lasts longer.
This means that overall it saves money. We say that replacing filament bulbs with energy-efficient bulbs is **cost-effective**.

What you need to remember *Copy and complete using the key words*

Making better use of energy
If we _____ energy, we both save money and protect the environment.
An energy-_____ appliance may be more expensive to buy, but it is cheaper to run.
If the overall cost is less, the purchase is _____.

6 How soon will it pay for itself?

> **REMEMBER**
>
> We can reduce the rate of thermal energy loss from buildings in many ways, including double glazing, loft insulation, cavity wall insulation and draught-proofing.
>
> The most effective method reduces the energy loss by the biggest percentage.

We can do lots of things to buildings to reduce thermal energy transfer. But before we spend money on things like double glazing or loft insulation, we need to know how much money this will save on heating bills.

It's useful to know how long it will take for the improvement to pay for itself.

This is called the **pay-back time**.

The shorter the pay-back time, the more **cost-effective** the improvement is.

1 **a** Some ways of reducing thermal energy transfer are more cost-effective than others. Explain, as fully as you can, what this means.

b Calculate the pay-back time for each of the three energy-saving ideas below.

c Write down the energy-saving ideas in the four pictures on this page in order, starting with the most cost-effective.

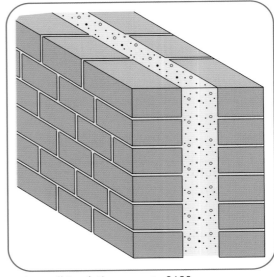

cavity wall insulation: costs £450
saves £75 per year

pay-back time = £450 ÷ £75 / year
= 6 years

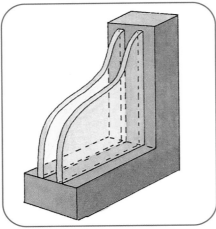

double glazing: costs £1200
saves £60 per year

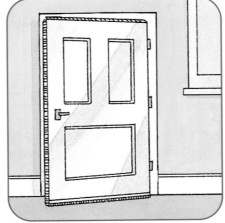

draught excluders: costs £25
saves £50 per year

loft insulation: costs £150
saves £150 per year

60 years ago, most people in the UK heated their homes using coal fires. Now, most people use gas fires or gas central heating.

2 **a** Look at the diagrams.
Then copy and complete the following.
cost of installing gas fire = _____
annual saving in fuel = _____
pay-back time = _____ ÷ _____ = _____

b How cost-effective is installing the gas fire compared with methods of reducing thermal energy transfer from a house?

c Write down <u>two</u> other advantages of gas fires over coal fires.

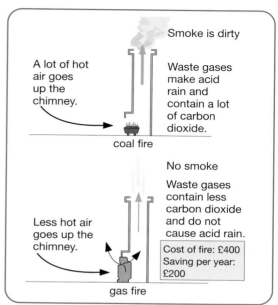

coal fire

Smoke is dirty

A lot of hot air goes up the chimney.

Waste gases make acid rain and contain a lot of carbon dioxide.

No smoke

Less hot air goes up the chimney.

Waste gases contain less carbon dioxide and do not cause acid rain.

Cost of fire: £400
Saving per year: £200

gas fire

It is easy to control the thermal energy output of a gas fire. It is also very easy to turn it on or off.

Old gas boilers are more expensive to run than modern energy-efficient boilers. Energy is also wasted if water is heated to a higher temperature than is needed. Fitting a condensing boiler and modern temperature controls can save up to 40% on heating bills.

3 **a** What feature of a condensing boiler makes it more efficient?

b Describe how it works.

4 How do temperature controls save energy?

5 What are the maximum and minimum pay-back times for installing an energy-efficient boiler?

6 A grant of £250 is available for installing an energy-efficient boiler.
How does this affect the pay-back time?

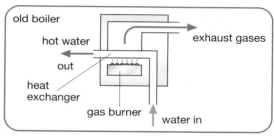

old boiler

hot water out

exhaust gases

heat exchanger

gas burner

water in

Thermal energy is transferred from the gas flames to water in the heat exchanger. A lot of thermal energy is wasted in the hot exhaust gases.

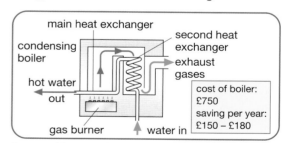

main heat exchanger

second heat exchanger

condensing boiler

exhaust gases

hot water out

gas burner

water in

cost of boiler: £750
saving per year: £150 – £180

A second heat exchanger transfers heat from the exhaust gases into the water. The gases cool until the water vapour in them condenses, giving up even more heat.

What you need to remember *Copy and complete using the key words*

How soon will it pay for itself?

The time taken for an energy-saving method to pay for itself is called the _____ .

The shorter this time is, the more _____ the method of saving energy is.

7 Review your energy efficiency

Saving energy saves money. It also helps the environment by reducing CO_2 emissions. If we don't reduce CO_2 emissions, global warming may lead to climate change.

A home energy survey

A home owner fills in an energy survey for her home.

1 Does the home owner have double glazing?

2 What is the pay-back time for draught-proofing her house?

3 Calculate the total amount the home owner could save each year by doing everything she can to improve energy efficiency.
How much will this cost?

Making decisions

The home owner cannot afford all the improvements she could make in one year. To help her decide what to do, she plots the survey data on three bar charts.

4 Which single improvement would save her the most on her energy bill?

5 Which are the <u>three</u> most cost-effective improvements she could make? Explain why.

6 The home owner decides she can only afford to spend £75 on energy-efficiency measures this year. How would you recommend she spends the money? Explain your answer.

Energy efficiency survey form

Measure	Already installed?	Annual saving if installed in future (£)	Cost (£)	Pay-back time (years)
Insulation				
cavity wall	✗	75	450	6
loft	✓	–	–	–
hot water tank	✗	20	15	0.75
double glazing	✓	–	–	–
draught-proofing	✗	50	25	0.5
Heating (ignore if not gas or oil central heating)				
condensing boiler and temperature controls	✗	150	750	5
Lighting				
energy-efficient bulbs in every room	✗	70	50	0.71
	TOTALS			

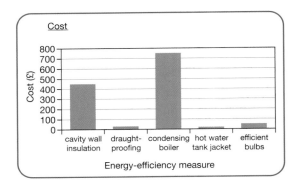

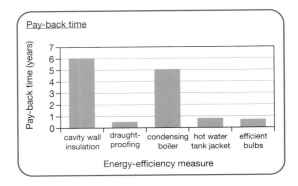

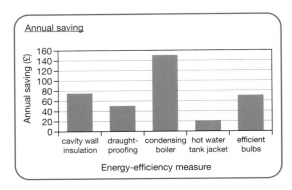

How energy efficient is your home?

Look at the table. It gives costs and savings for different energy-efficiency measures.

7 Check the energy efficiency of your home. You may need to ask a parent or carer for information. Do you have cavity wall insulation? What type of boiler do you have?

8 Use the data in the table to plot bar charts of the costs, savings and pay-back times for the energy-efficiency measures you could take.

9 For your home, suggest how you could save energy costs by spending

   a £100

   b £500

   c £2000.

	Annual saving (£)	Cost (£)
cavity wall insulation	75	450
loft insulation	150	150
double glazing	60	1200
draught-proofing	50	25
condensing boiler and temperature controls	150	750
hot water tank jacket	20	15
energy-efficient bulbs in every room	70	50

Energy efficiency – costs and savings.

Do you waste energy?

As well as insulating our homes and buying efficient appliances, we can save energy by using it with care.

10 Heating the water for a bath uses a lot of energy. How many times could you shower with the same energy?

11 You feel warm when you are watching TV. Should you take off your jumper or turn down the heating? Explain.

12 Copy and complete the checklist.

Do you ...	Yes	No
leave lights on when you leave the room?		
leave the TV and VCR on standby?		
fill the kettle to the top to make one cup of coffee?		
take a bath rather than a shower?		
make short journeys by car rather than walk or cycle?		

If you tick yes, then you are wasting energy!

Taking a shower uses only one-third as much hot water as a bath.

A thermostat controls the room temperature by switching the heating system on and off. Reducing the room temperature by just 1 °C can save up to 10% on heating bills.

What you need to remember

Review your energy efficiency

There is nothing new for you to <u>remember</u> in this section.

You are using the ideas you have met earlier.

You will sometimes be asked questions like these in tests and examinations.

1 Making use of electricity

Switched on to electricity

Electricity is a form of **energy**. This means you can make it work for you.

1 Look at the electrical appliances shown in the diagrams.
Copy the table below and fill it in.

Electrical appliance	What we use it for
	to play CDs
	to cook meals
	to read by
	to whip cream

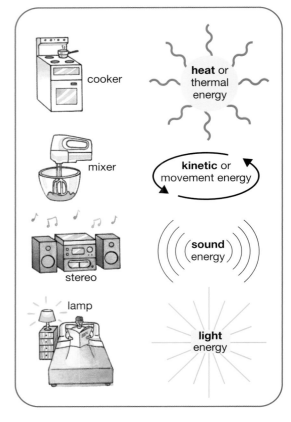

cooker

heat or thermal energy

mixer

kinetic or movement energy

stereo

sound energy

lamp

light energy

Why is electricity so useful?

We use electricity a lot because it is a very useful sort of energy. Electricity can be easily **transferred** as other kinds of energy. For example, a torch transfers electrical energy as light.

2 Copy the table on the right. Complete it using the names of other kinds of energy on this page.

Electrical appliance	What it transfers electricity as
cooker	heat (thermal energy)
mixer	
music centre	
lamp	

Using electricity in industry

Factories and offices also need a supply of energy.

3 Look at the picture of the factory.
Copy and complete the sentences.

The conveyor belt in the factory uses electricity to make the belt _____.
The fan heater transfers the electricity as two sorts of energy. It _____ up the air and then makes it _____.

conveyor belt used to move boxes

fan heater used to heat and move air.

More energy transfers

We design things to get useful energy from electricity. There is usually one main energy transfer we want. For example, a strip light is designed to transfer electrical energy as light.

Here is a way of showing this energy transfer:

strip light

electrical energy ⟶ light

4 Copy these energy transfer diagrams. Then complete them in the same way.

a electrical energy ⟶ movement

b electrical energy ⟶ sound

c electrical energy ⟶ heat

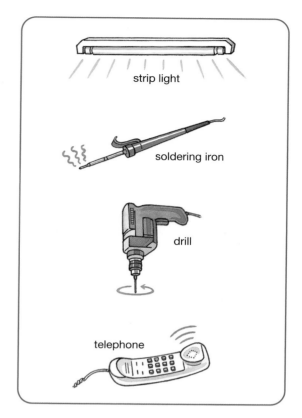

strip light

soldering iron

drill

telephone

Do you always get what you want?

Very often, you do not transfer all the electrical energy into the sort you want. There are other sorts of energy transfers that are not useful. For example:

- a light bulb produces more heat than light!
- a drill produces sound as well as movement from the motor.
- an electric motor gets hot as well as moving.

5 The electrical energy supplied to the computer is transferred as four different types of energy.

a Make a copy of the diagram and label it to show these <u>four</u> different types of energy.
b Which <u>three</u> types of energy transfer is the computer <u>designed</u> to make?
c Which energy transfer also happens but isn't really wanted?

What you need to remember *Copy and complete using the **key words***

Making use of electricity
We use a lot of electrical _____ in our homes and in industry.
Electricity can easily be _____ as other sorts of energy such as
_____ , _____ , _____ and _____ (or movement) energy.

You should know what energy transfers electrical appliances are designed to produce.

2 How much electricity do we use?

Electrical appliances transfer energy. How much energy they transfer depends on how **long** you switch them on for. It also depends on how **fast** they transfer energy.

Look at the pictures of the light bulbs.

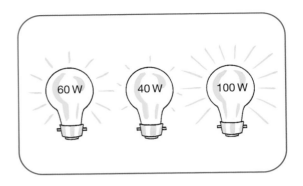

1 Which bulb is the brightest?

2 Which bulb transfers energy the fastest?

How fast something transfers energy is called its **power**. Power is measured in **watts** (W).

1000 watts is called a **kilowatt** (kW).

3 Look at the pictures of an electric heater. Copy and complete the table.

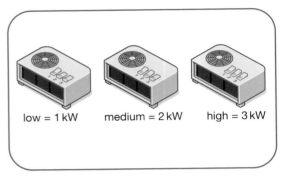

low = 1 kW   medium = 2 kW   high = 3 kW

Setting of heater	Power	
	watts	kilowatts
low		
medium		
high		

How much do electrical Units cost?

Jed lives in a flat. He uses a meter card to pay for his electricity. One evening the meter showed he had £1.90 credit. Jed fell asleep for three hours after leaving the heater on low. When he woke up there was £1.60 credit left.

Look carefully at the first two meters.

4 How many Units on the meter did the heater use in three hours on 'low'?

5 How much did each Unit cost?

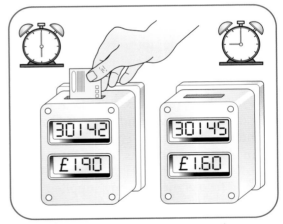

The meter reading shows the Units used.
The difference between the two readings shows how many Units have been used.

Jed felt cold so he turned the heater to 'high'. A friend arrived to talk to him. He was talking for nearly an hour. When the friend left Jed's credit had dropped to £1.30.

6 How many electrical Units did the heater use in one hour on 'high'?

How to work out electrical Units

The amount of electrical energy transferred is worked out by multiplying the **power** (in kilowatts) by the **time** (in hours).

This gives a **Unit** called the kilowatt-hour (kW h).

energy transferred = power × time
kilowatt-hours = kilowatts × hours
(kW h)   (kW)   (h)

7   How many Units would an electric heater set to 'medium' use in 1 hour?

8   Copy the table below and complete it.

The first row has been done for you.

You may need to change watts into kilowatts, and minutes into hours, before you work out your answers.

100 W = 0.1 kW
500 W = 0.5 kW
1500 W = 1.5 kW

30 minutes = 0.5 hours

Electrical appliance	Power in W	Power in kW	Time used	Number of Units used (kW × h = kW h)
electric heater on 'low'	1000	1	2 hours	1 × 2 = 2
electric heater on 'medium'	2000		2 hours	
light bulb	100		1 hour	
electric drill	500		2 hours	
hair dryer	1500		30 minutes	

Energy units
The normal unit of energy is the joule (J). Electrical energy can be measured in **joules**, but 1 joule is too small to use for measuring electrical energy in the home. We use the Unit (kW h) instead.

1 Unit = 3 600 000 J

What you need to remember *Copy and complete using the **key words***

How much electricity do we use?
Power is measured in _____ (W).
The name for 1000 watts is a _____ (kW).
How much electrical energy is transferred depends on:

■ how _____ an appliance is switched on for
■ how _____ the appliance transfers energy (its _____).

The energy used in an electrical appliance is worked out by multiplying the _____ (in kW) by the _____ (in hours):

energy transferred = power × time
(_____)   (kilowatts)   (hours)

A kilowatt-hour of electrical energy is called a _____.
We normally measure energy in _____ (J).

3 Paying for electricity

Counting the cost

To work out how much electricity costs, you need to know:

- how many Units (kW h) have been used
- how much each Unit costs.

total cost for electricity used = **number** of **Units** used × **cost** per **Unit**

1 Copy the table below and complete it. Each Unit costs 10p. The first row has been done for you.

Electrical appliance	Power in W	Power in kW	Time used in hours	Number of Units kW × hours	Total cost Units × 10p
heater (low)	1000	1	2	1 × 2 = 2	2 × 10p = 20p
heater (medium)			2		
light bulb			2		
electric drill			2		
hair dryer			2		

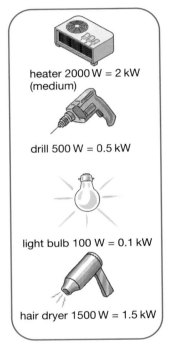

heater 2000 W = 2 kW (medium)

drill 500 W = 0.5 kW

light bulb 100 W = 0.1 kW

hair dryer 1500 W = 1.5 kW

2 Which appliance costs the most to use?

Working out electricity bills

It is always worth checking electricity bills, but you need information to do this.

Sometimes you may not be at home when the electricity meter reader calls, so you may get an 'estimated bill'.

Mrs Smith
42 Walker Road
Maviston

Maviston electricity company

Meter reading

This time	Last time	Units used	Pence per unit	Amount £	Standing charge £	Totals £
30340E	29210C	1130	10.0	113.00	14.30	127.30

Total exclusive of VAT   127.30
VAT   10.18

This bill is estimated. Please complete the enclosed pink card for an amendment.

Your customer number	You can phone us on	Period ending	Amount now due
03 3967 4721 60	0136 247 XXXX	12 Apr	£137.48

E against a meter reading means an estimate
C against a meter reading means it is your own reading

3 Look at the example bill.

a What is the 'This time' reading on the bill?
b What does the 'E' after this reading mean?

4 Which reading did Mrs Smith take herself ?

Here is the reading on Mrs Smith's meter when she received the bill.

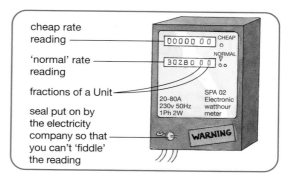

cheap rate reading ———

'normal' rate reading ———

fractions of a Unit ———

seal put on by the electricity company so that you can't 'fiddle' the reading ———

20-80A
230v 50Hz
1Ph 2W

SPA 02
Electronic
watthour
meter

WARNING

5 Was the estimated reading right?

6 Did Mrs Smith use more or less electricity than it says on the bill?

7 Copy the parts of the bill below. Then fill in all the missing numbers to make it a correct bill.

8 How much less is the new bill?

Meter reading		Units used	Pence per unit	Amount £	Standing charge £	Totals £
This time	Last time					
	29210C		10.0		14.30	
		Total exclusive of VAT				
		VAT				9.71
					Amount now due	

Half-price electricity

After about 11 o'clock at night, most businesses have closed and most people have gone to bed. This means that much less electricity is needed.

However, some power stations cannot be shut down, and they generate more electricity than is needed. The electricity companies sell electricity at a much cheaper price to persuade people to use more at night. Storage heaters are an example of appliances that use this cheap electricity.

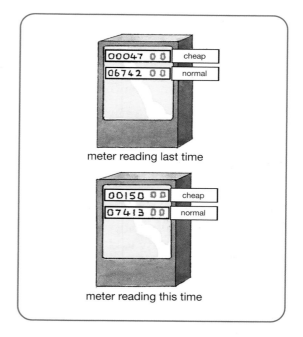

00047 0 0 cheap
06742 0 0 normal

meter reading last time

00150 0 0 cheap
07413 0 0 normal

meter reading this time

9 Look at the meter readings. Cheap rate electricity from this company costs 5p per Unit.
How much cheap rate electricity has been used?
What will this cost?

10 How much would it cost for the same amount of electricity on the 'normal rate' scale (10p per Unit)?

4 Understanding mains electricity

Most of the electricity we use comes from the **mains supply**. An underground cable connects the supply to the electricity meter in each house. Different circuits carry the electricity to lights, wall sockets and high power appliances such as the cooker.

> **1** What is the purpose of a circuit breaker?
>
> **2** Why are the lights and sockets in different circuits?

What does 230 V a.c. mean?

The average **voltage** of the mains electricity in the UK is **230 V**. This is much higher than the voltage of a battery and is high enough to kill you.

Mains electricity is a.c., which stands for **alternating current**. The mains current in the UK changes direction 50 times each second. We say that its frequency is 50 hertz (Hz for short).

> **3** Explain the difference between a.c. and d.c.
>
> **4** A TV made for use in the USA is marked 110 V 60 Hz. What is the voltage of the US mains? What is the frequency?

Changing voltage

Different electrical appliances need different voltages to work properly. It is easy to change the voltage of an alternating current using a **transformer**. Transformers do not work with direct current.

> **5** Give <u>one</u> reason why mains electricity is a.c. and not d.c.

To increase the voltage you need a step-up transformer. To reduce the voltage you need a step-down transformer.

> **6** Copy and complete the table.

	Voltage needed	What is used to produce this voltage from the mains?
personal stereo		step-_____ transformer
television		step-_____ transformer

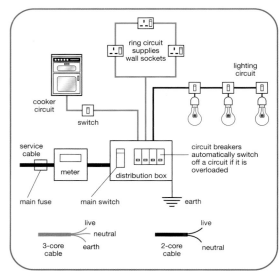

Lights, sockets and the cooker are in different circuits so no single circuit carries too much power.

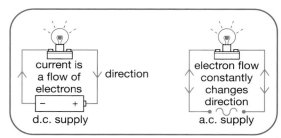

A battery supplies a direct current (d.c.). The current always flows in the same direction. An alternating current keeps changing direction. The number of times it changes direction each second is called its frequency.

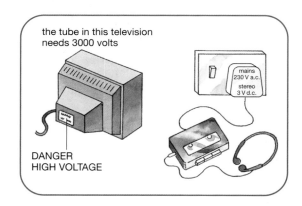

the tube in this television needs 3000 volts

DANGER HIGH VOLTAGE

How electricity reaches your home

Power stations generate electricity. All the power stations in the country are connected to a network of cables called the **National Grid**. The electricity is sent through the Grid to towns and cities.

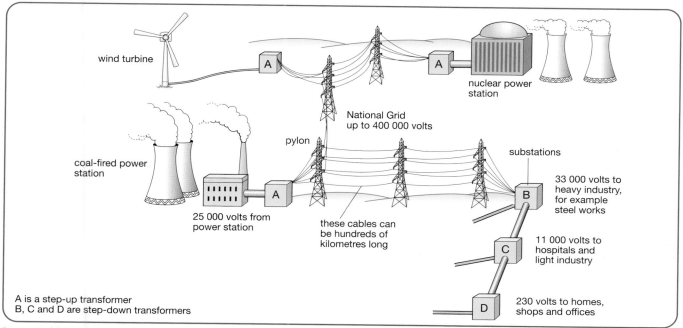

A is a step-up transformer
B, C and D are step-down transformers

Power cables carry electricity at very high voltages. These voltages are very dangerous, but the higher the voltage used, the less **energy** is wasted in the cables. Substation transformers reduce the voltage to make the electricity **safer** to use.

7
  a What voltage is used on the National Grid?
  b How is such a high voltage produced?
  c Why is such a high voltage used?

8 Describe, as fully as you can, what happens to electricity from the National Grid before it is sent to the people who use it.

What you need to remember *Copy and complete using the **key words***

Understanding mains electricity

The voltage of the _____ _____ in homes in the UK is
_____ .

The mains supply is an _____ _____ .
One advantage of a.c. is that the voltage can be changed with a _____ .
Electricity from power stations reaches us through the _____ _____ .
Electricity is sent through the Grid at a very high _____ so that less
_____ is wasted.
Before it reaches homes and factories, the voltage is reduced using transformers.
This makes the electricity _____ to use.

5 Choosing the right appliance

A heater for nan

Sophie's nan lives on her own. Her house is cold in winter. She has to light a coal fire every day, but now she finds it hard to carry the coal. Sophie wants to buy her nan some electric heaters. Nan needs a heater to keep warm when she is in the living room, a heater she can turn on when she's in the kitchen and one for her bedroom, so it is not too cold at night.

Sophie looks at the different types of heater in the catalogue.

1 Which heater has the highest power output?

2 Which heater will be cheapest to run on full power?

3 Which heater has no safety overheat cut-out?

4 If you were Sophie, which heaters would you buy for the three rooms? Write a short explanation of your choices.

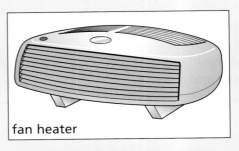

fan heater

- 2 kW output • two heat settings
- safety overheat cut-out
- instant heat

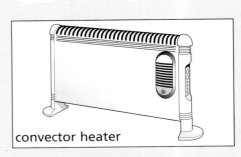

convector heater

- 3 kW output • variable thermostat automatically switches heater on and off to control room temperature • safety overheat cut-out • rapid heat • silent operation

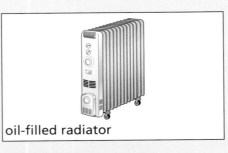

oil-filled radiator

- 500 W output • variable thermostat • safety overheat cut-out • one heat setting • silent operation • low running costs • slow warm up • ideal for maintaining background heat

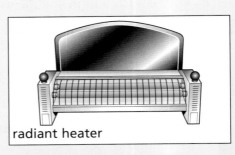

radiant heater

- 2 kW • two heat settings
- rapid heat • elements get very hot and glow brightly

Instant showers?

The village football team have a clubhouse next to the playing field. After training or a match, the players use the two shower cubicles. An electric immersion heater heats the water in the tank. To supply enough hot water for both showers they have to turn the heater on for 2 hours in advance.

5   What is the power of the heater?

6   How many Units of electricity are needed to heat the water for the showers?

7   If electricity costs 10p per Unit, how much does the hot water cost?

The club would like to reduce its electricity bill. Someone suggests they install two instant electric showers for the team to use, instead of the immersion heater.

8   If it takes on average 15 minutes for everyone to shower with two cubicles, how many Units of electricity will the two instant showers use?

9   What is the saving for each session?

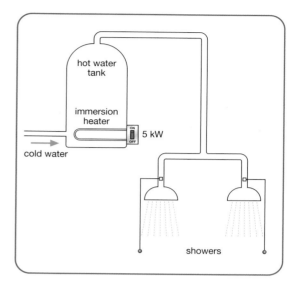

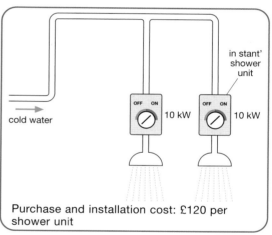

Purchase and installation cost: £120 per shower unit

> ### REMEMBER
>
> The pay-back time is the time taken for an improvement to pay for itself.

10   If the showers are used five times per week, what is the pay-back time for installing them?

What you need to remember

Choosing the right appliance
There is nothing new for you to <u>remember</u> in this section.
You have been <u>applying</u> ideas you have met before.
You may be asked to do this in tests and examinations.

> You need to be able to compare and contrast the advantages and disadvantages of using different electrical devices for a particular application.

Ideas you need from KS3

Energy to make electricity

Electricity gives us a useful form of energy, which we can transfer as many other types of energy.

Electricity has to be generated, and we need an energy <u>source</u> to do this. Because we must generate electricity using some other source of energy, we say that electricity is a <u>secondary</u> energy source.

Fuels as energy sources

The diagram shows the four main fuels (primary energy sources) we use to generate electricity.

1 Copy and complete these sentences.

To generate electricity you need some other
_____ of energy.
We can use fuels like _____ ,
_____ , _____ and
_____ fuel to generate electricity.
Coal, oil and gas are called _____ fuels.

How long can fuels last?

These fuels are non-renewable energy sources. This means that they can't be <u>replaced</u>.

2 Look at the bar chart of how long primary energy sources will last.
  a How long will coal, natural gas, oil and nuclear fuel last (at present rates of use)?
  b Which will last the longest?

The pie chart shows the energy sources that are used worldwide to generate electricity.

3 Copy the table headings below. Then complete the table, starting with the highest % and ending with the lowest. The first line has been filled in for you.

Energy source	% of world electricity generated
coal	39

4 Which of the energy sources on the pie chart is not a fuel?

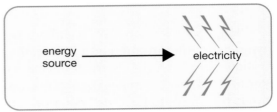

We always need some other energy source to make electricity.

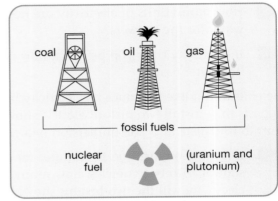

Fuels we use to generate electricity.

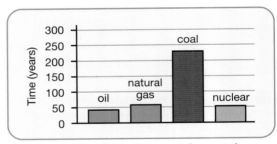

How long fuels will last if we use them at the present rate. (Nuclear fuel will last a lot longer if we use it in fast breeder reactors.)

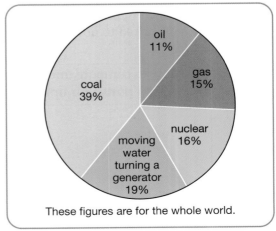

These figures are for the whole world.

Energy sources used to generate electricity.

Renewable energy sources

Fuels like wood are <u>renewable</u>. This means that they can be replaced.

Anything that we grow and use as a fuel is called biomass, for example wood. The energy for growing them comes from the Sun. Other renewable energy sources are sunlight, the wind, the waves, running water (hydro-electricity) and the tides.

Hydro-electric generators use water falling from behind a dam.

5 Which <u>three</u> ways of generating electricity use moving water?

6 Which renewable energy source
    a is used by solar cells?
    b consists of moving air?

Solar cells change sunlight into electricity.

Waves can turn generators.

The tides moving in and out of this tidal barrage can turn generators.

The wind turns generators.

Energy sources in the future

Fossil fuels and nuclear fuels will eventually run out.

7 What can we do to make fuels last longer before they run out?

8 What energy sources will we eventually have to depend on?

1 Using fuels to generate electricity

We use fuels to generate most of the electricity we use in Britain.

When we burn **fossil fuels** (coal, oil and gas) they transfer energy as heat. Nuclear fuels (for example **uranium** and **plutonium**) also produce **heat** as atoms are split up. This is called nuclear fission.

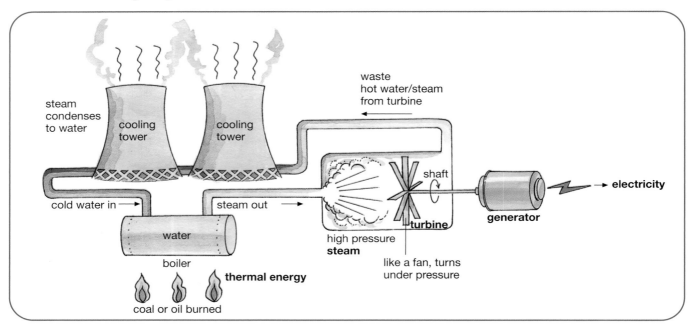

The diagram above shows how the heat (thermal energy) a fuel releases can generate electricity.

1. Write down the following sentences in the right order to explain how the power station works. Start with:

   Heat from the fuel boils water.
   - The shaft turns the generator.
   - Steam from the boiling water builds up a pressure.
   - The generator produces electricity.
   - A shaft connects the turbine to the generator.
   - The pressure turns the blades of the turbine.

2. What happens to the steam after it has been through the turbine?

3. a Which type of fuel does not burn to release energy?
   b What must happen to this fuel for it to release energy?

4. Look at the diagram on the right.
   What is different about a gas-fired power station?

In a nuclear power station, heat from the reactors is used to make steam. The fuel is used up in a nuclear reaction, but it does not burn.

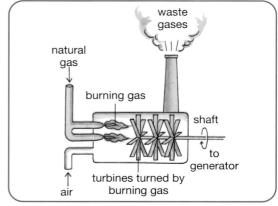

In a gas-fired power station there is no need to use steam. The hot burning gases drive the turbines directly.

What are the problems with using fuels?

When you **burn** a fuel, it produces waste.

This waste can pollute the atmosphere and soil, or you may have to store it until it is safe.

There is only a certain amount of each fuel in the Earth, so fuels are non-renewable. Once they are used up, they are gone **forever**.

The diagram shows the types of waste from a coal-fired power station.

5 **a** Write down <u>one</u> solid waste that has to be put somewhere.
    b Write down <u>four</u> types of waste that go into the atmosphere.

Look at the information in Fact file 1.

6 What do the cooling towers do?

7 For every 100 tonnes of coal a power station burns, how many tonnes are usefully transferred as electricity?

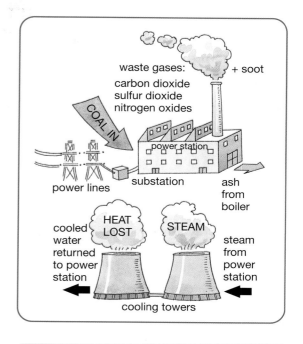

Fact file 1
Power stations are only about 30% efficient. Cooling towers change the steam back into water. This water is used again to make steam.

Why do we use fuels to generate electricity?

Fuels are plentiful (at the moment), but before the end of this century they may start to run out.

Power stations that use fuels can generate electricity at any time and in all sorts of weather.

8 Write down <u>three</u> advantages and <u>three</u> disadvantages of using <u>fuels</u> to generate electricity.

Fact file 2
Power stations that use fuels can be very big and can spoil the countryside. One power station can generate electricity for over a million people. Power stations that use fuels produce pollution.

What you need to remember *Copy and complete using the* **key words**

Using fuels to generate electricity
Coal, oil and gas are called _____ _____.
Examples of nuclear fuels are _____ and _____. Nuclear fission produces _____.
All these fuels are non-renewable – once they are used up, they are gone _____.
All non-renewable fuels transfer energy as _____ _____.
For coal and oil power stations, this energy is released when the fuels _____ and is used to boil water. This produces _____, which turns a _____.
Then this drives a _____ shaft, which produces _____.

2 Comparing fuels for electricity

Using fuels always produces waste. These wastes can pollute the air, the water and the soil. We can reduce some of this pollution, but this makes electricity more expensive.

The diagram and bar charts show some facts about the wastes from different fuels.

1 Look at the diagram. Copy and complete the table. The first line has been filled in for you.

Name of waste gas	What problem it can cause
sulfur dioxide	causes acid rain

Look at the bar charts.

2 **a** Which type of fuel produces no waste gases and very little solid waste?
   b Why does this fuel cause a very serious pollution problem?

3 **a** Which fuel produces the most solid waste?
   b Which fuel – coal, oil or gas – produces the least pollution?

4 **a** Which waste gas increases the greenhouse effect?
   b Which fuel causes the biggest increase in the greenhouse effect?

5 **a** Which two gases cause acid rain?
   b Which fuel produces most of the gases that cause acid rain?

6 Look at the amount of carbon dioxide produced by gas.
   How many times more carbon dioxide do coal and oil produce?

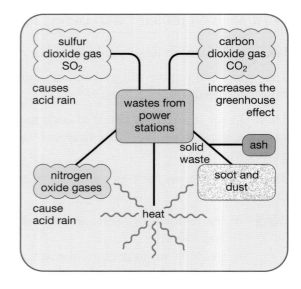

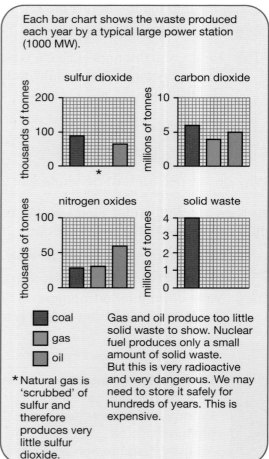

Each bar chart shows the waste produced each year by a typical large power station (1000 MW).

coal

gas

oil

*Natural gas is 'scrubbed' of sulfur and therefore produces very little sulfur dioxide.

Gas and oil produce too little solid waste to show. Nuclear fuel produces only a small amount of solid waste. But this is very radioactive and very dangerous. We may need to store it safely for hundreds of years. This is expensive.

How can we cut down air pollution?

Soot and dust are made of tiny particles. We can remove these from chimneys by attracting them using electric charges or by using filters. This makes the electricity a bit more expensive.

We can remove sulfur dioxide from chimneys with substances that absorb it. This makes the electricity up to 20% more expensive. It is far too expensive to remove the huge amounts of carbon dioxide from the waste gases.

Pollutant	How it is removed	Effect on cost of electricity
soot		
sulfur dioxide		

 7   Copy and complete the table.

Do nuclear fuels pollute?

Nuclear fuels don't burn when they release their energy. So nuclear power stations don't pollute the air with carbon dioxide or sulfur dioxide.

But small amounts of hazardous radioactive materials do escape into the surroundings. If there is an accident, much larger amounts of very dangerous radioactive materials can pollute a large area. Several countries are still affected by pollution from the accident at Chernobyl in 1986.

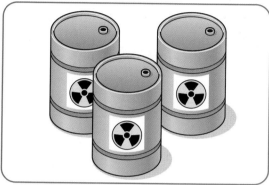

Nuclear power stations produce highly radioactive waste. Some of this can stay dangerously radioactive for thousands of years. So it has to be stored very carefully. This adds a lot to the cost of the electricity generated.

8   **a**   Write down <u>two</u> reasons why nuclear power stations may be a great threat to the environment.
     b   Write down <u>one</u> reason why nuclear power stations are less harmful to the environment than power stations burning coal or gas.

Comparing start-up times

Look at the bar chart.

9   Write down the four types of power station in order, starting with the shortest start-up time.

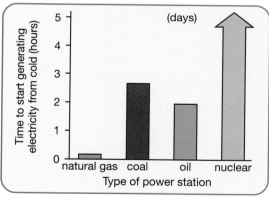

How long it takes to start up different types of power station.

What you need to remember

Comparing fuels for electricity
There is nothing new for you to <u>remember</u> in this section.

You should be able to compare the advantages and disadvantages of different fuels for electricity. These include:

- which types of waste are produced by which fuel
- whether the pollution by each type of waste can be reduced and how this can be done
- how controlling pollution affects the cost of electricity
- how the start-up times for power stations using different fuels compare.

3 Generating electricity with water

Water is always on the move. We can use this movement to drive turbines **directly**. The energy is **free** but it can be expensive to **capture** energy from water. It will never run out and it doesn't produce harmful waste.

The diagram shows three types of moving water that we can use to generate electricity.

1 Copy and complete the table.

Type of moving water	Which way the water moves	Why the movement keeps on happening
waves		the wind keeps on blowing across the sea
rivers	flows along to the sea	
tides		

Rain falls on the land and flows to the sea in streams and rivers. Rain keeps on falling because the Sun keeps on evaporating water from the sea.

The wind produces waves as it blows across the sea. As waves move along, the water moves up and down.

Tides make water rise and fall in estuaries twice a day. Tides keep happening because of the pull of the Moon's gravity as the Earth spins.

Hydro-electricity

We build dams across rivers. These trap a lot of water. We can use this trapped water to generate electricity. The diagram shows how we do this.

2 Write down the following sentences in the right order. The first one has been done for you.

- Water flows out through the bottom of the dam.
- The shaft of the turbine drives a generator.
- The generator transfers kinetic energy as electricity.
- The flowing water turns a turbine.

3 Copy and complete the energy flow diagram.

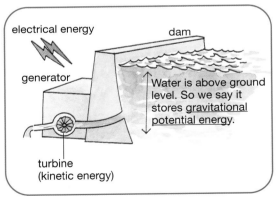

Falling water drives turbines, which turn **generators**.

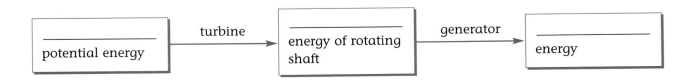

Good and bad news about hydro-electricity

Hydro-electricity supplies about 20% of the world's electricity without producing pollution. But in the UK there are only a few suitable sites for large hydro-electric plants. Most of the possible sites have been used. They supply about 1% of our electricity.

> **4** Write down <u>one</u> effect of hydro-electricity on the environment.

> **5** Hydro-electric generators are very useful if more electricity is suddenly needed. Explain why.

Electricity from tides

Tides make water flow into estuaries twice each day. We can trap this water behind a barrage. We can then use it to generate electricity when the tide goes out.

> **6** Where, in Britain, could a large **tidal** power station be built?

> **7** Write down <u>two</u> disadvantages of generating electricity from tides.

Electricity from waves

The diagram shows a small wave generator. No large generators have yet been made to stand rough seas.

> **8** What drives the turbine in the wave generator?

Land has to be flooded to make reservoirs.
Hydro-electric generators can be started in a few seconds.

You can only generate electricity at certain times each day.

Tides vary a lot in height.

Large estuaries like the Severn are important **wildlife** habitats. Wading birds find food in the mud. If you flood the estuary, they can't feed there.

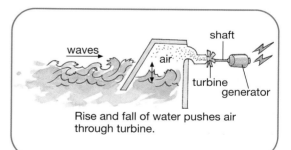

Rise and fall of water pushes air through turbine.

What you need to remember *Copy and complete using the **key words***

Generating electricity with water

Energy from these sources is _____ but it is expensive to _____.

Energy from the rise and fall of water owing to _____ and _____, and _____ _____ in hydro-electric schemes can drive turbines _____ to turn _____.

You can produce electricity when you need it from a _____ generator.

Reservoirs for these power stations flood _____.

You can generate electricity only at certain times each day using a _____ power station. Barrages for these power stations flood estuaries, destroying _____ habitats.

4 Generating electricity with wind

People have used the energy from the wind for thousands of years. But, during the past 300 years, steam engines, then petrol engines and then electricity took over from wind.

> **1** Write down <u>two</u> ways energy from the wind was used in the past.

We are now using wind energy again.

Wind is a renewable energy resource. It is a regular part of our weather, which is driven by energy from the Sun. So, as long as the Sun keeps shining, the wind will keep blowing.

This will help to make our stocks of non-renewable energy sources last longer.

Windmills like this were once used to grind wheat into flour.

The wind has been used to pump water.

A modern wind generator

The diagram shows a modern wind **turbine**. This turbine generates electricity.

> **2** Copy and complete the energy transfer diagram.

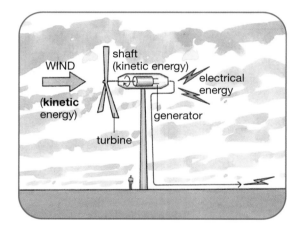

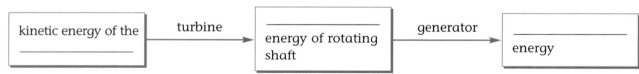

| kinetic energy of the _____ | —turbine→ | energy of rotating shaft | —generator→ | _____ energy |

Where should we put wind generators?

A large wind **generator** needs a wind of at least 5 metres per second before it will generate electricity. So we must put it in a place where there is plenty of **wind**.

Look at these maps of Great Britain.

> **3** Where are the best places for wind turbines? Answer in as much detail as you can.

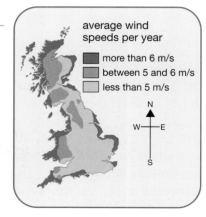

average wind speeds per year
- more than 6 m/s
- between 5 and 6 m/s
- less than 5 m/s

N
W—E
S

- high ground

Could wind generators provide all our electricity?

In 2005 there were more than 1200 wind turbines connected to the National Grid. These supplied just less than 1% of the UK's electricity. The government wants to raise this figure to 8% by 2010. This is the fastest growing way of using renewables to generate electricity.

We need many **hundreds** of wind generators to replace just one power station that uses coal.

The wind doesn't blow all the time, even on coasts and hills. Wind power is not always **reliable**, so we need some other way of generating electricity.

Wind **farms** use lots of turbines to transfer wind energy to electricity. Each wind turbine generates between 500 kW and 2 MW. (1 MW = 1000 kW.) A **coal-fired** power station generates about 1300 MW.

> **4** How many 2 MW wind turbines working at full power do we need to replace a power station that uses coal?

> **5** Write down <u>one</u> reason why wind cannot supply all the electricity we need.

Wind power could supply up to 40% of our electricity.

Wind generators and the environment

Wind generators do not release substances that **pollute** the air. But some people think that wind farms spoil the look of hills and coasts – this is called **visual** pollution. They object to changing a landscape that has been the same for centuries. Wind turbines also create some **noise** pollution as they turn.

Off-shore wind farms are more than 5 km from the coast, so they do not spoil the landscape. But they are more expensive to build and maintain than land-based wind farms.

> **6** Write down <u>one</u> advantage and <u>one</u> disadvantage of using wind power to generate electricity.

> **7** Write down <u>one</u> advantage and <u>one</u> disadvantage of off-shore compared to land-based wind farms.

What you need to remember *Copy and complete using the **key words***

Generating electricity with wind

The _____ energy of the wind can drive a _____ directly. This then drives a _____, which produces electricity.

Wind generators need to be on hills and coasts where there is plenty of _____.

You need _____ of wind generators to produce as much electricity as a _____ power station.

Large groups of wind generators are called wind _____. The wind does not blow all the time so wind power is not _____.

Wind turbines do not _____ the air, but by changing the landscape and making a sound they may create _____ pollution and _____ pollution.

5 Generating electricity from the Sun and the Earth

Solar cells

Solar cells are a very simple way of transferring energy from the Sun as electricity. There is only one energy transfer. Light is transferred directly as electricity.

But one problem is that solar cells are a very **expensive** way of making electricity.

Another problem is that solar cells will work only if the Sun is shining! Like the wind, they are not a reliable energy source.

1. Complete the energy transfer diagram below for a solar cell.

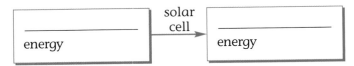

2. Look at the bar chart. To make each Unit (kW h) of electricity, which source of energy costs

   a the least?
   b the most?

3. One disadvantage of using solar energy cells to generate electricity is the cost.
   Write down <u>two</u> other disadvantages.

Why use solar cells?

Electricity from solar cells is expensive.

But there are times when they are worth using.

4. Write down <u>two</u> reasons why solar cells are used in satellites.

5. Where would you use a solar-powered pump? Explain why.

6. Why are solar cells suitable for calculators?

Calculators use only a very small amount of electricity. So you can use a very small solar cell instead of batteries.

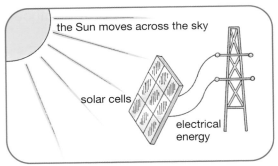

The solar cells must be at the correct angle to collect the most light energy.

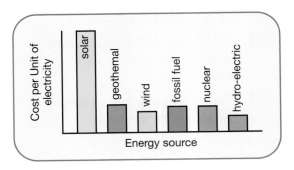

Satellites use solar cells. Solar cells weigh less than batteries and will work for many years.

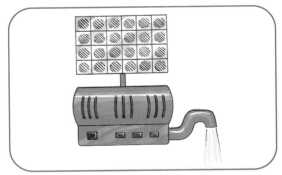

A solar-powered water pump for isolated villages. It is often too expensive to put power cables from power stations to **remote** places.

Geothermal energy

'Geo-' means 'from the Earth' and 'thermal' means 'heat'. So **geothermal** energy is heat from the Earth's rocks.

The rocks in the Earth contain **radioactive** elements like **uranium**. These elements give out radiation which transfers energy to the rocks as **heat**. This happens very slowly over billions of years.

At some places on the Earth, especially in **volcanic areas**, hot rocks heat water underground. Hot water and **steam** rise to the surface.

> 7 What do we call steam that spurts out of the ground?

> 8 Write down the names of <u>four</u> countries that use steam from the ground to generate electricity.

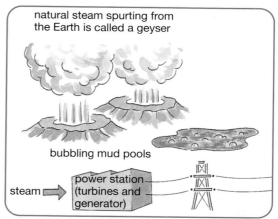

Natural steam is used to generate electricity in the USA, Italy, New Zealand and Iceland.

Making a heat mine

Engineers hope to be able to use geothermal energy even in places where there aren't any geysers. The diagram shows how they might be able to do this.

> 9 Copy and complete the sentences.
>
> In a 'heat mine', _____ water is pumped deep down into the ground.
> It passes through tiny cracks in _____ rocks and is turned into steam.
> This steam is used to generate _____ energy.

> 10 Write down <u>two</u> problems in using geothermal energy to generate electricity.

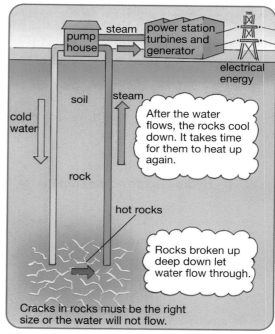

A heat mine.

What you need to remember *Copy and complete using the **key words***

Generating electricity from the Sun and the Earth
Energy from the Sun can be transferred as electricity using

_____ _____ .

Each Unit of electricity from a solar cell is very _____.
But solar cells will work for many years and are useful in _____ places on Earth and on _____. They are also useful in things that need very little electricity, such as _____.
_____ elements (like _____) in the Earth's rocks transfer energy as
_____. In some _____ _____, hot rocks heat water, and
hot water and _____ rise to the surface. The steam can drive turbines. This is
known as _____ energy.

6 A review of renewable energy sources

Many people agree that we need to use more renewable energy sources instead of non-renewable fuels.

1 Give <u>two</u> reasons why we must use less non-renewable fuel in the future.

But there are problems with using renewable energy sources, as well as advantages. The statements A to M on the right show some of these.

2 Match each of the renewable energy sources below with the statements.

The numbers in the brackets tell you how many statements you must match with each energy source. You need to use some of the statements more than once.

a Tidal barrages (4)

b Hydro-electric power stations (6)

c Wave generators (3)

d Geothermal (1)

e Solar cells (2)

f Wind turbines (2)

3 Which renewable energy source would you choose to generate electricity in these situations?
Explain each of your choices.

a In a desert region, for pumping water?
b In a mountainous region with many streams?
c In a country with many volcanoes and geysers?

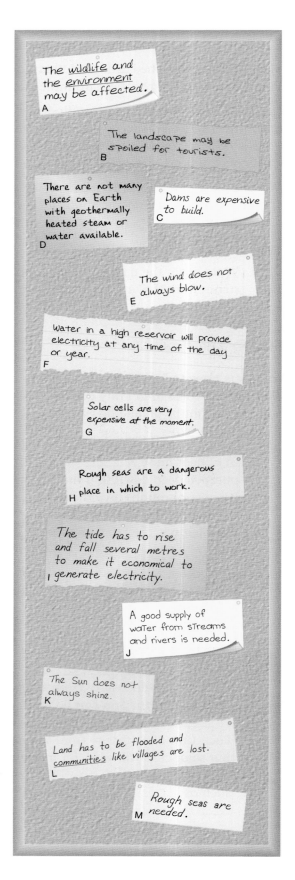

The wildlife and the environment may be affected.
A

The landscape may be spoiled for tourists.
B

There are not many places on Earth with geothermally heated steam or water available.
D

Dams are expensive to build.
C

The wind does not always blow.
E

Water in a high reservoir will provide electricity at any time of the day or year.
F

Solar cells are very expensive at the moment.
G

Rough seas are a dangerous place in which to work.
H

The tide has to rise and fall several metres to make it economical to generate electricity.
I

A good supply of water from streams and rivers is needed.
J

The Sun does not always shine.
K

Land has to be flooded and communities like villages are lost.
L

Rough seas are needed.
M

Choosing the best renewables for the job

Study the map of Arbril Island and read the 'Fact file' carefully. Then answer the questions.

Arbril Island

Fact file on Arbril Island

- Arbril is in the Southern Ocean between the Falklands and Antarctica.
- There is sunlight for six months of the year and then darkness for six months.
- The seas around the island are very rough. Sometimes it is impossible to travel to Arbril.
- The tides only rise and fall by less than a metre.
- Port Herbert is the main town. It relies on fishing as its main industry. It is on a sheltered part of the island.
- Soil is poor quality. But rainfall is high throughout the year.
- There are hot springs on the south-west of the island. They are difficult to reach over very high mountains.

Port Herbert needs a reliable electricity supply.
The old power station is coming to the end of its useful life.
It uses coal, which is very expensive to import.

4 Suggest <u>four</u> renewable energy sources which could be used.

5 For each energy source, suggest at least <u>one</u> problem to be solved.

6 a Copy the map. Then show on your map where you would build the new power station for each of your suggestions.
  b Give a reason for your choice of site in each case.

What you need to remember

A review of renewable energy sources
There is nothing new for you to <u>remember</u> in this section.
You have been <u>applying</u> ideas you have met before.
You may be asked to do this in tests and examinations.

You need to be able to compare and contrast the particular advantages and disadvantages of using different energy sources to generate electricity, including the place where the energy is needed.

7 Counting the cost of generating electricity

> **REMEMBER**
>
> To generate electricity we need to use some other energy source.
> We can compare these energy sources in various different ways, for example
>
> - how much electricity they are able to generate
> - whether or not they can generate electricity when we need it
> - how much pollution they cause.

Cost is another important factor when deciding what energy sources to use to generate electricity.

Cost per Unit

To work out the overall cost of each Unit of electricity from a certain energy source, we have to work out:

- the cost of **building** the system (the capital cost)
- the cost of **operating** and maintaining the system
- the cost, if any, of the **fuel** that is used.

We then need to share this cost between all the Units of electricity the system produces in its lifetime.

1 a Copy and complete the table for electricity generated by wind generators, by a nuclear power station, by a gas-fired power station and by a coal-fired power station.

System	Building cost (per Unit)	Fuel cost (per Unit)	Operating cost (per Unit)	Total cost (per Unit)
gas	2.3p	1.1p	0.3p	3.7p

b For each Unit of electricity, which system has

   i   the lowest building cost?
   ii the lowest fuel cost?
   iii the lowest overall cost?

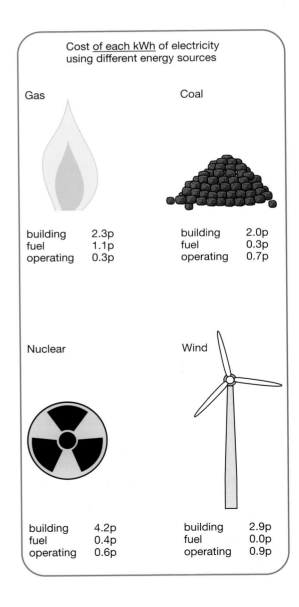

Cost of each kWh of electricity using different energy sources

Gas

building	2.3p
fuel	1.1p
operating	0.3p

Coal

building	2.0p
fuel	0.3p
operating	0.7p

Nuclear

building	4.2p
fuel	0.4p
operating	0.6p

Wind

building	2.9p
fuel	0.0p
operating	0.9p

Decommissioning costs

Electricity generating systems eventually wear out.
They must then be dismantled and removed.

This **decommissioning** costs money. We should also take
this into account when we calculate the cost of each Unit
of electricity.

> **2** Does decommissioning increase the cost of each Unit
> of electricity more for wind generators or for nuclear
> power stations?

Nuclear power stations don't pollute the air with
waste gases. But they produce radioactive waste
which will be dangerous for thousands of years.
The cost of storing this waste safely must be added
to other costs for electricity from this source.
Dismantling an old nuclear power station is very
expensive because of the radioactive material in it.

Environmental costs

Generating electricity also has other 'costs' that it is difficult
to put a figure on. For example, burning some fossil fuels
helps to create acid rain and the damage this causes costs
money to put right. Burning all types of fossil fuel produces
carbon dioxide, which increases the greenhouse effect. This
may change the climate and raise the level of the sea. The
cost of this could be enormous but is very difficult to estimate.

Some people think that we should tax things that damage
the **environment** to help to pay for the damage caused.

> **3** A person speaking on TV says that wind generators
> produce no pollution.
> Do you agree? Explain your answer.

> **4** When nuclear power stations are working properly,
> they produce very little pollution.
> Suggest why many people are still opposed to them.

Worn out wind turbines will be relatively cheap to
dismantle – they don't contain dangerous
materials. Wind farms don't pollute the air with
waste gases. But some people object to their
appearance and the noise they make. They might
be prepared to pay more for electricity to avoid
having wind generators in beauty spots.

What you need to remember *Copy and complete using the **key words***

Counting the cost of generating electricity
When comparing the advantages and disadvantages of ways of generating electricity the
_____ of each Unit is an important factor.
This includes the costs of _____ and _____ the system and the cost
of any _____ used.
The cost of _____ the system when it is worn out should also be taken into
account.
Some costs are difficult to estimate, for example the cost of the effect on the
_____, but they must be considered.

You need to be able to compare and contrast the particular advantages and disadvantages of using
different energy sources to generate electricity.

1 Why are there different colours of light?

Sunlight looks white but it is made up of many different colours. We can see all these colours in a rainbow.

Splitting light into a the rainbow

The diagram shows how you can split up white light into all the colours of the rainbow. The pattern of colours is called a **spectrum**.

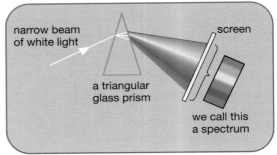

narrow beam of white light

screen

a triangular glass prism

we call this a spectrum

1 Copy and complete the sentences.

We can split up white light into many different colours using a glass _____.
This produces a _____.

Looking at the spectrum

Our eyes can pick out hundreds of different colours in a spectrum, but we usually group all these colours into a few broad bands.

These bands do not have sharp edges. Each band of colour shades gradually into the next one.

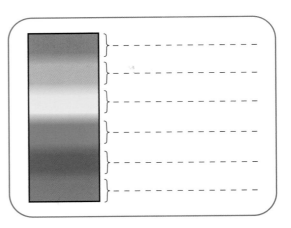

2 **a** Make a copy of the spectrum using coloured pens or pencils.

b Write the names of the following bands of colour on your diagram in the right order:

blue, green, orange, red, violet, yellow

How does light travel?

Light moves energy from one place to another.
It moves from place to place as a wave. You can compare the movement of a light wave from a bulb to your eye to the movement of a water wave across a pond.

3 Copy and complete the sentences.

Water waves and light waves carry

_____.

The length of one complete wave is the

_____.

_____ waves have a much shorter wavelength and travel at a much higher speed than _____ waves.

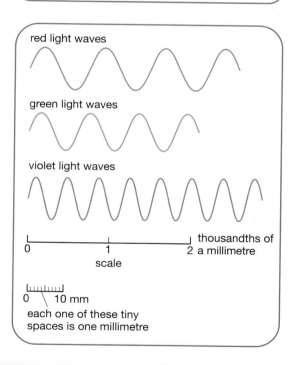

A dipper disturbs the water surface. A water wave travels away from the dipper. The wave carries energy. Some of the energy is transfered to the float as the wave passes.

speed: 0.4 metres per second

one complete wave

wavelength: 100mm

A light wave carries **energy** from a light bulb into your eye. Some of this energy is transfered to your nerves. This makes you see.

speed: 300 million metres per second

wavelength: less than one thousandth of a millimetre

What makes colours different?

Different colours of light have different **wavelengths**.

4 Look at the diagrams of red, green and violet light waves. Then copy and complete the following sentence.

Red waves have a _____ wavelength than violet waves.

The wavelengths of light waves are all very small.

5 How many violet waves are there

a in a thousandth of a millimetre?
b in a whole millimetre?

red light waves

green light waves

violet light waves

0   1   2   thousandths of a millimetre

scale

0   10 mm

each one of these tiny spaces is one millimetre

What you need to remember *Copy and complete using the key words*

Why are there different colours of light?

Light travels as waves and carries _____ from one place to another.
White light is a mixture of light of all _____ from red light waves to violet light waves.
When we split light up to make a _____ we spread the different wavelengths out into bands which we see as different colours.

2 More about waves

You already know that waves can have different wavelengths and travel at different speeds. But there is another way in which waves can be different from each other.

Another difference between waves

You can make a lot of waves each second or just a few waves each second.

If there are 10 waves each second, we say that the frequency is 10 hertz (Hz, for short).

The diagrams show what happens when you start to make water waves on calm water.

1 a How many complete waves are there after 1 second?
   b How many complete waves are there after 2 seconds?
   c How many complete waves are made during each second?
   d What is the frequency of the water waves?

Frequency and wavelength

The diagram shows what happens if you now make waves with double the frequency. The water is the same depth as before.

2 What happens to the wavelength when you double the frequency of the waves?

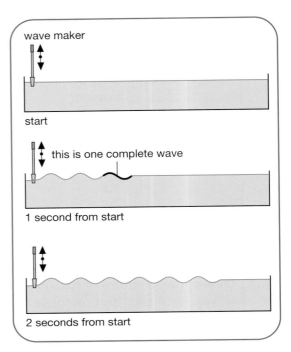

REMEMBER

This is the wavelength of a wave.

wave maker

start

this is one complete wave

1 second from start

2 seconds from start

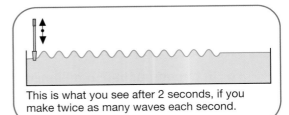

This is what you see after 2 seconds, if you make twice as many waves each second.

A formula for waves

The wave maker shown in the diagrams has a frequency of 10 hertz (Hz). This means that it makes 10 waves every second. If you look at the diagrams, you will see that by the end of 1 second the first wave has travelled a distance equal to 10 wavelengths. So the **speed** of the waves is 10 wavelengths per second.

If the wave maker is changed to a frequency of 4 Hz, the wave-speed is now 4 wavelengths per second.

In fact, for any frequency

wave-speed	=	**frequency**	×	**wavelength**
(metres per second, m/s)		(hertz, Hz)		(metres, m)

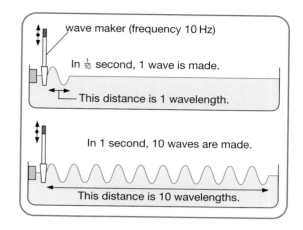

wave maker (frequency 10 Hz)

In $\frac{1}{10}$ second, 1 wave is made.

This distance is 1 wavelength.

In 1 second, 10 waves are made.

This distance is 10 wavelengths.

EXAMPLE

Some water waves have a wavelength of 6 m and a frequency of 0.5 Hz.
What is the wave-speed?

wave-speed = frequency × wavelength
= 0.5 Hz × 6 m
= 3 m/s

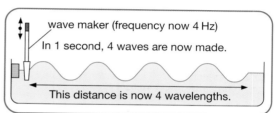

wave maker (frequency now 4 Hz)
In 1 second, 4 waves are now made.

This distance is now 4 wavelengths.

3 The student in the diagram makes waves that travel along a rope. She makes three waves in 1 second. Calculate the wave-speed. (Start by writing down the formula. Show all your working.)

0.4 m

3 waves in one second

4 **a** Write down the frequency and the wavelength of the wave on the string.
b Calculate the wave-speed.

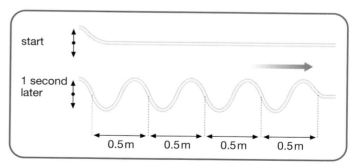

start

1 second later

0.5 m   0.5 m   0.5 m   0.5 m

What you need to remember *Copy and complete using the key words*

More about waves

All wavelengths of light travel at the same _____ in a vacuum.
All waves obey the wave formula

_____ = _____ × _____

3 Waves beyond the ends of the rainbow

White **light** is a mixture of many different colours.
Different colours of light have different wavelengths.

1   **a** Look at the diagram.
Then copy and complete the sentences.

Red light has the _____ wavelength.
Violet light has the _____ wavelength.

  b Make a copy of the diagram.
Make sure that the diagram is in the centre of
your page with plenty of room at both sides.
You will need to add things to it later on.

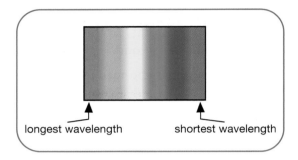

longest wavelength   shortest wavelength

Are there other waves we can't see?

Our eyes can only see certain wavelengths of light.
But there is also 'light' that we can't see.
This is because its wavelength is too long or too short.

The diagram shows how we can tell that these waves are
there, even though we can't see them.

2   **a** How do we know that there are waves outside the
red part of the spectrum?
  b What do we call these waves?

3   **a** How do we know there are waves outside the
violet part of the spectrum?
  b What do we call these waves?

Infra-red and ultra-violet waves are also called infra-red
and ultra-violet radiation.

4   Add infra-red and ultra-violet radiation to your
diagram of the spectrum.

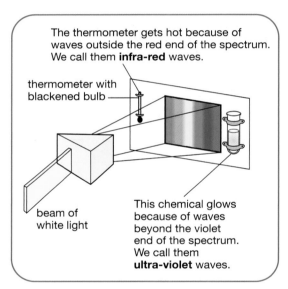

The thermometer gets hot because of
waves outside the red end of the spectrum.
We call them **infra-red** waves.

thermometer with
blackened bulb

beam of
white light

This chemical glows
because of waves
beyond the violet
end of the spectrum.
We call them
ultra-violet waves.

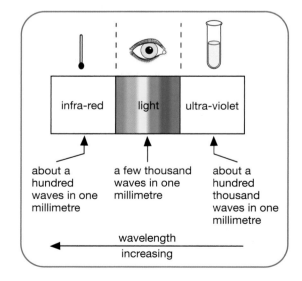

infra-red   light   ultra-violet

about a
hundred
waves in one
millimetre

a few thousand
waves in one
millimetre

about a
hundred
thousand
waves in one
millimetre

wavelength
increasing

Adding more waves to the spectrum

There are waves with longer wavelengths than infra-red waves.

There are also waves with shorter wavelengths than ultra-violet waves.

All of these waves are parts of a bigger spectrum, which we call the **electromagnetic** spectrum.

5 Add all these other types of waves to your diagram of the electromagnetic spectrum.

light	ultra-violet	**X**-rays	**gamma** rays

millions of waves in one millimetre   billions of waves in one millimetre

radio waves	microwaves	infra-red	light

waves a few centimetres to a few kilometres long   waves a few millimetres to a few centimetres long

How fast do electromagnetic waves travel?

All the different kinds of electromagnetic waves travel at the same **speed** as light through space. They all obey the **wave formula**:

wave-speed = frequency × wavelength

So the waves with the shortest **wavelength** also have the highest **frequency**.

6 Add the information about wavelength and frequency to your diagram.

7 Copy and complete the sentences.

Radio waves have the _____ wavelength and the _____ frequency. Gamma rays have the _____ wavelength and the _____ frequency.

REMEMBER

- In a vacuum (space), all electromagnetic waves travel at the same speed.
- This speed is 300 million metres per second.
- Electromagnetic waves are also called electromagnetic radiation.

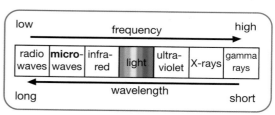

What you need to remember *Copy and complete using the* **key words**

Waves beyond the ends of the rainbow

The waves in the _____ spectrum can be grouped by wavelength and frequency.

_____ waves	_____ waves	_____- _____ waves	_____	_____ waves	_____-rays	_____ rays

long wavelength   red   violet   short _____

lowest _____   highest frequency

All types of electromagnetic radiation travel through a vacuum at the same _____.
All electromagnetic waves obey the _____ _____:

      wave-speed   =   frequency   ×   wavelength
    (metres/second, m/s)   (hertz, Hz)   (metres, m)

4 Electromagnetic waves and matter

There are many different types of electromagnetic waves.

1 Write down the names of <u>seven</u> different types of electromagnetic waves.

2 Write down <u>two</u> things that are the same about all the types of electromagnetic waves.

Electromagnetic waves travel easily through empty space (a vacuum).

But electromagnetic waves often bump into matter in the form of solids, liquids or gases.

The diagrams show what can happen when they hit matter.

3 What <u>three</u> things can happen when electromagnetic waves hit matter?

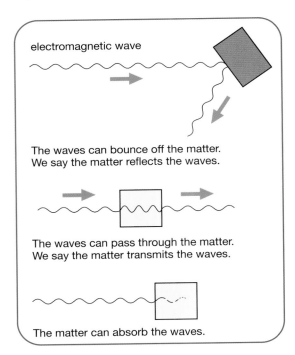

electromagnetic wave

The waves can bounce off the matter. We say the matter reflects the waves.

The waves can pass through the matter. We say the matter transmits the waves.

The matter can absorb the waves.

Absorbing electromagnetic radiation

Sometimes when radiation hits a solid, liquid or gas, some of the radiation is **transmitted** and some is **absorbed**.

This is what happens when light hits polythene.

The diagram shows how you can find out how much light polythene lets through.

4 Look at the graph. Then copy and complete the sentences.

The thicker the polythene is, the _____ light it lets through.
To absorb half of the light you need _____ mm of polythene.
A thickness of 4 mm of polythene lets through only _____ % of the light.

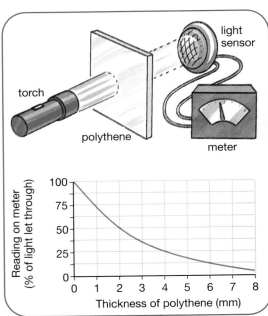

Different wavelengths do different things

The amount of electromagnetic radiation **reflected**, absorbed or transmitted depends on three things:

- the **wavelength** of the radiation
- the substance
- the type of surface.

5 What type of substance always reflects radio waves well?

6 How could you treat a metal surface to prevent it reflecting light?

7 Which wavelength radiation does water absorb more, long wavelength or short wavelength?

What happens to the energy?

Electromagnetic waves carry **energy** from one place to another. When waves are absorbed, this energy is transferred to the material that absorbs them.

8 A black surface absorbs the energy of light and infra-red radiation. What happens to this energy?

9 Some of the energy of radio waves is absorbed by an aerial. What happens to this energy?

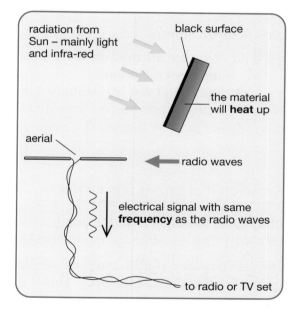

What you need to remember *Copy and complete using the key words*

Electromagnetic waves and matter

When electromagnetic waves hit a solid, liquid or gas they may be _____, _____ or _____ (or more than one of these). What happens depends on the _____ of the radiation, the substance and the type of surface.

Electromagnetic waves transfer _____. When the waves are absorbed by matter, this energy may make the matter _____ up.

When radio waves or microwaves are absorbed by an aerial, they produce an electrical signal with the same _____ as the waves.

5 Electromagnetic waves and living cells

When electromagnetic waves are absorbed, they transfer energy. This energy can damage cells or even kill them. Different **wavelengths** of electromagnetic radiation affect cells in different ways. You need to be able to evaluate

- the hazards of different types of electromagnetic radiation
- methods to reduce exposure to radiation.

Look for examples in the rest of this chapter.

Radiation that 'cooks' cells

Your cells become **hot** if they absorb infra-red radiation or microwaves. This heat can damage or kill the cells.

Look at the diagrams.

1 **a** Why are microwaves more dangerous than infra-red radiation?

b Why can't you accidentally damage your cells with the microwaves from a microwave oven?

Radiation that causes skin cancer

Ultra-violet radiation from the Sun is mainly absorbed by your skin. This can damage the molecules inside skin cells.

The cells can then start to multiply very quickly and also spread to other parts of the body. This is called **cancer** and may cause death.

2 What type of electromagnetic radiation usually causes skin cancer?

3 People with dark skins are less likely to get skin cancer. Why is this?

4 How can you protect yourself against skin cancer? Explain your answer.

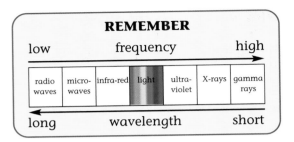

REMEMBER

low		frequency				high
radio waves	micro-waves	infra-red	light	ultra-violet	X-rays	gamma rays

long ← wavelength → short

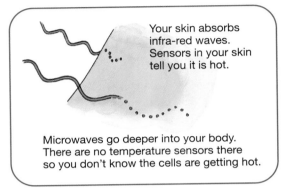

Your skin absorbs infra-red waves. Sensors in your skin tell you it is hot.

Microwaves go deeper into your body. There are no temperature sensors there so you don't know the cells are getting hot.

There's nothing to stop you putting your hand under a grill...

...but if you open the door of a microwave oven it switches off.

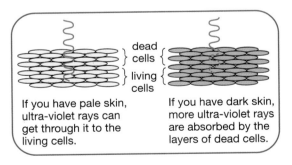

If you have pale skin, ultra-violet rays can get through it to the living cells.

If you have dark skin, more ultra-violet rays are absorbed by the layers of dead cells.

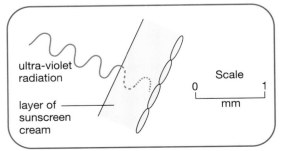

ultra-violet radiation

layer of sunscreen cream

Scale
0   1
      mm

Sunscreen cream protects your skin against cancer. It absorbs the ultra-violet rays.

Radiation inside people's bodies

X-rays can pass fairly easily through the soft parts of your body. Gamma radiation can pass quite easily through any part of your body.

Both types of radiation can cause cancer and **kill** cells.

Look at the diagram.

5   **a**   Why can X-rays and gamma rays cause cancer?
       b   Where in a person's body can these types of radiation cause cancer?

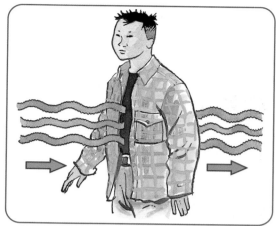

X-rays and gamma rays can pass through your body. But some are absorbed by your cells. This can cause cancer anywhere in your body.

Radiation dose

The amount of radiation your body gets is called the radiation **dose**. Small doses of electromagnetic radiation are not always harmful. You need at least a few minutes sunlight each day to stay healthy.

But large doses may damage your cells.

6   In which country is there a greater risk of skin cancer, Australia or the UK?

7   Suggest <u>one</u> reason for the higher risk.

8   'Slip on a shirt, slop on sunscreen and slap on a hat.' Explain how following this Australian advice reduces your radiation dose.

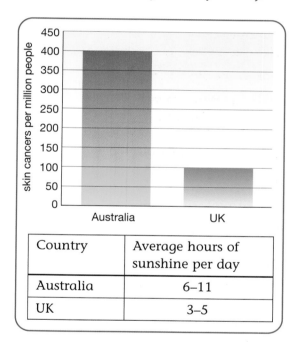

Country	Average hours of sunshine per day
Australia	6–11
UK	3–5

What you need to remember *Copy and complete using the **key words***

Electromagnetic waves and living cells
The effects of electromagnetic radiation on living cells depend on the _____ of the radiation and the _____ received.
Infra-red radiation and microwaves can damage cells by making them _____.
Ultra-violet radiation can damage the cells in your skin and may cause skin _____.

X-rays and gamma radiation can pass easily through your body. Where they are absorbed they may _____ cells or cause cancer.

6 Using light

Visible light is the only part of the spectrum we can see. We get most of our information about the world from the light that enters our eyes.

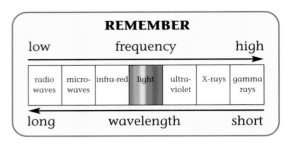

REMEMBER

low   frequency   high

radio waves	micro-waves	infra-red	light	ultra-violet	X-rays	gamma rays

long   wavelength   short

Traffic signals use light to **communicate** information.

Microscopes and telescopes use light to show details of tiny objects and distant stars and planets.

Cameras and video screens use light to record and display images.

High-power laser light cuts steel.

1 Write down <u>four</u> different ways we use light.

Reading information

The light from a laser travels in a very fine beam.

We can use a beam of laser light to read information from a bar code or a compact disc.

2 Copy and complete the sentences.

A bar code records a _____ that identifies a product. The _____ of the black bars varies. The laser beam is _____ by the black bars and _____ by the white spaces in-between. A _____ detects the pattern of reflections as the code is scanned.
Information is recorded on a CD as a pattern of _____ that _____ light.
The laser beam reads the information as the disc _____.

Laser light is reflected from the white parts of the bar code and absorbed by the black bars. A sensor detects the reflected light pattern as the code is scanned. The pattern depends on the width of the bars. A computer translates the pattern into a number that identifies the product.

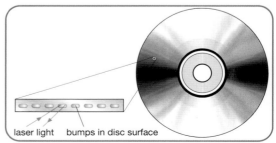

laser light   bumps in disc surface

A CD player works in a similar way. A pattern of microscopic bumps in the disc surface reflect the laser beam as the disc spins.

Seeing round corners

A doctor thinks a patient has a stomach ulcer, so she needs to look inside the patient's stomach. The diagram shows how she can do this.

3   What instrument does the doctor use?

4   Why does the instrument have this name?

The endoscope sends light round corners. The light waves travel down very thin fibres made from glass, called **optical fibres**.

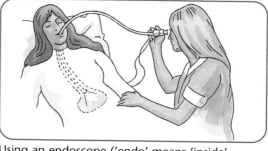

Using an endoscope ('endo' means 'inside', 'scope' means 'looking for').

How do optical fibres work?

Light waves travel through an optical fibre just like sound waves travel through a pipe. This is why you can use an optical fibre to send images and signals along **curved paths**.

5   Copy and complete the sentences.

Sound waves are _____ over and over again from the inside surface inside a pipe.
Light waves are _____ over and over again inside an optical _____.

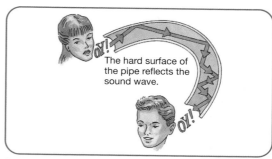

The hard surface of the pipe reflects the sound wave.

Sound waves travelling through a pipe.

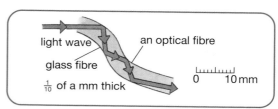

light wave   an optical fibre
glass fibre
$\frac{1}{10}$ of a mm thick   0   10 mm

Light waves travelling through an optical fibre.

Light hazards

Light from most everyday light sources is safe. But very bright light can damage your eyesight.

6   List <u>three</u> light sources that can cause eye damage if viewed directly.

7   Explain how you can protect your eyes from bright light.

Looking directly at the Sun can permanently damage your eyes.

DANGER

LASER RADIATION - AVOID DIRECT EYE EXPOSURE

Laser beams must never be directed into or towards eyes.

A welding torch makes metal white hot.
The operator must use a mask with a dark filter to protect his eyes from the high intensity light.

What you need to remember *Copy and complete using the **key words***

Using light
We use light to read and _____ information and to create images.
Light can travel along _____ _____ through _____ _____.

7 Using gamma radiation

You can kill living **cells** by giving them a high dose of gamma (γ) radiation. Smaller doses can damage cells. Damage to the cells of your body may cause cancer.

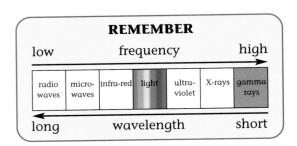

REMEMBER

Killing bacteria with gamma rays

We sometimes want to kill harmful **bacteria**.
We can do this using gamma radiation.

1   Write down <u>two</u> uses of gamma rays to kill harmful bacteria.

2   Using gamma rays, you can kill the bacteria on things inside completely sealed packets.

     a Why is this possible?
     b Why is this very useful?

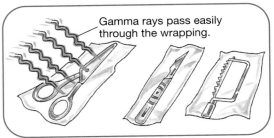

A surgeon's instruments must have no bacteria on them, so we sterilise them with gamma rays.

Killing cancer cells with gamma radiation

Doctors can use gamma rays to kill **cancer** cells inside a person's body, but they must be careful not to damage healthy cells. The diagram shows how they can do this.

3   Copy and complete the sentences.

The source of the gamma radiation _____ in a circle around the patient's body.
The cancer cells are at the _____ of this circle.
So the gamma rays hit the cancer cells all of the time.
But they only hit the healthy cells for _____ of the time.

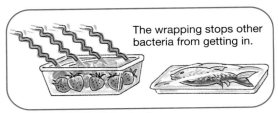

Bacteria make food go bad.
If we kill the bacteria, the food stays fresh longer.

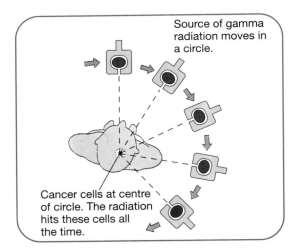

Source of gamma radiation moves in a circle.

Cancer cells at centre of circle. The radiation hits these cells all the time.

What you need to remember *Copy and complete using the **key words***

Using gamma radiation
Gamma radiation can kill living _____. It is used to kill harmful _____ in food or _____ cells inside people's bodies.

8 Using X-rays

X-rays can pass easily through some substances but not through others. To use X-rays safely and in a useful way, we need to know what substances they will, or won't, pass through.

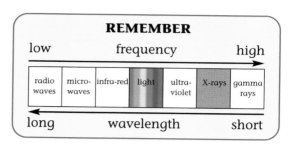

REMEMBER

low	frequency	high

radio waves	micro-waves	infra-red	light	ultra-violet	X-rays	gamma rays

long	wavelength	short

Taking an X-ray picture

The diagrams show how you can use X-rays to make a shadow **picture** of the **bones** inside a person's hand.

1 Copy and complete the sentences.

X-rays can pass easily through skin and flesh but not through _____ or _____.
Photographic _____ absorbs X-rays that fall on it.
These parts of the film then go _____ when the film is developed.

2 The X-ray picture shows a broken finger.
Which finger is this?

3 Doctors can use X-rays to see whether your lungs are healthy.
How do they know if there is diseased tissue in your lungs?

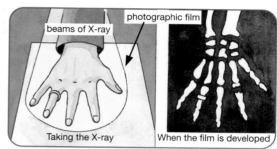

photographic film
beams of X-ray
Taking the X-ray | When the film is developed

The X-rays do not pass through the areas that show up as white. They are absorbed by these areas. You can't see the skin or flesh because X-rays pass through these easily and turn the film beneath black.

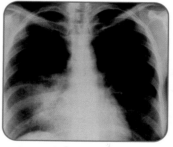

A chest X-ray. **Diseased** tissue absorbs X-rays more than healthy tissue does.

Using X-rays safely

X-rays can damage the cells of your body. Because metals **absorb** X-rays, they can be used to **protect** you.

4 Look at the photograph.
Then write down <u>two</u> other ways of reducing the risk of damaging the cells in people's bodies with X-rays.

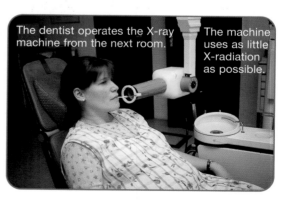

The dentist operates the X-ray machine from the next room. The machine uses as little X-radiation as possible.

What you need to remember *Copy and complete using the **key words***

Using X-rays
X-rays do not pass through the _____ in your body.
X-rays pass through skin and flesh, but do not pass so easily through _____ tissue.
Doctors can use X-rays to make a shadow _____ of the inside of your body.
Metals _____ your body because they _____ X-rays.

9 Using ultra-violet radiation

The Sun sends out lots of **ultra-violet** (UV) radiation, some of which falls on the Earth. Most of this is absorbed by the Earth's atmosphere but some of it gets through.

1   You get a lot of ultra-violet radiation if you go skiing in the mountains.
Write down <u>two</u> reasons for this.

Ultra-violet radiation and your body

The diagrams show some of the effects ultra-violet rays can have on your body.

2   Write down
a   <u>two</u> reasons why people might want to let ultra-violet rays on to their skin
b   <u>two</u> ways in which ultra-violet radiation can harm your body.

You can read more about the harmful effects of ultra-violet rays on page 276.

Changing ultra-violet radiation into light

Some substances can **absorb** the energy from ultra-violet radiation and use it to produce **light**. We say that these substances are **fluorescent**. The diagrams show some uses for fluorescent substances.

3   Write down <u>two</u> uses for fluorescent substances.

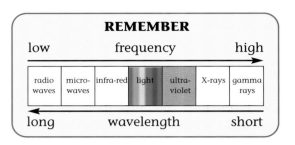

Ultra-violet rays are partly absorbed as they travel through the air.

White and shiny surfaces reflect ultra-violet rays.

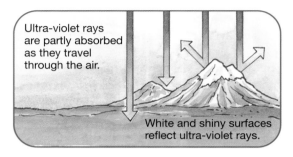

Ultra-violet rays absorbed by your skin are used to make vitamin D, but they can also cause skin **cancer**.

Ultra-violet rays can damage your eyes. So you have to wear dark glasses. Sunbeds can give people with pale skin a **tan**.

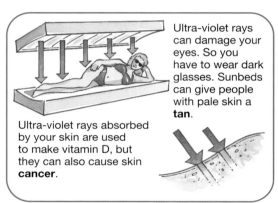

You can put invisible marks on to valuable things.

a strip light

in light

in UV rays

JO BLOGGS
07129643

energy sent out as light waves

UV waves absorbed by fluorescent substance

Using fluorescent substances.

What you need to remember *Copy and complete using the* **key words**

Using ultra-violet radiation

Radiation from the Sun, or from a sunbed, can give pale skins a _____.

But it can also damage skin cells and cause skin _____.

These things happen because of _____ (UV) radiation.

Some substances _____ ultra-violet radiation and use the energy to produce

_____. We say that these substances are _____.

10 Using infra-red radiation

Hot things send out **infra-red** (IR) radiation, and when things **absorb** infra-red radiation they get hot.
So infra-red rays are often called heat rays.

Infra-red radiation can be used for cooking, for example in toasters and grills.

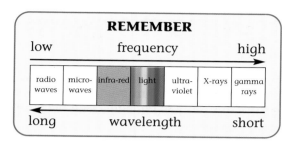

1 An electric toaster has a shiny surface between the heating elements and the outer case.
Write down <u>two</u> reasons for this.

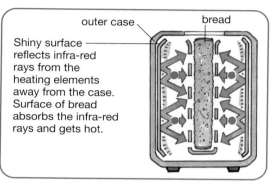

Shiny surface reflects infra-red rays from the heating elements away from the case. Surface of bread absorbs the infra-red rays and gets hot.

How a toaster works.

Infra-red rays for lazy people

You can change channels on a **television** set, or switch on a **DVD** player, using a remote control. The diagram shows how this works.

2 **a** How is your instruction carried to the television set or DVD player?
b Why must you point the remote control at the television set or DVD player?

Infra-red telephone calls

Long-distance telephone messages used to be sent as electrical signals through copper wires. They are now mainly carried by infra-red rays inside **optical** fibres.

3 Write down <u>two</u> advantages of using the optical fibres.

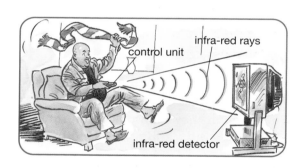

The cable of optical fibres has a much **smaller** diameter but it can still carry the same number of telephone calls.

copper wires
optical fibres

With copper wires, the signal gets weak. You need to boost the signal every 4–5 km. With optical fibres, there is less **weakening** of the signal

What you need to remember *Copy and complete using the **key words***

Using infra-red radiation

Toasters and grills cook food using _____ (IR) radiation.
Foods become hot when they _____ this radiation.
Infra-red rays are used to control a _____ set or a _____ player, and to send telephone messages along _____ fibres.
This is better than sending electrical signals along wires, because the cable has a _____ diameter and there is less _____ of the signal.

11 Using microwaves

We use microwaves for cooking, and to carry TV and mobile phone signals for **communications**. To make good use of microwaves, we need to know what will reflect, transmit or absorb them.

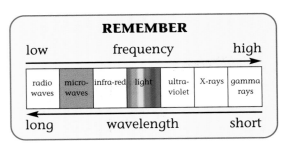

Microwave ovens

The diagram shows how a microwave oven works.

1   Copy and complete the sentences.

The case of a microwave oven is made of

_____.

This _____ microwaves.
Food contains _____ molecules. These _____ microwaves and become hot.
The food is put into containers made of
_____, _____ or
_____. These materials allow
microwaves to pass through them very easily.
We say that they _____ the microwaves.

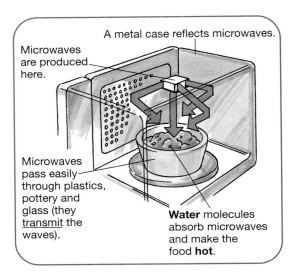

A metal case reflects microwaves.

Microwaves are produced here.

Microwaves pass easily through plastics, pottery and glass (they <u>transmit</u> the waves).

Water molecules absorb microwaves and make the food **hot**.

Satellite television

The diagram shows how television **satellites** use microwaves with certain wavelengths.

2   **a**   What wavelengths of microwaves are used for satellite television?
    b   Why are these wavelengths used?

3   Copy and complete the sentences.

We use a _____ dish to collect enough microwaves for a strong signal.
This _____ the microwaves on to an aerial.
The aerial transfers energy from the microwaves as an _____ signal.

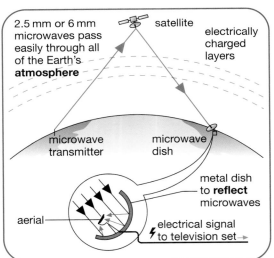

2.5 mm or 6 mm microwaves pass easily through all of the Earth's **atmosphere**

satellite

electrically charged layers

microwave transmitter

microwave dish

metal dish to **reflect** microwaves

aerial

electrical signal to television set →

What you need to remember *Copy and complete using the **key words***

Using microwaves
In microwave ovens, the microwaves are strongly absorbed by _____ molecules in food. The energy from the microwaves makes the food _____.
Metal things _____ microwaves, even if they are full of small holes.
Some microwaves can pass easily through the Earth's _____.
We can use these microwaves for _____. They carry information to and from _____ and within mobile phone networks.

12 Using radio waves

The main use for radio waves is **communications**.
They carry **radio** and **television** signals from transmitters
to receivers. When we use any kind of waves, we need to
know what will reflect them, what will transmit them and
what will absorb them.

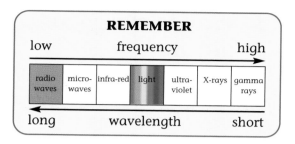
Transmitting and absorbing radio waves

The diagrams show why radio waves are suitable for
broadcasting radio and television programmes.

1. What substances will radio waves pass through
easily?

2. What happens when radio waves are absorbed by
an aerial?

3. Why can't you send a radio message to or from a
submarine?

Reflecting radio waves

The Earth's atmosphere has electrically charged layers.
One of the electrically charged layers **reflects** radio waves
with long wavelengths.

The diagram shows how we can use these reflections.

4. Why is it useful to be able to reflect long wavelength
radio waves?

5. What is the wavelength of these radio waves?

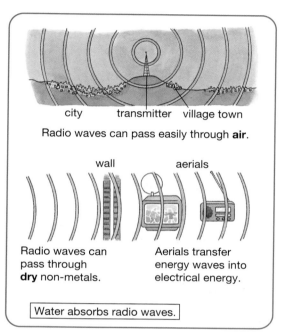

city   transmitter   village town

Radio waves can pass easily through **air**.

Radio waves can pass through **dry** non-metals.

Aerials transfer energy waves into electrical energy.

Water absorbs radio waves.

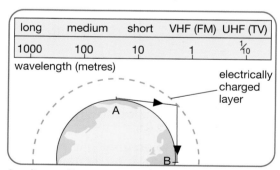

long	medium	short	VHF (FM)	UHF (TV)
1000	100	10	1	1/10

wavelength (metres)

electrically charged layer

Sending radio waves round the **curved** surface of
the Earth.

What you need to remember *Copy and complete using the* **key words**

Using radio waves

Radio waves can pass easily through _____ and through _____
non-metals.

This is what makes them useful for _____ . They can carry _____
and _____ programmes.

A layer in the Earth's atmosphere _____ radio waves with long wavelengths.

We use this property to send radio waves around the _____ surface of the Earth.

13 Why is everything going digital?

In recent years, the companies that provide telephone services and transmit TV programmes have been changing over to **digital** signals.

> **1** Write down the names of <u>two</u> other common digital devices, besides mobile telephones and satellite TV receivers.

To understand what digital signals are, and why they are used, it is easiest to start by looking at the type of signal that digital signals are replacing. These are called **analogue** signals.

What are analogue signals?

Speech and music are sound waves that travel through the air. A microphone transfers the energy of a sound wave to a changing electric current. We call this a signal.

> **2** Copy and complete the sentences.
>
> The signal from the microphone changes
> _____. It follows the same
> _____ as the sound wave. We call a
> signal that varies continuously to carry information
> an _____ signal.

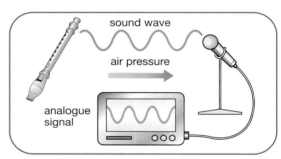

A sound wave causes air molecules to move to and fro. The microphone signal follows the same pattern as the sound wave. It changes **continuously** (without breaks).
Analogous means 'similar'. Because the microphone signal follows the same pattern as the wave, we call it an analogue signal.

A problem with analogue signals

When you listen to an analogue radio station, on the VHF or medium wave bands for example, the signal may sometimes be spoilt by **interference** (noise).

> **3** Name <u>four</u> sources of noise in analogue radio signals.
>
> **4** Why is noise more of a problem when you are a long way from an analogue transmitter?

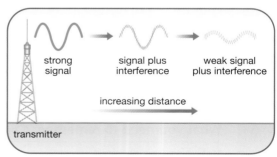

As well as the signal you want, the aerial picks up noise from other transmitters, electrical machinery, thunderstorms and outer space.
The signal you want is weak when you are a long way from the transmitter. You must turn up the volume to hear it. This means you hear more of the noise too.

What are digital signals?

A digital signal is a series of on–off pulses that are a code for the information it carries.

To change an analogue sound signal into a digital signal, special circuits measure the height of the signal thousands of times per second. This gives a list of numbers.

> **5** What is the format of the numbers in a digital signal?

> **6** Why is a digital signal discrete?

> **7** What is the name for a single digit in the signal?

Some advantages of digital signals

The aerial of a digital receiver picks up interference in the same way as an analogue receiver. Because the digital signal is discrete, the receiver can separate the signal from the interference. The receiver can then reproduce the signal without interference.

> **8** An analogue copy of a videotape is never as good as the original.
> A digital copy of a DVD is identical to the original.
> Explain these observations.

Digital radio and television signals are affected less by interference than analogue signals. **Computers** use binary code to process information in digital form. Text, sound, pictures and video can be stored, copied and transmitted digitally without errors or loss of quality.

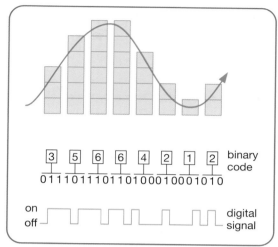

A digital signal is a list of numbers in binary code. Every number is a series of 0s and 1s. These digits are called bits. A digital signal does not vary continuously. It is either on (1) or off (0). We say that a digital signal is **discrete**.

What you need to remember *Copy and complete using the **key words***

Why is everything going digital?

Communications signals may be _____ or _____ .

An analogue signal changes _____ . A digital signal is _____ (on–off).

Digital information can be stored and processed by _____ .

Digital signals are less affected by _____ than analogue signals and so can be copied and transmitted without errors.

14 How safe are mobile phones?

Scientists know that some types of electromagnetic radiation are definitely harmful to our bodies.

Some people, including some scientists, think that the radiation emitted by mobile phones may harm our bodies.

1 Which types of electromagnetic radiation are definitely harmful

   a because they can cause cancer?
   b because they can kill cells by cooking them?

2 **a** What type of radiation do mobile phones emit?
   b Why is the radiation from mobile phones unlikely to kill cells by cooking them?

Do mobile phones cause cancer?

Several surveys have been done, in Sweden and in the USA as well as in the UK, to see if there is a link between mobile phones and brain cancer.

3 Write down <u>two</u> reasons why these surveys do not show a definite link between mobile phones and brain cancer.

Can microwaves cause cancer?

Many scientists do not believe that microwaves can damage cells in a way that causes cancer.

The diagram shows how other scientists have tried to prove them wrong.

4 **a** What did these other scientists do?
   b What did their experiments show?

> **REMEMBER**
> - Cells in our bodies may be killed or made cancerous by gamma radiation, X-rays and ultra-violet radiation.
> - Cells can also be damaged by strong infra-red or microwave radiation, which 'cooks' them.

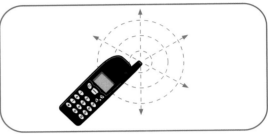

Mobile phones emit microwaves. These are very <u>weak</u> compared with those from a microwave oven.

> ## Mobile phones and brain cancer
> Some surveys show a very slight increase in brain cancer amongst people who use mobile phones. However:
>
> - not all surveys show this
> - the number of cases is very small
> - there was a decrease of other types of cancer in mobile phone users.

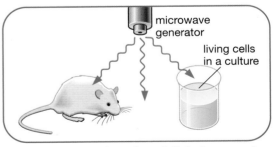

Some experiments have found slight increases in cancer. Others have found no difference or even a decrease in cancer.

Mobile phones and the media

Reports in newspapers and on TV are sometimes made very dramatic so that they grab people's attention. This means that they are not always very fair or balanced.

In the article opposite, the reported facts are all correct but the headline is only an opinion.

5 **a** Why is the headline only an opinion?
   b What would have to be done to show a definite link between mobile phone masts and brain cancer?

Man killed by microwaves

Just one year after a mobile phone mast was put up near his house, John Smith (47) developed a brain tumour. Six months later, he was dead.

His widow, Mary Smith (45), is campaigning to get all mobile phone masts removed from places close to where people live and work.

Should you use a mobile phone?

Many of the things that we do have some risk. For example, every time you cross the street there is a risk that you might get knocked down. So we always have to balance the benefits of whatever we want to do against the risks.

6 Given that there might be a health risk with mobile phones, which do you think is the best policy?

   a Never use a mobile.
   b Use a mobile only in real emergencies.
   c Use a mobile mainly for texting, not for talking.
   d Use a mobile whenever you feel like it and for as long as you like.

Are power lines a health hazard?

Some people, including some scientists, believe that living close to high voltage power lines can cause leukaemia (a blood cancer). Others disagree.

As with mobile phones, there is no definite evidence either way about power lines.

7 What do you think should be the government's policy about power lines?

Power lines give out very low frequency, very long wavelength radiation.

What you need to remember

How safe are mobile phones?
There is nothing new for you to <u>remember</u> in this section.

You need to be able to evaluate information about the possible risks from radiation and methods for reducing exposure.

1 What are atoms made of?

All substances are made of atoms.
Atoms are made of even smaller particles.

What's inside an atom?

In some substances, all the atoms are the same.
These substances are called elements. Gold is an element.

The diagram shows what each atom of gold is made of.

1 Each gold atom contains three different kinds of particles.

a What are the <u>three</u> different kinds of particles called?

b Which of these particles have an electrical charge?

2 Copy and complete the sentences.

A gold atom has no electrical charge.
This is because the positive (+) charges of the
_____ are exactly balanced by the
_____ (−) charges of the electrons.
Atoms have the same number of protons and electrons.

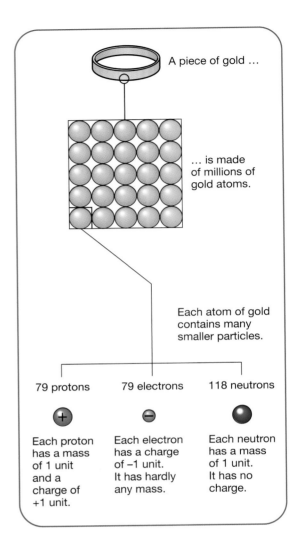

A piece of gold …

… is made of millions of gold atoms.

Each atom of gold contains many smaller particles.

79 protons	79 electrons	118 neutrons

Each proton has a mass of 1 unit and a charge of +1 unit. | Each electron has a charge of −1 unit. It has hardly any mass. | Each neutron has a mass of 1 unit. It has no charge.

The Christmas pudding model of an atom

The particles inside atoms are very, very small.

You can't see them even with a very powerful microscope.

But scientists once thought that atoms were probably made like a Christmas pudding.

3 Look at the diagram. Then copy and complete the sentences.

Scientists thought that the smaller bits that make up atoms, such as _____ and
_____, filled up all the space in an atom, just like currants and raisins in a
_____ _____.

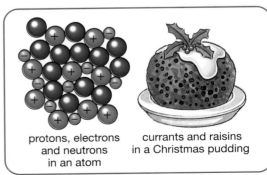

protons, electrons and neutrons in an atom | currants and raisins in a Christmas pudding

Christmas pudding model of an atom.

Testing the Christmas pudding model

When scientists tested their idea about atoms, they found out that they were wrong.

You can make gold into very thin sheets, just a few atoms thick. This is called gold leaf. Ernest Rutherford and his students tried firing some very fast particles at a sheet of gold leaf.

The diagrams showed what the scientists expected to happen and what actually happened.

4 **a** What did the scientists expect to happen?
  b What actually happened?

This test meant that scientists had to change their minds about how atoms were made. The Christmas pudding model predicted that all the particles should pass straight through the gold. But the experiment showed that this prediction was false.

very fast particle — thin sheet of gold (just a few atoms thick)

Scientists expected all the particles to go very easily through the gold sheet ...

... just like a bullet through tissue paper.

gun   bullet   tissue paper

But some of the particles bounced back!

thin sheet of gold

A new model of an atom

Scientists now think that atoms are mainly empty space. The protons and neutrons are in a very small dense **nucleus**. Electrons move about in the space around the nucleus.

5 Where is most of the mass of an atom concentrated?

6 How does this model explain why a few of the fast-moving particles bounced back from the gold leaf?

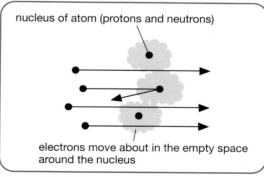

nucleus of atom (protons and neutrons)

electrons move about in the empty space around the nucleus

New model of atom.

The nucleus is tiny. If the whole atom was the size of a football stadium, the nucleus would be smaller than a pea. But more than 99.9% of the atom's mass is in the nucleus.

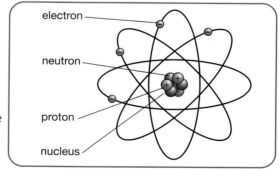

electron

neutron

proton

nucleus

What you need to remember *Copy and complete using the **key words***

What are atoms made of?
Atoms have a small _____ made of _____ and _____.
Particles called _____ move around in the empty space around the nucleus.

2 What is radioactivity?

Some substances give out invisible radiation.
This radiation can darken a photographic film and make certain substances glow. We say that the substances that emit this radiation are **radioactive**.

Radioactive substances emit radiation all the time.

There is **nothing** you can do to stop this.

> **1** Look at the diagrams. Write down what happens to the amount of radiation a radioactive substance emits
>
> **a** when you heat it up or cool it down
> **b** when you dissolve it
> **c** when you break it up into small pieces.

You can't make a radioactive substance emit radiation faster or slower. This makes it different from other kinds of radiation, which you <u>can</u> control.

> **2** **a** What can you do to a substance to make it emit light?
> **b** How can you make a substance emit less infra-red radiation?

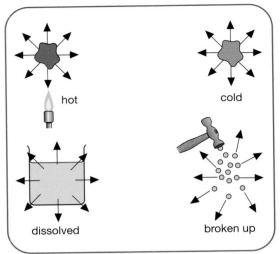

Nothing you can do to a radioactive substance changes how much radiation it emits.

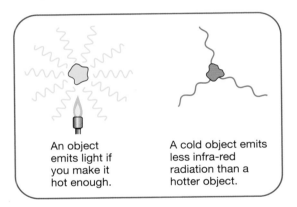

An object emits light if you make it hot enough.

A cold object emits less infra-red radiation than a hotter object.

How do we know that radioactive substances emit radiation?

You can't see, hear or feel the radiation from radioactive substances, but there are ways of detecting it.
The diagrams show how you can do this.

> **3** Write down <u>two</u> ways of detecting the radiation from a radioactive substance.
>
> **4** Which would be the best way
>
> **a** of measuring how <u>fast</u> a radioactive source is emitting radiation?
> **b** of telling how much radiation a person has been exposed to during a whole week?
>
> **5** Even when it isn't near a radioactive source, a Geiger counter gives a small reading. Why is this?

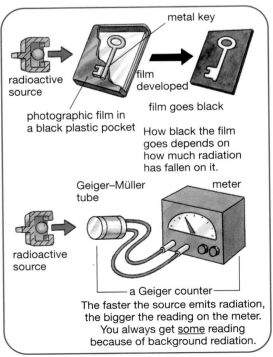

metal key

radioactive source

photographic film in a black plastic pocket

film developed

film goes black

How black the film goes depends on how much radiation has fallen on it.

Geiger–Müller tube

meter

radioactive source

a Geiger counter

The faster the source emits radiation, the bigger the reading on the meter. You always get <u>some</u> reading because of background rediation.

Detecting radiation.

Where does the radiation come from?

The radiation from radioactive substances comes from the **nuclei** of the atoms. This is why we also call it **nuclear radiation**.

6 Why do heating, dissolving and chemical reactions not affect the rate at which radioactive substances emit radiation?

The processes at the bottom don't change the nuclei at the centre of atoms. So they don't affect the emission of nuclear radiation.

What is an isotope?

All the atoms of a particular element have the same number of protons in their nuclei. In some elements, different atoms have different numbers of neutrons. We call these different atoms isotopes.

7 What does the number 14 tell us about the isotope carbon-14?

8 How many protons and neutrons are there altogether in the most common isotope of uranium?

Two different isotopes of carbon.

Isotope	Natural abundance
uranium-234	0.006%
uranium-235	0.72%
uranium-238	99.27%

Some isotopes of uranium.

Why are only some isotopes radioactive?

In most atoms the nucleus doesn't change. We say that these atoms have a stable nucleus.
But some atoms have an unstable nucleus.
Sooner or later, an unstable nucleus will emit radiation. The nucleus changes when it does this, and we say that the nucleus decays.

9 What is a radio-isotope?

10 Write down the names of <u>one</u> stable and <u>one</u> unstable isotope of iodine.

Some stable isotopes.

carbon-12
oxygen-16
cobalt-59
iodine-127
lead-208

Some radio-isotopes.

carbon-14
cobalt-60
strontium-90
iodine-131
uranium-238
americium-241

Radio-isotopes (also called radionuclides) are unstable. They emit nuclear radiation and decay.

What you need to remember *Copy and complete using the **key words***

What is radioactivity?
Some substances give out _____ _____.
This radiation comes from the _____ of atoms.
There is _____ that can be done to stop the emission of this radiation.
These substances are _____.

3 Three types of radiation

Radioactive substances emit three main types of radiation. These are called **alpha** (α) radiation, **beta** (β) radiation and **gamma** (γ) radiation.

We know that there are three different types of radiation because we need different thicknesses of material to block them.

Look at the diagram.

1 Which kind of radiation does thin paper block?

2 Which type of radiation passes through the greatest thickness of material?

3 What thickness of aluminium blocks beta radiation?

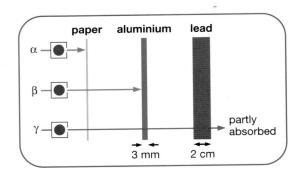

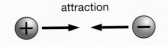

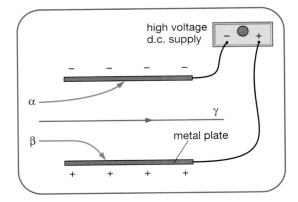

REMEMBER

A positive charge attracts a negative charge

attraction

Another difference between α, β and γ radiation

The diagram shows what happens when α, β and γ radiations pass between metal plates with positive and negative charges.

4 How are the plates given a charge?

5 Which type of radiation doesn't have an electric charge?

6 What kind of charge must α radiation have?

7 What kind of charge must β radiation have?

Magnets may affect radiation too

A movement of charge is an electric current. When a magnet is placed near an electric current, a force pushes the current. This is how an electric motor works.

8 Which type of radiation is not affected by the magnetic force? Why is this?

9 The magnetic force deflects α radiation and β radiation in opposite directions.
What does this tell you about their electric charges?

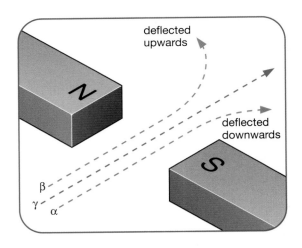

What are alpha, beta and gamma radiation?

By measuring the effects of electric and magnetic forces on the three types of radiation, scientists have discovered what they are.

10 Copy and complete the sentences.

An alpha (α) particle is a
_____ nucleus. It has a mass
of _____ mass units and an
electric charge of _____.
A beta (β) particle is an
_____. It has a mass of
_____ _____ and
an electric charge of _____.
Gamma (γ) radiation is a form of
_____ radiation. It has a very
short _____.

An α particle is a **helium** nucleus.

A β particle is a fast-moving **electron**. It is emitted from the <u>nucleus</u> of an atom.

Symbol	Name	Mass (mass units)	Charge (charge units)
+	proton	1	+1
●	neutron	1	0
–	electron	almost 0	−1

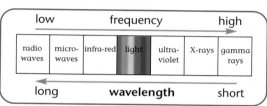

The **electromagnetic** spectrum

Which type of radiation is emitted?

Different radioactive sources emit different kinds of radiation. Some substances may emit more than one of the three types.

11 What type of radiation does the isotope polonium-210 mainly emit?

12 Name <u>two</u> radio-isotopes that are sources of β radiation only.

13 Name a radio-isotope that emits both α and γ radiations

Radio-isotope	Radiation emitted
carbon-14	β
cobalt-60	β and γ
strontium-90	β
iodine-131	β and γ
radium-226	α and γ
polonium-210	α (99%)

What you need to remember *Copy and complete using the **key words***

Three types of radiation
Radioactive sources emit three main types of radiation: _____ particles, _____ particles and _____ rays.
Alpha particles are absorbed by _____. They are _____ nuclei with a mass of 4 mass units and a charge of +2.
Beta particles are absorbed by a few millimetres of _____. They are _____ with a mass of almost zero and a charge of −1.
Gamma rays are only partly absorbed by 2 cm of _____. They are _____ radiation with a very short _____.

4 Alpha, beta, gamma: what are the dangers?

It is dangerous to expose your body to the radiation from radioactive sources. If the radiation is **absorbed** by living cells, it can **kill** them or make them **cancerous**.

There are three main types of radiation from radio-isotopes: **alpha** (α), **beta** (β) and **gamma** (γ).

Which type is most dangerous depends on whether the source of the radiation is inside or outside your body.

Look at the diagrams.

1 Which type of radiation is most harmful when the radio-isotope that emits it is inside one of your body's living cells?

2 Which type of radiation is least harmful when the radio-isotope that emits it is inside one of your body's living cells?

3 Which type of radiation is most harmful when the source of the radiation is outside your body?

4 Which type of radiation is least harmful when the source of the radiation is outside your body?

Explain your answers.

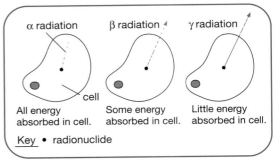

Source inside a cell.

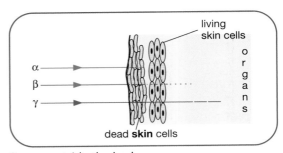

Source outside the body.

What amount of nuclear radiation is safe?

The amount of radiation your body gets is called your radiation dose.

The graph shows how the risk of cancer depends on the size of your dose of nuclear radiation.

5 Copy and complete the sentences.

The bigger the dose of radiation your body gets, the _____ the risk of cancer.

The graph suggests that there is some risk of cancer even with a very _____ radiation dose.

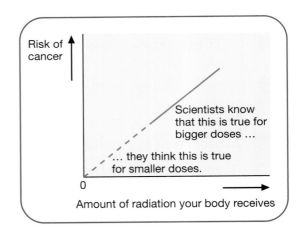

Shielding the radiation from radioactive sources

We need to stop the radiation from radioactive sources from reaching our bodies. To do this, we must shield the radioactive sources with substances that absorb the radiation.

6 a What are small, not very strong radioactive sources used for?

    b How are these radioactive sources shielded?

7 a Where would you find large and very powerful radioactive sources?

    b How are these radioactive sources shielded?

Thick layers of metal and concrete are needed so that almost all of the gamma radiation is absorbed.

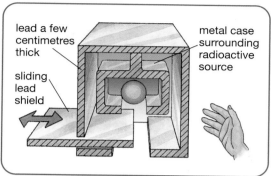

Shielding a small radioactive source (for killing bacteria or cancer cells).

Checking radiation doses

People who work with radioactive materials often wear film badges. They can then check how much radiation their bodies have received each week.

8 Look at the diagram below.

What does the developed film tell you?

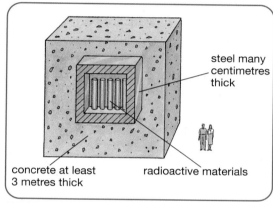

Shielding large, very powerful radioactive sources in nuclear power stations.

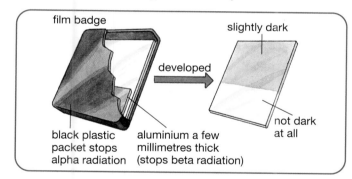

When the film is developed, it goes dark in the places where the radiation has been absorbed. The film goes darkest where the most radiation has fallen.

What you need to remember *Copy and complete using the* **key words**

Alpha, beta, gamma: what are the dangers?

Nuclear radiation can _____ living cells or make them _____.

A source of _____ radiation is very dangerous when it is inside the body.

The alpha particles are _____ by living cells.

Alpha sources are less dangerous outside the body because alpha particles are absorbed by dead _____ cells. _____ particles and _____ rays can penetrate the skin.

You should be able to evaluate

- hazards associated with different types of nuclear radiation
- measures that can be taken to reduce exposure to nuclear radiation.

5 Using nuclear radiation

Nuclear radiation can be dangerous, but it can be very useful too. We use gamma radiation to **kill** bacteria and to **treat** cancer, for example.

We can use small amounts of radio-isotopes to find out what happens to substances inside the bodies of plants and animals. The picture shows an example.

Radio-isotopes used in this way are called **tracers**.

> **1** What type of radiation should the iodine radio-isotope emit?
> Give <u>two</u> reasons for your answer.

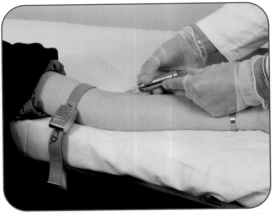

A doctor injects her patient with a radionuclide of iodine.
After a few hours, she can measure the uptake of iodine by her patient's thyroid gland. She does this with a radiation detector outside the patient's body.

REMEMBER

- Alpha radiation is very easily absorbed. Inside your body it can cause serious damage to your cells.
- Beta radiation can pass quite easily through the soft parts of your body.
- Gamma radiation can pass through your body very easily indeed.

A use for alpha particles

The picture shows a smoke detector. Smoke detectors like this are common in homes. They save many lives by giving an early warning of fire before people are overcome by smoke.

> **2** What radio-isotope is used in the smoke detector?

> **3** Which type of nuclear radiation does this isotope emit?

> **4** How does this radiation allow the smoke particles to be detected?

> **5** Give <u>two</u> reasons why radiation from the source is not harmful to people in the home.

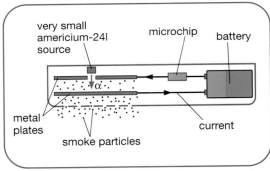

The α particles **ionise** air molecules between the plates by knocking electrons from them. The ions and electrons carry an electric current. Smoke particles trap the ions and electrons so the current falls. The microchip detects the change and triggers the alarm.

Thickness measurement

Radioactive substances can help us to make things into thin sheets.

For example, aluminium cooking foil is very thin. So it only <u>partly</u> absorbs beta radiation.

The thicker the foil is, the more beta radiation it absorbs. We can use this idea to control the **thickness** of aluminium foil when we are making it.

The diagram shows how we can do this.

6   Write down the following sentences in the right order. The first one has been done for you.

■ A thin sheet of aluminium is sent between two rollers.
■ A radioactive source sends β radiation through the foil.
■ Pressure on the rollers squeezes the aluminium sheet into thin foil.
■ The aluminium foil is now made a little thicker.
■ A signal from the control box reduces the pressure on the rollers.
■ If the foil is too thin, too much β radiation gets through to the control box.

7   Look at the diagram. Then explain why α radiation and γ radiation are not suitable for controlling the thickness of aluminium foil.

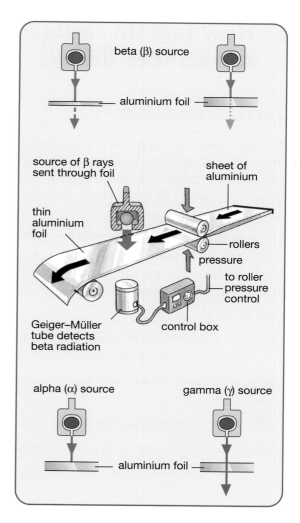

beta (β) source

aluminium foil

source of β rays sent through foil

sheet of aluminium

thin aluminium foil

rollers

pressure

to roller pressure control

Geiger–Müller tube detects beta radiation

control box

alpha (α) source

gamma (γ) source

aluminium foil

What you need to remember *Copy and complete using the **key words***

Using nuclear radiation
We use gamma radiation to _____ bacteria and _____ cancer.
A smoke detector contains a weak source of alpha radiation. The alpha particles _____ air molecules.
The _____ of aluminium foil is measured with beta radiation as it is made.
Radio-isotopes can be used as _____ to follow the movement of substances in animals and plants.

You should know and understand why particular types of nuclear radiation have particular uses.

6 How fast do radioactive substances decay?

Looking at radioactive decay

You can never tell when a particular radioactive atom will emit radiation and decay. It is a random process. But a sample of radioactive material usually contains billions of radioactive atoms so, on average, it emits radiation at a fairly steady rate.

An atom that produces radiation is called a 'parent' atom. Over a period of time, the sample of radioactive material gradually becomes less radioactive. This is because the number of parent atoms gets smaller as the atoms decay.

Look at the diagram.

1 How many parent atoms are there in the sample at the start of the experiment?

2 What is the **count rate** on the Geiger counter at this time?

3 How many radioactive atoms are left after 1 hour?

4 What is the count rate on the Geiger counter now?

Start	1 hour later
4 000 000 radioactive atoms	2 000 000 atoms
G–M tube	G–M tube
200 counts per second	100 counts per second

Half-life

The time it takes for the number of parent atoms to decrease by one half is called the **half-life**. In this time the count rate from the sample (its radioactivity) will also decrease by one half.

5 What was the half-life of the sample in the experiment above?

6 **a** What is the half-life of the radio-isotope shown on the graph?
  b What fraction of the parent atoms are left after
    i two half-lives?
    ii three half-lives?
  c Plot a similar graph using the data in the table. Find the half-life of this radio-isotope.

Different radio-isotopes have different half-lives. Half-lives can vary from a tiny fraction of a second to billions of years.

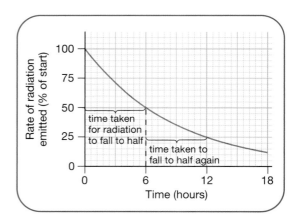

Rate of radiation emitted (% of start)	100	80	60	40	20
Time (hours)	0	3	7	13	23

Using radioactive substances to tell dates

As the radioactive atoms in a substance decay, the substance emits less radiation. You can use this idea to **date** things.

7 Look at the graph.
Some archaeologists find a piece of wood in an ancient tomb. The carbon in the wood is only 60% as radioactive as the carbon in some new wood. How old is the piece of wood from the tomb?

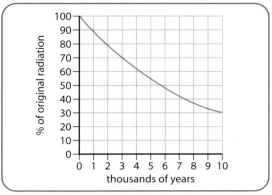

Decay graph for radioactive carbon

Dating Moon rock

Potassium-40 atoms are radioactive. They have a very long half-life. They decay to stable atoms of argon-40.

A sample of Moon rock brought back to Earth by the Apollo astronauts contained potassium-40 atoms when it was formed. Some of these atoms have now decayed into argon-40.

The table shows how we can find the age of the rock by comparing the numbers of potassium and argon atoms it contains now.

Scientists found that there were seven times as many argon atoms as potassium atoms in the rock.

8 How many half-lives have passed since the rock was formed?

9 How old is the rock?

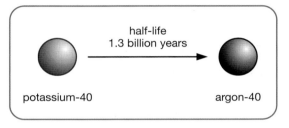

Number of half-lives that have passed	Potassium-40 (%)	Argon-40 (%)	Ratio potassium:argon
0	100	0	1 : 0
1	50	50	1 : 1
2	25	75	1 : 3
3	12.5	87.5	1 : 7
4	6.25	93.75	1 : 15

What you need to remember *Copy and complete using the key words*

How fast do radioactive substances decay?

The _____ of a substance is the time it takes for the number of radioactive atoms to halve.

In this time the _____ _____ from the substance will also halve.

We can use the half-life to _____ rocks and objects that contain radioactive atoms.

7 Choosing and handling isotopes

We use radio-isotopes in different ways. We use them to measure the thickness of materials, as tracers, and to produce radiation to treat cancer. We even use them in the home as parts of smoke alarms.

These diagrams show some more ways we can use isotopes.

Engineers place a radiation source in a pipeline to check the weld (joint) between two pieces of pipe.

1 How is the radiation detected?

2 How are cracks in the weld shown?

3 Why must the radiation be able to pass through steel?

Scientists use a radioactive tracer to investigate the take-up of fertiliser by a plant.

4 Why would an alpha source <u>not</u> be suitable?

5 Why must the half-life of the tracer be short?

The Cassini space probe has a radioactive heat source to generate electricity. The source transfers its energy as heat as its radiation is absorbed.

6 Why must the source have a half-life of a lot longer than 7 years?

This table gives properties of some radio-isotopes.

Isotope	Radiation(s) emitted	Half-life
phosphorus-32	β	14 days
cobalt-60	β and γ	5.3 years
plutonium-238	α	86 years

7 Choose a suitable isotope for each of the <u>three</u> applications shown.
Explain your choice.

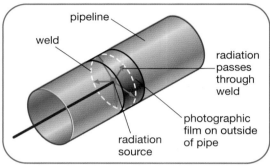

The film records the radiation that passes through the weld. Cracks absorb less radiation than solid metal. They show up as dark areas on the film.

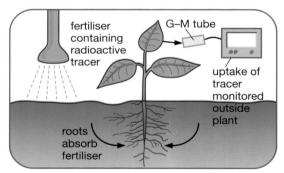

The tracer must have a short half-life so it does not stay in the environment after the experiment is finished.

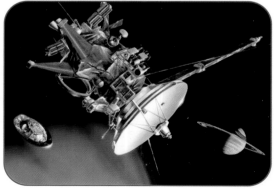

The Cassini space probe took 7 years to reach Saturn. It transmitted images of the planet back to Earth.

Reducing exposure

A teacher is demonstrating radioactivity experiments to her class. The radiation sources she uses are very weak, but she still follows strict safety procedures to make sure her dose and the doses of her students are as small as possible.

The teacher keeps the time each source is out of its box to a minimum. She replaces it in the box when she's not using it.

The sources are in sealed capsules to prevent any leakage of radioactive material.

A perspex screen absorbs beta radiation. Alpha radiation is absorbed by the air between the source and the students.

The box is lead-lined to absorb the radiation from the sources.

The teacher handles the sources with tweezers, not her fingers. This increases the distance between her fingers and the source. Keeping her fingers at least 10 cm from the source can reduce the dose they receive by 10 000 times!

The students sit well back from the demonstration.

The radiation from a source spreads in all directions. The further you are from the source, the smaller the radiation dose you receive.

At the end of the lesson the teacher counts the sources to make sure they have all been returned to the box. Then she locks the box in a metal box in the store room. It is not kept in a room in which people sit or work regularly.

8 List <u>three</u> ways in which you can minimise the dose from a radioactive source.

9 Where should radioactive sources be kept when not in use?

10 Explain how the dose received from a source depends on distance.

11 Why are radioactive sources for school use sealed in capsules?

What you need to remember

Choosing and handling isotopes
There is nothing new to <u>remember</u> in this section.

You should be able to evaluate radioactive sources for particular uses, including as tracers, in terms of the types of radiation emitted and their half-lives. You should be able to evaluate measures that can be taken to reduce exposure to nuclear radiations.

1 The Universe

Astronomers use telescopes to observe planets, stars and galaxies. They measure their movements, and the radiation they give out. In this way they have discovered how far away the planets, stars and galaxies are, and what they are made from.

What is a star?

Our Sun is a **star**. It is a huge ball of very hot, glowing gas.

1 How does the Sun produce its energy?

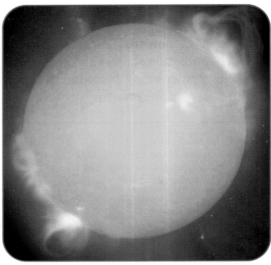

In the centre of the Sun, nuclear reactions give off vast amounts of energy. This energy radiates out from the Sun as heat and light.

What is a planet?

The Earth is a **planet**. Planets are smaller and colder than stars. The Earth and eight other major planets orbit the Sun in almost circular paths.

2 List the planets in the solar system.

3 Name some other objects in the solar system besides the Sun and the planets.

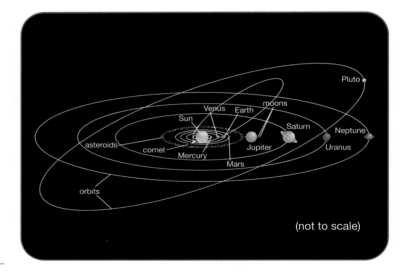

(not to scale)

How far away is the nearest star?

The Sun is the nearest star to Earth.

Light travels <u>very</u> fast, but it still takes light about 8 minutes to reach us from the Sun.

The next nearest star is called Proxima Centauri.

4 How long does it take light to reach us from Proxima Centauri?

5 How many times further away from us is Proxima Centauri than the Sun?

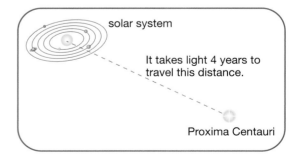

solar system

It takes light 4 years to travel this distance.

Proxima Centauri

What is a galaxy?

A **galaxy** is a group of many billions (thousands of millions) of stars. Our Sun is just one of billions of stars in our galaxy. Our galaxy is just one of billions of galaxies in the Universe.

Some galaxies are beautiful spirals, like our galaxy. Others are round or cigar-shaped.

6 Look at the top photograph. How many galaxies can you see?

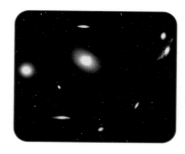

This shows part of the Virgo cluster. It takes light about 40 million years to reach us from these galaxies.

How big is the Universe?

Stars in a galaxy are often millions of times further apart than the planets in the solar system.

Galaxies are often millions of times further apart than the stars inside a galaxy.

Astronomers often tell us how far away things are by saying how long it takes the light from them to reach us. If it takes 1 year for the light reach us, the distance is 1 <u>light-year</u>.

7 What is the name of our galaxy?

8 Where in our galaxy is the solar system?

9 Copy and complete the table.

Object	How long it takes light from the object to reach us
Sun	
nearest other star	
Virgo cluster	

Our Sun is in a galaxy called the Milky Way. The sun is about two-thirds of the way out from the centre of our galaxy. It takes light about 100 000 years to cross the Milky Way.

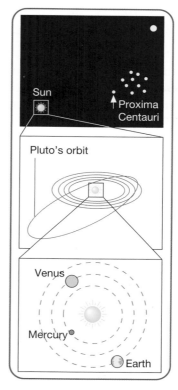

It takes 4 years for light to travel to the Sun from the nearest star.

It takes light about 10 hours to cross the solar system.

It takes light 500 seconds travel from the Sun to the Earth.

What you need to remember *Copy and complete using the **key words***

The Universe

The Earth is a _____. There are nine planets in our _____ _____. The planets orbit the Sun, which is our nearest _____.
The Sun is just one of billions of stars in our _____, which is called the Milky Way.
There are billions of galaxies in the Universe.

2 Observing the Universe

A new view

In 1610 the Italian scientist Galileo was the first person to observe the stars and planets with a telescope. He saw that there were many more stars than people could see with the naked eye.

At that time, the Catholic Church taught that the Sun and all the stars and planets moved around the Earth. Galileo's observations suggested that the planets moved around the Sun.

1 What did Galileo discover about Jupiter?

2 Why did Galileo's theories get him into trouble with the Catholic Church?

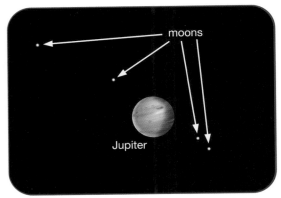

Galileo observed the planet Jupiter through his telescope. He saw at least four moons in orbit around it.

Telescopes today

In 1668, Isaac Newton invented a telescope which used a curved mirror rather than a lens. Most modern astronomical telescopes are based on his design. A large circular mirror with a curved surface collects the light from the stars. The mirror reflects and concentrates the light to form an image.

3 What is the ideal shape for a telescope mirror?

4 Write down <u>two</u> reasons why a large diameter mirror is better than a smaller diameter mirror.

5 How do astronomers observe the images formed by their telescopes?

6 What is the purpose of a spectrometer?

Telescope problems

The amateur astronomer in the picture uses a telescope in a back garden near London. The image is good, but it is not perfectly clear.

7 Describe <u>three</u> problems with using a telescope for astronomy in Britain.

Light pollution masks faint stars.
Air pollution makes the image hazy.
Cloud cover often prevents observations.

Top of the range telescope

The William Herschel telescope is powerful telescope used by British astronomers. It is 2426 m above sea level on La Palma, one of the Canary islands.
La Palma is much nearer the Equator than the UK is. The skies are clear all year round. At the high mountain observatory, there is very little air or light pollution. The atmosphere is thinner there than at sea level.

8 List <u>three</u> advantages of putting a telescope in a remote high mountain area nearer the Equator.

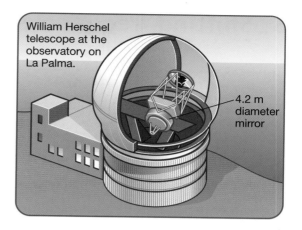

William Herschel telescope at the observatory on La Palma.

4.2 m diameter mirror

Space telescope

The USA used the Space Shuttle to launch the Hubble **space** telescope in 1990. The Hubble telescope's main mirror is 2.4 m in diameter. It's not as big as some telescopes on **Earth**, but its images are clearer.

9 Why are images from the Hubble so clear?

10 What is the disadvantage of space-based telescopes compared with those on Earth?

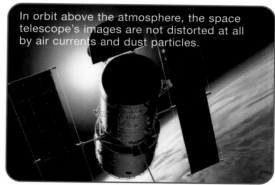

In orbit above the atmosphere, the space telescope's images are not distorted at all by air currents and dust particles.

The Hubble telescope has cost about 100 times more to build and maintain than the William Herschel telescope.

Other telescopes

Astronomers don't just observe the Universe with telescopes that detect **visible light**. They build telescopes that detect other parts of the electromagnetic spectrum too.
Radio telescopes have discovered pulsars (spinning neutron stars) and radio-galaxies that emit vast amounts of energy. X-ray telescopes can detect the X-rays from a supernova (exploding star) and from matter falling into a black hole.

11 Why are radio telescopes so large?

12 Name <u>two</u> objects in space that emit radio waves.

13 Why must X-ray telescopes be in space?

14 Name <u>two</u> objects an X-ray telescope can observe.

A radio telescope has a huge dish to collect very weak **radio waves** from distant stars and galaxies.

The Earth's atmosphere absorbs **X-rays**, so an X-ray telescope has to be in space.

What you need to remember *Copy and complete using the **key words***

Observing the Universe
We can observe the Universe from the _____ or from _____.
Telescopes may detect _____ _____ or other electromagnetic
radiations such as _____ _____ or _____.

You need to be able to compare and contrast the advantages and disadvantages of using different types of telescope on Earth and in space.

3 Shifting frequencies

> **REMEMBER**
> ■ The wavelength is the length of one complete wave.
> ■ The frequency is the number of waves passing a point in 1 second.

The diagram shows a train sounding its whistle.

The sound wave travels through the air with a certain **wavelength** and **frequency**.

1 Write down the wavelength and frequency of the sound when the train is stationary.

When the train is moving, the wavelength and frequency of the sound change. The waves are bunched up in front of the train and spread out behind.

2 What are the wavelength and frequency in front of the moving train?

What are the wavelength and frequency behind the moving train?

When a wave source moves <u>towards</u> an observer, the frequency is <u>higher</u> and the wavelength is <u>shorter</u>.

When a wave source moves <u>away</u> from an observer, the frequency is <u>lower</u> and <u>wavelength</u> is longer.

Stationary train

sound wave wavelength = 0.34 m

number of waves each second = 1000

Moving train

wavelength behind train = 0.37 m sound wave wavelength in front of train = 0.31 m

number of waves each second = 917

number of waves each second = 1100

Speed trap

A police speed gun uses electromagnetic waves to measure the speed of a vehicle.

4 What kind of electromagnetic waves does the speed gun use?

5 What happens to the wavelength and frequency of the reflected waves when the vehicle is moving towards the detector?

6 How do the changes in frequency and wavelength depend on the speed of the vehicle?

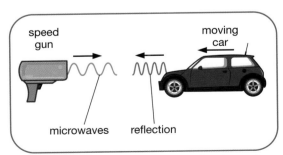

speed gun moving car

microwaves reflection

The waves reflected from a car moving towards the speed gun are bunched together. They have a higher frequency and a shorter wavelength than the waves given out by the gun. The faster the car is moving, the bigger the shifts in frequency and wavelength.

Red-shift

Astronomers examine the light from a star or a galaxy by splitting it up into a spectrum. They can tell from these spectra that distant galaxies are moving away from us.

The spectra of stars and galaxies have patterns of dark lines. These are the 'fingerprints' of different elements.

In the spectrum of the light from a distant galaxy, the lines of particular elements are shifted towards the red part of the spectrum. This is called a **red-shift**.

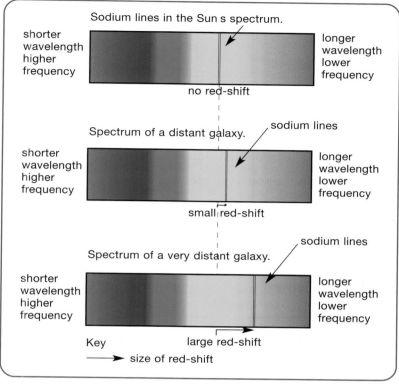

Sodium lines in the Sun s spectrum.

shorter wavelength higher frequency

longer wavelength lower frequency

no red-shift

Spectrum of a distant galaxy.

sodium lines

shorter wavelength higher frequency

longer wavelength lower frequency

small red-shift

Spectrum of a very distant galaxy.

sodium lines

shorter wavelength higher frequency

longer wavelength lower frequency

Key

large red-shift

size of red-shift

7 What does the red-shift show has happened to the wavelength and frequency of the light from the galaxy?

8 What does this shift tell us about the movement of the galaxy?

9 What kind of shift would you expect if a galaxy was moving towards us?

A red-shift shows us that a galaxy is moving away from us.

A more distant galaxy has a **bigger** red-shift.
This tells us that it is moving away faster.

10 Copy and complete the sentences.

The light from distant galaxies shows a red-_____.
This tells us that the galaxies are moving
_____ _____ us.
More distant galaxies have _____ red-shifts.
This tells us that they are moving away
_____.

4 How did the Universe begin?

Expanding Universe

Astronomers have measured the distance to different galaxies. They have also measured the speed at which they are moving away from us.

1 How can astronomers find the distance to a galaxy?

2 How can they find the speed of a galaxy?

The table gives some of results for the speeds of galaxies at different distances.

Galaxy location	Distance from Earth in millions of light years	Speed away from Earth in thousands of kilometres per second
Virgo	52	1
Ursa Major	650	15
Corona	950	20
Bootes	1700	39
Hydra	2600	61

Astronomers find the distance to a galaxy by measuring the brightness of certain stars. The further away the galaxy, the dimmer the stars. Astronomers can tell how a galaxy is moving by looking at the colour (wavelength) of the light. If there is a red-shift, the galaxy is moving away from us. The bigger the shift, the faster it's moving away.

3 Plot a graph of speed against distance.
Draw a line of best fit.

4 What can you say about the speed of distant galaxies compared to those that are closer to Earth?

In 1929, Edwin Hubble discovered that the further away galaxies are from us, the faster they are moving away. This suggests that the whole Universe is **expanding** (getting bigger).

The picture shows a model of an expanding Universe.

5 Copy and complete the sentences.

As the Universe expands, all the galaxies get _____ apart.
The greater the distance between two galaxies, the _____ they move away from each other.

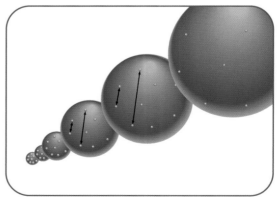

All the galaxies get further apart as the Universe expands.
More distant galaxies move away from each other faster than nearby galaxies.

The big bang theory

Measurements of red-shift from distant galaxies show that the Universe is expanding. This suggests that the whole Universe began from a very small initial **point**. Scientists believe that the whole Universe started with a huge explosion of matter and energy from this point. This is called the **big bang** theory.

6 Explain what is meant by the 'big bang' theory.

7 Give <u>two</u> pieces of evidence that suggest the big bang happened in this way.

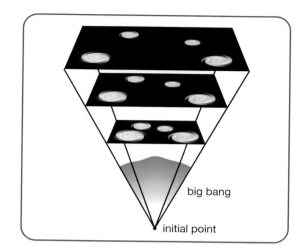

The age of the Universe

By measuring the speeds of many galaxies and their distances from us, astronomers have calculated when the 'big bang' happened. They think that it was probably about 15 billion years ago.

Look at the time line for the Universe below.

8 How long ago did the first galaxies begin to form?

9 How long ago did our Sun form?

10 What is the age of the Earth?

The big bang theory predicts that heat radiation left over from the initial explosion should be found throughout the Universe. Sensitive radio-telescopes have found this radiation.

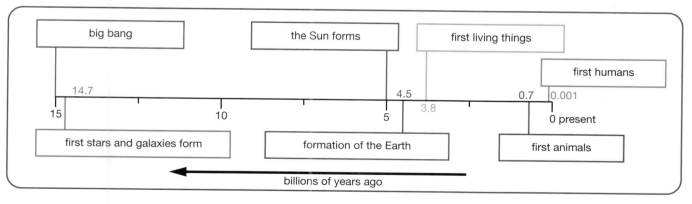

billions of years ago

What you need to remember *Copy and complete using the **key words***

How did the Universe begin?

The bigger red-shift of more distant galaxies is evidence that the Universe is

_____.

This evidence supports the _____ _____ theory.
The big bang theory is that the Universe began from a very small initial _____.

How science works

■ Introduction

Throughout this book, you will have come across examples of how science works.

Scientists

■ try to explain the world around us
■ gather evidence to try to solve problems
■ argue about the reliability and validity of evidence
■ make discoveries that lead to technologies that are important for society and for the environment.

You can identify the main sections that are concerned with **How science works** by looking at the **What you need to remember** boxes which have no blank spaces for you to fill in.

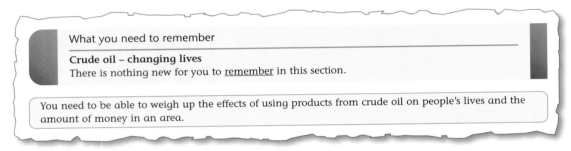

What you need to remember

Crude oil – changing lives
There is nothing new for you to <u>remember</u> in this section.

You need to be able to weigh up the effects of using products from crude oil on people's lives and the amount of money in an area.

Here are some examples of the sorts of issues you need to think about.

■ You need to be able to compare and contrast the particular advantages and disadvantages of using different energy sources to generate electricity.

■ You need to be able to evaluate evidence about environmental issues such as global warming. You need to ask yourself whether the data are valid and reliable.

■ You need to be able to weigh up the good and bad points about new fuels.

■ You need to be able to evaluate information about possible risks from radiation and methods of reducing exposure.

■ You need to be able to describe and explain some of the problems and benefits of using hormones to control fertility, including IVF.

You can learn the skills of dealing with these sorts of issues.

The following pages draw together some of the skills that you will need for your work in class, for tests and examinations and for the centre-assessed unit.

■ The centre-assessed unit

As part of your normal work in class, you will be asked to

■ carry out practical activities on a particular topic
■ use the data you collect in a written test taken under examination conditions.

■ Gathering evidence – observing

Careful observation is a key part of good science. Observing doesn't just mean looking. It can involve all your senses.

You observe similarities and differences when you classify objects or organisms. To do this, you need to be able to recognise which observations are useful for your purpose and which are not. For example, classifying flowers according to the arrangement of petals is useful in biology, but classifying according to colour isn't.

Observing patterns can lead to investigations.
For example, noticing the differences in cooling rates of tea in different teapots could lead to an investigation of the pots and a search for the cause of the differences.

Observations of an object, a living thing or something that happens.

↓

Questions

↓

Investigations to try to answer these questions, including making

■ further observations
■ measurements
■ experiments

■ Designing an investigation

Suppose you were investigating the effects of surface colour on cooling by radiation.

You could do this by allowing hot water to cool in two metal cans – one painted white and the other painted dull black. You could measure the time taken for each sample to cool by 30 °C.

Your investigation must be a <u>fair test</u>. So you need to keep everything but the surface colour of the cans the same.

You need to

■ use the same kind and size of can
■ use the same quantity of water in each can
■ cover both cans in the same way to reduce heat loss by convection and evaporation
■ place both cans in a similar situation (if one can is in sunlight and the other in shade, the results will not be valid)
■ begin recording at the same starting temperature (80 °C say).

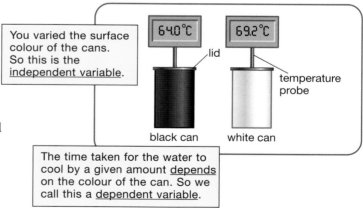

You varied the surface colour of the cans. So this is the <u>independent variable</u>.

64.0 °C   69.2 °C

lid

temperature probe

black can   white can

The time taken for the water to cool by a given amount <u>depends</u> on the colour of the can. So we call this a <u>dependent variable</u>.

The variables that you control (keep the same) are the <u>control variables</u>. The quantity of water and the starting temperature are two of the control variables.

Gathering evidence – measuring

We use our senses to observe differences between objects and organisms and to observe changes. However, we can support our observations and increase the accuracy of the information we gather by measuring – but only if we measure accurately.

Validity of data

When you are planning an investigation, you need to think about whether the data you collect or the measurements you make are going to give you the information that you need. For example, if you want to compare the amounts of gas and electricity used by houses with and without insulation, you must look at meter readings for a full year, not just for the summer months.

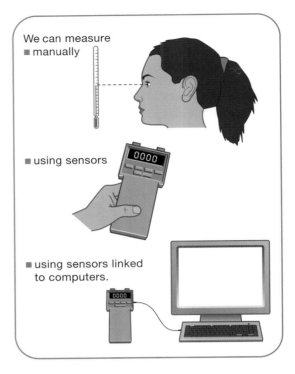

We can measure
- manually
- using sensors
- using sensors linked to computers.

Reliability

The way that you make your measurements affects their reliability. If you and others can obtain the same results in repeats of the experiment, then your results are reliable.

Things that affect reliability include

- the type of instrument you select and use
- whether the instrument was accurate
- whether it was set up correctly
- who took the measurements
- whether or not measurements were repeated to obtain mean values.

Sophie measures the length of a bench with a cheap plastic tape measure. She can read the tape to the nearest millimetre, so her measurement is <u>precise</u>. But the tape has stretched so her result is <u>not accurate</u>.

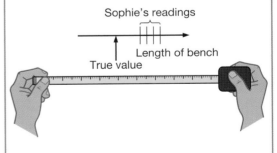

The readings are close together but the mean is not the true value.

Mohan is measuring the bench with a wooden rule which only has centimetre divisions. He must estimate the readings between the divisions. His rule is not as <u>precise</u> as Sophie's tape, but is more <u>accurate</u> because it has not stretched.

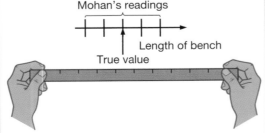

The readings vary, but the mean is close to the true value.

■ Presenting data

You will often be asked to record data in a table as you carry out an investigation. Then, you may need to present this data in a way that allows you to pick out any patterns most easily.

So, in your coursework and in tests and examinations, you will need to be able to

- <u>design</u> tables for your results and complete them accurately
- <u>present</u> data in several different ways, for example as bar charts and line graphs
- <u>choose</u> the best way of presenting data for different types of datasets.

The best way to present your data depends on the types of variables you are dealing with.

Types of variables

- <u>Independent variable.</u> This is a variable that you decide to alter. In the example on page 313, we varied the surface colour of the can.

- <u>Dependent variable.</u> This is the variable that you measure. In this example, we measured and recorded the time for the sample to cool by 30 °C.

- In this example, the independent variable is <u>discrete</u> (black or white), so you could choose a bar chart to present your results.

- The independent variable goes on the x-axis.

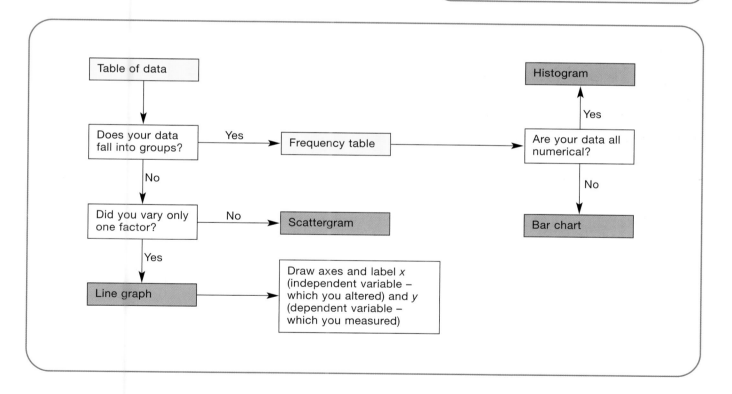

■ Drawing bar charts

> **REMEMBER**
>
> You use bar charts when the data falls into distinct groups or categories. We say that the variable is a <u>categoric variable</u>.

Continuous and categoric variables

Suppose you were investigating carbon dioxide emissions.
You could

- investigate the change in carbon dioxide concentration over time. Both of these variables are <u>continuous</u> so you should present the data as a line graph.
- investigate the carbon dioxide emissions in different parts of the world. You would then have separate sets or categories of data. You have a <u>categoric</u> variable so you should present data as a bar chart.

You may be asked to draw a bar chart.

Choose sensible scales that allow you to use at least half the page, and label the axes.

Remember

- to look carefully at the scale
- to draw the bars the same thickness and equally spaced out
- to draw the top of each bar with a thin straight line
- to label each bar, or draw a key.

The bar chart shows how much carbon an average person puts into the air in different parts of the world.

You may be asked to compare carbon emissions in North America and Africa.

You could say that the average person in North America is responsible for more carbon emissions than a person in Africa.

A better answer is to say that the average person in North America is responsible for 15 times the carbon emissions of the average person in Africa.

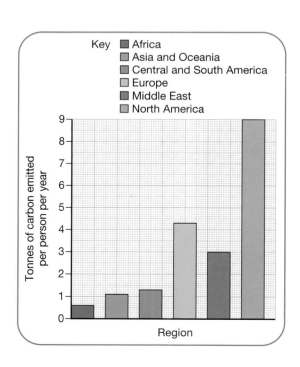

■ Drawing line graphs

■ Choose sensible scales for the axes. (You should use more than half of the available squares along each axis.)

■ Label the axes (for example, *Time taken for completion of reaction (min)*).

■ Mark all the points neatly and accurately …

… like this 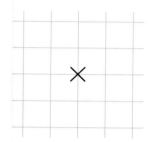   … or like this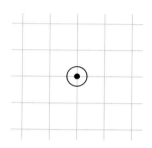

■ Use a pencil to draw your line so you can rub it out if you don't get it right first time.

■

If …	Then …
… the points are close to being a straight line or a smooth curve …	… draw the 'best fit' straight line or smooth curve.
… the theory suggests that the change is smooth …	
… there is a point that is obviously wrong …	… ignore it. Indicate that you did so.

■ Interpreting line graphs

When you are reading off values from a graph make sure you do the following.

■ Check the scales on the axes so that you know what each small square on the grid represents.

■ Remember to quote units in your answer. (You can find these on the axis where you read off your answer. You can still quote the correct units even if you don't understand what they mean!)

■ Be as precise and accurate as you can
  – when describing trends or patterns
(in the example, if you're asked what happens to the temperature of liquid 2 between 0 and 3 minutes, *'decreases steadily'* is a better answer than *'decreases'*)

  – when specifying key points
(in the example, saying *'there is no temperature change in liquid 2 between 4 and 7 minutes'* is better than saying *'the temperature stayed the same for 3 minutes'*)

  – when making comparisons
(in the example, if you're asked to compare the cooling curves of the two liquids *'liquid 2 became a solid at 49°C whereas liquid 1 became solid at 55 °C'* is better than saying *'liquid 2 became solid at a lower temperature than liquid 1'*).

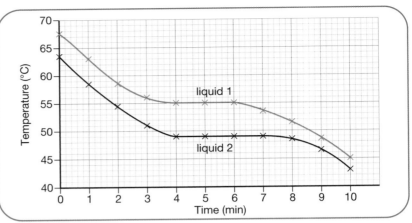

The graph shows the results of an experiment about cooling liquids. As the liquids cool, they become solid. While this is happening there is no temperature change.

■ Pie charts

Where does the nitrate go?

The pie chart shows what happens to the nitrate in fertiliser added to soil.

You may be asked to read the data from a pie chart and put it into a table like this.

What happens to the nitrate in fertiliser	%
in harvested crop	68
becomes organic nitrogen in soil	16
leached out by rain	14
nitrate in soil	2

You may be asked to complete a pie chart.

Draw thin, straight lines. Remember to add all the labels, or provide a key.

> Get plenty of practice handling data in these ways so that you'll
> - do well in your coursework
> - do the right thing even if you're nervous in an examination.

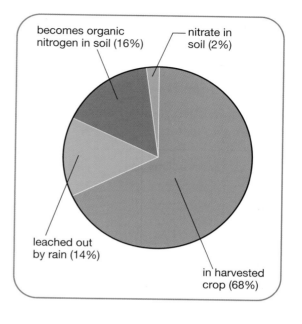

■ Sankey diagrams

What happens to the energy?

The diagram shows what happens to each 100 J of energy from petrol when it burns in a car engine.

Remember that all the energy must be transferred in some form.

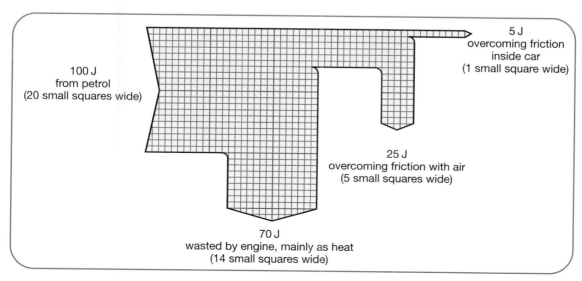

■ Identifying patterns in data

You have already seen that presenting data in suitable graphs and charts can help you to identify patterns. You have also learnt how to describe some of them.

Line graphs often show whether or not there is a correlation between two factors.

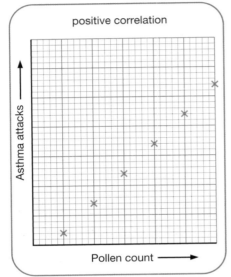

positive correlation

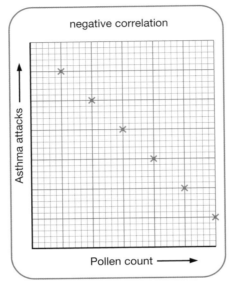

negative correlation

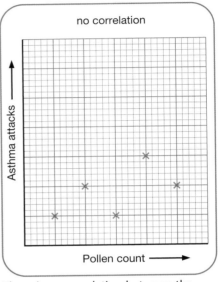

no correlation

As the pollen count rises, so does the number of asthma attacks. This is a positive correlation. The factor (pollen count) may or may not be a cause of asthma attacks.

The number of asthma attacks falls as the pollen count increases. This is a negative correlation. The factor (pollen count) may or may not be a cause of the fall in the number of asthma attacks.

There is no correlation between the number of asthma attacks and the pollen count.

If there is a correlation between two factors, then this suggests that one <u>may be</u> a cause of the other.

But to say that one <u>causes</u> the other, you need

■ further evidence
■ some backing from theory to show how the factor could cause the other.

So, some links that you observe are <u>causal</u> but others may be due to other factors. For example, data show a link between ice cream sales and asthma. But it is an <u>associated factor</u>, summer conditions, that leads to both increased ice cream sales and the increase in pollen count.

Other links are just due to <u>chance</u>.

Pollen <u>could be</u> a cause of asthma attacks because it can irritate the lining of the nose and bronchial tubes. This could cause narrowing of the tubes and, as a result, the breathing difficulties of an asthma attack. However, other investigations have shown that many factors, including air pollution and stress, affect the rate of asthma attacks.

So, you <u>cannot</u> say that pollen is <u>the</u> cause of asthma attacks.

- Evaluation – including the validity and reliability of evidence

You need to be able to evaluate information in science. You will have learnt some of the skills at KS3, and you need to continue to extend and practise them.

For example, when you evaluate an investigation, you are probably used to thinking about

- the strengths and weaknesses of your plan
- whether the data or information you gather is valid and reliable (see page 314)
- checking for anomalies in data (data that do not fit the pattern) and suggesting reasons for them
- suggesting improvements for future investigations.

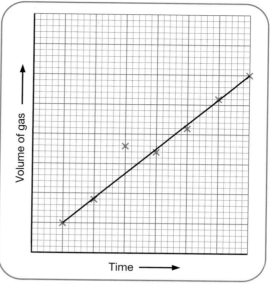

One point doesn't fit the pattern, so it's ignored. It's an <u>anomalous result</u>.

You need to be able to do these things in relation to the work of others too. For example, in Chemistry, on pages 196–199, you evaluate the evidence for theories about how features of the Earth's crust such as mountains developed.

> **How to evaluate information is a skill that you can learn**
> You need this skill in your everyday life too.
> For example
>
> - to judge what you read in the newspapers, hear on the radio or see on TV. You need to be able to recognise whether what you are reading is fact or opinion, as you did on pages 288–289
> - to judge the ideas of others
> - to have confidence in your own ideas because you have thought about the evidence that supports them.

Is it risky to live near pylons?

Food additive linked to cancer!

Should you give up eating tuna?

Is this vaccine safe?

Which is less harmful to the environment, petrol or diesel?

Should there be an environment tax on carrier bags?

Do we need nuclear energy?

Sunbed users risk cancer!

You may have to make decisions about these issues. You'll need to be able to judge the information you are given and to find out more information for yourself.

■ How society judges evidence

As individuals, we have to look at evidence and evaluate it in relation to the decisions we make

- about our own lives
- about the lives of our families
- when we serve on juries
- when we vote.

> If you are evaluating research that seems to cast doubt on the idea that there is a link between sugar and tooth decay, you need to know who paid for the research – it might have been a sugar producer.

> There is no clear evidence of a link between childhood leukaemia and living close to pylons. But parents are likely to be concerned by even the suggestion of a risk to their children, and may wish to take action.

Social factors sometimes influence whether scientific evidence and new theories are accepted.

For example, it sometimes depends on

- what ideas are fashionable at the time
- who put forward the new ideas.

> Darwin wasn't keen to publish his ideas about evolution because they seemed to go against the ideas about creation in the Bible (see pages 88–89).

> It took a long time for people to take Wegener's ideas about the Earth's crust seriously. One problem was that he was a meteorologist, not a geologist (see pages 198–199).

Sometimes people just don't want to accept evidence.

> People continue to use sunbeds and mobile phones despite safety concerns. They may feel that the benefits they gain from them now outweigh any long-term risks.

> Doctors accepted Doll and Hill's evidence about smoking and large numbers gave up. But, at first, most other people didn't want to admit that there might be a link.

So, you need to be aware that decisions aren't always based on evidence alone.

Revising

You are more likely to remember things if you

- review your work regularly. The first time you revise should not be for an examination.
- revise actively rather than just reading through notes. You'll find that it helps to stop your mind wandering. For example, you could make brief notes or a chart of key points, memorise formulas and plan answers to questions. Notes and charts are useful for last-minute revision.

■ Using this book

See if you know which words go into the **What you need to remember** boxes for the pages you are revising.

Try to do this without looking at the text or diagrams on the pages. Then, if there is anything you can't remember, read the text and look at the diagrams to find the answer.

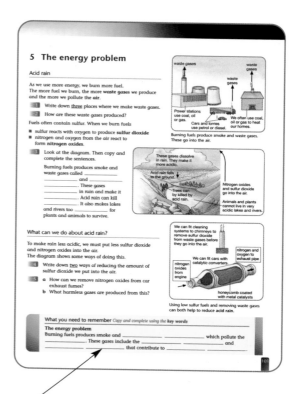

What you need to remember *Copy and complete using the **key words***

The energy problem
Burning fuels produces smoke and _____waste_____ _____gases_____ which pollute the _____air_____. These gases include the _____sulfur_____ _____dioxide_____ and _____nitrogen_____ _____oxides_____ that contribute to _____acid_____ _____.

Remember that

- the key words are printed in bold type like this: **Pesticides** and **herbicides** are two examples of these chemicals.
- you can check your answers at the back of the book (pages 329 to 344).

You can also use the **What you need to remember** boxes for a last-minute review of the things that you need to <u>know</u>.

But you don't just have to <u>remember</u> the scientific ideas, you also need to be able to <u>use</u> them. You may be asked to do this in a situation you haven't met before.

Tests and examinations

In tests, you will be assessed on

- your knowledge and understanding of
  - science
  - how science works.

- your ability to apply your
  - skills
  - knowledge
  - understanding.

In the centre-assessed unit, you will be assessed on your practical, enquiry and data-handling skills.

In the external assessment tests, you will answer either multiple choice questions (Science A) or short answer written questions (Science B).

Both Science A and B questions are based on

- science knowledge and understanding
- the way science works
- application of knowledge and understanding to new situations.

Answering multiple choice questions

Only one of the alternatives will be correct.

Another may be almost correct and the rest will be wrong.

If you are not sure of the answer, rule out the ones that you know are wrong, then make a sensible guess.

Farmers sometimes add lime to the soil in their fields. They do this mainly to:

A Increase the calcium in their crops

B Make the soil less acid – correct

C Get rid of moles

D Increase the calcium supply for grazing animals.

The count rate from a radioactive isotope decreases from 80 to 20 counts per second in 10 minutes. The half-life of the sample is:

A 10 minutes

B 8 minutes

C 5 minutes

D 2.5 minutes

Answering short answer questions based on what you should know

Three hormones control the maturing of an egg in an ovary and then its release. Which of the three hormones directly causes the release of an egg in the middle of the menstrual cycle?

If you're not sure of the answer

You might be tempted to write down several answers in the hope that one of them is right. This is a bad idea. In most cases, you'll automatically get no marks.

If you write FSH or LH as your answer to this question, you will score 0 marks even though LH is the correct answer.

You must make up your mind as to what you think is the most likely answer. If you change your mind later, you can cross out the old answer and write the new one.

Answering short answer questions in which you use your knowledge in a new situation

When microorganisms feed and grow they produce waste. If you add the right microorganisms to warm milk in a vacuum flask, they produce a waste acid. This turns the milk into yoghurt in less than a day. Write down two reasons why this happens quickly.

Two possible answers are that the milk contains water and that it is warm. Oxygen probably isn't the reason because it happens in a sealed container. You could also say

- the milk contains plenty of food for the microorganisms
- the microorganisms reproduce quickly (like microorganisms which cause diseases inside your body).

■ Calculations

Even if you get the wrong answer to a calculation, you can still get quite a lot of marks.

To gain these marks, you must have gone about the calculation in the right way. But the person marking your answer can only see that you've done this if you write down your working neatly and set it out tidily so it's quite clear what you have done.

Look at the example in the Box.

A potato has a mass of 150 grams. All of the water in the potato is evaporated in a cool oven. The dry matter in the potato has a mass of 7.5 grams.
What is the percentage of water in the potato?

Always set out your class work and homework calculations like this so that you get into good habits.

Then you'll still do calculations in the right way even under the pressure of examinations.

Answering short answer questions involving calculations

Mass of water in potato $= 150\,g - 7.5\,g$

$= 142.5\,g$

So fraction of potato that is water $= \dfrac{142.5\,g}{150\,g}$

So percentage of potato that is water $= \dfrac{142.5\,g}{150\,g} \times 100\%$

$= 95\%$

You gain marks for these steps even if you make a mistake.

How to write a balanced symbol equation

Step 1. Write down the word equation for the reaction (see page 121).

Step 2. Write down the formulas for the reactants and products.

Step 3. Check to see if the equation is balanced. Count the atoms on both sides of the equation.

(You do not need to write this down.)

If the equation is not balanced, you need to go on to Step 4.

Step 4. Balance the equation. Do this by writing a number in front of one or more of the formulas. This number increases the numbers of all of the atoms in the formula.

Step 5. Check that the equation is now balanced.

If it isn't, go back to Step 4.

1 **a** Write down the word equation and the unbalanced symbol equation for the following reaction:

   calcium + water → calcium + hydrogen
                                hydroxide

   $Ca \ + \ H_2O \ \to \ Ca(OH)_2 + \ H_2$

   b Balance the symbol equation.
   c Add state symbols to your equation

2 Write balanced symbol equations for these reactions. Show all the steps.

   a potassium + chlorine → potassium chloride
   b copper oxide + hydrogen → copper + water

Formulas you need for question 2

chlorine	Cl_2
hydrogen	H_2
potassium chloride	KCl
copper oxide	CuO
water	H_2O

Example: the reaction between sodium metal and water

sodium + water → sodium + hydrogen
                            hydroxide

$Na \ + \ H_2O \ \to \ NaOH + \ H_2$

Reactants		Products
1	sodium atoms	1
2	hydrogen atoms	3
1	oxygen atoms	1

The equation is not balanced because the number of hydrogen atoms is not the same on each side.

We can balance the hydrogen atoms by doubling up the water and sodium hydroxide.

$2Na + 2H_2O \to 2NaOH + H_2$

2NaOH means 2 Na atoms, 2 O atoms and 2 H atoms.

This means 4 H atoms and 2 O atoms. So the O atoms also balance (two on each side).

This 2 is then needed so that there are 2 Na atoms on each side.

Check:

Reactants		Products
2	sodium atoms	2
4	hydrogen atoms	4
2	oxygen atoms	2

The equation now balances. There are the same numbers of each type of atom on each side.

Adding state symbols

When you have balanced an equation, you should then add state symbols. For example:

$2Na(s) + 2H_2O(l) \to 2NaOH(aq) + H_2(g)$

Remember: (s) = solid
               (l) = liquid
               (g) = gas
               (aq) = in solution in water

Periodic table

The periodic table of elements

Group 1	Group 2												Group 3	Group 4	Group 5	Group 6	Group 7	Group 0
						1 **H** hydrogen 1												4 **He** helium 2
7 **Li** lithium 3	9 **Be** beryllium 4												11 **B** boron 5	12 **C** carbon 6	14 **N** nitrogen 7	16 **O** oxygen 8	19 **F** fluorine 9	20 **Ne** neon 10
23 **Na** sodium 11	24 **Mg** magnesium 12												27 **Al** aluminium 13	28 **Si** silicon 14	31 **P** phosphorus 15	32 **S** sulfur 16	35.5 **Cl** chlorine 17	40 **Ar** argon 18
39 **K** potassium 19	40 **Ca** calcium 20	45 **Sc** scandium 21	48 **Ti** titanium 22	51 **V** vanadium 23	52 **Cr** chromium 24	55 **Mn** manganese 25	56 **Fe** iron 26	59 **Co** cobalt 27	59 **Ni** nickel 28	63.5 **Cu** copper 29	65 **Zn** zinc 30		70 **Ga** gallium 31	73 **Ge** germanium 32	75 **As** arsenic 33	79 **Se** selenium 34	80 **Br** bromine 35	84 **Kr** krypton 36
85 **Rb** rubidium 37	88 **Sr** strontium 38	89 **Y** yttrium 39	91 **Zr** zirconium 40	93 **Nb** niobium 41	96 **Mo** molybdenum 42	[98] **Tc** technetium 43	101 **Ru** ruthenium 44	103 **Rh** rhodium 45	106 **Pd** palladium 46	108 **Ag** silver 47	112 **Cd** cadmium 48		115 **In** indium 49	119 **Sn** tin 50	122 **Sb** antimony 51	128 **Te** tellurium 52	127 **I** iodine 53	131 **Xe** xenon 54
133 **Cs** caesium 55	137 **Ba** barium 56	139 **La*** lanthanum 57	178 **Hf** hafnium 72	181 **Ta** tantalum 73	184 **W** tungsten 74	186 **Re** rhenium 75	190 **Os** osmium 76	192 **Ir** iridium 77	195 **Pt** platinum 78	197 **Au** gold 79	201 **Hg** mercury 80		204 **Tl** thallium 81	207 **Pb** lead 82	209 **Bi** bismuth 83	[210] **Po** polonium 84	[210] **At** astatine 85	[222] **Rn** radon 86
[223] **Fr** francium 87	[226] **Ra** radium 88	[227] **Ac*** actinium 89	[261] **Rf** rutherfordium 104	[262] **Db** dubnium 105	[266] **Sg** seaborgium 106	[264] **Bh** bohrium 107	[277] **Hs** hassium 108	[268] **Mt** meitnerium 109	[271] **Ds** darmstadtium 110	[272] **Rg** roentgenium 111								

Elements with atomic numbers 112–116 have been reported but not fully authenticated

* The Lanthanides (atomic numbers 58–71) and the Actinides (atomic numbers 90–103) have been omitted. The mass numbers of **Cu** and **Cl** have not been rounded to the nearest whole number.

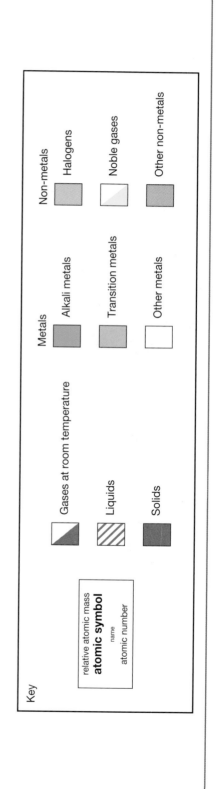

Key

relative atomic mass
atomic symbol
name
atomic number

Gases at room temperature

Liquids

Solids

Metals

Alkali metals

Transition metals

Other metals

Non-metals

Halogens

Noble gases

Other non-metals

Formulas that you must remember and be able to use

■ Energy

The cost of using an electrical appliance is given by

cost = number of kilowatt-hours × cost per kilowatt-hour

(Note: one kilowatt-hour of electricity is also called a Unit.)

Energy transferred from the mains supply is measured in kilowatt-hours or Units

energy transferred	=	power	×	time
(kilowatt-hours, kW h)		(kilowatts, kW)		(hours, h)

The energy transferred by an electrical device can be calculated as follows

energy transferred	=	power	×	time
(joules, J)		(watts, W)		(seconds, s)

You can calculate the efficiency of an energy-transferring device as follows

$$\text{efficiency} = \frac{\text{useful energy transferred by device}}{\text{total energy transferred by device}}$$

(Note: an efficiency is just a number; it has no units. You can state an efficiency as an ordinary fraction, a decimal fraction or a percentage, for example 3/4 , 0.75 or 75%.)

■ Waves and radiation

Wave-speed, wavelength and frequency are related as follows

wave-speed	=	frequency	×	wavelength
(metres per second, m/s)		(hertz, Hz)		(metres, m)

Biology

1 Responding to changes

1 Survival

You need sense organs to detect **stimuli** – to make you aware of changes in your **environment**. Sense organs contain special cells called **receptors**. Different receptors detect different stimuli. Some are sensitive to touch, to **pressure** or to temperature. Others detect light, **sounds**, changes in position and chemicals.

You don't need to know the structure and function of sense organs such as the ear and eye.

2 Making decisions – coordination

Your **nervous** system allows you to react to your surroundings and **coordinate** your behaviour. Information from receptors passes along **sensory** neurones in **nerves** to your spinal cord and brain. Your brain coordinates the response. It sends nerve impulses along **motor** neurones to the **effectors** that respond. There is a tiny gap called a **synapse** between one **neurone** and the next.

3 Automatic responses

Fast, **automatic** responses to stimuli are called **reflex** actions. Impulses pass from receptors to effectors via sensory, relay and **motor** neurones. At junctions between neurones, there are tiny gaps called **synapses**. Nerve impulses reach effectors very rapidly and cause the response. If the effector is a muscle, it responds by **contracting**. If it is a gland, it responds by releasing or **secreting** a chemical.

4 Keeping things the same in your body

For it to work properly, everything inside your body must be kept at a **constant** level. Special glands in your body produce chemicals called **hormones** to control the amounts of water, ions and **sugar** in your blood. Your **bloodstream** carries hormones to their **target** organs.
You lose water from your **lungs** in your breath. You lose water and ions from your skin in **sweat** and from your kidneys in **urine**. For **enzymes** to work at their best, your body **temperature** must be kept constant.

You need to be able to evaluate the claims of manufacturers about sports drinks.

5 The menstrual cycle

The pituitary gland secretes the hormones **FSH** and **LH**. FSH affects the ovaries. It stimulates them to make **eggs** mature and to produce hormones including **oestrogen**. Oestrogen from the ovaries makes the lining of the **womb** thicken. It also inhibits FSH production and causes the release of the hormone LH by the **pituitary gland**. LH stimulates the **ovaries** to release an egg at about the middle of the **menstrual cycle**.

6 Using hormones to control pregnancy

Some women use **hormones** to control their **fertility**. FSH is a fertility **drug** for women who don't produce enough **FSH** of their own. It helps a woman to become **pregnant** by stimulating her ovaries to make eggs mature. Oral **contraceptive** pills contain hormones that inhibit FSH production. They stop **eggs** maturing.

You should be able to describe and explain some of the problems and benefits of using hormones to control fertility, including IVF.

2 Keeping healthy

1 A healthy diet

A healthy diet contains the right balance of the different **food groups** and the right amount of **energy**. We say that a person whose diet is not balanced is **malnourished**. A malnourished person may be too fat, too thin or have a **deficiency disease**.

2 Energy balance

The rate at which chemical reactions happen in your cells is called your **metabolic rate**. It depends on

- how active you are
- the proportion of **muscle** to fat in your body
- your genes (**inherited** factors).

Exercise increases your metabolic rate and it stays high for some time after you finish exercising. If you take regular exercise, you are likely to be **fitter** than people who don't. The less exercise you take and the warmer it is, the less **energy** food you need.

3 More about body mass

In the developed world many people eat too much and take too little **exercise**. They easily become **overweight** and develop health problems. People who are **obese** are at greater risk of getting diseases linked with excess weight such as **arthritis, diabetes, heart disease** and **high blood pressure**. In the developing world, some people have **health** problems linked to lack of food. They may have poor resistance to **infection**. Women may have irregular **periods**.

4 How can you lose body mass?

There is nothing new for you to <u>remember</u> in this section.

You need to be able to evaluate claims made by slimming programmes.

5 Diet and heart disease

Processed foods often contain a high proportion of **fat** and **salt**. For about 30% of the population, too much salt can cause an increase in **blood pressure**. The fat in your diet and inherited factors affect the amount of **cholesterol** your **liver** makes. Two types of **lipoproteins**, LDL and HDL, carry cholesterol around your body. High levels of LDL (bad) cholesterol increase your risk of blood vessel damage and **heart disease**. HDL (good) cholesterol protects your arteries. Eating polyunsaturated and **monounsaturated** fats may lower blood cholesterol and help to improve the LDL / HDL balance that is important for heart health. Eating **saturated** fats can increase blood cholesterol.

3 Our bodies and drugs

1 People and drugs

A substance that can change the way your body works is called a **drug**. Many drugs come from **natural** substances. **Indigenous** (native) peoples usually know about their local sources of drugs and have used them for thousands of years. Some drugs are beneficial but can also **harm** our bodies. Some people use drugs for **recreation**. Some are more harmful than others. Some are legal, some **illegal**. The overall impact of **legal** drugs on health is much greater than the impact of illegal drugs, because more people use them.

You need to be able to evaluate the different types of drugs and why some people use illegal drugs for recreation.

2 What's your poison – alcohol?

Alcohol can damage organs such as your **brain** and **liver**. It also affects your **nervous system**. Your **reactions** become slower and you may lose self-control. You may even lose consciousness and go into a **coma**.

3 Legal but harmful – tobacco

Tobacco smoke contains

- **nicotine** – an addictive substance
- **carcinogens** – substances that cause cancer
- **carbon monoxide** – which reduces the amount of oxygen your blood can carry.

When a pregnant woman smokes, the fetus can be deprived of **oxygen** so the baby may have a low **birth mass**.

4 Smoking and lung cancer

There is nothing new for you to <u>remember</u> in this section.

You need to be able to explain how the link between lung cancer and smoking gradually became accepted.

5 Addiction

Drugs change the **chemical** processes in people's bodies so they may become dependent or **addicted** to them. They may suffer **withdrawal symptoms** without them. **Heroin** and **cocaine** are very addictive.

You need to be able to evaluate studies about links between cannabis use, health and addiction to hard drugs. You need to be able to evaluate the different ways of trying to stop smoking.

6 Making sure medicines are safe

Scientists **test** new medicinal drugs in the laboratory to make sure they are not **toxic**. Then they do **trials** on human volunteers to find any **side-effects**. Sometimes drug tests fail to show up problems. **Thalidomide** is a drug that was developed as a sleeping pill. Doctors discovered that it also helped to relieve **morning sickness** in pregnant women. Sadly, when pregnant women took it, their babies were born with abnormal **limbs**. The drug was banned. Recently, doctors have started to prescribe it to treat **leprosy**.

7 Drugs to prevent problems

There is nothing new for you to <u>remember</u> in this section.

You need to be able to evaluate the effects of statins on cardiovascular disease.

4 Infectious diseases

1 The problem of infection

There is nothing new for you to <u>remember</u> in this section.

You need to be able to relate the contribution of Semmelweiss in controlling infection to solving modern problems with the spread of infection in hospitals.

2 Invading microorganisms

Microorganisms such as **bacteria** and **viruses** can get into your body. They may multiply rapidly, releasing **toxins** (poisons) into your tissues. These make you feel ill. Viruses can **reproduce** only inside living cells. The newly produced viruses burst out of the cells, causing **damage**. The microorganisms that cause **disease** are called **pathogens**. **White blood cells** help to defend our bodies against them.

3 How do we treat diseases?

Doctors prescribe some medicines to help relieve **symptoms** of a disease. For example, **painkillers** relieve aches and pains but they don't kill the **pathogens**. **Antibiotics**, including **penicillin**, kill bacteria inside the body. They can't kill **viruses** because they live and reproduce inside cells. It's hard to find drugs that will kill them without damaging body **tissues**.

4 Bacteria and viruses change

Many strains of bacteria, including **MRSA**, have become **resistant** to antibiotics as a result of **natural selection**. To prevent even more bacteria developing resistance, it is important not to **over-use** antibiotics.

You need to be able to relate epidemics and pandemics of diseases such as bird flu (a virus infection) to mutation of bacteria and viruses.

5 Immunity and vaccination

Having a disease makes you **immune** to another infection by that disease. You can also become immune by being **immunised**. Doctors and nurses put small amounts of **dead** or **inactive** forms of a pathogen into your body as a **vaccine**. We call this **vaccination**. After vaccination, your body responds to future infection by the pathogen as though you have already had the disease.

6 Humans against microorganisms

When pathogens get into your body, your white blood cells help to defend you against them. Some white blood cells take pathogens into their cells. We say they **ingest** them. Some produce **antibodies** to destroy particular viruses or bacteria. Others make **antitoxins** to counteract the poisons (toxins) the pathogens release. Having a disease, or being vaccinated against it, makes you **immune** to that particular disease. When you meet it again, your body responds fast enough to stop you being ill. An example of a vaccine is **MMR**, which is used to protect children against measles, mumps and rubella.

You need to be able to evaluate the advantages and disadvantages of being vaccinated against a particular disease.

7 How has the treatment of disease changed?

There is nothing new for you to <u>remember</u> in this section.

When you are given information, you need to be able to explain how treatment of disease has changed as a result of increased understanding of antibiotics and immunity.

5 Adaptations

1 Surviving in different places

Animals and plants are **adapted** for survival in the conditions in which they normally live. Adaptations for life in the Arctic are different from those for survival in the **desert**.

You need to be able to use these and similar ideas to suggest how other animals are adapted to the conditions in which they live.

2 Adapt and survive

To survive, organisms need to obtain **materials** from their surroundings and from the other plants and animals that live there. Animals and plants may be **adapted** in special ways to cope with particular features of their habitats. Examples of adaptations are **thorns**, poisons and **warning colours** to deter **predators**.

You need to be able to use these and similar ideas to suggest how organisms are adapted to the conditions in which they live.

3 **Different places, different plants**
There is nothing new for you to <u>remember</u> in this section.

You need to be able to explain why plants and animals live where they do.

4 **Why weed the garden?**
Plants need the right conditions to grow well. They need materials such as **water** and **nutrients** from the soil and plenty of **light**. They **compete** with each other for these things.

You need to be able to suggest what plants are competing for when you are given information about a particular habitat.

5 **Competition between animals**
Animals of one species often **compete** with each other. They also compete with members of other **species**. They compete for **food**, water, a **mate** and **territory**.

When you are given information about a particular habitat, you need to be able to suggest what the animals in it are competing for.

6 Genes

1 **Who do you look like?**
Young plants and animals have similar characteristics to their **parents**. This is because parents pass on information to their young in the form of genes in their **sex cells (gametes)**. Different **genes** control the development of different **characteristics**.

2 **Passing on genes**
Living things are made of **cells**. The **nucleus** of a cell contains many pairs of **chromosomes**. Chromosomes carry the **genes** that control the **characteristics** of animals and plants.

3 **Two kinds of reproduction**
In sexual reproduction, male and female sex cells or **gametes** join (fuse). The cell produced **divides** to produce a new individual. The offspring from sexual reproduction have a mixture of **genetic information** from two parents, so they vary. **Asexual reproduction** involves one **parent**. So there is no fusion of gametes, no mixing of genetic information and no variation in the offspring. We call these **genetically** identical offspring **clones**.

4 **Using asexual reproduction**
We can grow more plants from parts of older plants. We call them **cuttings**. Cuttings from the same plant all have exactly the same **genes**. Plants with exactly the same genes are **genetically** identical. We call them **clones**. Taking cuttings helps us to produce new plants **quickly** and **cheaply**.

5 **More about cloning**
Modern cloning techniques include:

- **tissue** culture. This is growing new plants from small groups of cells.
- **embryo** transplants. Scientists separate the cells from a developing animal embryo before they become specialised. Then they **transplant** the identical embryos or **clones** into the wombs of host mothers.
- producing embryos by fusion of nuclei from **adult** cells with egg cells.

You may be asked to interpret information about cloning techniques and to consider economic issues concerning cloning.

6 **Genetic engineering**
Scientists can find a useful gene in an animal or plant and 'cut' it out using **enzymes**. They can make copies of the gene and **transfer** them to the cells of organisms such as bacteria. They can also transfer genes into the cells of animals and plants at an early stage of their **development** so that they develop with the characteristics that they want. For example, they do this to produce **GM** crops with particular features. All these are examples of **genetic engineering**.

You may be asked to interpret information about genetic engineering techniques and to consider economic, social and ethical issues concerning genetic engineering, including GM crops.

7 **Advances can cause problems**
There is nothing new for you to <u>remember</u> in this section.

You need to be able to interpret information about cloning techniques and to consider economic, social and ethical issues concerning cloning.

7 Evolution

1 Change in nature

We can observe change in **species**. We call the remains of ancient species **fossils**. Most scientists agree that fossils provide **evidence** of how much (or how little) species have changed. They also show that many ancient life forms have died out or become **extinct**.

You need to understand that there are questions that scientists can't answer, for example, whether or not living things separated in time belong to the same species.

2 Three billion years of life

Scientists think that simple life forms developed on Earth over 3 **billion** years ago. Then they changed or **evolved** to produce all the species that are alive today plus lots of species that are now **extinct**. Scientists study similarities and differences between species. This helps them to see how closely **related** they are. This helps them to understand evolutionary relationships between species.

3 Some puzzles

There is nothing new for you to <u>remember</u> in this section.

You need to understand that there are questions that scientists cannot answer and to be able to suggest reasons why scientists can't be sure about the origin of life on Earth.

4 Explaining change

Individuals in a species **vary** because of differences in their **genes**. Those with characteristics best suited to their **environments** are the most likely to survive, breed successfully and pass on their genes to the next generation. The least suited die. Over a period of time a species changes. This is **evolution** by **natural selection**.

You need to be able to identify differences between different theories of evolution and to suggest reasons for different theories.

5 New tricks and old

We can learn from **fossils** how much (or how little) plants and animals have **changed** since life began on Earth. Species may become extinct if the **environment** they need to survive changes. Extinction can also happen because of new **predators**, new **diseases** or new **competitors**.

You need to be able to interpret evidence about evolutionary theory just as you have done in this section and those before it.

6 How new features arise

Sometimes genes change to produce new forms. We call these changes **mutations**. They may cause more rapid change in a **species**. Mutations increase the amount of **variation** in a population. A species with a varied population is more likely to survive a change in the **environment**. It is more likely to include individuals with **characteristics** suited to the environment. These individuals are likely to survive, **breed** successfully and **pass on** their genes.

8 Sustainable development

1 Humans take over

Humans reduce the amount of land available for other animals and for plants by cutting down trees and using the land for **farming** and **building**, taking stone from **quarries** and dumping waste in **landfill** sites. All these things can destroy the **habitats** of animals and plants and reduce **biodiversity**.

You need to be able to analyse the effects of humans on the environment just as you have done here.

2 More people, more problems

As the human **population** and the **standard** of living increase, so does our effect on the **environment**. Loss of forest and other habitats leads to reduction in **biodiversity**. Some of the plants and animals lost may have been of use in the future. We use up **raw** materials, including **non-renewable** energy sources faster. We also produce more waste. Unless we handle the **waste** carefully, we will cause more pollution of the air, **land** and **water**.

3 **Sustainable development**

We need **sustainable** development to improve the quality life of **people** now and in the future and to avoid damaging the **environment**. To manage sustainable development, we need to plan at **local**, regional and global levels.

You need to be able to weigh evidence and form balanced judgements about environmental issues including sustainable development. Think about sustainable development as you study the environmental issues in the following sections.

4 **Make poverty history**

There is nothing new for you to <u>remember</u> in this section.

You need to be able to form balanced judgements about sustainable development.

5 **The energy problem**

Burning fuels produces smoke and **waste gases** which pollute the **air**. These gases include the **sulfur dioxide** and **nitrogen oxides** that contribute to **acid rain**.

6 **Are we changing the climate?**

Methane and **carbon dioxide** in the Earth's atmosphere absorb most of the **energy** that the Earth radiates. Some of this energy is re-radiated to the Earth's surface. It keeps the Earth warmer than it would otherwise be. This is called the **greenhouse effect**. The amounts of methane and carbon dioxide in the **atmosphere** are increasing. This may be increasing the **average** temperature of the Earth. We call it **global warming**.

You need to be able to evaluate methods of collecting environmental data and to analyse and interpret the data about environmental issues such as global warming. You need to ask yourself whether the data is valid and reliable.

7 **More about global warming**

Burning **fuel, deforestation** and decay of waste by **microorganisms** all <u>add</u> carbon dioxide to the air. Trees <u>remove</u> **carbon dioxide** from the air and 'lock it up' in their wood. So fewer trees means less carbon dioxide is removed from the atmosphere. Keeping cattle and growing rice increase the amount of **methane** in the air. Greater amounts of carbon dioxide and methane in the Earth's atmosphere may cause **global warming**. As well as causing quite big changes in the Earth's **climate** it may lead to a rise in **sea level**.

You need to be able to weigh evidence and form balanced judgements about environmental issues such as global warming.

8 **Waste can pollute water**

Humans are producing more and more waste. Unless we handle it properly we will cause more pollution. We pollute water with untreated **sewage**. Farmers use **fertilisers** to make their crops grow better. The **pesticides** and **herbicides** they use to protect their crops are **toxic**. All these chemicals drain from the land into the water. Dissolved waste gases such as sulfur dioxide make the water **acidic**.

9 **Indicators of pollution**

We can use **indicator** organisms to show how much pollution there is, including

- **lichens** as indicators of air pollution
- invertebrate animals as indicators of **water pollution**.

You need to be able to evaluate methods of collecting environmental data and consider their validity and reliability.

10 **Looking to the future**

There is nothing new for you to <u>remember</u> in this section.

You need to be able to form balanced judgements about sustainable development.

Chemistry

1 Building materials from rocks

1 Limestone for building

Limestone is a type of **rock**. It is very useful for **building** because it is easy to cut into blocks. Many other useful building materials can be made from limestone, for example **glass**, **cement** and **concrete**.

2 Where do we get limestone from?

We get limestone from places called **quarries**.

You need to be able to use information like this to say how using limestone affects local people, the environment and the amount of money in an area.

3 What's it all made from?

All substances are made from tiny **atoms**. If the substance has atoms that are all of one type we call it an **element**. There are about 100 different elements. We use letters to stand for elements. We call these **symbols**. For example, Na stands for one atom of **sodium** and O stands for one atom of **oxygen**. The periodic table shows all of the elements. Each column contains elements with similar **properties**. We call each column a **group**.

4 What's in limestone?

Limestone contains a chemical **compound** called **calcium carbonate**. The **formula** of a compound shows the number of atoms it contains. The formula for calcium carbonate is $CaCO_3$.

5 Heating limestone

When we heat limestone strongly in a kiln it breaks down into **quicklime** and **carbon dioxide**. We call this kind of reaction **thermal decomposition**. The chemical name for quicklime is **calcium oxide**.

6 Describing reactions 1

We can describe a chemical reaction using a **word equation**. The substances that react are the **reactants**. The new substances that are produced are the **products**.

7 Using quicklime

When you heat limestone, it decomposes into **quicklime** and carbon dioxide. Many other **carbonates** decompose in a similar way when you heat them. Quicklime (calcium oxide) reacts with cold water to form **slaked lime** (calcium hydroxide). We can use slaked lime to make **mortar**.

You need to be able to weigh up the advantages and disadvantages of using materials like cement for building.

8 Cement and concrete

We heat limestone and clay together in a hot kiln to make **cement**. A mixture of cement, sand, rock and water gives **concrete**. The water **reacts** with the cement and makes the concrete set solid.

You need to be able to weigh up the advantages and disadvantages of using materials like concrete for building.

9 Glass in buildings

We can use limestone to make **glass**. To make the glass we heat a mixture of limestone, **sodium carbonate** and **sand**.

10 Describing reactions 2

For a chemical reaction, we can write a word equation and a **symbol equation**. We replace the name of each chemical with a **formula**. In a symbol equation, (s) stands for solid, (l) stands for **liquid**, **(g)** stands for gas and **(aq)** stands for aqueous solution. Atoms do not appear or disappear during chemical reactions. The **mass** of the products is the same as the mass of the **reactants**. This means that when we write an equation it must be **balanced**.

You need to be able to explain what is happening to the substances in this topic using ideas about atoms and symbols. You can learn more about balancing equations on page 326.

11 Chemical reactions up close

In the centre of an atom there is the **nucleus**. Around the nucleus there are particles called **electrons**. Atoms react with atoms of other elements to produce **compounds**. They do this by **sharing** electrons with another atom or by **giving** or **taking** electrons. We say that the elements have made **chemical bonds**.

2 Metals from rocks

1 On your bike!

There is nothing new for you to <u>remember</u> in this section.

You need to be able to use information like this to work out the advantages and disadvantages of making things out of metal.

2 Where do we get metals from?

Metals are found in the Earth's **crust**. Most metals, except gold, are found joined with other **elements** as **compounds**. Rocks containing metal compounds are called **ores**.

You need to be able to think about the effects that mining metal ores can have on the environment.

3 Extracting metals from their ores

To split up a metal from its ore we need a **chemical reaction**. We say we **extract** the metal. To extract iron we heat **iron oxide** with **carbon**. We do this in a **blast furnace**. When we remove the oxygen from a metal oxide we call it **reduction**. We can put metals in order to show how reactive they are, or their **reactivity**. We can only extract metals using carbon if they are **below** it in the reactivity series.

4 Is it worth it?

It is important to decide if it is worth extracting a metal from its ore. We say it must be **economic** to extract the metal. This changes over time.

You need to be able to use information like this to think about the effects of mining and making use of metal ores on local people and the amount of money in an area.

5 Iron or steel – what's the difference?

Iron from the blast furnace is about 96% iron. It contains impurities which make it **brittle**. We remove these impurities to make pure **iron**, which is quite **soft**. The layers of atoms in pure iron can **slide** over each other. Steels are a mixture of iron with other **metals** or with the non-metal element **carbon**. We say that steels are **alloys**. The different sized atoms **disrupt** the layers in the iron. The layers don't **slide** over each other so easily. We can add carbon to steel to make it **harder**. Low carbon steels are easy to **shape** while high carbon steels are **hard**. Stainless steel is an alloy which does not **corrode** easily.

You need to be able to explain how the properties of other alloys are related to the way in which the atoms are arranged just like you did for steel.

6 More about alloys

We can make metals more useful to us by mixing them with other metals. Many of the metals we use are mixtures, or **alloys**. Pure copper, gold and aluminium are quite soft. We can add small amounts of other metals to these metals to make them **harder**. Scientists often develop new alloys, for example **shape memory alloys**. We can bend this type of alloy and the metal will still return to its original **shape**.

You need to be able to weigh up the advantages of using smart materials like shape memory alloys.

7 The transition metals

We find the transition metals in the **central block** of the periodic table. Transition metals have all of the usual **properties** of metals. They are good conductors of **heat** and **electricity**. They are also easy to **shape**. **Copper** has properties that make it useful for plumbing and wiring. We use transition metals like iron as structural materials because they are **strong**.

8 Extracting copper

We usually use **electricity** to extract copper. We call this process **electrolysis**. Some ores contain only small amounts of the metal. We call these **low grade** ores. We can use **bacteria** to help us extract copper from these ores. New methods of extracting copper have less effect on the **environment** than traditional mines.

9 Aluminium and titanium

Aluminium and titanium are very useful metals. This is because both metals have a **low density** and they will not **corrode** easily. However, aluminium and titanium are both **reactive** metals. Extracting them from their ores is very **expensive**. This is because

- there are many **stages** to the extraction
- the process uses a lot of **energy**.

10 New metal from old

We should reuse or **recycle** metals instead of extracting them from their ores. Extracting metal affects our **environment** and uses up substances which we cannot **replace**. It is also **expensive** because it uses large amounts of **energy**.

You need to be able to use information like this to consider the effects of recycling metals on the environment, local people and the economy.

3 Getting fuels from crude oil

1 Crude oil – a right old mixture

Crude oil is a **mixture** of a very large number of compounds. A mixture is made from two or more **elements** or **compounds**. The substances in a mixture are not joined together with a chemical bond. The chemical properties of each substance in the mixture are **unchanged** so we can **separate** them. Evaporating a liquid and then condensing it again is called **distillation**. Separating a mixture of liquids into different parts is called **fractional distillation**. The liquids in the mixture must have different **boiling points**.

2 Separating crude oil

We separate crude oil into fractions by **fractional distillation**. The oil evaporates in the fractionating tower. Different fractions condense at different **temperatures**. The fractions we collect contain molecules of a similar **size**. The fractions in crude oil have different **properties** which depend on the size of the molecules.

3 What are the chemicals in crude oil?

Crude oil contains many different **compounds**. The smallest part of a compound is called a **molecule**. Most of the compounds in crude oil are **hydrocarbons**. This means that the molecules are made from atoms of **hydrogen** and **carbon** only. Many of these hydrocarbons are compounds called alkanes. We can show the structure of **alkanes** like ethane in two ways:

- by writing the molecular formula C_2H_6
- by drawing the structural formula

$$H-\overset{\displaystyle H}{\underset{\displaystyle H}{C}}-\overset{\displaystyle H}{\underset{\displaystyle H}{C}}-H$$

The alkanes have the general formula C_nH_{2n+2}. We say that they are **saturated** hydrocarbons. The more carbon atoms there are in an alkane molecule, the higher its **boiling point**.

4 Burning fuels – where do they go?

How we use hydrocarbons as fuels depends on their **properties**. When we burn fuels we make new substances that are mainly **gases**. Most fuels contain carbon and hydrogen. When they burn, they produce **carbon dioxide** and **water** vapour.

5 It's raining acid

Many fuels contain atoms of sulfur. When we burn the fuel, we make the gas called **sulfur dioxide**. This gas can cause **acid rain**. To stop sulfur dioxide from getting into the air we can remove

- the **sulfur** from the fuel **before** we burn it (e.g. in vehicles)
- the **sulfur dioxide** from the waste gases **after** burning the fuel.

6 Global warming, global dimming

When we burn fuels we produce large amounts of the gas **carbon dioxide**. This is making the Earth warmer. We call it **global warming**. Burning fuels also releases tiny **particles** into the air. These may be reducing the amount of sunlight that reaches the ground. We call this **global dimming**.

You need to be able to weigh up the effects of burning hydrocarbon fuels on the environment. This is also covered on pages 160 and 166.

7 Better fuels

There is nothing new for you to <u>remember</u> in this section.

You need to be able to weigh up the good and bad points about new fuels.

8 Using fuels – good or bad?

There is nothing new for you to <u>remember</u> in this section.

You need to be able to weigh up the effects of using fuels on the environment, local people and the amount of money in an area.

4 Polymers and ethanol from oil

1 Crude oil – changing lives

There is nothing new for you to <u>remember</u> in this section.

You need to be able to weigh up the effects of using products from crude oil on people's lives and the amount of money in an area.

2 Making large molecules more useful

Large hydrocarbon molecules are not very **useful** as fuels. We can break them into smaller, more useful molecules. We call this **cracking**. We heat the large molecules to make them **evaporate**. We pass the vapours over a hot **catalyst**. We separate and collect these smaller more useful molecules. The large molecules **break down** to make smaller ones. We call this **thermal decomposition**.

3   Small molecules
Some of the small hydrocarbon molecules we make by cracking are useful as **fuels**. The small molecules belong to two groups, the **alkanes** and the **alkenes**. Alkenes contain a double bond between two carbon atoms. We say they are **unsaturated**. We can show the structure of an alkene like ethene in two ways:

■ by writing the molecular formula C_2H_4
■ by drawing the structural formula

The general formula for the alkenes is C_nH_{2n}.

4   Making ethanol
Ethanol is a very useful chemical. We can make ethanol by reacting **ethene** and **steam**. We pass the vapours over a **catalyst**.

You need to be able to weigh up the advantages and disadvantages of making ethanol from renewable and non-renewable sources.

5   Joining molecules together again
We can use alkenes to make long molecules or **polymers**. Examples of polymers are **poly(ethene)** and **poly(propene)**. We call the small alkene molecules which join together the **monomers**. Different monomers make polymers with different **properties**. The properties of a polymer also depend on the **conditions** that we use to make it, such as the temperature and pressure.

6   Useful polymers
Polymers have many uses. New uses for polymers are being developed. For example

■ **hydrogel** polymers which absorb water
■ **smart** polymers which respond to changes
■ **dental** polymers for repairing teeth
■ **shape memory** polymers which change shape when they are heated
■ **waterproof** polymer coatings for fabrics.

7   Polymers and packaging
Polymers are very useful as **packaging** materials.

8   What happens to waste polymers?
Many polymers are not broken down by **microorganisms**. We say they are not **biodegradable**.

You need to be able to weigh up how using, throwing away and recycling polymers can affect people, the environment and our economy.

5   How can we use plant oils?

1   Plants – not just a pretty face
Many plants contain **plant oils** which can be very useful to us. We can use plant oils for **fuels**, **food** and many other things too. Plant oils can come from the **seeds**, **nuts** and **fruits** of the plant. To extract the oil we often have to **crush** the plant material. Then we have to either **press** it to squeeze out the oil or remove it by **distillation** using steam. Finally we remove any **water** or **impurities** from the plant oil.

2   Plant oils for food
Plants give us oils which we call **vegetable oils**. They are very important to us as **foods**. Like other fats and oils, they give us lots of **energy**. They also contain important **nutrients**. We can cook using vegetable oils. This increases the amount of **energy** in the food.

You need to be able to weigh up the effects of using vegetable oils in our food. You need to think about their effects on our diet and health. You will continue this on page 188.

3   Changing oils
We can **harden** vegetable oils if we react them with **hydrogen**. In this reaction we use a **nickel catalyst** at 60 °C. We say that the hardened oils are **hydrogenated**. They now have a **higher melting point** and are solid at room temperature. We use the hardened oils to make **spread** like margarine and for making **cakes**. Vegetable oils can contain **carbon–carbon** double bonds. We say that they are **unsaturated**. We can detect these double bonds using chemicals like **bromine** or **iodine**.

You need to be able to weigh up the effects of using vegetable oils in foods and the impact that they can have on our diet and health.

4   Emulsions
Oil won't **dissolve** in water but we can mix oil and water together to make an **emulsion**. Emulsions are **thicker** than oil or water. They are useful to us because they have special **properties**. Emulsions have a good **texture** and **appearance**. They are also good for **coating** foods. We use emulsions to make foods like **salad dressing** and **ice cream**.

5   Additives in our food
Much of the food we eat is processed and contains **additives**. Additives are put in food to improve its **appearance** (how it looks), its **shelf life** (how long it lasts) and its **taste**.

6 Any additives in there?

We can find out if a food contains additives by looking on the list of **ingredients**. Many additives which are allowed in our food have been given **E-numbers**. We can find out which additives are in our food using **chemical analysis**. We can detect and identify artificial colourings using **chromatography**.

You need to be able to weigh up the good and bad points about using additives in food.

7 Vegetable oils as fuels

We can burn vegetable oils as **fuels**. They could be used to **replace** some of our fossil fuels. Vegetable oils will not run out. We say that they are **renewable**.

You need to be able to weigh up the good and bad points about using vegetable oils to produce fuels.

6 Changes in the Earth and its atmosphere

1 Ideas about the Earth

When the Earth was formed it was very **hot**. Scientists once thought that features on the Earth's surface such as **mountains** formed because of **shrinking** of the Earth's crust as it cooled.

2 Ideas about Earth movements

The Earth's crust is made up from a number of large pieces. We call them **tectonic plates**. The plates **move** as a result of **convection currents** in the mantle. Convection currents happen because the mantle is heated up by natural **radioactive** processes.

You need to be able to explain why scientists didn't agree with the theory that the crust moves (continental drift) for many years.

3 Effects of moving plates

Tectonic plates move only a few **centimetres** a year. But when they move, it can be **sudden**. The movements can cause **disasters** like **earthquakes** and **volcanic eruptions**. These happen at the places where the plates **meet**.

You need to be able to explain some of the reasons why scientists can't predict earthquakes.

4 Predicting disasters

There is nothing new for you to <u>remember</u> in this section.

You need to be able to explain some of the reasons why scientists can't predict volcanic eruptions.

5 Where did our atmosphere come from?

For the first billion years after the Earth formed, there were lots of **volcanoes**. These produced **gases** which made up the early **atmosphere**. The **water vapour** that was made condensed to form the **oceans**. The early atmosphere was mainly made from **carbon dioxide** gas. There was very little **oxygen**, which living things need. This is like the atmosphere of **Venus** today. There may also have been **water vapour** and small amounts of **methane** and **ammonia**.

6 More oxygen, less carbon dioxide

As plants began to grow on the Earth, they used up **carbon dioxide** and produced **oxygen**. Over billions of years the **carbon** in the carbon dioxide became **locked up** as

■ **fossil fuels** like coal and oil
■ carbonates in **sedimentary** rocks.

So, the concentration of carbon dioxide in the atmosphere fell.

You need to be able to explain some ideas about how our atmosphere has changed and to weigh up some of the evidence to support these ideas.

7 Still changing – our atmosphere

Burning fossil fuels is increasing the concentration of **carbon dioxide** in the atmosphere.

You need to be able to explain some ideas about how our atmosphere has changed and to weigh up some of the evidence to support these ideas, including the effects of human activities on the atmosphere.

8 The atmosphere today

This table shows the gases in our atmosphere.

Gas	Amount
nitrogen	about 4/5 (80%)
oxygen	about 1/5 (20%)
noble gases	small amounts
carbon dioxide	very small amount

There is also a small amount of **water vapour** in the atmosphere. The noble gases are in **Group 0** of the periodic table. They do not react with anything so we say they are **unreactive**. We can use the noble gases to make **electric discharge tubes** and **filament lamps**. We can use **helium** to fill balloons because it is **less dense** than air.

Physics

1 How is heat transferred?

1 Thermal radiation

Infra-red rays can travel through empty **space**. Another name for empty space is a **vacuum**. Heat radiation is also called **thermal** radiation. A **dark, matt** surface is good at absorbing and emitting infra-red radiation. A **light, shiny** surface is poor at absorbing and emitting infra-red radiation. Light, shiny surfaces are good at **reflecting** radiation. The hotter something is, the more **infra-red** energy it radiates.

2 Using the Sun's energy

There is nothing new for you to <u>remember</u> in this section.

3 Explaining conduction, convection and radiation

Conduction is the transfer of heat from particle to **particle** through a material. **Convection** is the transfer of heat in **fluids** by the movement of the particles in a convection current. **Radiation** is the transfer of heat by electromagnetic **waves**. No substance is required between the objects that emit and absorb the radiation. Radiation is emitted and absorbed by **charged** particles.

4 What factors affect heat transfer?

The rate of heat transfer through a material or to and from an object is affected by different factors. These include

- the **dimensions** and shape of an object
- the kind of **material**
- the **temperature difference** between an object and its surroundings.

A good conductor has a higher **conductivity** than a poor conductor. A **large surface** area transfers heat more quickly than a smaller one. A thin sample transfers heat more quickly than a **thick** one. The higher the temperature difference, the greater the rate of heat transfer.

5 Keeping warm outdoors

There is nothing new for you to <u>remember</u> in this section.

6 Reducing heat loss from buildings

Heat can be lost from buildings by conduction through the **ceilings**, **walls**, **floors** and **window glass**. It is also lost by convection because of **draughts**. You can save heat by **insulating** the loft, fitting draught excluders, putting in cavity wall insulation and **double glazing**. Some methods reduce the amount of heat loss by a bigger percentage (%) than others. So we say that they are more **effective**. Materials that are used for **insulation** often contain air. This air is trapped so it can't move about. A gas, such as air, is a very poor **conductor**.

2 Using energy efficiently

1 Does energy get used up?

Energy can't be **created** or **destroyed**. It can only be transferred into other forms. All the energy we use will finally **spread out** as thermal energy. We cannot re-use this energy and so we need an energy **source** to supply the energy we need.

2 How is energy wasted?

Energy can be wasted by **friction**, poor insulation and poor **design**. We try to transfer energy in the most **efficient** way. Any energy that is not transferred usefully is **wasted**.

3 How efficiently is energy transferred?

If a device is 100% **efficient** then it transfers all the energy it uses to useful energy. A real device always **wastes** some energy. You can work out the efficiency of a device with the formula

$$\text{efficiency} = \frac{\text{useful energy out}}{\text{energy in}}$$

You need to be able to calculate the efficiency of a device, just like you have done on this page.

4 Keeping track of energy

Some of the energy you put into a device will be transferred in a **useful** way but some of it will be **wasted**. The useful energy plus the wasted energy always adds up **exactly** to the energy you put in. All the energy eventually ends up as **thermal energy**, which makes everything a bit **warmer**.

5 Making better use of energy

If we **conserve** energy, we both save money and protect the environment. An energy-**efficient** appliance may be more expensive to buy, but it is cheaper to run. If the overall cost is less, the purchase is **cost-effective**.

6 How soon will it pay for itself?
The time taken for an energy-saving method to pay for itself is called the **pay-back time**. The shorter this time is, the more **cost-effective** the method of saving energy is.

7 Review your energy efficiency
There is nothing new for you to <u>remember</u> in this section.

3 Why are electrical devices so useful?

1 Making use of electricity
We use a lot of electrical **energy** in our homes and in industry. Electricity can easily be **transferred** as other sorts of energy such as **heat**, **light**, **sound** and **kinetic** (or movement) energy.

You should know what energy transfers electrical appliances are designed to produce.

2 How much electricity do we use?
Power is measured in **watts** (W). The name for 1000 watts is a **kilowatt** (kW). How much electrical energy is transferred depends on:

- how **long** an appliance is switched on for
- how **fast** the appliance transfers energy (its **power**).

The energy used in an electrical appliance is worked out by multiplying the **power** (in kW) by the time (in hours):

$$\begin{array}{ccc} \text{energy transferred} & = & \text{power} \quad \times \quad \text{time} \\ \textbf{(kilowatt-hours)} & & \text{(kilowatts)} \quad \text{(hours)} \end{array}$$

A kilowatt-hour of electrical energy is called a **Unit**. We normally measure energy in **joules** (J).

3 Paying for electricity
An electrical Unit is a **kilowatt-hour** (kW h). You can work out the cost of electrical energy used by using this equation:

$$\begin{array}{ccc} \text{total cost for} & = & \textbf{number of} \quad \times \quad \text{cost per} \\ \text{electricity used} & & \textbf{Units used} \quad \text{Unit} \end{array}$$

4 Understanding mains electricity
The voltage of the **mains supply** in homes in the UK is **230 V**. The mains supply is an **alternating current**. One advantage of a.c. is that the voltage can be changed with a **transformer**. Electricity from power stations reaches us through the **National Grid**. Electricity is sent through the Grid at a very high **voltage** so that less **energy** is wasted. Before it reaches homes and factories, the voltage is reduced using transformers. This makes the electricity **safer** to use.

5 Choosing the right appliance
There is nothing new for you to <u>remember</u> in this section.

You need to be able to compare and contrast the advantages and disadvantages of using different electrical devices for a particular application.

4 How should we generate the electricity we need?

1 Using fuels to generate electricity
Coal, oil and gas are called **fossil fuels**. Examples of nuclear fuels are **uranium** and **plutonium**. Nuclear fission produces **heat**. All these fuels are non-renewable – once they are used up, they are gone **forever**. All non-renewable fuels transfer energy as **thermal energy**. For coal and oil power stations, this energy is released when the fuels **burn** and is used to boil water. This produces **steam**, which turns a **turbine**. Then this drives a **generator** shaft, which produces **electricity**.

2 Comparing fuels for electricity
There is nothing new for you to <u>remember</u> in this section.

You should be able to compare the advantages and disadvantages of different fuels for electricity. These include:

- which types of waste are produced by which fuel
- whether the pollution by each type of waste can be reduced and how this can be done
- how controlling pollution affects the cost of electricity
- how the start-up times for power stations using different fuels compare.

3 Generating electricity with water
Energy from these sources is **free** but it is expensive to **capture**. Energy from the rise and fall of water owing to **waves** and **tides**, and **falling water** in hydro-electric schemes can drive turbines **directly** to turn **generators**. You can produce electricity when you need it from a **hydro-electric** generator. Reservoirs for these power stations flood **estuaries**. You can generate electricity only at certain times each day using a **tidal** power station. Barrages for these power stations flood estuaries, destroying **wildlife** habitats.

4 Generating electricity with wind

The **kinetic** energy of the wind can drive a **turbine** directly. This then drives a **generator**, which produces electricity. Wind generators need to be on hills and coasts where there is plenty of **wind.** You need **hundreds** of wind generators to produce as much electricity as a **coal-fired** power station. Large groups of wind generators are called wind **farms.** The wind does not blow all the time so wind power is not **reliable.** Wind turbines do not **pollute** the air, but by changing the landscape and making a sound they may create **visual** pollution and **noise** pollution.

5 Generating electricity from the Sun and the Earth

Energy from the Sun can be transferred as electricity using **solar cells.** Each Unit of electricity from a solar cell is very **expensive.** But solar cells will work for many years and are useful in **remote** places on Earth and on **satellites.** They are also useful in things that need very little electricity, such as **calculators. Radioactive** elements (like **uranium**) in the Earth's rocks transfer energy as **heat.** In some **volcanic areas,** hot rocks heat water, and hot water and **steam** rise to the surface. The steam can drive turbines. This is known as **geothermal** energy.

6 A review of renewable energy sources

There is nothing new for you to <u>remember</u> in this section.

You need to be able to compare and contrast the particular advantages and disadvantages of using different energy sources to generate electricity, including the place where the energy is needed.

7 Counting the cost of generating electricity

When comparing the advantages and disadvantages of ways of generating electricity the **cost** of each Unit is an important factor. This includes the costs of **building** and **operating** the system and the cost of any **fuel** used. The cost of **de-commissioning** the system when it is worn out should also be taken into account. Some costs are difficult to estimate, for example the cost of the effect on the **environment,** but they must be considered.

You need to be able to compare and contrast the particular advantages and disadvantages of using different energy sources to generate electricity.

5 Using waves

1 Why are there different colours of light?

Light travels as waves and carries **energy** from one place to another. White light is a mixture of light of all **wavelengths** from red light waves to violet light waves. When we split light up to make a **spectrum** we spread the different wavelengths out into bands which we see as different colours.

2 More about waves

All wavelengths of light travel at the same **speed** in a vacuum. All waves obey the wave formula

wave-speed = frequency × wavelength

3 Waves beyond the ends of the rainbow

The waves in the **electromagnetic** spectrum can be grouped by wavelength and frequency.

radio micro infra-red light ultra-violet X gamma

All types of electromagnetic radiation travel through a vacuum at the same **speed.** All electromagnetic waves obey the **wave formula**:

wave-speed	=	frequency	×	wavelength
(metres/second, m/s)		(hertz, Hz)		(metres, m)

4 Electromagnetic waves and matter

When electromagnetic waves hit a solid, liquid or gas they may be **reflected, absorbed** or **transmitted** (or more than one of these). What happens depends on the **wavelength** of the radiation, the substance and the type of surface. Electromagnetic waves transfer **energy.** When the waves are absorbed by matter, this energy may make the matter **heat** up. When radio waves or microwaves are absorbed by an aerial, they produce an electrical signal with the same **frequency** as the waves.

5 Electromagnetic waves and living cells

The effects of electromagnetic radiation on living cells depend on the **wavelength** of the radiation and the **dose** received. Infra-red radiation and microwaves can damage cells by making them **hot.** Ultra-violet radiation can damage the cells in your skin and may cause skin **cancer.** X-rays and gamma radiation can pass easily through your body. Where they are absorbed they may **kill** cells or cause cancer.

6 Using light

We use light to read and **communicate** information and to create images. Light can travel along **curved paths** through **optical fibres**.

7 Using gamma radiation

Gamma radiation can kill living **cells**. It is used to kill harmful **bacteria** in food or **cancer** cells inside people's bodies.

8 Using X-rays

X-rays do not pass through the **bones** in your body. X-rays pass through skin and flesh, but do not pass so easily through **diseased** tissue. Doctors can use X-rays to make a shadow **picture** of the inside of your body. Metals **protect** your body because they **absorb** X-rays.

9 Using ultra-violet radiation

Radiation from the Sun, or from a sunbed, can give pale skins a **tan**. But it can also damage skin cells and cause skin **cancer**. These things happen because of **ultra-violet** (UV) radiation. Some substances **absorb** ultra-violet radiation and use the energy to produce light. We say that these substances are **fluorescent**.

10 Using infra-red radiation

Toasters and grills cook food using **infra-red** (IR) radiation. Foods become hot when they **absorb** this radiation. Infra-red rays are used to control a **television** set or a **DVD** player, and to send telephone messages along **optical** fibres. This is better than sending electrical signals along wires, because the cable has a **smaller** diameter and there is less **weakening** of the signal.

11 Using microwaves

In microwave ovens, the microwaves are strongly absorbed by **water** molecules in food. The energy from the microwaves makes the food **hot**. Metal things **reflect** microwaves, even if they are full of small holes. Some microwaves can pass easily through the Earth's **atmosphere**. We can use these microwaves for **communications**. They carry information to and from **satellites** and within mobile phone networks.

12 Using radio waves

Radio waves can pass easily through **air** and through **dry** non-metals. This is what makes them useful for **communications**. They can carry **radio** and **television** programmes. A layer in the Earth's atmosphere **reflects** radio waves with long wavelengths. We use this property to send radio waves around the **curved** surface of the Earth.

13 Why is everything going digital?

Communications signals may be **analogue** or **digital**. An analogue signal changes **continuously**. A digital signal is **discrete** (on–off). Digital information can be stored and processed by **computers**. Digital signals are less affected by **interference** than analogue signals and so can be copied and transmitted without errors.

14 How safe are mobile phones?

There is nothing new for you to <u>remember</u> in this section.

You need to be able to evaluate information about the possible risks from radiation and methods for reducing exposure.

6 Radioactivity

1 What are atoms made of?

Atoms have a small **nucleus** made of **protons** and **neutrons**. Particles called **electrons** move around in the empty space around the nucleus.

2 What is radioactivity?

Some substances give out **nuclear radiation**. This radiation comes from the **nuclei** of atoms. There is **nothing** that can be done to stop the emission of this radiation. These substances are **radioactive**.

3 Three types of radiation

Radioactive sources emit three main types of radiation: **alpha** particles, **beta** particles and **gamma** rays. Alpha particles are absorbed by **paper**. They are **helium** nuclei with a mass of 4 mass units and a charge of +2. Beta particles are absorbed by a few millimetres of **aluminium**. They are **electrons** with a mass of almost zero and a charge of −1. Gamma rays are only partly absorbed by 2 cm of **lead**. They are **electromagnetic** radiation with a very short **wavelength**.

4   **Alpha, beta, gamma: what are the dangers?**
Nuclear radiation can **kill** living cells or make them **cancerous**. A source of **alpha** radiation is very dangerous when it is inside the body. The alpha particles are **absorbed** by living cells.
Alpha sources are less dangerous outside the body because alpha particles are absorbed by dead **skin** cells. **Beta** particles and **gamma** rays can penetrate the skin.

You should be able to evaluate

- hazards associated with different types of nuclear radiation
- measures that can be taken to reduce exposure to nuclear radiation.

5   **Using nuclear radiation**
We use gamma radiation to **kill** bacteria and **treat** cancer. A smoke detector contains a weak source of alpha radiation. The alpha particles **ionise** air molecules. The **thickness** of aluminium foil is measured with beta radiation as it is made.
Radio-isotopes can be used as **tracers** to follow the movement of substances in animals and plants.

You should know and understand why particular types of nuclear radiation have particular uses.

6   **How fast do radioactive substances decay?**
The **half-life** of a substance is the time it takes for the number of radioactive atoms to halve. In this time the **count rate** from the substance will also halve. We can use the half-life to **date** rocks and objects that contain radioactive atoms.

7   **Choosing and handling isotopes**
There is nothing new for you to <u>remember</u> in this section.

You should be able to evaluate radioactive sources for particular uses, including as tracers, in terms of the types of radiation emitted and their half-lives. You should be able to evaluate measures that can be taken to reduce exposure to nuclear radiations.

7   The Universe

1   **The Universe**
The Earth is a **planet**. There are nine planets in our **solar system**. The planets orbit the Sun, which is our nearest **star**. The Sun is just one of billions of stars in our **galaxy**, which is called the Milky Way. There are billions of galaxies in the Universe.

2   **Observing the Universe**
We can observe the Universe from the **Earth** or from **space**. Telescopes may detect **visible light** or other electromagnetic radiations such as **radio waves** or **X-rays**.

You need to be able to compare and contrast the advantages and disadvantages of using different types of telescope on Earth and in space.

3   **Shifting frequencies**
If a wave source is moving relative to an observer there will be a change in the observed **wavelength** and **frequency**. There is a **red-shift** in light observed from most distant galaxies. The further away galaxies are, the **bigger** the red-shift.

4   **How did the Universe begin?**
The bigger red-shift of more distant galaxies is evidence that the Universe is **expanding**. This evidence supports the big bang theory. The **big bang** theory is that the Universe began from a very small initial **point**.

Biology

Some words are used on lots of pages. Only the page numbers of the main examples are shown. You will find the *italic* words in the definitions elsewhere in the Glossary/index.

F

fat part of our food which we use for energy and for making cell membranes   20, 23, 28

fertilise, fertilisation when a male *sex cell* joins with a female *sex cell* to start a new plant or animal; it forms a single *cell* which gets half its *chromosomes* from each parent   16, 77

fertilisers you add these to soil to provide the minerals plants need to grow; some are natural, e.g. manure; others are artificial, e.g. potassium nitrate   107

fertility a measure of the ability to *reproduce*   18

food group a class of foods such as *carbohydrates, fats* or *proteins*   21

fossils remains of plants and animals from a very long time ago   83, 84–85, 90

FSH a *hormone* made in the *pituitary gland* that makes *eggs* mature in the *ovaries* and makes the ovaries secrete *oestrogen*   17, 18

G

gamete another name for a *sex cell*; a *cell* with half the usual number of *chromosomes* for a *species*   68, 72

genes these control the *characteristics* of plants and animals; they are passed on by parents in *chromosomes*; they are made of *DNA*   69, 70–71, 78–79, 89, 92

genetic engineering transferring *genes* from the *cells* of one living organism into the cells of a different organism   78–79, 81

genetic information the information coded in *genes*   70, 72

genome the name for an organism's complete set of *genes*   71, 78

global warming an increase in the average temperature on Earth   102–103, 104–105

GM crops genetically modified plants – that is, they have *genes* added, changed or removed   79

greenhouse effect the warming effect of *greenhouse gases* on the Earth   103

greenhouse gases gases such as *methane* and *carbon dioxide* that stop some of the thermal energy escaping from the *atmosphere*   99, 103, 104

H

habitat the place where a plant or animal lives   60, 95, 96, 111

HDL cholesterol a *fat* in the body; sometimes called 'good' *cholesterol*   29

heart disease *disease* when the heart doesn't work properly; often used to mean coronary heart disease, in which one or more arteries to the heart *muscle* is blocked   28, 42

herbicides weedkillers   106–107

heroin an *addictive drug*; a depressant   31, 38

high blood pressure *blood pressure* that is higher than normal; it increases the risk of kidney, heart and circulation problems   25

Hill, Bradford (1897–1991)   36–37

hormones chemicals *secreted* in small amounts which *coordinate* the growth and activities of living things   14, 17, 18–19, 74, 76

I

immune, immunity when your body stops you catching a particular *infection*   52, 55

immunised, immunisation injected with dead or weakened *pathogens* to make you *immune* to them   53

indicator organism an organism that indicates or tells you something about a place   108–109

indigenous native to an area   30

infect, infection when *microorganisms* get into your body and cause a *disease*   44–45, 56

infertile unable to produce offspring   18

ingest to take in food   55

inherited passed on in the *genes* from parents   68

O

obese very fat   25

oestrogen *hormone* made in the *ovaries*   17

ovaries where female *gametes* and the *hormones* oestrogen and progesterone are made   16–17, 18, 19, 72

P

painkillers *drugs* that relieve pain, e.g. paracetamol   48, 49

pandemic a worldwide outbreak of a *disease*   50

Pasteur, Louis (1822–1895)   45

pathogens *microorganisms* that cause *disease*   46, 55

penicillin an *antibiotic*; it kills *bacteria* in and on the body   48, 51

period loss of lining of the *uterus* (*womb*) about once a month if an *egg cell* is not *fertilised*; another name for menstruation   16

pesticides chemicals which kill pests   106–107

pituitary gland gland in the base of the brain that produces *hormones* including *FSH* and *LH*   16, 17

placebo a 'dummy' pill that may help someone feel better   43

pollute, pollution when the *environment* is contaminated with undesirable materials or energy   101, 106–107, 108–109, 111

polyunsaturated fat a type of *fat* that may help to lower blood *cholesterol*   28

population all the plants or animals of one *species* which live in a particular place   82, 93, 96

predator an animal which eats other animals   61, 91

pregnant, pregnancy expecting a baby   16, 18–19, 35

proteins part of our food which we need for growth and repair; *genes* control the order of the *amino acids* which make up proteins   20

R

receptors sensory *cells* – that is, cells which detect *stimuli*   8–9, 12

recreation leisure activity   31

recycle, recycling when materials are used over and over again   99, 110

reflex action a quick automatic response to a *stimulus*; no thought is needed   12–13

relay neurones connector *neurones* in the *central nervous system*   12, 13

reproduce, reproduction when organisms *breed* or make offspring   72–73

retina layer of light-sensitive *cells* lining the eye   8

S

saturated fat *fat* in the diet that may increase the risk of *heart disease*   28, 29

secrete to pass a useful substance out of a *cell* or gland   13, 17

selective breeding when we *breed* only from the plants or animals which have the *characteristics* we want; also called artificial selection   76, 81

Semmelweiss, Ignaz (1818–1865)   44

sense organs organs which detect *stimuli*, e.g. the eyes   8–9

sensory neurones *neurones* which connect *receptors* to the brain and spinal cord   11, 12, 13

sewage watery waste containing organic material which goes into the sewers   106

sex cells *cells* which join to form new plants or animals (also called *gametes*)   68, 72

sexual reproduction *reproduction* in which two *gametes* join to form a new *cell*; the offspring produced *vary*   72, 76

side-effects unpleasant effects of a treatment or *drug*   19, 40, 54

slimming controlling diet and using exercise in order to lose body mass   26–27

smallpox a serious *virus infection* – now wiped out   52, 53

species we say that plants or animals which can *breed* with each other belong to the same species; members of a species *vary* because they *inherit* different combinations of *genes*   67, 83, 84, 89, 93

sperm (cell) the male *gamete* (*sex cell*)   68, 72

standard of living extent to which the material needs of a person or a group are met   97

statins *drugs* for lowering blood *cholesterol*   43

stimuli changes in the surroundings to which living things respond; one is called a stimulus   8

sulfur dioxide a poisonous gas that *pollutes* the air and is one of the causes of *acid rain*   101, 109

sustainable development development in a way that won't damage the Earth and will let development keep going   98–99, 100, 108

sweat watery fluid *secreted* by sweat glands; evaporation of sweat cools the body   14

symptoms what a patient feels and describes about an illness, e.g. a headache or nausea   48

synapse a tiny gap between one *neurone* and the next   11, 12

T

target organs organs that a *hormone* or a *drug* acts on   14

taste buds groups of *cells* on the tongue that are sensitive to some chemicals   9

territory an area occupied and defended by an animal or a group of animals   66

thalidomide a *drug* that was found to prevent development of the limbs of a fetus; now used to treat *leprosy*   41

tissue culture growing *cells* in dishes in a laboratory; plant *clones* can be produced this way   76, 79

toxic poisonous   40, 106

toxins substances which are poisonous (*toxic*)   47

transplant to move from one place to another   77

tuberculosis a serious *bacterial infection*; also called TB   48, 56–57

U

urine the liquid excreted by the kidneys; it contains water, salts and urea   14

uterus where a baby develops before birth; also called the *womb*   17, 77

V

vaccinated, vaccination when a dead or weakened *pathogen* is injected to make the person *immune* to that *disease*   52–53, 54, 57

vaccine made from dead or weakened *pathogens*; this is used to produce *immunity* to the pathogen, and protection from the *disease*   52–53, 54

vary, variation to show differences   81, 87, 89, 92–93

viruses *microorganisms* which can only live inside other *cells*   46, 50, 53

vitamins substances in food which we need in very small amounts to stay healthy; not eating enough can cause *deficiency diseases*   21

W

Wallace, Alfred Russel (1823–1913)   88

warning colours colours that warn a *predator* that an animal is poisonous or unpleasant in some way   61

waste unwanted products of a reaction or process   97, 101, 107

white blood cells *cells* in blood which help to destroy *microorganisms* and the *toxins* they produce   47, 55

withdrawal symptoms unpleasant *symptoms* when a person doesn't get the *drug* they are *addicted* to   38

womb another word for *uterus*   16–17, 77

Chemistry

Some words are used on lots of pages. Only the page numbers of the main examples are shown. You will find the *italic* words in the definitions elsewhere in the Glossary/index.

A

acid, acidic a *solution* that has a *pH* of less than 7   119, 137

acid rain rain which may have *sulfur dioxide* and *nitrogen oxides* dissolved in it; this makes the rain more *acidic*   160–161

additives substances added to food to improve its *shelf life*, appearance or taste   191, 192–193

alcohol a substance that is produced by *fermentation* using *yeast*, e.g. in beer and wine   153, 165, 174

alkanes a family of *saturated hydrocarbon compounds*, including *methane*, with the *general formula* C_nH_{2n+2} 156–157, 172

alkenes a family of *unsaturated hydrocarbon compounds*, including *ethene*, with the *general formula* C_nH_{2n} 172–173, 176–177

alloy a mixture of *metals*   140, 141, 142–143, 148

alternative fuel a *fuel* we can use instead of *fossil fuels*   164–165

aluminium a lightweight *metal* that is *extracted* from its *ore* by *electrolysis*   132, 133, 142, 143, 148–149

ammonia a *gas* made from *hydrogen* and *nitrogen*; its *formula* is NH_3 118, 205

(aq) short for *aqueous*; used in *symbol equations*   128

aqueous dissolved in *water*   128

atmosphere the layer of *gases* above the Earth's surface   162, 163, 204–205, 206, 208–209, 210

atoms the smallest *particles* of an *element*   116, 129–130, 131

B

bacteria a type of *microorganism*; we can use certain bacteria to help us to *extract copper* from *low grade ores*   147, 181, 207

balanced when an equation is balanced, the *products* contain the same number of each type of *atom* as the *reactants*   129

biodegradable a biodegradable substance will rot because it can be broken down by *microorganisms*; natural fibres like cotton are biodegradable   181, 182

biodiesel a *hydrocarbon fuel* made from *plant oils*   164, 194

blast furnace a furnace used to *extract iron* from its *ore*   136, 140

boiling point the *temperature* at which a *liquid* boils   153, 154–155

brittle brittle materials break easily; the opposite of *tough*   140, 141

bromine we can use a *solution* of bromine (bromine water) to test if a substance contains *double bonds*   189

burn, burning when a substance reacts with *oxygen* releasing thermal (heat) energy   158–159, 160

C

calcium carbonate the chemical name for *limestone*; its *formula* is $CaCO_3$ 119, 120, 122, 128, 207

calcium hydroxide the chemical name for *slaked lime*   118, 122, 129

calcium oxide the chemical name for *quicklime*   118, 120, 122, 128–129

carbon a non-metal *element* that is found in living organisms and in *fossil fuels*, e.g. *crude oil*, and in *carbonate* rocks like *limestone*   116, 136–137, 163, 206–207

carbon dioxide a *gas* produced when substances containing *carbon burn*; the *atmosphere* contains a small amount of carbon dioxide; its *formula* is CO_2 118, 130, 160, 162, 205, 206–207, 208–209

N

nickel catalyst a *catalyst* made from nickel which we use when we *harden vegetable oils*   188

nitrogen a not very *reactive gas* that makes up about $\frac{4}{5}$ (80%) of the air   205, 210

nitrogen oxides *compounds* of *nitrogen* and *oxygen* that help to cause *acid rain*   209

noble gases *unreactive gases* in *Group* 0 of the *periodic table*; the *atmosphere* contains small amounts of the noble gases   205, 210–211

non-renewable supplies of a non-renewable substance will eventually run out, e.g. *fuels* like *petrol*   164, 182

nucleus the central part of an *atom*   130

nutrients foods needed by animals, or minerals needed by plants   186

O

ore a *compound*, often an *oxide*, from which a *metal* is *extracted*   134–135, 136, 138–139, 147

oxides *compounds* of *oxygen* and another *element*   134, 136–137, 146, 160

oxidise, oxidation when *oxygen* combines with another *element*, usually to form an *oxide*   206

oxygen a *gas* making up about $\frac{1}{5}$ (20%) of the air; when substances *burn* they *react* with oxygen to produce *oxides* of the *elements* they contain   130, 159–160, 205, 206, 210

P

particles
1 the very small bits that scientists think everything is made of
2 when *hydrocarbon fuels burn* they often release tiny particles of *carbon* into the air; these may cause *global dimming*   163, 164, 167

periodic table a table of the *elements* that has similar elements placed in the same column or *group*   117, 144–145, 210

petrol a widely available *fossil fuel*   154, 155, 158, 161, 164, 165

pH a scale that tells you how *acidic* or alkaline a *solution* is   178

plant oils oils from plants; they can be used for food and as *fuels*   184–185, 186–187

plastics *compounds* usually made from *crude oil*; they are *polymers*   176, 181, 182–183

pollute, pollution when the *environment* is contaminated with undesirable materials or energy   135, 161, 166

poly(ethene) a *plastic* or *polymer* made from the *monomer ethene*   176–177

polymers substances which have very long molecules, e.g. *plastics*   176–183

poly(propene) a *plastic* or *polymer* made from the *monomer* propene   177

polythene the everyday name for *poly(ethene)*   176, 182

pressing applying pressure, e.g. to crushed plant material in order to extract *plant oils* 185

products the substances that are produced in a *chemical reaction*   121, 129

properties what substances are like, e.g. chemically *reactive* or *tough*   117, 144, 148, 155, 177, 180

Q

quarries places where we can dig a substance (usually a rock) out of the ground   114–115, 135

quicklime a substance made by heating *limestone*; its chemical name is *calcium oxide*   120, 122, 129

R

radioactive giving out energy in the form of radiation; the Earth's *mantle* is heated by the breakdown of radioactive substances   197, 199

react, reaction when chemicals join or separate   121, 122, 128–129

reactants the substances you start off with in a *chemical reaction*   121, 129

sulfur dioxide a *gas* that can produce *acid rain* 160–161

symbol a short way of writing an *element*, e.g. C = *carbon*   116

symbol equation this shows the *reactants* and *products* of a *chemical reaction* using their *formulas* and *state symbols*   128–129

T

tectonic plates very large pieces of the Earth's *crust* and upper part of the *mantle* which slowly move   198–199, 200

temperature a measure of the thermal (heat) energy contained in an object   162, 178, 179, 208–209

thermal decomposition a reaction that uses thermal (heat) energy to break down a substance into new substances   120, 170

titanium a *transition metal* which has high *strength*, low *density* and good resistance to *corrosion*   132, 133, 148–149

tough, toughness tough materials don't break or crumble when you hit them; the opposite of *brittle*   140

transition metals *metals* in the central block of the *periodic table*; they do not belong to any of the *groups*   144–145, 148

tsunami a series of giant waves caused by an *earthquake* or *volcanic eruption* under the sea 202–203

U

unreactive not able to take part in *chemical reactions*   210–211

unsaturated in an unsaturated *hydrocarbon molecule*, two of the *carbon atoms* are linked by a *double bond*; these bonds can open up to link with other atoms, making the hydrocarbons *reactive*   172, 188, 189

V

vapour a *gas* produced when a *liquid evaporates* 152, 153, 154, 174

vegetable oils another name for *plant oils* 186–187, 194–195

Venus a planet; the *atmosphere* on Venus today is similar to that on the Earth 4000 million years ago   205

viscous a *liquid* which is viscous is hard to pour 170

volcanic eruptions when lava, volcanic ash and *gases* come out onto the surface of the Earth 200, 202

volcanoes mountains or hills formed from lava or ash during a *volcanic eruption*   200, 202, 204

W

water a *compound* of *hydrogen* and *oxygen*; its formula is H_2O 118, 129, 159, 204

water vapour *water* in the form of a *gas* 204–205, 210

waterproof polymers *polymers* which *liquid water* cannot get through, e.g. Goretex   179

Wegener, Alfred (1880–1930) the first person to come up with a developed theory of *continental drift*, which led to our present theory of *plate tectonics*   198, 200

word equation this shows the *reactants* and *products* of *chemical reactions* using their names 120, 121, 129

Y

yeasts *microorganisms* which produce *alcohol* from sugar, e.g. in beer and wine   174

Physics

Some words are used on lots of pages. Only the page numbers of the main examples are shown. You will find the *italic* words in the definitions elsewhere in the Glossary/index.

A

absorb, absorption to soak up or take in 215, 274–275, 276, 281, 282, 296, 297

absorber a surface that soaks up the energy from the *waves* (or *radiation*) that strike it 215

a.c. short for *alternating current* 248

acid rain rain that is more acidic than usual because of dissolved *sulfur dioxide* or *nitrogen oxides* 239, 256, 267

alpha (α) one of the types of *radiation emitted* when the *nucleus* of a *radio-isotope decays*; it consists of *particles*, each of which is the nucleus of a helium *atom* 294–296, 298

alternating current an electric *current* that constantly changes direction with a particular *frequency*; *a.c.* for short 248

aluminium a silvery metallic element with low density 217, 294, 299

analogue signals signals that vary continuously and which can have any values of amplitude or *frequency* (between upper and lower limits) 286–287

atmosphere the layer of gas that surrounds the Earth 255, 282, 284, 285, 307

atoms all substances are made of atoms; atoms have a *nucleus* that is made up of *protons* and *neutrons* and that is surrounded by *electrons* 290–291, 293, 300–301

attract, attraction the force that pulls things together, e.g. *magnets* or opposite electrical *charges* 257, 294

B

bacteria a type of microorganism 216, 280

beta (β) one of the types of *radiation emitted* when the *nucleus* of a *radio-isotope decays*; it consists of *particles* called *electrons* 294–296, 299

big bang the name of the theory which says that the *Universe* started with a huge explosion from a tiny point and has since been expanding from that point 311

billion 1 000 000 000 or a thousand million 305

biomass wood and other recently grown plant materials used as an *energy source* 253

C

cancer a disease in which abnormal body *cells* multiply in an uncontrolled way 276–277, 280, 288–289, 296

capital cost the cost of materials, equipment and labour when building, for example, a *power station* 266

carbon dioxide a gas produced when most *fuels* burn; carbon dioxide in the *atmosphere* helps to keep the Earth warm (the *greenhouse effect*); adding more carbon dioxide to the atmosphere makes the Earth warmer (global warming) 239, 240, 255, 256

Cassini space probe an unmanned space probe sent to study the planet Saturn 302

cells (biological) the basic units from which living things are built 276–277, 280, 288, 296

charged particles *particles* that possess an electrical *charge* 219

charges electrical charges can be *positive* or *negative*; electric *currents* are caused by moving charges 219, 257, 285, 290, 294

Christmas pudding model an old model for the *atom* in which the *particles* fill up all the space, like currants and raisins in a Christmas pudding 290–291

circuit breaker a device that protects an electric circuit by switching off a *current* if it is too big; it is then reset 248

coal-fired power station a *power station* in which *thermal energy* (heat) from burning coal is transformed into electrical energy 255, 256–257, 261

communications methods used for exchange of information, e.g. the telephone network or internet 284–285

conduction
1 electrical – the flow of an electric *current* through a substance
2 thermal – the transfer of *thermal energy* (heat) from the hotter parts of a substance to colder parts without the substance itself moving 212, 218, 220, 224

conductivity a property of a substance that tells you how well it conducts (carries) heat or electricity 220, 222, 230

conductor a substance which readily allows electricity or *thermal energy* (heat) to pass through it (*conduction*); metals are good conductors 212, 217, 218, 220, 225

conserve to save; not to waste 236

convection the transfer of *thermal energy* (heat) by the movement of a liquid or gas 213, 218, 224

cooling towers used in many *power stations* to change steam back to water after it has passed through *turbines* 254, 255

copper a reddish metal that is a good *conductor* and is easily made into wires 217, 220, 283

cost-effective more than able to repay the cost of setting up; things that are cost-effective usually have a short *pay-back time* 237, 238

count rate the number of counts per second – especially counts recorded by a *radiation* detector, e.g. a *Geiger counter* 300

current a flow of electric *charge* 248, 294, 298

curved paths paths that are not straight lines but curved, e.g. like an arc of a circle 279

D

d.c. short for *direct current* 248

decay what happens to the unstable *nucleus* of a *radio-isotope atom* when it *emits radiation* 293, 300–301

decommissioning the process of dismantling a building when its useful life is over, e.g. a *power station* 267

digital signals signals that have only two values – on or off (1 or 0) 286–287

direct current an electric *current* that always flows in the same direction; *d.c.* for short 248

discrete separate, not continuous like an *analogue signal*; *digital signals* are discrete 287

dose the amount or quantity received 277, 303

double glazing windowpanes with two sheets of glass separated by an air gap 225, 238

E

efficiency the fraction (or percentage) of the energy supplied to a device that is usefully transferred by it 232–233, 240–241

efficient an efficient device usefully transfers a large proportion of the energy supplied to it (or a larger proportion than other devices) 232, 236–237

electromagnetic radiation *radio waves, microwaves, infra-red radiation, visible light, ultra-violet radiation, X-rays* and *gamma radiation* 219, 308

electromagnetic spectrum the different types of *electromagnetic radiation* arranged in order of their *wavelengths* or *frequencies* 273, 309

electromagnetic waves *waves* that travel at the speed of light through empty space; all the different forms of *electromagnetic radiation* are electromagnetic waves with different *wavelengths* and *frequencies* 219, 273, 274–275, 276–277, 308

electrons tiny *particles* with a *negative charge* (–1) and very little *mass*; in an *atom*, electrons move around the *nucleus*; they move when a *current* flows through a solid substance (usually a metal) 218, 248, 290–291, 295, 298

emit, emission the sending out of *radiation*, e.g. by *radioactive* substances   215, 292, 294–295

emitter a surface or object that *emits radiation*   215

endoscope a device used by doctors to see inside patients' bodies; light travels along bundles of *optical fibres*   279

energy efficient light bulb a light bulb designed to use less energy than a *filament lamp*   237

energy source something that supplies energy, e.g. to generate electricity   226, 252–253, 262, 264–265

environment the surroundings in which we live   267, 302

F

filament lamp a lamp that *emits* light because a metal filament becomes very hot when an electric *current* passes through it   219, 232, 234, 237

fission see *nuclear fission*

fluids a general term for liquids and gases; states of matter that can flow   218

fluorescent able to *absorb ultra-violet radiation* and re-emit the energy as light   232, 234, 282

fossil fuels *fuels* that formed in the Earth over millions of years from the remains of dead animals and plants, e.g. coal, oil and natural gas   236, 252, 254, 267

frequency the number of complete *waves* or vibrations each second; frequency is measured in units called *hertz* or cycles per second   248, 270–271, 273, 275, 308–309

friction a force which acts on an object in the opposite direction to the direction it is moving (or tending to move)   230

fuels substances that release energy when they are burned; *nuclear fuels* release energy by the splitting of their *nuclei* (*nuclear fission*) in a nuclear reactor   227, 252–257

G

galaxy a group of *billions* of *stars*; the *Universe* is made up of billions of galaxies   305, 307, 309, 310–311

Galileo Galilei (1564–1642)   306

gamma (γ) one of the types of *radiation emitted* when the *nucleus* of a *radio-isotope decays*; it consists of very short *wavelength*, very high *frequency, electromagnetic waves*   273, 277, 280, 294–297

gas-fired power station a *power station* in which *thermal energy* (heat) from burning gas is transformed into electrical energy   254, 256, 257

Geiger counter used to measure the *radiation emitted* by *radioactive* substances; a Geiger-Müller tube detects the radiation   292, 299, 300

generator a machine that transforms *kinetic* (movement) *energy* into electrical energy   254, 258–261, 263

geothermal energy *thermal energy* (heat) from inside the Earth; it is produced by the natural *decay* of *radio-isotopes*, including *uranium*   263

gravitational potential energy the energy that is transferred either to an object when it is lifted against the force of *gravity* or from an object as it falls because of gravity   227, 258

gravity the force of *attraction* between two objects because of their *mass*; for this force to be big enough to be noticeable, at least one of the bodies must have a very large *mass*   258

greenhouse effect the Earth being kept warm by gases such as *carbon dioxide* in the *atmosphere*; burning *fossil fuels* produces more carbon dioxide and so increases the greenhouse effect   256, 267

H

half-life the time it takes for the *radiation emitted* by a sample of a *radio-isotope* to fall to half of its original rate or for half of the original radio-isotope *atoms* to *decay*   300–301, 302

heat transfer the movement of *thermal energy* (heat) from one place or object to another   212, 220–221

hertz the unit of *frequency*; the number of complete vibrations, oscillations or cycles per second; *Hz* for short   248

Hubble, Edwin (1889–1953)   310

Hubble space telescope an astronomical *telescope* located in *orbit* around the Earth; Hubble was launched by the Space Shuttle in 1990   307

hydro-electricity electricity generated using the *gravitational potential energy* of water stored behind a dam   258–259

Hz short for *hertz*   248

I

infra-red radiation *radiation* that transfers *thermal energy* (heat) from hot objects; a form of *electromagnetic radiation*   214–215, 216, 217, 219, 272–273, 276, 283

insulation material which is a poor *conductor* of heat (has a low *conductivity*); used to reduce the transfer of *thermal energy* (heat) in or out of an object or place   217, 221, 222–223, 224–225, 230, 238

insulator a substance which does not allow electricity or *thermal energy* (heat) to pass through it by *conduction*   212, 220, 225

interference unwanted signals that spoil a radio signal   286–287

ionise to give an *atom* or a molecule an electrical *charge* by the addition or removal of *electrons*   298

isotopes *atoms* of the same element that have different numbers of *neutrons* in their *nucleus*   293, 302–303

J

J short for *joule*   245

joule energy or work is measured in joules; 1 joule is the work done when a force of 1 newton moves through a distance of 1 metre; *J* for short   245

K

kilowatt 1 kilowatt is 1000 *watts*; *kW* for short   244

kilowatt-hour 1 *Unit* of electricity; 1 kilowatt-hour is the energy transferred in 1 hour by an appliance with a *power* of 1 *kilowatt*; *kW h* for short   245

kinetic energy the energy an object has because it is moving   227, 229, 231, 258, 260

kW short for *kilowatt*   244

kW h short for *kilowatt-hour*   245

L

laser a light source that produces light of a single *wavelength* (colour) concentrated into a pencil-thin beam   278, 279

light pollution stray light that interferes with astronomers' observations of the night sky, e.g. from street lamps   306

light-year the distance that light travels in 1 year; it is used as a unit for the very large distances to *stars* and *galaxies*   305, 310

M

magnets these *attract* iron and steel and can attract or repel other magnets   294

mains supply the electricity that is supplied to our homes   248

mass the amount of matter in an object; mass is measured in units called kilograms (kg)   290, 291

microwaves *electromagnetic radiation* with a *wavelength* between the wavelengths of *radio waves* and *infra-red radiation*; they are used for cooking, by *mobile phones* and to send signals (e.g. for TV) to and from artificial *satellites*   276, 284, 288

mobile phones these send and receive signals using *microwaves*   288–289

radiation dose a measure of how much harmful *radiation* a person's body receives in a certain time   277, 296–297, 303

radioactive emitting *alpha*, *beta* or *gamma radiation*   256, 257, 292–297, 300–301

radio-isotope an unstable *atom* that *decays* and emits *radiation*; another word for radio-isotope is radionuclide   293, 295, 296, 298, 300, 302

radionuclide see *radio-isotope*

radio telescope a *telescope* that collects and analyses *radio waves emitted* by distant objects   307, 311

radio waves long *wavelength electromagnetic radiation* that we use to carry radio and TV signals   273, 285, 307

red-shift the shift of the lines in the *spectrum* of light from distant *galaxies* towards the red end of the spectrum, indicating that the galaxies are moving away from us   309, 310, 311

reflect, reflection the bouncing back of *waves* (or *radiation*) from a barrier or a boundary   215, 274, 275, 284, 285, 306, 308

renewables *energy sources* that are constantly being replaced and so will not run out   253, 260–261, 264–265

Rutherford, Ernest (1871–1937)   291

S

satellites objects that move in an *orbit* around the Earth or another *planet*; the Moon is a satellite of the Earth; there are also artificial satellites   262, 284

secondary energy source an *energy source* that has been generated from another energy source; e.g. electricity is a secondary energy source which can be generated from *fossil fuels* or sunlight   252

solar cells these transfer energy from the *Sun's radiation* directly as electricity   262

solar cooker a cooker powered by the energy of sunlight   216

solar panels these *absorb* energy from the *Sun's radiation* and transfer it as *thermal energy* (heat)   217

solar system a *star* together with any *planets* and other objects that *orbit* the star   304, 305

spectrum
1 visible spectrum – what you get when you split up white *visible light* into all the different colours (*frequencies*, *wavelengths*) that it contains, e.g. with a prism   268, 278, 306
2 see *electromagnetic spectrum*

speed the distance travelled in a certain time; a measure of how fast something moves   271, 273, 310–311

stars very large objects, like the *Sun*, that *emit radiation* because of the nuclear fusion reactions that occur inside them   304–305, 306, 307, 309, 310, 311

start-up time how long it takes to start up a *power station* and get it generating electricity   257

sulfur dioxide a gas that is produced when many *fuels* burn; it is one of the causes of *acid rain*   256–257

Sun the Earth's local *star*   214, 216–217, 226, 304–305, 306, 309, 311

T

telescope an instrument that uses lenses or mirrors to collect and focus light (or other *radiations*) from distant objects; the radiation may be focused to form an image or separated into a *spectrum*   306–307

thermal energy the energy an object has because it is hot; the hotter an object is, the more *kinetic energy* its *particles* have   212, 224–225, 229, 230, 234–235, 238–239, 254

thermal radiation *electromagnetic radiation* given out by an object because of its temperature; the *Sun*, for example, *emits* a great deal of *infra-red radiation* and *visible light*   214–215, 219

thermostat a device designed to maintain a constant temperature by controlling the heat supply in response to temperature changes, e.g. in a room   241, 250

tidal barrage a dam built across a river estuary so that electricity can be generated from the *tides*   259

We are grateful to the following for permission to reproduce photographs:

Cover Image, Alfred Pasieka / SPL; 8, David Lyons / Alamy; 13, CC Studio / SPL; 18, Piers Morgan / Rex; 19, 178t, Owen Franken / Corbis; 20, The Vegetarian Society; 23t, Dr Don Fawcett / SPL; 23m, Astrid & Hanns-Frieder Michler / SPL; 23b, R. Bowen, Colorado State University; 24, Dominique Derda / France 2 / Corbis; 25t, Sheila Terry / SPL; 25bl, 29, 47, CNRI / SPL; 25bc, 43, Saturn Stills / SPL; 25br, Phototake Inc. / Alamy; 26t, Eitan Simanor / Alamy; 26b, Michael Donne / SPL; 30, Dr Morley Read / SPL; 32, Parrot Pascal / Corbis Sygma; 34, United Phosphorus Limited; 35, Graham Portlock / Pentaprism; 37, Report Of The Royal College Of Physicians, 1962 – Smoking And Health, Royal College Of Physicians, London; 38, Ralph Morse / Getty; 40, Samuel Ashfield / SPL; 41t, Georgina Harrison / Rex; 41b, Science Museum; 42t, Julie Reza / Wellcome Trust; 42b, Rob Lewine / Corbis; 45t, topfoto.co.uk; 45m, BSIP, Girand / SPL; 45b, Ian Miles – Flashpoint Pictures / Alamy; 48t, 49, 53t, H. Rogers / Trip; 48m, 281m, 281b, Michael Wyndham Picture Collection; 48b, 167, Simon Fraser / SPL; 50, Ted Horowitz / Corbis; 51, 147t, Eye Of Science / SPL; 52t, 98, Reuters; 52b, 88t, 88tm, 88bm, 88b, Mary Evans Picture Library; 53b, B. Seed / Trip; 56t, 194, SPL; 56tm, 56b, Wellcome Library, London; 56bm, Prof. Peter Molan, Honey Research Unit, University Of Waikato; 57t, B. Lake / Trip; 57ml, S. Grant / Trip; 57mr, Peter Menzel / SPL; 57b, N. Price / Trip; 61m, Geoff Dore / naturepl.com; 61b, Holt Studios International Ltd / Alamy; 62m, Geoff Kidd / A-Z; 62b, Phil Gates; 64l, WorldThroughTheLens / Alamy; 64m, Geogphotos / Alamy; 64r, The Garden Picture Library / Alamy; 66t, Andy Myatt / Alamy; 66m, David Newham / Alamy; 67tl, Niall Benvie / OSF; 67tr, 95m, 114, Malcolm Fife; 71, Biophoto Associates; 76m, 76b, Dr F. Taylor / Geoscience Features Picture Library; 77l, Chris Westwood / Environmental Images; 77r, Sarah Rowland / Holt Studios International; 79t, Philippe Plailly / Eurelios / SPL; 79b, Nigel Cattlin / Holt Studios International; 81t, Royal Botanic Gardens Kew; 81b, International Potato Center (Cip); 82, David Fox / OSF; 84t, W. Higgs / Geoscience Features Picture Library; 84m, John Reader / SPL; 86m, Tom McHugh / SPL; 86b, Ralph White / Corbis; 89l, Jonathan P. Scott / Planet Earth Pictures; 89r, Thomas Dressler / Planet Earth Pictures; 93t, Simon Fraser / RVI, Newcastle-Upon-Tyne / SPL; 93b, Bill Longcore / SPL; 94, Alan Beatty / Ecoscene; 95t, Keith Wheeler; 96, Christopher Jones / Life File; 97, 267t, Paul Thompson / Ecoscene; 100t, Nick Hanna / Alamy; 100b, Peter Dean / Agripicture; 106t, 107, Nick Hawkes / Ecoscene; 106m, Alexandra Jones / Ecoscene; 106b, J Whitworth / A-Z; 109l, 109r, Cuboimages Srl / Alamy; 109m, 241m, Imagestate / Alamy; 110t, David Crausby / Alamy; 110b, 182b, Justin Kase / Alamy; 111l, Jean Martin; 111r, David Woodfall / Getty; 112t, Angelo Hornak / Corbis; 112ml, Sandro Vannini / Corbis; 112mr, Alan Schein Photography / Corbis; 112b, Peter Adams Photography / Alamy; 113t, 113m, 118, 207, 211m, 211b, Andrew Lambert; 113bl, K. Handke / Zefa / Corbis; 113bm, Richard Klune / Corbis; 113br, Mark Thomas / SPL; 116, Goodshoot / Alamy; 119t, 144m, 144b, 148m, 176, 262b, Andrew Lambert Photography / SPL; 119bl, 119br, John Pettigrew / Cambridge University Press; 121t, 121tm, 121bm, 121b, David Acaster; 124t, 124m, British Cement Association; 126m, V&A Images / Victoria & Albert Museum; 126b, Vanessa Miles / Alamy; 127t, Lenny Lencina / Alamy; 127bl, 127br, Mayang Murni Adnin (http://www.mayang.com/); 131, Simon Belcher / Alamy; 132t, Hulton-Deutsch Collection / Corbis; 132m, 132b, Bettmann / Corbis; 133t, Mark A. Johnson / Corbis; 133m, John Terence Turner / Alamy; 134t, 134m, 134b, The Natural History Museum, London; 135l, Jim Winkley / Ecoscene; 135m, Susan Cunningham / Panos Pictures; 135r, 160m, Erik Schaffer / Ecoscene; 136, Ace Stock Limited / Alamy; 142tl, K-Photos / Alamy; 142tr, Stockdisc Classic / Alamy; 142b, 160t, 188, Vanessa Miles; 143, Pascal Goetgheluck / SPL; 146, Charles O'Rear / Corbis; 147m, Wayne Lawler / SPL; 148t, TRH Pictures / Boeing; 148bl, C. Rennie / Trip; 148br, 178bm, Dr P. Marazzi / SPL; 149, James L. Amos / Corbis; 155, Esso Petroleum Company Ltd; 161l, 190tl, 190tr, 190m, Jeremy Pembry / Cambridge University Press; 161r, Robert Brook / SPL; 162l, Jeremy Walker / SPL; 162r, Steve Allen / SPL; 163, Dave Reede / Agstock / SPL; 164t, BSIP Chassenet / SPL; 164m, Anthony Cooper; Ecoscene / Corbis; 164b, James King-Holmes / SPL; 165t, Kenneth Murray / SPL; 165m, Jack Dabaghian / Reuters / Corbis; 166t, Stefano Sarti / Empics; 166b, 253ml, 253bl, Martin Bond / SPL; 168, Paul Souders / Corbis; 169, Dean Conger / Corbis; 172, Van Parys / Corbis Sygma; 174l, M. Barlow / Trip; 174r, Desiree Navarro / Getty Images; 177, Reuters / Corbis; 178tm, Maximilian Weinzierl / Alamy; 178b, CSIRO Textile and Fibre Technology; 179t, Tim Beddow / SPL; 179m, Dr Jeremy Burgess / SPL; 179b, Stockshot / Alamy; 180, Ripesense Ltd; 181t, Craig Aurness / Corbis; 181m, View Pictures Ltd / Alamy; 181b, Roger Ressmeyer / Corbis; 182tl, Andrew Paterson / Alamy; 182tr, 184m, Comstock Images / Alamy; 183t, Photofusion Picture Library / Alamy; 183m, Andrew Butterton / Alamy; 183b, Stockbyte Silver / Alamy; 184t, Robert Golden / ABPL; 184b, Rix Biodiesel Ltd; 185t, Lena Trindade / Brazilphotos / Alamy; 185b, Jonathan Blair / Corbis; 186, Cordelia Molloy / SPL; 187t, Norman Hollands / ABPL; 187m, Gary Houlder / Corbis; 187b, Sam Stowell / ABPL; 190br, Maximilian Stock Ltd / ABPL; 190bl, Tony Robins / ABPL; 191ml, ATW Photography / ABPL; 191mr, Joy Skipper / ABPL; 191b, Anthony Blake / ABPL; 192t, Eddie Gerald / Alamy; 192m, David Marsden / ABPL; 192b, Steve Lee / ABPL; 195t, B. W. Hoffman / AGStock / SPL; 195m, G. P. Bowater / Alamy; 201, AFP / Getty Images; 202t, Patrick Robert / Sygma / Corbis; 202m, Wesley Bocxe / SPL; 203m, Spencer Platt / Getty Images; 203bl, 203br, Jane Beesley / Oxfam; 206, Dr B. Booth / Geoscience Features Picture Library; 209, D. A. Peel / SPL; 211t, TRH Pictures / US Navy; 214, D. Phillips / SPL; 216, Alex Bartel / SPL; 220, Tony Camacho / SPL; 223t, Tim Pannell / Corbis; 232m, Noble Phil Noble / PA / EMPics; 229t, Clive Mason / Getty Images; 229m, Torleif Svensson / Corbis; 236, Jon Bower / Alamy; 241b, John Lamb / Getty Images; 253t, Jon Wilkinson / Ecoscene; 253mr, Chinch Gryniewicz / Ecoscene; 253br, Ian Pickthall / Ecoscene; 260l, 267m, Anthony Cooper / Ecoscene; 260r, David Walker / Ecoscene; 261t, Kevin King / Ecoscene; 261b, Mark Baigent / Alamy; 262m, 302, 307m, NASA / SPL; 268, Photograph By Andrew Davidhazy, Rochester Institute Of Technology; 278, Stock Image / Alamy; 279l, Jerry Lodriguss / SPL; 279r, R. Maisonneuve, Publiphoto Diffusion / SPL; 287, Royalty-free / Corbis; 298, Chris Priest / SPL; 301, Larry Miller / SPL; 304t, Detlev van Ravenswaay / SPL; 305t, 305m, NOAO / SPL; 307bl, Ken Biggs / SPL; 307br, David Ducros / SPL; 310, NASA / ESA / STSCI / SPL; 311, Julian Baum / SPL

Abbreviations: ABPL, Anthony Blake Photo Library; OSF, Oxford Scientific; Rex, Rex Features; SPL, Science Photo Library. Letters used with page numbers: b, bottom of the page; l, left-hand side of the page; m, middle of the page; r, right-hand side of the page; t, top of the page.

Picture research: Vanessa Miles.